A REVIEW ON MARXIST AND LEFT DEBATES

A REVIEW ON MARXIST AND LEFT DEBATES

Zeng Zhisheng

Translated by Wedo Translation & Interpretation Co. Ltd.

CANUT INTERNATIONAL PUBLISHERS
Berlin, London

Originally published as The Latest Studies by Western Scholars on Marxism Issues in 2006 by China Renmin University Press.

Original Chinese Edition Copyright 2006 by Zeng Zhisheng

ISBN 7-300-07561-4

English Print edition: A Review on Marxist and Left Debates

Copyright 2011

ISBN: 978-3-942575-07-2

English Digital Edition:

ISBN: 978-3-942575-10-2

Published by
Canut International Publishers
Yorck Street. 66
10965 Kreuzberg Berlin-Germany

Canut International-London
12a Guernsey Road E11
London 4BJ –England-UK
URL: http://www.leftreader.com
E-Mail: canut@leftreader.com

CONTENTS

PUBLISHER'S NOTE

Marxist theories require constant development and enrichment. This can only be possible through withstanding the critique raised by contemporary trends of thoughts and also absorbing and uniting with their enlightening aspects. In the next pages readers will find a preface written by the author Zeng Zhisheng himself for the Chinese edition which describes the content and aim of the book. In the recent decades Chinese Marxists have been closely following the theoretical trends in the other parts of the world and desire to develop a dialog and a debate. This book includes one of the outstanding research results made by them-renown names in Chinese academia- on current Marxist trends outside China. The author mainly opts for descriptive attitude and tries to clarify the relations between main theoretical trends rather than debating with them. Yet reader will be able to observe the level of research achievements and keen efforts given by them to form an analytical frame.

The book explicitly reflects the optimism shared by Chinese Marxist academia for the bright future of global Marxism which is not baseless when we consider re-flourishing Marxist, left and socialism studies in almost every part of the globe. As capitalism is globalised and it spreads to every corner of the world and forces many old classes and strata into the ranks of working class and as the intellectual qualities of working class rises, critique against capitalism and old world order includes more and more progressive thoughts thus Marxism wins new fellows. The vigorous debates and researches in the book demonstrate that Marxism and socialist schools have the intrinsic nature to develop themselves with the demands of times.

Readers interested in the fate of current Marxism, socialism, democratic political civilization, humanly natural environment, feminist movement and free self-development of nations will find ample stimulating material and ideas in this book.

Finally I specially thank China Renmin University Press and our translators for their generous efforts through realization of this book.

Deniz Kizilcec

March 2011, Berlin

ACKNOWLEDGEMENTS

This book was planned and designed by the School of Marxism Studies, Renmin University of China. In the beginning, Prof. Duan Zhongqiao has presided over the work together with Prof. Huang Jifeng and Zeng Zhisheng who have also participated to determine the research direction and content design. In the later stage, as Prof. Duan Zhongqiao was assigned for another task and Prof Zeng Zhisheng has undertaken his part in the project.

In addition to the above three scholars, those who have participated this research project also include Prof. Zhou Xincheng from Renmin University of China,

Dr. Gao Yachun – instructor in Heilongjiang University and Wang Miao - doctoral student from Renmin University of China. Zeng Zhisheng has written Chapters 3, 5, 8 and 9; Duan Zhongqiao, Chapters 1 and 4; Gao Yachun, Chapter 2; Zhou Xincheng, Chapter 6; Wang Miao, Chapter 7; Huang Jifeng, Chapter 10. Zeng Zhisheng as the chief editor has determined the name of the book.

Canut Publishers have organized the English edition in cooperation with the original publisher Renmin University Press. The book was first published by Renmin University Press in December 2006.

CHAPTER II

THE EXPLOITATION THEORY OF ROEMER

In the school of Analytical Marxism arisen, John E. Roemer, an American famous economist and also professor of the Political Science Faculty of Yale University, is an important representative figure. His prominent contribution to the school of Analytical Marxism is that he has used the research methodology of modern Western economics to make a major revision to the traditional exploitation theory of Marxism and put forth an exploitation theory based on non-labor theory of value.

Roemer points out that most part of Marx's thought has been very important for more than one century, because Marx had provided the argumentation for the immorality of the capitalist system. In the face of the proposition that capitalism is morally neutral as tub-thumped by contemporary neoclassical economists, an important mission of Marxist economics is to morally challenge the validity of capitalist economic system.

To a large extent, Marx's condemnation of capitalism centers on capitalists' exploitation to workers. However, the concept of exploitation has two meanings: One is the exploitation in a technical sense, i.e.: some people's expropriation of some other people's labor from the perspective of fact judgment; the other is the exploitation in a moral sense, i.e.: some people's unjust use of some other people from the perspective of value judgment[1].

On this basis, Roemer thinks that Marx's exploitation theory has two problems although it contains the condemnation of capitalist morality. Firstly, Marx's theory is based on the labor theory of value, while the labor theory of value is false,

---

1   John E. Roemer: Free to Lose. An Introduction to Marxist Economic Philosophy, translated by Duan Zhongqiao and Liu Lei, Beijing, Economic Science Press, 2003, p 4-5.

so the exploitation theory based on the labor theory of value is questionable. Nevertheless, although the labor theory of value is false, the capitalists in fact exploit workers in a technical sense as described in Marx's exploitation theory is a reality. This fact can also be proved by the methodology of modern Western economics. Secondly, to say the least, even if the labor theory of value is correct, the exploitation theory based on it in a technical sense is not adequate to morally criticize capitalist system, because at most such exploitation theory is a fact description rather than a value judgment. Just out of the above consideration, Roemer has put forward an exploitation theory based on non-labor theory of value, aiming to morally criticize capitalism.

1. THE NON-LABOR THEORY OF LABOUR

What is capitalist exploitation? In Marx's illustrations, capitalist exploitation refers to the unpaid expropriation of the surplus value of workers' production by the capitalists. Concretely speaking, in a capitalist society, the labor power of workers becomes a commodity; as capitalists possess all means of production, while workers do not own them, and workers have to sell their labor power to capitalists; same as other commodities, the value of workers' labor as a commodity is also decided by the socially necessary labor time spent on its reproduction. Therefore, worker's labor power is a special commodity which can produce a value greater than its own value; capitalists buy worker's labor power in the labor market. But the workers will produce a value greater than the value of their labor power during the production. However, the amount that capitalists pay to workers is only the value of their labor power. The difference between these two amounts is the surplus value. The surplus value is expropriated by capitalists without payment. This is the capitalist exploitation described by Marx. Undoubtedly, Marx's theory of capitalist exploitation is based on labor theory of value.

Like many modern Western economists, Roemer also suggests that the labor theory of value to be false and exploitation theory based on labor theory of value can hardly hold water. But at the same time, Roemer argues that the capitalists' exploitation of workers as exposed by Marx de facto exists and this exploitation can be demonstrated with the microeconomic equilibrium model of mainstream bourgeois economics. In order to prove it, Roemer has designed a standard microeconomic equilibrium model. In this model, competition, market-clearing price and wage rates decide such a result: some people are exploited and some are exploiters[2].

The microeconomic equilibrium model designed by Roemer is a simple economic model for production of only one kind of commodity (we call it Model A for short). Imagine a society of 1000 agents. In this society, only one kind of

---

2   *Ibid.*, p.9.

commodity – corn is produced and consumed. The production of corn needs the input of labor and seed-corn only; each agent owns same skill and production capacity and possesses the available corn production technique and knowledge; all agents have a preference of subsistence, or in other words, once they have achieved a given level of corn for subsistence (suppose it is one unit) and have renewed their original endowment of seed-corn, and he assumes they would rather prefer leisure or continue to work and consume more corn.

Let's suppose the society has 500 units of seed-corn as capital in the beginning; and two corn production techniques are available: one technique is the farming technique and the other is the factory technique. If farm technique is adopted, one unit of corn will be produced with 3 days' labor and without seed-corn; if factory technique is adopted, two units of gross corn products or one unit of net corn products (the products after renewing one unit of seed-corn) will be produced by one day's labor and one unit of seed-corn. The production cycles with these two techniques are both one week (seven days).

Let's further suppose they have equal initial capital (seed-corn) and each agent owns a half unit of seed-corn as capital. On the basis of the above given conditions, including agent preference, production techniques and initial capital is equal too , the equilibrium solution (optimal result) to this economic model is that each agent works two days, including 1/2 day at factory and 1 1/2 days at farm. More specifically, one agent produces corn with factory technique in 1/2 day, sows 1/2 unit of its seed-corn and obtains one unit of gross corn products. Of the one unit of corn, a half unit is used to renew the seed-corn initially owned and the other half unit is for consumption by himself. As the amount of corn which meets his subsistence is one unit, he has to produce 1/2 unit more corn in other place. Therefore, he goes to a farm. In the farm, without seed-corn as capital, he spends 1 1/2 days producing 1/2 unit of corn. Roemer said people might ask: By what technique corn can be produced only with labor? Perhaps farm technique includes picking wild corn in forest. This production process can produce corn, but it needs more labor to produce the same amount of corn when compared with the factory technique. However, the concrete form of production technique has nothing to do with the issue per se. The importance is to assume there are two ways to maintain subsistence in this economy. One is to use capital to carry out production. The so-called capital refers here to a rare and non-labor input. In this model, it is seed-corn. The other is farm technique with which every person can carry out production no matter whether they own the capital or not[3].

Roemer has commented that the equilibrium solution in the above model is self-sufficiency, for there is no exchange transaction between agents. Everybody works for themselves. They neither sell labor to others nor hire others' labor. Nobody sells his corn to others.

---

3   *Ibid.*

Based on this equilibrium solution, Roemer puts forth the concept of socially necessary labor time for the reproduction in the society. He says, with given techniques, seed-corn as capital and consumption need, the needed socially necessary labor time for production of 1000 units of corn is 2000 days, or specifically speaking, the socially necessary labor time for production of one unit of corn is 2 days. In a more general sense, the socially necessary labor time for the production of a certain amount of corn is the total labor for production of this amount of corn and also includes reproduction of the seed-corn consumed in this process. In terms of the above model, the society will firstly use all of its seed-corn capital in factory production and spend 500 labor days producing 500 units of net corn products. The rest 500 unit of corn will be produced through 1500 labor days in the farms. The socially necessary labor time is reflected by the labor for the total corn consumption needed by all agents.

On the basis of socially necessary labor time, Roemer gives a definition of exploitation in a technical sense: "Exploitation is said to exist if in a given economy some agents must work more time than is socially necessary (longer than the socially necessary labor time) to earn their consumption bundles and others work less time than the socially necessary time to earn their bundles."[4] The former are the exploited, while the latter are exploiters. According to this definition, no exploitation exists in Model A, because everybody's labor time is just equal to socially necessary labor time.

The premise of Model A is an equal capital (seed-corn). If it is not equal, what will happen? On the basis of Model A, Roemer puts forward another model (we call it Model B for short): Now suppose that among the 1000 agents in Model A, there are 10 rich agents, each with 50 units of corn, and 990 poor agents, who have no seed-corn and only own labor power ; besides, the utility function of each agent in this model – a function between the consumed corn and the consumed labor, is that nobody wants to spend more time in obtaining corn unless they can obtain corn without performing additional labor. Other conditions in Model B are the same as those of Model A.

Because initial seed-corn in Model B is unequal, in this case the self-sufficient pattern in the Model A cannot realize an equilibrium (cannot realize the optimal selection of the rich and the poor), because the result of this pattern will only be as follows : Each poor agent without property will work three days in the farm to obtain one unit of corn, while each rich agent with property will work with his one unit of seed-corn one day at factory to produce one unit of net corn product for their consumption. However, if there will be labor market and the rich agents can become capitalists and can hire the labor of the poor agents, both the rich and the poor may do better and equilibrium can be realized. Roemer points out that

---

4   *Ibid*, p. 34.

the solution for the realization of an equilibrium is to keep wage rate at 1/3 unit of corn per day. It will not work if the wage is higher than this value, because the daily income in the farm is 1/3 unit of corn, if the wage by the factory is higher than that in the farm, all of the poor will work in the factory, but the factory does not have enough seed-corn for them. Nor will it work, if it is lower than this value, because in this case, the poor would rather prefer farm than work at factory. Therefore, the only feasible wage rate which can eliminate labor market is 1/3 unit of corn/day. At this wage rate, none of the poor will mind whether s/he works in the farm or factory, because the actual income in these two places is same. With the wage rate of 1/3 unit of corn per day, the 990 poor agents are all willing to do any amount of labor for capitalists in 0 to 3 days. Their labor is available in any time period from 0 to 3×990=2970 days. The number of poor agents hired by the rich agents is just enough to make full use of the seed-corn owned by the rich agents, i.e.: 500/3 poor agents. These poor agents will work in the factory and each will spend three days' labor and earn one unit of corn. The rest 823.33(990-500/3) poor agents will still work in the farm and each will earn one unit of corn needed by them. These rich agents – capitalists work 0 day that means they do not work. The poor agents hired by them produce 1000 units of corn for them and 500 units of corn will be used to renew their original seed-corn capital, 500/3 units of corn will be used to pay wages, and the remaining 2/3×500=333.33 units of corn will be their profit.

Based on his definition of exploitation in a technical sense, Roemer states that exploitation exists in Model B. Because in this model, the necessary labor time is still 2 days (it will not change with the changes in the distribution of initial seed-corn, because the calculation of socially necessary labor time has nothing to do with the initial capital distribution. It only relies on total consumption, technique, and the available total capital and labor), each capitalist works zero day and each of the workers and peasants needs to work 3 days.

Therefore, Roemer believes that his micro-economic equilibrium model can also describe capitalists' exploitation of workers as described by Marx: the labor performed by workers is more than the socially necessary labor time, so they are exploited; the labor performed by capitalists is less than socially necessary labor time, so they are exploiters. Hence, Roemer further declares that the description of exploitation has nothing to do with labor value, but traditional Marxism considers exploitation closely related to labor value, thus closely related to the transactions in the labor market. In order to confute the Marxist argument that the description on the exploitation in a technical sense should be based on the labor theory of value, Roemer has designed another model called "isolated capital market" (we call it Model C for short). He wanted to prove that the exploitation that is realized through the medium of labor market can also be fully demonstrated in an economic model without labor market.

Suppose there is an isolated labor market in the above model (Model B) and the agents in the market exchange their labor with each other. Suppose there is also an isolated capital market (Model C), where the techniques, agents and initial capital are identical to those in the isolated labor market (Model B), and the only difference is that the people there have not yet established a labor market, or for some reason, they reject the labor hiring system, but the people in the isolated capital market accept capital borrowing and lending. Concretely speaking, in the isolated capital market, there are also 1000 agents and tangible capital – that means 500 units of seed-corn, thus 10 rich agents own 50 units of corn, and the rest 990 poor agents only possess labor power. Same as the isolated labor market, the isolated capital market also has two techniques: if farm technique is adopted, one unit of corn will be produced with 3 days' labor and without any seed-corn; if factory technique is adopted, two units of brut corn is produced or one unit of net corn will be produced with one day's labor and one unit of seed-corn. People may borrow or lend seed-corn among each other, but they must only work for themselves. The preference of subsistence is the same as that in the isolated labor market: everybody only wants to reproduce his initial tangible capital and consume one unit of corn. After that is earned, they prefer leisure. Of course, it would be better if they can get more corn without laboring.

What is the equilibrium solution for this model? It is that ten rich agents are willing to lend seed-corn to the poor agents at a weekly interest rate of 66%. At this rate, if a poor agent borrows three units of corn from a rich agent, s/he can use three days' labor to produce six units of corn. S/he has to repay three units of corn as principal and pay two units of corn as interest. In the end, s/he will keep one unit of corn for self consumption. This arrangement is not different from his three days' work at farm, so he will certainly not mind it, while the rich agent who lends corn will be satisfied with this arrangement, too, because in this transaction, he obtains two units of corn without performing any labor. It should be noted that at this interest rate, the seed-corn of the rich agents is not enough to lend to all poor agents, we can only assume each of the 500/3 poor agents borrows three units of corn, while the rest 823.33 peasants will stay to work in the farm. As the arrangement in the latter has no real difference from that in the former, the latter (823.33 peasants) will have no objection to this arrangement. Can the interest rate be lower? No, it cannot, because if so, every poor agent would prefer to borrow capital (because obviously, they could obtain more corn and more leisure than what they obtain in the farm work), but the seed-corn capital is not enough to enable all the peasants work in the factory. Can the interest rate be higher? Neither, because if so, no poor agents would prefer to borrow corn and the rich agents will have to work. Therefore, the only interest rate which can make an equilibrium between supply and demand is 66%.

Roemer concludes, that just as the previous labor market model, the capital market model also contains exploitation in this equilibrium model where the ten rich agents are still exploiters and live from the interest rate without work, while the 990 poor agents are the exploited, no matter where they work, in the factory or in the farm. The difference is that in the isolated capital market model, capital borrowing substitutes selling of labor, and capital lending substitutes hiring of labor.

Of course, the proletarians in the isolated capital market may perhaps work in factories they control, while the proletarians in the isolated labor market perhaps work under the supervision of foremen employed by capitalists, but it is not the key issue. In terms of the issue of exploitation we are interested in, the condition in the isolated capital market is completely the same as that in the isolated labor market. Roemer claims that the model of the isolated capital market indicates that the labor power or wage exchange in the labor market is not an indispensable part of the theory of exploitation, because exploitation can also exist in a capital market without a labor market.

All in all, according to Roemer, to demonstrate the capitalist exploitation in a technical sense as described by Marx, the labor theory of value is not indispensable, because the micro equilibrium model of the mainstream bourgeoisie economics can explain this kind of exploitation, too.

2. DEFINING EXPLOITATION BY PROPERTY RELATIONS

Why does exploitation appear in Model B and Model C? Roemer attributes it to two reasons: relative scarcity of capital and secondly different ownerships of tangible capital. With respect to the first reason, if the capital is sufficient in relation to the available labor, the rate of profit will decline and subsequently exploitation will perish. With respect to the second reason, when capital (whether it is something produced in the past or natural resource expropriated by individuals) becomes private property and is distributed unequally, exploitation will appear in the market process.

According to Roemer's definition of exploitation in a technical sense, workers are exploited, because the amount of labor embodied in the consumption goods they can purchase with their wages is less than the amount of labor they have expended. Capitalists are exploiters, because the amount of labor embodied in the commodities they purchase with their profit is more than the amount of labor they have expended. Roemer has asked why people are interested in the exploitation in a technical sense and why people need the measurement of exploitation.

In his view, Marx's theory of exploitation as a kind of mathematical measure has both descriptive and normative purposes: With descriptive purpose, exploitation is used to explain the existence of profit; but with normative purpose, exploitation is used to indicate that workers are unfairly treated by capitalists. However, he believes if capitalist exploitation is an important concept; it should be free of normative considerations. In his model above, the occurrence of exploitation results from the unequal distribution of the ownership of tangible capital (seed corns). In this case, exploitation on workers seems unfair; it is because people believe that the initial distribution of tangible capital which causes exploitation is unfair[5]. That is to say, for Roemer, if the exploitation theory is not connected with unfairness of value judgment, its explanation will not serve the purpose of morally criticizing capitalism.

Model D:

In order to demonstrate his view, Roemer gave two examples which include exploitation in a technical sense, but which can hardly be considered as unfair.

The first example (we call it Model D for short) is different from Model A only at one point. In this model D, social agents are divided as Class H and Class S, as a labor (H)iring class and a labor (S)elling class. Each agent in the labor selling class firstly uses his 1/2 unit of corn at factory to produce 1/2 unit of net corn products; s/he further sells his labor power at a wage rate of 1/3 unit of corn/day to the three persons who hire him to process their 1 1/2 units of seed-corn and earn 1/2 unit of corn as wages. In this case, he will work two days in total and earn one unit of corn. When the labor seller spend 1 1/2 days producing 1 1/2 units of corn, he only obtains 1/2 unit of corn as his wage, the labor hirers will obtain 66% profit by relying on their capital, i.e.: each labor hirer obtains 1/3 unit of corn as net profit. For consumption, a labor hirer needs one unit of corn, so he must work two days in the farm to obtain another 2/3 unit of corn. In this case, the agents in labor hiring class work only in the farm, while the agents in labor selling class work only in the factory.

For Roemer, in view of their property relations and final benefits, this arrangement (supposing there is not any particular harm to work for others) does not show any moral unfairness. Everybody works two days and consumes one unit of corn. However, this arrangement embodies an exploitation described by Marxism, because a labor seller produces one unit of corn working a day in the factory, but he only gets a wage equal to 1/3 unit of corn, and his surplus labor is expropriated by the owner of the seed-corns. For Roemer, if people adopted this traditional concept, the exploitation described by Marxism cannot not be used as a mathematical measure to prove unfairness morally, because the agents in the

---

5   *Ibid*, p. 62.

society will certainly show indifference to the social division of labor pattern realized in the Model D – everybody works two days for self subsistence, 1/2 day in the factory and 1 1/2 days in the farm. Of course, the social division of labor in this arrangement contains nothing immoral. Therefore, exploitation which can be morally condemned does not exist in this described arrangement[6]. This example indicates exploitation exists from the perspective of Marx's surplus labor theory, but it does not exist observed by the moral perspective.

Model E:

Let's see the second example (we call it Model E for short). Assume there are two persons – Karl and Adam, they have the following preferences on corn and labor: Karl rather prefers to consume 2/3 unit of corn without work than to consume one unit of corn and work for only one day. Adam rather prefers to consume 3 1/3 units of corn and work for 4 days than to consume 3 units of corn and only work for 3 days. These two preferences are both reasonable. Comparatively speaking, Karl attaches more importance to leisure. Karl rather prefers less corn in order to work less; while Adam attaches more importance to corn consumption. He rather works one more day extra after three days' of his labor in order to get more corn.

Now let's suppose the production techniques in this model are still farm technique and factory technique as those in Model A. Let's further suppose that the initial distribution of capital is unequal: Adam has 3 units of corn, while Karl has one unit of corn. Same as the conditions described above, neither of them want to reduce their initial corn reserves. What will happen?

They both can work for self subsistence. In other words, Karl produces one unit of net corn through spending one day in the factory processing his one unit of corn (capital); in the same way, Adam gets 3 units of corn and by working 3 days. However, this arrangement is not the best one for both of them.

Now let's suppose Karl prefers hiring Adam at a daily wage of 1/3 unit of corn. This is an attractive offer to Adam, because his second best (other) opportunity is to work one day in the farm to produce 1/3 unit of corn. In this case, the result will be: Karl hires Adam to process his one unit of corn, pays 1/3 unit of corn as wage to Adam and keeps 2/3 unit of corn as profit for his consumption, thus reaches his aim of less work. Adam firstly uses his own corn to produce 3 units of net corn through 3 days' labor, and then works one day for Karl to earn 1/3 unit of corn as his wage. In the end, he has 3 1/3 units of corn by 4 days' labor. Although this result also realizes equilibrium (they are both satisfied), exploitation appears, because Karl does not work and lives sheer by exploiting the labor of

---

6   *Ibid.*, p. 142.

Adam. However, Karl is poor, while Adam is rich. In this case, for whom should we show moral sympathy? Not Adam of course.

This example indicates that the exploitation in a technical sense is not necessarily a moral concept. Thus only when exploitation is the result of the unfair and unequal distribution of the means of production (initial capital), can we consider it as an immoral thing. Thus Roemer concludes, what people really care is the inequality of wealth distribution, and the exploitation in a technical sense is misleading.

Roemer believes that the inequality Marx tries to demonstrate and calls it as exploitation, is the inequality which is caused by difference in the ownership of means of production. By this token, the exploitation in a technical sense, demonstrated by Marx based on the labor theory of value, and the exploitation in a technical sense, calculated by him through comparing socially necessary labor time with the labor expended by a person will become a useful mathematical measure only when it fundamentally reflects the inequality in the initial distribution of wealth. Besides, only when the initial distribution of wealth can be proved as acquired by immoral means can the exploitation caused by it can be evaluated as immoral. For Roemer, as a general mathematical measure of inequality, the surplus value theory and accordingly its exploitation research methodology on the basis of surplus value are unsuccessful[7].

Based on the above argumentation, Roemer holds that exploitation should be defined directly with property relations rather than through surplus value theory because it is only roundabout and finally an unsuccessful route, and it will be more convincing if people's moral criticism at capitalism is established directly on the basis of property relations, rather than proving it through the veil of the theory of exploitation. Moreover, from his point of view, it is not difficult to define exploitation directly with property relations. Instead of employing the labor value theory, exploitation can be re-defined through the inequality of initial wealth. For this, he gave another model (we call it Model F for short):

Model F:

Imagine a society in which the agents own w_i initial wealth, and suppose the following activities realized through the market exchanges: After those exchanges, agent i obtains yield y_i in the end. w_i or y_i can be regarded as certain commodity bundles – they stand for initial capital and final output, respectively. If someone is better off when the initial distribution of wealth is equal, we will define him as 'exploited'; on the contrary, we will define him as 'exploiter'. To express this model in non-mathematical language: Roemer assumes a society with a certain

---

7   *Ibid*, p. 145.

number of agents, each with a certain amount of initial wealth (wi), and then supposes each agent in the end obtains a certain amount of yield (yi) corresponding to his initial wealth after market exchanges; if the initial wealth of each agent in the society is equally distributed, the final gain of each agent will either increase or decrease; the ones with increased gain are defined as the exploited, while the ones with decreased gains are defined as the exploiters.

For Roemer, if agent i is better off in product distribution (in his gains) in connection with the initial ownership of the means of production, better off than he is in the product distribution (his gains) in real life, it means he is exploited[8]. If not, it will mean, he exploits others. Taking the real capitalist society for example, if equal distribution of the means of production is assumed , the condition of the workers will become better, while the condition of the capitalists will become worse, so in the real capitalist society workers are exploited and capitalists are exploiters. This is Roemer's definition of exploitation based on property relations (PR) and for Roemer, his definition of exploitation is different from the definition based on surplus value, "because it does not involve labor value, but involves the fundamental problem which people are much more concerned, i.e.: the outcome caused by unequal distribution of transferable asset ownership which effects final distribution of yields". In addition, it is also a definition which corresponds to reality, as it judges the exploitative character of a distribution by comparing it with another probable possible distribution pattern. Moreover, his theory is oriented towards welfare. In other words, if the condition of a person is better under certain circumstances which correspond to reality, he is exploited; otherwise, he exploits others.

Roemer thinks that his PR definition on exploitation is tenable, because in all of the aforesaid examples, except the two non-immoral exploitation examples (Model D and Model E), his PR definition of exploitation is also consistent with the traditional Marxist definition of exploitation based on surplus value. Moreover, in these two examples, his PR definition but not the definition based on surplus value gives the correct answer In Model D, according to his PR definition, no one is exploited; in Model E, Adam is exploiter and Carl is the exploited, but if they start with two units of corn after a later re-distribution of initial capital, then in terms of final welfare Adam will suffer, while Karl will benefit.

Roemer stresses that his PR definition of exploitation enables people to pay explicit attention to such a view: exploitation is the loss of a person and such loss is caused by unequal initial distribution of property. A person will be considered unfairly treated if he does not possess equal property in the form of transferable means of production; whether he is exploited or not is determined by the comparison between his gain in current system and what he gains under initial equal

---

8   *Ibid*, p. 146-147.

distribution of the transferable property. To further strengthen the explanatory power of his theory, Roemer has also explained how to evaluate the status of the jobless persons in the capitalist society. For him, according to the definition based on surplus value theory, these jobless will be considered exploiters, because the amount of labor embodied in the commodities they obtain is more than the amount of labor they expend, but according to the PR definition, they will be considered as the exploited, for they will undoubtedly become better off if the wealth is redistributed equally and every person possesses equal share of tangible capital. In this issue, if people want appeal for the conclusion that the jobless in capitalist society are exploited, obviously the PR definition will be a better choice.

3. CAPITALIST EXPLOITATION AND CAPITALIST PRIVATE OWNERSHIP

For Roemer the key purpose of Marx's research on the issue of exploitation was to reveal the unfairness of capitalist private ownership. And the people should concentrate their attention on the moral reasonableness of the initial ownership of capital, because the decisive factor for the existence of exploitation is the initial distribution of property. In a more general sense, it is the private ownership on the means of production, which causes a great inequality in wealth distribution and this has accumulated generation by generation. Labor market or exploitation, neither of them is the source of inequality and unfainess Marx was concerned about[9].

In capitalism, the initial unequal property ownership was determined by means of robbery, occupation or theft. For this, Marx had devoted an elaborate dissertation in the chapter: primitive accumulation, in volume 1 of Capital. Roemer has pointed out that the unequal capital ownership established by those ugly means was obviously unfair. If the initial distribution of capital is unfair, then the capitalists' exploitation on workers caused by it will be unfair, too. However, some defenders of capitalism argue that the unequal distribution of capital can be achieved through morally irreproachable ways, for example: different rate of time difference (preference between labor and leisure) or different talent for entrepreneurship talents, different risk propensity, or simply luck. Roemer has refuted these arguments one by one.

In regard to the rate of time preference, Roemer admits if people have different time preferences, exploitation can appear after a short time. The example about Karl and Adam is evident, but whether we see this exploitation as an immoral thing or not depends on the reasons of time preferences. Neo-classical economists are inclined to regard time preferences from an aspect of individualism thus something for which individual should bear the consequences. Roemer objects

9   *Ibid.* p. 118.

to this view. For Roemer, attributing time preferences to people's independent choice is false, because thrift is caused by culture, while culture is formed by the objective conditions faced by the people[10]. He has also pointed out that Marxists also consider time preferences as determined by the society, and it is impossible to defend exploitation and inequality on the basis of time references and furthermore differences in time preference among persons or groups is caused by previous unequal conditions. To confront the arguments of neo-classical economists Roemer puts forth three contra arguments: firstly, the initial status as different amount of ownership was all established through theft and brutal force in capitalism. Secondly, it is a fact that people indeed have different time preferences and these differences will continuously exist in capitalist society, but these differences are formed as a response to inequality and oppression- unfair history-. If this is true, it is incorrect to claim it is the initial root for the unequal wealth. Thirdly, even if they assume there is some inherited or inborn differences among people related to time preferences, then why should we make benefit from that or why should those people suffer for that[11]

In regard to entrepreneurship talent, advocates of capitalism often argue that profit is a reward for entrepreneurship talent. People with this ability have discovered the labor organization and commodity producing methods which could not be discovered by others. Thus, reward to this rare skill is profit. For this argument, Roemer has raised two doubts: firstly, is talent for entrepreneurship really a rare skill? In his opinion, this rarity is more likely caused by the fact that majority of the people do not have the opportunity to develop their talent for entrepreneurship in the capitalist society. Secondly, even if the talent for entrepreneurship is rare, is it proper that it should be so highly rewarded by capital accumulation? In his opinion, entrepreneurs neither need (in terms of their functions in production) nor have the right to claim profit. When we think in terms of the need aspect, even if entrepreneurs are not given huge rewards, they will still continue to apply their talent, for example: the income of the managers in large Japanese companies is much lower than that of their counterparts in the United States. Therefore, the reward for them should be an amount just enough to make them play their role as entrepreneurs.

Why do entrepreneurs not have the right to claim profit? This is because their talent is the result of the cultural or hereditary factors from which they should not gain benefit. Actually, their talent for entrepreneurship mostly depends on how they were grown up together with their class or familial backgrounds. If someone's talent for entrepreneurship is caused by those mutual interactions in a certain circumstances or due to his family background, while are proletarians not so lucky? Then the advantage of the former can be evaluated as the result of

10   *Ibid.* p. 69.
11   *Ibid.* p. 71.

unequal opportunities and this result as unequal opportunity can be attributed to a certain society. Some people may claim that talent for entrepreneurship is not learnt but inborn, or in other words, some people are naturally born having the abilities to acquire those talents for entrepreneurship, while others not, and conclude that the entrepreneurs should have the right to obtain profit. Roemer argues that this view is in fact based on the principle of inborn self-ownership, i.e.: that means a person should be given the ownership of income which his inborn skills can acquire. However, this principle is doubtful. Firstly, this hereditary character forms an unequal opportunity. Should we tolerate this inequality? Secondly, even if we admit this principle, we cannot draw the conclusion: having the talent for entrepreneurship, they should get huge profit as reward, because they may obtain rewards for this ability through other means, for example: praising them for their rare talent so that they are satisfied to some extent.

In regard to risk propensity, some scholars argue that investment is actually risky decision, so it should be rewarded. They presuppose that there are essentially two kinds of people: people willing to take risk and people unwilling to take risk. Among the people who take risks, only some become capitalists but many may go bankrupt. Proletariat comprises of those who are unwilling to take risk or those who took risk but has ended up with failure. Their surplus labor–capitalist profit is the premium they should pay to capitalists for the risk the capitalists take for them. In other words, it is the risk taken by capitalists which guarantees workers' stable wages and unworried sleep, so workers should pay capitalists because capitalists are gambling for them. Roemer thinks this view is extremely incredible. He said many workers also dream to become capitalists and are willing to take some risk, but they cannot, because they either lack the opportunity to enter capital market or lack the ability of entrepreneurs in some aspects -perhaps also including the possession of good relationships as social capital-. Besides, strictly speaking, the risks in workers' life is not lower than capitalists', for they are facing many risks like occupational diseases, unemployment and post-retirement poverty, which capitalists and managers do not face.

In regard to luck, some people argue that luck is a legitimate way to obtain property, so the highly unequal initial capital distribution caused by it should be considered as fair and just. Roemer pointed out that the most important luck is heritage, for people obtain different amounts of tangible capital ownership through it. Inheritance can be studied from both perspectives; the inheritor and that of the successor. If the wealth of the inheritor is legitimately obtained through labor, skill, his time preferences and risk propensity and saved by him , he should have the right to dispose these properties by his own will. But evaluated from the perspective of the next generation, i.e.: the potential successor is perhaps in those circumstances which extremely contain unequal opportunities. Roemer believes that equal opportunities aspect is a powerful argumentation to refute the proposition that luck is a legitimate means to obtain property. In other words, the property obtained by luck should belong to everybody rather than some certain individuals, because after all, no one can do anything which should inevitably rewarded by luck.

In short, in the real capitalist society, all the capital obtained by so-called morally irreproachable means has in fact to do with unfair initial capital distribution. Therefore, many inequalities in the real capitalist society are caused by the robbery and plunder which had occurred generations ago. One example is heritage. The unequal distribution of capital is unfair from the very beginning and it is the real cause of exploitation, and manifests that capitalist exploitation is unfair.

Roemer's above arguments aim to clarify that the capitalist private ownership of the means of production should be eliminated in order to eliminate capitalist exploitation. Whereas, some scholars argue that since capitalist exploitation is the result of the private ownership of the means of production and unequal ownership on them, the elimination of capitalist exploitation can be realized through equally distributing private property while retaining private property and market, i.e.: establishing "people's capitalism". Roemer has clearly rejected this view from the following aspects:

4. CRITIQUE OF PEOPLE'S CAPITALISM

Firstly, the market system itself has the problem of low efficiency. Roemer has argued that the reason why advocators of "people's capitalism" propose to retain market system is based on the hypothesis of neo-classical economics that market system, this "invisible hand", is the most efficient mechanism. Contrarily, Marxism believes that the market system in itself has the problem of low efficiency. Its typical manifestation is that in the current capitalist society, there is massive unemployment occurring from time to time plus a huge amount of idle capital assets especially during crises. Why is the hypothesis of neoclassical economics not realized? Roemer thinks it is because many conditions are required in order to ensure that "invisible hand" plays an effective role, whereas the market economy actually ruins a substantial part of those necessary conditions which enable the "success" of the market. If "people's capitalism" still insists to retain market system, it should inevitably face the problem of low efficiency, too. Roemer also specifically notes that his criticism on private property ownership is based on the major criticism made by Marx's historical materialism and historical materialism has proved that the economic structure adopting private ownership on transferable property is no longer the best choice for the emancipation and further development of productive forces.

Secondly, the equal re-distribution of the means of production cannot fully correct the mistakes originating from the previous unequal distribution. Roemer has commented : if we suppose that "people's capitalism" will be realized by offering everybody an equal share of national assets (transferable capital), still considerable inequality will appear in the later generation, if each individual keeps his/her former advantages of his/her skills and risk preferences and if thrift remain as before . This is because people's current preferences and skills are largely the result of previous unfair wealth distribution and cannot be changed magically by the new redistribution. Therefore, the redistribution of "people's capitalism" cannot correct the mistakes made by capitalism in the past.

Thirdly, the existence of private ownership and market system only marginally promote people's self-realization and emancipation. Roemer argues that people's preferences and values are not solely determined by the class they belong to and the wealth they possess, but also determined by the economic structure in which they live. Private ownership and the market system leads to commodity fetishism as described by Marx, i.e.: the consciousness (Germ. Bewusstsein) that both materials and people are evaluated based on their market value in the market system and accordingly equated. As "people's capitalism" still retains private ownership and market system, it will hamper people's self-realization and real emancipation.

Fourthly, the equal redistribution of private property cannot eliminate inequality, because some people can still obtain great benefits caused by the unequal initial distribution. Different people possess different inherent endowment. This difference is either inborn or obtained by luck, but obtaining benefit from endowment is morally unreasonable, because people should not become owners of their endowments. Although "people's capitalism" distributes private property equally, it is still an economic system which enables people to reap benefit from their inborn luck.

Roemer has commented: "it is not necessary that all of the above four reasons should be fully convincing, but any of them is powerful enough to refute the idea of correcting capitalist exploitation through people's capitalism".

All in all, Roemer argues that the way to eliminate the inequality resulting from different ownerships over external world is not to equalize the ownership of these properties but to adopt public ownership. This needs the elimination of a specific type of private property rights"[12], i.e.: elimination of capitalist ownership on the means of production.

The above describes the major thoughts of Roemer's exploitation theory based on non-labor theory of value. Certainly, in Roemer's theory, the criticism against

---

12   *Ibid.* p. 118.

the value orientation of capitalist system is clear-cut and his criticism is novel and intensive. It serves as an important reference for the vitality and development of Marxism today. However, Roemer's theory also has some obvious problems. On the one hand, although Marx's labor theory of value is facing many challenges, it is still an irreplaceable scientific theory for the analysis of capitalist exploitation in our era. Roemer has claimed that the labor theory of value was false without giving any convincing proofs and his conclusions are hardly acceptable. On the other hand, the main value of Marx's theory on capitalist exploitation is to reveal the capitalist production mode and the specific laws of the capitalist society generated by it, whereas Roemer claims that the only value of this theory is to indicate the inequality of capitalist exploitation. Thus obviously, he puts the cart before the horse. Moreover, in terms of his research methodology, Marx's research on the issue of exploitation adopts a holistic approach which proceeds from class relations, while Roemer adopts individualistic rational approach proceeding from isolated individuals. Thus his research method is also doubtful. Therefore, Roemer's criticism at capitalist exploitation evaluated as a whole fails to be fully scientific.

REFERENCES

• John E. Roemer: Free to Lose: An Introduction to Marxist Economic Philosophy, translated by Duan Zhongqiao and Liu Lei. Beijing, Economic Science Press, 2003.

CHAPTER II

STUDIES ON SOCIALISM AND DEMOCRACY

In recent years, people more frequently inquire on democracy and democratic politics and the relations between socialism and democracy, especially the relations between globalization and democracy .The policies by radical democracy and New Left movement, the issues of contemporary democracy and revolution have become hot topics[1]. In this chapter I will review these ideas and debates.

1. GLOBALIZATION AND DEMOCRACY

Does Globalization Cause the Crisis of Democracy?

The issue of the relations between globalization and democracy has aroused universal attention. By and large, people show two remarkably different attitudes towards it. Some people believe that globalization causes the depreciation and crisis of democracy; some people believe that globalization promotes democracy, because it abandons autocratic nation-states. Below we will analyze these views, respectively.

"Is globalization the cause for the crisis of democracy?" This is a question asked by German scholar Fritze Scharpf. His answer is positive. In his sense,

---

1   Main relevant works after mid 1980s: Ernesto Laclau and Chantal Mouffe: Hegemony and Socialist Strategy: Towards a Radical Democratic Politics (1985); Robert A. Dahl: Introduction of Economic Democracy (1985); Samuel Bowles and Herbert Gintis: Democracy and Capitalism: Property, Community, and the Contradictions of Modern Social Thought (1986); Carol C. Gould: Rethinking Democracy: Freedom and Social Co-operation in Politics, Economy, and Society (1988); Chantal Mouffe Editor in Chief: Dimensions of Radical Democracy: Pluralism, Citizenship, Community (Phronesis) (1992); Douglas Lummis: Radical Democracy (1996); George Labica: Révolution et Démocratie (2003).

globalization is the cause for the depreciation of democracy. Scharpf believes that since economic globalization, economic transnational integration is being strengthened with each passing day, and although the socialism in Eastern Europe has collapsed, the Western democracy did not win, instead it is drawn into trouble, because economic transnational integration eliminates the abilities developed by nation-states after the Second World War in "taming capitalism by means of democracy". Therefore, his conclusion is: the deficit of democracy in the globalized transnational politics is inevitable. Globalization is the cause for crisis of democracy.

According to Scharpf's analysis, globalization contributes to the crisis of democracy mainly from the following aspects:

(1) Following the globalization of the capital markets, the distribution relations becomes more favorable for employers, whereas the national economic policy loses the ability of guaranteeing sufficient employment by the Keynesian demand management method. Meanwhile, the internationalization of commodity and labor markets triggers competition and every government compete to attract enterprises and capital inflows to protect or enlarge their "economic bases". This competition prompts the governments to release taxes for enterprises and capital inflows, and also they restrict the social regulations on labor relations. As the taxes from labor income and consumption expenditures cannot be raised at discretion, the welfare expenditures by governments are restricted and social security system is narrowed. The consequence of the above phenomenon is the comeback of mass unemployment and poverty which was partly alleviated after the Second World War. In politics, the most serious result is that the status of the middle class which includes skillful technical workers and clerks becomes fragile. The continuity of this trend will lead to a crisis of democracy, because it not only impairs the interests of an overwhelming majority of people but also endangers social morality and awareness. In a word, the social problems resulting from unrestricted economy have weakened people's trust in democratic politics as a whole[2].

(2) Transnational politics almost always embody complicated multilateral negotiations. The result is that today no negotiation partner can unilaterally decide who will assume political responsibility or demand from any of its partners that; it should alone assume political responsibility. In the international negotiations, it is not that all negotiation partners acquire legal certification according to the Western concept by means of democracy. Even if their (actors') legitimacy is recognized, they should be responsible for politically separated constituency groups. As there are no political links among these separated groups, they cannot be considered as the "foundation" of integral democracy.

---

2   Fritze Scharpf: Democracy in Transnational Politics, Ullrich Baker et al.: Globalization and Politics, Beijing, Central Compilation & Translation Press, 2000, p. 126-127.

(3) Due to economic globalization and Europeanization, democratic politics faces triple challenges: firstly, the postwar welfare states are bygone. Secondly, the competition for "economic bases" implies a general loss of welfare in Western industrial states. Lastly, economic integration worsens domestic distribution. On the one hand, as some people obtain adequate opportunities to invest in all parts of the world, the power distribution between capital and labor changes. On the other hand, the competition for "economic bases" directly generates a second problem in the distribution sphere, i.e.: the competition by low-cost labor states firstly damages the low-quality labor force in high-cost labor states. No doubt, the industrialization of threshold states will increase the demand for capital goods and high-quality labor services.

Based on the above analysis, Scharpf believes that the Western democracy could not celebrate its victory and instead went into big trouble after the failure of socialism in Eastern Europe. The ever-increasing economic transnational integration since 1970s is the main reason, because this integration eliminates the ability developed by nation-states in decades after the Second World War in "taming capitalism by means of democracy". One should not expect that the social policy goals can be realized by transnational means, because it is impossible that transnational politics can obtain legitimacy by domestic democracies from within states but it can only be the product of multilateral negotiations among states. Obviously, Scharpf is pessimistic towards the trend of intensified globalization after the failure of socialism in Soviet Union and Eastern Europe. He thinks that this trend does not promote and expand democracy and on the contrary it makes democracy more deficient and weaker, and this deficiency and weakness is mainly caused by the emergence of multinational corporations which weaken the politics of nation-states and secondly this weakening depreciates the democratic traditions accumulated by nation-states over a long time.

Another German scholar Ullrich Baker made a profound study on the dilemma of democracy brought by globalization and how to get rid of it. On this issue, Baker thinks that in the sense of Niklas Luhmann, political monopoly exists in territorial states, while territorial states are losing influence in the process of globalization. Therefore, "world society" means a non-political society without world politics, world parliament and world government. This society is a completely decentralized society. It does away with the legitimacy which is broken down into countless self reproduction, self regulation and democracy. Baker objects Luhmann's above views. Firstly, a modern state represents a kind of organization of social space. Inside it, every aspect of sociality is established on the principle of territorial sovereignty. Therefore, the "world society" in Luhmann's sense is a Western world society in essence and a world society excluding the Third World. Secondly, the theory of "world society" does not realize that today a great many new political actors which transcend nation-states are acquiring power in terms of quality and quantity. These actors are considered "non-political", because they enormously effect the shaping of power relations, legislation, lifestyle, laboring modes, global society, and virtual world of nation-state society. Thirdly, it is difficult to understand the view that world society is a society without world state and world government, because from the economic perspective, it is impossible that there is a world economic department managing huge economic trusts which engage in transnational activities. In the policy range of world states, world economy is an actor without opponent; it transcends the reference framework and intervention by nation-states and is deemed as a "non-political" force.

However, it can create and develop its own political forces in the political vacuum created as a result of transcending the nation-states. It also implies that world society is a post-political world on the surface appearance, but just for this reason, it is highly political in the sense it gets rid of the political relations designed by nation-states.

Baker concludes that in the era of globalization, it is not very easy to get rid of this democracy dilemma because on the one hand, this dilemma cannot be smoothly solved in the direction of "cosmopolitan democracy. [...] and on the other hand, all the attempts to extremalize the activity fields of democracy in nation-states ignore the unique realities and self motives of transnational activity sphere , its power field, objective problems, conflicts and so on. In addition, these attempts also absolutize and exaggerate the historical institutional tradition of nation-states, national economy and parliament democracy[3].

Therefore, Baker proposes "world citizenship initiative", i.e.: "a world party", "the values and goals of world citizenship initiative and activity of world citizens". In other words, it should be based on the values and traditions of all human cultures and religions and realize that it should assume obligations considering the globe as a whole – respect freedom, differences and tolerance. World party is quite different from any previous party in the nation-state based on its own values, traditions and based on self-solidarity. World citizenship initiative regards global issues as the center of its political vision and political actions. Through concrete alternative policies, it programmatically and institutionally opposes the priority unbendable to nation-states. Its goal is always to open and reform the political system of nation-states in order to solve the problems in "global sphere and level". World citizenship initiative or world citizen party certainly has different sources, for example from France, Canada, USA, Poland, Germany, Japan, China and South Africa. Although different states have different views, they cooperate with each other and strive to realize the values and a system of cosmopolitism. Today, the problem before us to solve is to realize the democracy of transnational non-political politics. In the end, Baker put forth a slogan: The world citizens in the whole world, unite![4]

---

3   Ullrich Baker et al.: Globalization and Politics, p. 32-33.
4   *Ibid.*, p. 70.

Globalization generates "Empire"

Another concept opposing against the above view is argued by post-Marxist American scholars Michael Hardt and Italian scholar Antonio Negri. In their book *Empire*: they have argued that the globalization of capitalist mode of production and exchange means that economic relations have become more autonomous from political controls, and consequently political sovereignty has declined. While still important, the sovereignty of nation states has progressively declined. The primary factors of production and exchange – money, technology, labor and commodities – move with increasing freedom across national boundaries; hence the nation state has less and less power to regulate these flows and cannot impose its authority over the economy. Even the most powerful nation states should no longer be regarded as supreme and sovereign authorities, neither outside nor even within their own borders[5]. Therefore, they have argued that a new form of state – "empire" emerges:

Empire is emerging before us. In past decades, the colonial system was abandoned and the Soviet Union and its allies, restricting the formation of a global market has finally collapsed. We can witness the irresistible and irreversible globalization of economic and cultural exchanges. Following the formation of the global market and the global production lines, the order of globalization, a new logic and structure of ruling system, simply to express, a new form of sovereignty is emerging. Empire is a political object. It effectively controls global exchanges. It is the top authority which rules the world.

Michael Hardt and Antonio Negri explain the logic behind their ideas: under the circumstances of globalization, sovereignty has taken a new form, composed of a series of national and supra-national organisms united under a single logic of rule. This new global form of sovereignty is called "empire". This kind of "empire" is completely different from "imperialism". Imperialism was the expansion of their sovereignty by European nation-states, which exceeded their own boundaries, while "empire" emerges while imperialism declines. Compared with imperialism, empire does not have a center of power and does not rely on fixed boundaries and limits. It is a ruling machine without center and boundary. Michael Hardt and Antonio Negri envisage that firstly, empire is a hypothetic system which successfully covers spatial integrity or in other words really rule the whole "civilized" world. No national border can limit its increasing dominion. Secondly, the concept of empire expresses that it is not rather a historical regime which originates from conquest as an order which successfully terminates history and hence permanently fixes the existing situation. In other words, empire does not stand for the rules which are fleeting in historical movements but stands for a

---

5   Michael Hardt and Antonio Negri: Empire – Introduction, Nanjing, Jiangsu People's Publishing House, 2003.

system which has not temporary boundaries and is beyond history and at the end point of history. Thirdly, the rules of empire control the social order extended to each layer of group world. Empire not only governs a territorial population, but also creates a world where it settles itself; not only rules human associations but also directly seeks human dominion. The object it rules is the complete social life, so empire represents a typical form of life power. Fourthly, the practice of empire is always bathed in blood, but the concept of empire has always been propagated as offering peace – a perpetual and universal peace beyond history[6]. Michael Hardt and Antonio Negri also believe that empire manages hybrid identities, flexible hierarchies and plural exchanges through modulating networks of command. In this way, the obvious colors of nation states on the original world map of imperialism have been incorporated and mixed into a global rainbow of the empire.

Michael Hardt and Antonio Negri have argued that this ideal road of "empire" and the process of globalization provide a new possibility for freedom struggles. The "living subjects" of the empire may even independently create "anti-imperialism" and the struggle against, resist and overthrow empire and the struggle for establishing a real alternative will constantly waged inside the empire. Through these struggles, a new democratic form and a new constitutional power will be created and one day the original empire may even be transcended.

For Michael Hardt and Antonio Negri, in the society of empire, the production of subjectivity is tending not to be restricted by any concrete location. Following the universal meltdown of boundaries, the functions of system are broadened and deepened. The social system of empire can be considered to be formed in the flow process consisting of the generation and fall of subjectivity. In the process of modernization, developed capitalist states output their institutional forms, and colonists sing the song of praise for them and believe that these systems constitute the basis of the new civil society. By contrast, in this postmodern process, the output of the system causes a universal institutional crisis. The system of empire is like a software program with virus and constantly adjusts and destroys the institutional forms around it. Today an empire-controlled society is going to become the order dominant in all regions. The control means of the empire in fact consists of three stages with clear demarcation: The first stage is the stage of tolerance. It represents the facets of magnificence and liberty of the empire. In this stage, the empire turns a blind eye to everything and accepts people of all skin colors without discrimination. It sets aside differences, thus realizing a universal tolerance. This approach means taking out all the potentials that comprise subjects, generating a neutral power space and making the establishment and legitimacy of a universal authority view possible. The core of the empire will be formed by this new authority view. The second stage is a stage of differentiation.

6   *Ibid.*

It involves the recognition on the accepted differences. This second stage was particularly obvious after the end of the Cold War. Developments which were deemed as transformation from socialism to capitalism were supported by the global regime. These differences are considered cultural rather than political so that they will play a role as a uniform force in peaceful areas. The third stage is the stage of manipulation. In this stage, these differences are manipulated and hierarchically differentiated. Colonial force seeks and determines authentic and separate identity, while the empire becomes prosperous with the help of flow and jumble.

Michael Hardt and Antonio Negri use "decline" to define the empire sovereignty. That is to say, on the one hand, empire is not pure but a hybrid body; on the other hand, the rules of the empire play their roles mainly through separation and deconstruction. Separation and deconstruction happen at every moment of the empire society, but it does not mean that the empire goes to its doom. The crisis of modern sovereignty is not interim or particular but a normal state of modernity. Likewise, decline is not the deviation of empire sovereignty but its soul. The power of empire is established on the basis of destroying and separating all determined ontological relations.

Thus it can be seen, the "empire" envisaged by Michael Hardt and Antonio Negri is a sheer utopia divorced from reality and an illusion of Post-modernisms, because this kind of empire will be a hybrid and plural, anarchical state. The core content of the book *Empire* is to illustrate the vicissitude of the forms of social and political power during capitalist globalization, and argues that under the circumstances of globalization, the sovereignty of nation-states are declining, but sovereignty has taken a new form and is composed of a series of national and supra-national organisms united under a single logic of rule. This new global form of sovereignty is defined as "empire".

Since the book *Empire* was published by American Harvard University Press in 2000, it has attracted wide attention from the ideological circles. Some Post-modernisms have praised it as the *Communist Manifesto* rewritten in our times (Slovenian philosopher Slavoj Zizek) and as the next great thought (New York Times). It has even gained favor from European rightists. European rightists regard empire a politically authoritative model that substitutes nation state, because it represents a selective model for the organization of political life; the ultimate political goal of European New Right should be to create a Europe made of numerous national communities, regions and free cities and hundreds of flags. The only model which can maintain a decentralized political body with diversified cultures could be the decentralized political structure of empire. Some people have criticized this book and considered it as a "global nonsense" and the *City of God* distorted by Post-modernisms (Alan Wolf).

Certainly, in their book, Michael Hardt and Antonio Negri perceive incisively the new changes brought to human society by globalization: apart from economic changes, more importantly, it also brings new major changes in politics and power structures. Globalization shatters all deep-rooted political powers and the one substituting them is a superpower – surpassing imperialism–– empire, which is bigger and stronger than any power. However, the "empire" in the sense of Michael Hardt and Antonio Negri is a described as a thing transcending substance. It is a kind of "spiritual kingdom" or in the current popular phrase "virtual kingdom". In this "spiritual kingdom" or "virtual kingdom", people enjoy sufficient democracy, because they can freely deconstruct this "empire" and then reconstruct it. The assumptions and descriptions by Michael Hardt and Antonio Negri remind me online PC games.

2. RADICAL DEMOCRACY STRATEGY BY NEW LEFT

Laclau and Mouffe's Theory of Radical Democracy

"Radical democracy" is an important concept introduced by post-Marxists Ernesto Laclau and Chantal Mouffe in their book *Hegemony and Socialist Strategy: towards a Radical Democratic Politics*[7].

According to the analysis of Laclau and Mouffe, radical democracy has emerged since democracy and socialism both have failed. "Democracy", initially which was conceived as the actions of the masses, was the leading factor in the historical confrontations of the era and had dominated European political life between 1789 to 1848. In that period, the "people" who were almost non-organized have carried out barricade battles in 1789 and 1848, the Chartism in Britain, and created the Mazzini and Garibaldi Movements in Italy. But after 1850s, the leading actors have become trade unions and the social democratic parties. However, later on, due to the complication and institutionalization of the capitalist society, "promise" people becoming the masters of their country was not realized but at the same time became more difficult to realize. As analyzed by Gramsci, capitalism has become a shelter and fort of a civil society and enables the factors that can be unified among the people to be re-separated and combined. The fundamental defect of social democracy has made it impossible that workers become the subjects of history.

Laclau and Mouffe believe that Marx had analyzed the phenomenon of social differentiation by applying his theory of class hostility, whereas this theory has caused serious defects since the very beginning: class hostility cannot make a

---

7   The book of Laclau and Mouffe was published in 1985. Before it, books and articles on this thought have appeared in 1960. American scholar Douglas Lummis had once commented that he has discussed on the topic of radicalness and democracy with his friends as early as 1980, and has published an article titled Democratic Radicalism in 1982 and the book Radical Democracy in 1996.

society divided into two opposite camps and cannot make itself a boundary of differentiation and hostility in political field. In conclusion, the changes brought by Marxism into the political principle based on social differentiation have in fact inherited the essential characteristics of Jacobinism, i.e.: the hypothesis on the unique fields where fundamental separation factors and party politics can be formed. The continuity between Jacobinist and Marxist political theories on radical democracy is doubted by the new left program of radical democracy. A new political theory can be established only on the basis of refusing converging separation points and refusing struggles based on a unified political space and recognizing the pluralism and inclusiveness of the society.

Laclau and Mouffe have reviewed the history of democratic revolutions. They have analyzed that there were anti-capitalist radical struggles in the 19th century, but they were not proletarian struggles. Labor movements which could be strictly called as the product of capitalism have only appeared in Britain till mid 19th century and Europe till late 19th century, but this kind of labor movements had less and less doubts or opposition against capitalist production relations and instead they have only focused to reform production relations. Comparing with the previous radical struggles, this trend was a retrogression; therefore it was called "reformism". Therefore this affiliation in this period —between workers and capitalists —have formed a unified/common discourse however it was to some extent regarded as two different legitimate stances. In the late period of the First World War and the period of radical labor movements after the this war, a series of new circumstances have emerged, such as: paralysis of social order, militarization of factories, adoption of Taylor production management system and the changes in the roles of skillful workers in production, all have affected the organizational crisis of hegemonic power and changes in the attitudes of traditional workers. In the 20 years after the Second World War, "the new capitalist symptom of joviality" has appeared. It seemed to have an unlimited absorbing and assimilating capacity persuading people to struggle for partial system changes and it seemed that any potential of antagonism could be alleviated and assimilated into a homogeneous and unitary society. Welfare state could meet numerous social demands, but it was embattled in some complicated and recurrent contradictions. Under these consequences egalitarian struggles and democratic revolutionary activity were generated from new sources, newer directions and new fields. This can be termed as the democratic revolution by "New Social Movements". In this new era social relations were commercialized and bureaucratized. On the other hand, there occurred an ideological change towards freedom and democracy has caused a constant expansion struggles for equality. These are the key factors for the deepening of democratic revolution. Meanwhile, the emergence of "democratic consumption culture" has triggered new struggles and it plays an important role in resisting old affiliations. For Laclau and Mouffe, these "new confrontations" are quite diversified and pluralistic and now the basic conditions of democracy should be explored and understood as radical and plural democracy, this should be the new concept.

What is radical and plural democracy? Many scholars consider "radicalism" a heterodox behavior and a trend of extremism in political ideas and actions. Generally, it may also refer to the extremist fraction of the Left wing, i.e.: Extreme Left, or Ultra Revolutionary. The "radicalism" in the sense of Laclau and Mouffe is based on "pluralism". In other words, it will be radical if the opposing subject admits the principle of pluralism and denies the principle of unitariness; vice versa, to be radical the opposing subject should admit pluralism. Therefore, they have argued that the concept of subject should not retrogress to the principle of affirmation, obedience and unity. As long as this approach is accepted, pluralism will be deemed a radical concept. The pluralism of unity embodies effectiveness in this principle and only in this range, pluralism can be radical[8].

Laclau and Mouffe have argued that in the face of the offensive of Conservative and Right forces, the choice of Left should be to completely orient itself to democratic revolution and develop a chain of equals in the anti-oppression struggles. Left should not to give up the ideology of freedom and democracy but deepen and expand them in the direction of radical and plural democracy[9]. In many cases, overthrowing an old oppressive system by means of violence is the condition for the development of democracy, but the connotations of traditional revolutions have gone quite beyond this. And they have caused some fundamental features i.e.: establishing a centralized system of rule through which the society was "reasonably" re-organized. But this old tradition contradicts with the pluralism and openness required by radical democracy. Laclau and Mouffe have further explained this idea arguing on the hypothesis of the classic concept of socialism which has asserted that the elimination of private ownership on the means of production will eliminate all forms of affiliations in the entire new historical era, but the real facts have not proved that. Although socialism is a part in the program of radical democracy, as facts have proved the other way round was not and cannot be the same. Therefore, Laclau and Mouffe have written that when setting the socialization of the means of production as one of the goals in the strategy of radical and plural democracy, people should insist that this kind of socialization should not only include workers' autonomous management and control on them. More crucially, all subjects should equally participate in the decision making: what to be produced, how to produce and in what form the products will be distributed. Only under these circumstances, can the social control on the products be created. The main limitation of the previous traditional left view is that it has transcendentally attempted to determine the representatives of changes, the layers of effectiveness in social field, fracture factors and privileges.

---

8   Ernesto Laclau and Chantal Mouffe: Hegemony and Socialist Strategy: Towards a Radical Democratic Politics, p.186.

9   *Ibid.*, p.198.

Just as Mouffe has written in his book *Return of the Politics*, the strategy of radical democracy will generate a new hegemony. This hegemony will be the comprehensive product of maximum possible quantity of democratic struggles[10]. Mouffe has also argued that what they need is a kind of "hegemony" of democratic values. It requires the diversity of democratic practices and institutionalizing them in more and more diversified social relations, thus the diversity of subject status can be shaped through the matrix of democracy. This kind of hegemony can never be abandoned. Laclau wrote in his book *Identity and Hegemony: The Role of Universality in the Constitution of Political Logics*: "What is 'hegemony'?" A "hegemonic" method fully accepts the following viewpoint; ethical factor is a universal factor in a community. It is a factor which surpasses any exclusivist universality. "Hegemony" embodies an inner tension in the relation between ethics and norms and also is a method by which we explain this uncertain input process. Laclau has also written that it is necessary to stress that "hegemony" is an ethical method. It depends on the fundamental ethical decision to be accepted[11].

Laclau has defined the four dimensions of "hegemony" as follows:

(1) The imbalance of power is constructive.

(2) Hegemony can only exist because universality/particularity dichotomy is eliminated; universality exists only because it is reflected in a particularity and destructs it. On the contrary, if a particularity cannot become a place where universality displays its effect, it cannot become politics.

(3) Hegemony is inclined to produce a void signifier. When the incommensurability between universality and particularity is maintained, this signifier will enable the latter to become a representative of the former.

(4) The field in which hegemony is expanded can be such a field: the generalization of representative relations is the condition for the structure of social order[12].

Laclau has argued that among the four dimensions, the first dimension stresses the dependency of universality on particularity. This is because in a traditional revolutionary movement, due to Marx's political model, the condition in which a special group (proletariat) declares its goal as the goal of the whole universal

---

10   Chantal Mouffe: Return of the Political, Nanjing, Jiangsu People's Publishing House, 2001, p. 20.
11   Ernesto Laclau: Identity and Hegemony: The Role of Universality in the Constitution of Political Logics, please refer to Judith Butler et al.: Contingency, Hegemony, Universality: Contemporary Dialogues on the Left, p. 79, Nanjing, Jiangsu People's Publishing House, 2004, p. 218-219.
12   Ernesto Laclau: Structure, History and Politics, please refer to Judith Butler et al.: Contingency, Hegemony, Universality: Contemporary Dialogues on the Left, p. 218-219.

community inherently embodies the idea that another (opposite) group exists and this other is deemed as a public evil. The second dimension above stresses and explains the role of universality. This is the first dimension of the power inherent in universal emancipation strategy. The conditions of universality set a fundamental repulsion in advance. In the sense of Laclau and Mouffe, the real emancipation should include the elimination of power. That is to achieve a kind of universality which does not depend on particularity, i.e.: as the "human emancipation" defined by Marx. It includes and represents an even a higher human ideal which is harmonious as a whole, i.e.: realizing a fully harmonious and transparent society. This society will be fully free in a self-specified sense.

In the relation between the logic of democracy and the design of hegemony, Laclau and Mouffe have argued that the logic of democracy is not enough to form any hegemony, because it is only the identical replacement of more extensive social relations as demanded by equalitarianism and it is only the logic which aims eliminating unequal affiliations. It is not a social demonstrative logic, so it cannot establish any form of nodes reconstructing social structure. However, if the subversive factors of the logic of democracy and the affirmative factors of the social system are no longer united by any anthropological basis and this anthropological basis turns them into the reverse side of a front and into a single process, then any possible form of unity between them will be occasional and thus become the result of connection process per se. It is just the following circumstance: no design of hegemony absolutely can be established in the logic of democracy. Instead, it must consist of a series of demonstrative social organization schemes[13].

Laclau and Mouffe believe that today democratic revolution is the source of a new social system and in this system power will be "emptied". Therefore, the modern democratic society will be built into a society in which power, law and knowledge is messed up by radical non-determinist actors and society becomes an uncontrollable adventurous theatre; as a result, any effort for institutionalization could not be realized, and the known is still uncertain due to the unknown elements and it is quite true that we cannot also define things occurring today[14]. Therefore, according to the thinking mode of radical democracy, the reconstruction of a new democratic revolutionary strategy requires the abandonment of the abstract illusion of universalism which does not differentiate individual human natures. Today, this illusion has become a major obstacle blocking the future development of democratic revolution. The differences radical democracy requires us to admit—particularity, diversity and heterogeneous – in fact this should include all things repulsed by the traditional abstract concept of human.

---

13   Ernesto Laclau and Chantal Mouffe: Hegemony and Socialist Strategy: Towards a Radical Democratic Politics, p. 211-212.
14   Chantal Mouffe: Return of the Political, p. 12.

The strategy of radical democracy should try to protect the current democratic system, and extend its applicability to many new social relations. Its purpose is to create another aspect in the liberal and democratic tradition, which will no longer approach to people's rights under the framework of individualism but prefer truly visualizing/realizing "democratic rights". This will generate a kind of new hegemony which will be the complex total sum of maximum possible quantity of democratic struggles. Thus we can understand that the hegemony defined by Laclau and Mouffe is hegemony with "democratic values". This new democratic practice requires diversity and should be institutionalized within all diverse social relations in the society so that the diversity of the subjects can be shaped through the matrix of democracy. This strategy requires the existence of diversity, pluralism and conflict, while the hegemony achieved by radical democracy can never be abandoned , because it does not need/require any society ruled by the unitary logic of democracy.

Douglas Lummis and Radical Democracy

For Lummis, "democracy" is a term which refers "belonging to the people", a term intrinsically including criticism and a term referring to revolution. But it was plagiarized by rulers to conquer legitimacy for their rule. Now it is the time to take it back and restore its critical and radical power. Although the history of its use is a history of hypocrisy and treachery, democracy is still a pure word in a sense and it still contains a commitment yet to be fulfilled till present era. Thus, Lummis aims to give a true meaning for "democracy". The term should be used to describe democratic things only. It means identifying and discarding the distorted essence and eliminating hypocritical use of this term.

The first step of Lummis' work is to research the history of the concept of "democracy" and define it anew.

Re-define "people": (A) Democracy is usually defined as government by the people. Lummis thinks that the traditional way to evade the radical connotation of this word is excluding slaves, some races, the poor or other groups which narrows the scope of the concept. Usually, in a state when the upper class claims that they support the "rights of people", the "people" they refer here only includes themselves; when they propagate democracy, they never mean democracy for slaves and servants but for middle and upper classes.

Re-define "people": (B). Sometimes, a ruling party or a party seeking political power claims it is democratic but actually they re-define "people" as those "who support their party". The government they establish describes the manipulated people who support it as "reliable mouthpieces-commonsense- of the people".

Re-define "people": (C). Another variant of the above case is that as long as a party has correct consciousness, it thinks it represents the soul and ideas of the people. When such a party claims to be people's power and claims it represents people's voice (but the "people" here are abstract rather than concrete humans"), the problem arises. Such power is different from the power enjoyed by people.

Subsequently, Lummis has analyzed the discourses on democracy.

"Democracy is to care for people's welfare". Lummis believes that a party and a king may both care for people's welfare policy, but their rule is still autocratic, because democracy does not mean that people are blessed by a kind or a just ruler, instead the meaning of democracy is that "people rule themselves"

"Democracy is to have a ruler supported by the people". But this may easily be confused with democracy. For example, a ruler obtains support by offering promises, but it is not democracy. This is not democracy; people should not transfer their rights to someone in exchange with given promises.

"Democracy is development" (A). Some people claim that democracy is a modern and progressive governance system of the future which will be the end point of an automatic historical development process. In fact, democracy is one of the oldest ruling forms, the spirit of democracy has appeared from time to time in history and people have indeed fought for it. If we expect to obtain democracy through waiting, we will wait for it forever.

"Democracy is development" (B). Some people claim that economic development itself is democratic. If economic development means that people assume their control on the centers of economic power — lands, factories, corporates and banks, it makes sense; but if economic development only means increase of wealth, no matter how good this development is, it will not be a democracy. Democracy is a form of political rule rather than a mode of economic development.

"Democracy is a pronoun of American constitutional and democratic system". Some elements in the American constitutional system have high value, but they should not be regarded as the definition of democracy. America has not solved the problem of economic democracy – and the democracy in the workplace yet, Americans have not found a method which can surpass the anti-democratic imperialism in their country yet, they have not solved the problem of ever-increasing domestic power centralization in Washington yet and it is extremely likely that they have forgotten their long tradition of radical democracy.

"Democracy is free elections". Free election is a very important democratic method under some circumstances, but under some other circumstances, election can be used and becomes a route through which some demagogues or landlords can seize power[15].

Lummis has observed the discourses about democracy and made a profound analysis on the essence of bourgeoisie democracy. Meanwhile, he has also analyzed the democracy in the era of Soviet Union. "Some Marxists think that democracy has been achieved or transcended by socialism/communism, i.e.: when the private ownership on means of production is abolished, the issue of democracy will automatically die out together with state and politics." But the historical experience indicates that a new economic system can guarantee nothing, and the people in socialist countries have to achieve democracy through struggle. Therefore, Lummis thinks that in today's world, mankind has never obtained true democracy, and the democracy in the past was not true democracy, either. Then what does true democracy refer to?

Lummis has argued that "democracy is common sense" , but regarding democracy as common sense does not mean that it is agreed by all people in the same way; regarding democracy as common sense means that the concept of democracy is simple and it is not an abstract philosophy and should be expressed with an ordinary language. Democracy also means government by the people. People should unite themselves into an entity. Only through this entity, can power be grasped with principle. "Democracy demands consensus" is close to this meaning. The word of democracy is the combination of demos (people) and kratia (power). Who are demos? What is kratis? What kratis should demos have? How do demos arrange their kratis? Through which systems and regulations should it be guaranteed? Lummis argues that democracy is not an arrangement by any special political or economic system. Instead the actual situation could be so that the alleged political or economic system may or may not be good for democracy. Democracy describes a kind of idea, rather than a method to realize this idea. It is not a form of governance but the goal of governance; it is a historically existing system, rather than a historical cause. Lummis has sharply explained that usually, the standard definitions for democracy all deviate from the above basic ideas. In the Oxford English Dictionary democracy is defined as "government by the people". In the Columbia Encyclopedia, democracy is described as "a government where the people participate in managing the activities of the state".

The problem here is that the term "power" is substituted by the term "government", thus the definition in Columbia Encyclopedia also deviates from the true meaning of democracy; and limits democracy as the "activities of the state". For Lummis, "The government of the people, by the people, and for the people" as defined by Abraham Lincoln can be a supplement to his above ideas, but it is not an accurate definition of democracy, either[16].

---

15 Lummis: Radical Democracy, p. 8-11.

16 *Ibid.*, p. 14-15.

Lummis thinks that among many versions of democracy, such as: liberal demo-
cracy, social democracy, democratic socialism, Christian democracy, people's de-
mocracy and popular democracy, "radical democracy" is the best, because firstly,
this pattern of democracy aims to align with those people who have claimed or
claim themselves as radical democrats whose deeds and practice are consistent
with their past and current attitudes; secondly, the modifier "radical" is accen-
tuation. Radical democracy means the democracy which is in its essential and
elementary form and fundamental democracy, exactly speaking, it is democracy
itself[17].

Lummis also thinks that the hidden meaning of the term "radical" helps to explain the essence and elements of democracy. Democracy is politically radical and
"left". "Left" is a political metaphor and originates from the French Constituent
Assembly held in 1789. "Left" means "standing on the side of the people".
Democracy also contains other important meanings ; criticizes all forms of centralization of powers in the hands of extraordinary leaders, bureaucrats, classes,
troops, companies, parties, trade unions, technologies, and so on. In terms of
definition, democracy is the anti-thesis against all these powers. Observing the
governments and economic institutions in today's world, radical democracy is
subversive everywhere, not only in the regimes of military dictatorships but also
in those so-called democratic states and authoritarian states. Lummis thinks the
term "radical" in radical democracy also has the meaning of "stock" and "basic", so radical democracy is the basis, the root of all powers, the basis of all
regimes, and the root term for all political terms[18]. Democracy is basic politics[19].
Therefore, in the sense of Lummis, "radical democracy" is "basic politics" or
"stock" of politics; is "basic democracy", or "democracy itself", and is an important element of politics. Obviously, it is remarkably different from the ordinary
meaning of radical as "rapid" or "extreme".

Lummis has further illustrated the content of radical democracy. He thinks that
radical democracy can be understood in two aspects. One belongs to the domain
of reality and the other belongs to the domain of value. All powers stem from
people's judgment on relevant realities. This judgment indicates that political power does not stem from ruler but the ruled; there will not be a king unless many
people agree to be its subjects; when each and everyone decides not to be a subject, nobody can become a king. Therefore, the value judgment is that those who
generate power should also possess the power[20]. However, democracy brings a dilemma for us. On the one hand, people are free and deserve respect: they should
be what they are without being intervened. On the other hand, if people want to

---

17   *Ibid.*, p. 16-17.
18   *Ibid.*, p. 18.
19   *Ibid.*
20   *Ibid.*, p. 30.

control power, they must turn themselves into an entity through which power is controlled in principle (only). This dilemma becomes more complicated in a multi-cultural world. For example, democrats living in a country outside Europe are blamed by two critics: a new colonist snob says "there democracy is immature" and "these people are not ready for democracy and do not have a democratic political culture". The anti-colonial or an anti-imperialist conventionalist elites say it is cultural imperialist attempt to introduce democracy based on different values. For this, the correct answer by democrats should be democracy is common sense[21].

Therefore, Lummis highly favors Foucault's theory of power. Foucault has criticized that the society is a concrete right to rule the people. Lummis thinks that this criticism is the very foothold and starting point of radical democracy and firmly disagrees with the famous definition of democracy given by Joseph Alois Schumpeter in 1942 as "democratic method is an institutional arrangement in order to realize political decision and an individual obtains the power of political decisions through winning people's vote". Lummis neither agrees with Benjamin Barber's democracy definition engraved in pre-political marble which is established on a mistake-free basis. Lummis expresses even stronger disagreement with the "pre-political democracy" with a meaning and essence limited to ontology as argued by Laclau and Mouffe in *Hegemony and Socialist Strategy: Towards a Radical Democratic Politics*. In fact, Lummis writes that Chapter 1-Democracy in Marx's early work *Critique of Hegel's Philosophy of Right* is the closest to the manifesto of radical democracy, but it is a great pity that since after Marx became a communist, he had never in detail illustrated on the issue of democracy again. After Marx became a communist, he has also not discarded his initial understanding of democracy but has sublimed that approach. In Marx's understanding of communism, that democracy approach is not only maintained but also given more prominent meaning. Nevertheless, for Lummis the elaborate illustration on democracy in *Critique of Hegel's Philosophy of Right* is unique among Marx's works. Lummis has highly appreciated and reviewed Marx's early theories on democracy, but his several evaluations indicate that he could not perceive the essence and requirements of democracy as analyzed by Marx in that era.

In *Critique of Hegel's Philosophy of Right*, Marx had written with a keen insight: "In monarchy the whole, the people, is subsumed under one of its modes of existence, the political constitution; in democracy the constitution itself appears only as one determination, and indeed as the self-determination of the people. In monarchy we have the people of the constitution, in democracy it is the constitution of the people. Democracy is the resolved mystery of all constitutions."[22]

---

21   *Ibid.*, p. 32-33.
22   Collected Works of Karl Marx and Frederick Engels, Chinese Version 1, Vol.1, Beijing, People's Publishing House, 1965, p.281.

Marx had continued: "democracy starts with man and makes the state objectified man", "democracy is the essence of every political constitution, socialized man under the form of a particular constitution of the state"[23], while "Hegel proceeds from the state and turns man into the subjectified state"[24]. Today, we can see that Marx's words have no much difference from Lummis' theory of radical democracy. However, these views inevitably bear the impression of early Marxist democrats, while when Marx joined a deeper practice and study, his thoughts became more complete and mature and no longer remained in abstract democracy. In *Communist Manifesto*, Marx had written: "the first step in the revolution by the working class is to raise the proletariat to the position of ruling class to win the battle of democracy"[25]. Marx has believed that if the proletariat is not to be raised to the position of ruling class, democracy will be only an empty word. Therefore, after deeper revolutionary practice, Marx has naturally paid more attention to the issues of establishment of the proletarian regime and proletariat dictatorship and wrote less on the issue of democracy. In comparison, Lummis is only limited to the prate of democracy and radical democracy. Marx has insisted underlined that democracy should not be described as a system or a package system but a state/ phase of existence, and that struggle for democracy is not designing abstract systems on democracy but to change that existence–state of things-[26]. Lummis himself has also stressed that radical democracy not better introduce some kind of new ethics of heroism related to this world – he suggested radical democracy only requires better use of our owned tentative virtues. To achieve radical democracy, we need to have confidence in these common sense virtues. The democratic beliefs and common sense beliefs are established by the people who do not destroy their own brothers and off springs. Obviously, the radical democracy in Lummis' sense is established and acquired by relying on "common sense virtues" and "common sense belief" and does not require any fighting spirit and sacrificing spirit of heroism, not to say aims to establish a new social system; democratic belief is radical democracy. Belief in it is enough. Whereas, this kind of democracy is unavoidably kind of fantasy, apart from providing a little common sense of democracy for the people.

---

23   Ibid.
24   Ibid.
25   Marx and Engels Selected Works, Edition 2, Vol.1, p. 293.
26   Lummis: Radical Democracy, p. 157.

3. LEBICA AND DEMOCRATIC REVOLUTION

Famous French Marxist researcher George Labica has published his work
Révolution et Démocratie in 2002. In this book, Professor Labica has expressed his
new ideas on issues of democracy and revolution in the new era. "Democracy has
become a core topic of debate today and this debate is shared by most countries
and regions in the current world". Below we will introduce this book.

Cosmopolitan Demand for Democracy

The demand for democracy has to do with both the changes in the old-style
democracy and the termination of autarchy prevalent in most Third World countries as well as the collapse of "realistically existent" socialism. The demand for
democracy among some people, young people in particular, is full of illusions. For
example, in Algeria, people even regard not finding banana in the market as a sign
of socialism. In Albania, many people have fled from their motherland and went
into exile in France. The democracy imagined by them is American-style democracy and is to own a villa with a swimming pool, beautiful women, money, cars
and so on. In Russia, during the first presidential election, people have discussed
Western democracy, as if the democracy introduced by their decades' practiced
social system was completely ludicrous. Does the cosmopolitan demand for democracy have a close relation with market cosmopolitism? The answer is positive,
because it seems that market has produced a unique political form of democracy,
and these two mutually interact. For example, in China, markets and power are
both incompatible.

Democracy cannot be reduced to an acceptable program in any time. It is the fruit
of tradition and practice on the basis of social struggles. In history, democracy
was considered the most effective and acceptable system by market and capital. In
fact capitalism and democracy are confused. In the form and content of national
reconciliation, under conditions of the cosmopolitan demand for democracy, will
democracy be fruitless? Liberalism which is of no help to democracy arouses
and triggers the demand for nationalism, racism and also religion here and there.
From ancient Greece to today, has there been never a democracy without exer-
cising "exclusion". "Greek model of democracy" was established based on the
concept of elite citizens. This concept excludes a majority of people – aliens, slaves and women. Of course, our democracy is more advanced than the Athenian
democracy, but exclusion also exists in caucus activities. For example, in France,
women were given the right to vote only in recent 50 years, but regardless of so-
lemn vow, alien laborers have never obtained the right for election, even the right
for limited expression. Today all democracies are fragile. In a democratic system,
all political and social forces opposite to democracy use democratic process and
freedom in order to ascend to the throne of power. The Nazi system not long

before was established in this way. Same case has happened in Algeria recently, too. In Algeria, the emerging democracy movement was accused and labeled as a threat by "anti-democratic forces" and was suppressed by force. In countries like France and Italy, the political and ideological schools which are adverse to democracy have become a practical danger. Russia which was once granted by the certificate of democracy by Western powers is now severely criticized by them. Does democracy have no restriction? We still do not know. Once bourgeoisie is under threat, it will resort to fascism without hesitation. Is not democracy a manipulation or manipulated? The act that covers its anarchic essence under the pretext of "market laws" and serves only to commercialization of profit maximization is easily adapted to commercial transactions of selling own organs and own children for survival.

Model of Democracy

Labica dissertates, is it correct to talk on democracy-model or democratic models? Can the so-called advanced democracy offered to the states, nations and political groups desiring or strongly demanding democracy assume this role? We think that the discourse of law is a matter of significance; it adds a weight through terms like "lawful state", "human rights", "international law" and others. But the idea of "model" is also embodied in them. But unfortunately, things are not so simple. The "national laws" formulated by Prussian state had not the least democracy at all. However, in 1970s, this word had become precious, because it was used by the United States to fight against "socialist world" in the ideological sphere. Today, "lawful state" is not dried up in terms of emotions and desire, but in fact its content has been emptied. So is the concept of "human rights". The human rights loudly voiced by some people and respected globally do not play a model role at all in fact. Let's observe the recent events: the "new world pattern" generated after Panama, Nicaragua, Grenada and Gulf and Iraq wars, nothing is left except the most fundamental law. Whenever bourgeoisie faces to must make a real judgment on democracy, it will block the road for democracy. For instance, France did so in 1793, 1848 and 1871. Our democratic model also has another phenomenon – political repulsion, which is a phenomenon characterized by depoliticization and by majority refusing and indifferent for voting. As known to all, the leaders of the most powerful states in the world are voted by 30% of their electorates. In France, in some precincts, nearly 60%~65% of the people abstain, people prefer fishing to voting, they are indifferent to state affairs, and analysts believe with reason that this shows the corruption of democracy.

Diseases of Democracy

Labica concludes that except utopia, there is never illusory democracy. The badly concocted freedom and equality are still inseparable from land and property. Since 1989, no democratic system is free from diseases, ours is even more so. Below he explains this issue with several examples:

• The so-called "great poverty" is presented as a new discovery in the new 21th century.
• The justice of class (which is damaged due to its negating laws) and media are all submitted to the states or private power.
• Some democracies are degraded by inequalities and deterioration by cultural signifiers such as occupation, tax, wage differences, education and knowledge (here another great discovery is "illiteracy").
• Excessive plunder on the Third World through impossibly payable debts have caused recurrent famine and deaths.
• Racism bounds back through policies for immigrants; military adventures of neo-colonialism.
• Everything from media culture to financial market is subjected to the interests of North America.
• Secret acts and bargains on military, economic and international affairs.
• Political-financial scandals are not merely accidental events indicating the general level and prevalence of power corruption; scientific research is also subordinated to monopoly interests.
• World-wide natural imbalances.
• Highly commercialized consumption turns Europe into a "frozen earth", causing massive destruction of necessities[27].

After enumerating the morbid facts generated by bourgeois democracy, Labica points out that these facts indicate that the capitalist "modern" democracy is suffering from destruction. Therefore, people should not cherish any illusion. No capitalist society can be considered as democratic. Capitalism is indeed an anti-democratic system.

Labica believes that current world is a world full of violence. In the two "world-wide" wars, tens of millions of people were killed. In the countless "local" wars afterwards, such as the wars in Vietnam, Algeria, Cambodia, North Korea, Iran & Iraq, Rwanda, and Congo. Besides these acts with obvious violence, Labica thinks that there are also practices with unobvious violence, for example: force millions of child laborers to work, force them to go to the battlefields and even force them to become prostitutes. Moreover, at present, TV stations open TV channels for dogs, cats and other pets, while the basic health conditions for ordinary people cannot be guaranteed. Taking Paris for example, the water used in

---

27   George Labica: Révolution et Démocratie, p. 124-125.

the rich district 16 is cleaner than that in the poor district 20. HIV/AIDS could be cured or at least its threat could be diminished, but the monopolistic structure in the medicine industry causes extremely high medicine prices and no improvement in the situation and meanwhile medical research on it is hindered. The price of this circumstance is: the death toll exceeds the total death toll of world wars. Environmental pollution is also a kind of violence. Opulence and shortage, this pair of terms also have got a byname "theory that productive forces decide everything". It has turned the Aral Sea into a dead sea of carbon dioxide. Another kind of violence is emerging, too. It is the violence occurring in labor relations. It not only involves the group of new poor laborers but also involves the universal phenomenon called "moral abuse". In Heinz Lehmann's book titled Labor Abuse has such a title: Moral abuse, daily evil-doing violence, labor abuse, agony of France, terror of labor, violence in labor, misery and violence on children, and so on. 5000 people a day or 2 million people a year die from harsh working conditions in the world. In a word, globalization polishes violence and presents it as sweet fruits deserved by the privileged. Globalization firstly, attacks the ruled and exploited in the world, then even all living men and women, because the owners and masters do not guarantee their lives. Therefore, the discourse of security which generates violence and the discourse of terrorism is both violence, the war as politics is itself violence, labor abuse is violence, market is violence, corruption is violence, justice of a class is violence, TV is violence, and unemployment and exclusion are violence. Then who brings about all these violence? The answer is that capital creates the violence during job. This is the revolutionary answer[28].

The "participants of the 68 Movement" had ever shouted: the only solution: revolution. No doubt, they were reasonable and meanwhile too advanced. In today's world, this solution has become necessary. Why revolution? How to bury current system? Facing bitter lessons, our unquestionable answer is: that the road, means and goal of revolution are democracy. Neo-liberalism is the enemy of democracy. Widespread commercialization reduces personal individual space to a maximum and even their organs are deprived and sold, followed by the sale of their wives and children. Among the illegal human trafficking, sex and slave trade alone involves 800,000-900,000 people and USD 7-8 billion of yearly profits. These figures even keep rising. Neo-liberalism also means the acceptance of market democracy by the grave diggers of capitalist policy. In order to maximize profits, all powers are given to economy, and the policies to regulate it are refused. "Citizens" are nothing but puppets manipulated by corporate shareholders. Therefore, Labica thinks that democracy and revolution are closely related, and they are historically and theoretically inseparable. Since *Communist Manifesto* was published, Marx and Engels had emphasized the inseparability of the two. They said: "the first step in the revolution by the working class is to raise the proletariat to the position of

---

28   *Ibid.*, p. 124-125.

ruling class to win the battle of democracy."[29] Obviously, this stage is a stage as the most thorough break with all old traditional systems. Therefore, democracy is the best weapon to terminate private property. Engels had once commented: "Democracy would be totally valueless to the proletariat if it were not immediately used as a means adopt those thorough measures directed against private property and ensure the livelihood of the proletariat."[30] Therefore, communists have summed up their theory into one sentence: eliminate private property. Communists strive for the solidarity and unity of all democratic parties in the world[31], although the proletariat is the only thorough revolutionary class, it by no means exclusively starts the revolution against private ownership of property. Only after communists are closely united with petty bourgeoisie, peasants and a possible part of bourgeoisie, can the revolution win. Lenin had also believed so. During the first revolution in Russia in 1905, he put forth the slogan of "establishing a democratic republic" and believed that proletariat was an advanced democratic fighter, the class status of the proletariat made it a thorough democrat, what proletariat will lose is only its chains, while what it can obtain with the help of democratic system is the whole world[32]. Lenin had written; "Whoever wants to reach Socialism by a different road, rather than that of political democracy, will inevitably arrive at conclusions that are absurd and reactionary both in the economic and the political sense."[33] His expressions have the significance of education. According to this logic, obtaining political power will become an impassable mission, proletarian dictatorship will become the final form of the new democratic state, and this form in fact is only a "semi-state", "joint state", "non-state state" or "cheap state". "The Soviets of Workers and Peasants are a new *type* of state, a new and higher *type* of democracy, a form of the proletarian dictatorship, a means of administering the state *without* the bourgeoisie and *against* the bourgeoisie. For the first time democracy is here serving the people, the working people, and has ceased to be the democracy for the rich […]."[34]

Labica thinks that current globalization also causes two world-wide consequences. One is the emergence of world proletariat. They are the new workers under capitalist production relations. They are the vast ruled masses. They have only one and only enemy – neo-liberal politics. The other is the dominion, particularly the dominion brought by super imperialism. It utmost blocks any space free from the

---

29   Marx and Engels Selected Works, Edition 2, Vol.1, p. 293.

30   Engels: The Principles of Communism, please refer to Marx and Engels Selected Works, Edition 2, Vol.1, p. 239-240.

31   Marx and Engels Selected Works, Edition 2, Vol. 1, p. 286; 307.

32   Lenin: Two Tactics of Social-Democracy in the Democratic Revolution, please refer to Selected Works of Lenin, Edition 3, Vol. 1, Beijing, People's Publishing House, 1995, p. 558.

33   *Ibid.*, p. 537.

34   Lenin: Letter to American Workers, please refer to Selected Works of Lenin, Edition 3, Vol. 3, Beijing, People's Publishing House, 1995, p. 568.

control of hegemony and has realized its control in many fields—finance, trade, military, diplomacy, science, technology, communication, food, culture, health and etc. Therefore, the course of revolution is unpredictable, while its outlines only exist in its own files. If some people learn only from revolution and all its files, the difficulty will be how to teach others. Here in this book (by Lebica. Tr) only its purpose is contained. The struggle for democracy cannot do without specific conditions–those concrete power relations in the spheres of state and class struggle-, such as: the "weakest link" theory, such as national commune/convention during French Revolution, and the dual power structure of Soviet/interim government during Russian Revolution in February 1917. The current cosmopolitism has aroused opposition of more and more people in each country. The name of the resistance movement is "anti-cosmopolitism".

Labica is a famous French leftist Marxist researcher and political activist. He is also a guest professor of many universities including Renmin University of China and Cuban Havana University. After the "9•11" event, he wrote a series of articles and works to disclose and criticize the imperialist misdeeds of the United States and some Western countries – their fake democracy discourse and real invasionism, and fake anti-terrorism discourse and real expansionism. Undoubtedly, his words represent the just voice of the people who love peace and progress in the world.

4. SOCIALISM AND DEMOCRACY

Scholars also have discussed much on the issue of relations between socialism and democracy. Joelle Fishman, member of the National Commission of US Communist Party, has argued in his book *Working Class Democracy versus Capitalist Democracy* that: "a powerful communist party is critical for expanding democracy, communists are an important force struggling for democracy, and socialism is the only road to win and ensure sufficient democracy. Employer and capitalist are the same things. They never want workers to have the least understanding on socialism and public ownership. In fact, fascism is a terrorist ruling form by bourgeoisie, while socialism is a democratic system extended and expanded by the working class." "In the sense of American government, democratic states are those states which allow multinational corporations to exploit them without restriction. In the sense of working class, democracy means the power of working class, including economic ownership and adopting political delegation. This is socialism. People's participation is the fundament for democracy. A mass party can unite working class to oppose the threat of fascism and the danger of war and on this basis, to realize the real sublation of capitalism".

Fishman believes that to achieve sufficient democracy, class struggle must be the basis, and without class struggle, it will be impossible to achieve sufficient democracy[35], because in the capitalist United States, the economic and political system determining our life does not include a democratic control at all. Corporations decide most of the government affairs and affect all social issues. What is more, constitution and legal system forbid the government to intervene in corporate policies to a large extent. The capitalist class obstructs people from meaningful democratic participation through their mass organizations, and reduces democracy to voting. By contrast, socialism encourages people to participate in all kinds of public organizations and local community and government organizations managed by themselves and without full grassroots participation, socialism cannot be operated".

Fishman's democracy approach and ideas on future American socialism shows certain commonness shared by the communist party organizations in Western developed countries. Quite number of communists or leftists in developed capitalist states argues that the main reason for the failure of socialism in Soviet Union and Eastern Europe was that these countries did not give real emphasis to the democratic superiority of socialism, and that they have adopted highly centralized centrally planned economic systems and highly centralized centralism in politics. Therefore, many of them have explored various democratic solutions, economically and politically.

American scholar David Schweickert has suggested a socialist model completely different from former Soviet Union in order to supersede capitalism. This socialist model should be an "economic democracy" model. It should consist of three main elements:

(1) Commodity and service markets same as the capitalist society in essence;

(2) Employing workplace democracy to supersede capitalist labor wage system;

(3) Exercise democratic management on investments to supersede capitalist capital market[36].

Schweickert has argued that socialism with "economic democracy" has three characteristics: firstly, every enterprise is democratically managed by workers. However, although workers manage the factory, they do not own the means of production, because these means of production are collectively owned by the society. If an enterprise gets into trouble, the workers can freely try a re-organization or leave this company and find jobs elsewhere, but they cannot sell the

35 Joelle Fishman: Working Class Democracy Versus Capitalist Democracy, published in Foreign Theoretical Trends, 2000 (1), p. 24.
36 David Schweickert: Marx's Democratic Critique of Capitalism and Its Implications for China's Developmental Trajectory, published in Journal of Teaching and Research, 2005 (10), p. 16.

company unless it is bankrupt. Secondly, daily economy is a kind of market economy: raw materials and consumer goods are exchanged by the prices decided by supply and demand. As socialism adopts market economy, companies purchase raw material, machines and equipment from other companies and then sell their products to other enterprises or consumers. Enterprises try their best to make profit, but the profit here is different from the capitalist profit. Secondly, new investments are regulated and decided by the society and designed according to a democratic plan which also considers the market circumstances. This characteristic is critical for this socialist model. The workers' autonomous management eliminates the commodity feature of labor force as well as the "alienation" caused by this[37]. Therefore, this kind of socialism may also be called "market socialism with economic democracy".

For Schweickert market socialism with economic democracy is an economic system with three basic structures: workers' autonomous management, social control on investments, and commodity and service markets. They are essentially different when compared with capitalism: labor hired by capital, ownership of productive means, and commodity, service, capital and labor markets in capitalism. In his book *Against Capitalism*, Schweickert also demonstrates in detail that the model of market socialism with economic democracy is superior to capitalism in every aspect: it is more equal, because it eliminates incomes from property ownership ; it is more democratic because it extends democracy downward to factories and upward to the formulation of the policies for macro-economic development; it also boldly demonstrates the probably only most devastating feature of contemporary capitalism (globalism)– excessive free flow of capital throughout the world because this enables capital to rapidly move to all parts of the world and to those regions where maximum return is expected. This endangers jobs and ruins local communities and generates a great number of migrants.

Schweickert has analyzed China's socialist economic reforms and has argued that China has generally done well in adopting economic democracy. He has commented that Deng Xiaoping's early reforms were not fully consistent with the model of economic democracy, but his ideas on reform practice includes basic socialist elements such as: the main means of production should be owned by the public, the public should control the allocation of resources and under these conditions socialism can have and establish markets and operate this tool effectively. Therefore, the practice of establishing township and village enterprises have proved successful, and reforms related to peasants has supplemented this practice. Schweickert argues that his theoretic model socialism with economic democracy provides a conceptual framework for socialists to understand the profile of China's current situation, and he also raises some realistic topics for discussion.

---

37   David Schweickert: Against Capitalism, Beijing, China Renmin University Press, 2002, p. 72-73.

Schweickert has concluded: For China, the ideal economic system will be a socialist system, and the ideal political system will be democratic politics[38].

Adam Schaff, former member of the Central Committee of Polish United Workers' Party and famous philosopher, asserts that socialist democracy should be a "plural" – a multi-party system-, and has argued that the socialist democracy of the future should develop this kind of democracy. For Schaff the future socialism as a new mode of socialism should adapt to new conditions and requirements and also should adapt to the new era of social life. After evaluating past practices he has written: "the realization of socialist system requires corresponding objective and subjective conditions. Ignoring this basic law of social development and establishing socialism arbitrarily will inevitably end up with failure. Secondly, without social consensus and without social endorsement on socialist revolution as advocated by Gramsci, no socialism can be realized. Thirdly, neither a society without democracy nor liberal democracy without people holding different political views can exist. Without an institutionalized social supervision and political pluralism, there will not be democracy. Fourthly, if you do not want democracy to become an empty talk, you must endow democracy with practical contents which should be based on creating corresponding economic conditions. Therefore, social autonomy should be adopted. Social autonomy may prevent exploitation of human on the basis of private ownership on the means of production".

Schaff's approaches on socialist and Marxist-Leninist democracy has triggered sharp raised by many communist and left thinkers. His mistakes were mainly critiqued as follows: firstly, he mistakenly evaluates capitalist democratic system as the "true democracy", thus concluding that without political pluralism, there will not be democracy; and no liberal democracy without people holding different political views can exist. But facts clearly refute his ideas. Secondly, he claims socialist democracy should be plural, i.e.: multi-party system. Thirdly, he considers democracy and freedom something contradictory with Marxism-Leninism, and even describes Marxism-Leninism as the basis of communist/fascist practice.

The above left views and critics on socialist democracy offer valuable insight for Marxists. The democracy analyzed by the American communist Fishman is defined as working class possessing two powers, economic ownership and political control by its own representatives. This is also socialism. This view concisely explains the essence of socialism. American left wing scholar Schweickert has proposed the model of "socialism with economic democracy", which should bring true democracy for workers in an economic sense, i.e.: democratic management, reasonable distribution relations and reasonable investment. This is also

38   David Schweickert: Marx's Democratic Critique of Capitalism and Its Implications for China's Developmental Trajectory, published in Teaching and Research, 2005 (10), p. 21.

a creative approach. But I cannot agree with Schaff's formulation as "without political pluralism, there will not be democracy", nevertheless his idea; "if you do not want democracy to become an empty talk, you must endow democracy with real practical content which should be based on creating corresponding economic conditions" is a realistic critique to current democracy.

REFERENCES

• Michael Hardt and Antonio Negri: Empire. Nanjing, Jiangsu People's Publishing House, 2003.
• George Labica: Révolution et Démocratie. French Cherry Season Press, 2003.
• Marx and Engels: Communist Manifesto. Beijing: People's Publishing House, 1997.
• Marx & Engels Selected Works, Edition 2. Vol. 1. Beijing, People's Publishing House, 1995.
• Chantal Mouffe: Return of the Political. Nanjing, Jiangsu People's Publishing House, 2001.
• David Schweickert: Against Capitalism. Beijing, China Renmin University Press, 2002.

CHAPTER III

DEBATES ON FUTURE SOCIALISM

After the collapse of socialism in Soviet Union and Eastern Europe, Marxists and socialists have increased their research efforts on the issue of socialism and have become very active in late 1990s. This is mainly manifested by the facts that more and more people join the debate on the issues of socialism and its future, the international symposia receive more attendees and their contents are getting richer. For example, the "Socialist Conference" based in New York, USA holds regular meetings every year since 1996 with above 1000 attendants each time in general; French "Marx International Conference" (Espace Marx) is held once every two years since 1995 with above 1000 attendants each time. In addition, the "World Social Forum" (WSF) which has emerged also attracts much attention and thousands even ten thousands participate WSF events each time. Besides, there are also various kinds of large commemorations and international symposia.

These numerous international assemblies have contributed much to the debate on the issues of socialism and its future, involving dozens of topics. This indicates that people's enthusiasm for socialism did not fully ebb with the upheaval of Soviet Union and Eastern Europe, and on the contrary it has begun to rise vigorously in specific context. The debated issues related to socialism are diversified. Here we will mainly introduce the views debating on the issues of future socialism.

1. DEVELOPMENT TREND OF SOCIALISM

At his speech titled "The 21st Century Socialist Vision", Sean Sayers from British University of Kent has argued that capitalist society has encountered great changes in the second half of the 20th century, and practices an important transformation not predicted by Marx and has developed into a global system. The term "globalization" exactly describes the fundamental changes in the capitalist system in recent years. In a sense, globalization is not a novel phenomenon, but has existed in different development stages of capitalism. The new nature of contemporary globalization is that currently, almost the whole globe is controlled by a unitary economic system. Following the collapse of Soviet Union and the reform in the Chinese economic system, global economic separation has ended. Since 1914, for the first time the globe has been covered by a unitary economic system for the first time. The global market has become an all-pervasive force. It is no longer possible for an economy to develop in isolation; it will lead to poverty and backwardness if it pursues a policy discarding the global market.

Sayers points out, in several important aspects, the history in the past 100 years did not progress forward as envisaged by Marx. The developed capitalist society manifests an unexpected tenacity. Its success in economy and its democratic system in politics have shown more vitality than expected by Marx or other early socialists. Even contrary to Marx's anticipation, in many countries, working class neither was pauperized nor became the force of revolution. If Marxist critique on capitalism is to be continuously applied in today's world, it must take these realities into consideration.

Sayers continues, after communist system has collapsed in Soviet Union and Eastern Europe, capitalism has restored and adjusted its system in the above spheres, but we cannot therefore say that history has reached its final stage. The economic and social conditions causing capitalist crises still exist, so do the immanent contradictions of capitalism as demonstrated by Marx. No doubt, compared with the era of Marx, a significant change has taken place on the class attributes of contemporary capitalist society. Marxists should take a new look at this issue, but we have no reason to abandon the point of view that class hostilities are the basic characteristic of capitalist society. As the inherent contradictions of capitalism are still there, we have no reason to think that capitalism represents the last stage of history. In the 21st century, we will see a development prospect that will surpass this historical stage.

In the epoch of globalization, what strategy should socialism adopt? Sayers thinks that even in the epoch of globalization, it is not necessary for socialism to adopt a global development strategy, because although the capitalist order in the world now looks as if a seamless iron plate, this situation will change. World economy is made up of several trade blocs (Europe, East Asia and America).Among these blocs, competition and conflicts will break out. Perhaps this may create conditions for the emergence and development of independent socialist states among them.

In the end, Sayers points out, the practice of socialist bloc and other countries (for example China) in the 20th century indicates that an economic sphere independent from the world capitalist free market can be viable. These socialist countries have covered vast regions and possessed sufficient resources. Their failure and collapse cannot become a reason for economic non-subsistence. For the failure, political and economic mistakes should be blamed. Sayers concludes: the forces fighting against capitalist system on the globe will not die out but will grow, develop and spread. Socialism is still the mission of the 21st century[1].

Many scholars have conducted numerous analyses on capitalism. First of all, many versions of models defining and exploring on the stages of capitalism were developed. Some scholars suggest that capitalism has entered into the era of "turbo capitalism" and "post Fordism", some think that it has entered into the era of "post capitalism" or "late capitalism"; some argue that today we are in the era of "new capitalism" and "global capitalism" or "financial capitalism", and so on. American scholar Arif Dirlik points out, following the failure of socialism in the S.U and Eastern Europe and the opening of China and their return to capitalism, it seems that there is no place without the presence of capital in the world except a few negligible exceptions, so today's capitalism is "global capitalism". The basic characteristics of Dirlik's "global capitalism" is characterized firstly by new international division of labor and globalization of the production process ; secondly, production is decentralized, new high-tech "Hanseatic League" is emerging, and it becomes increasingly difficult to determine which state or region is indeed the center of global capitalism; thirdly, economies of multinational corporations have substituted national markets to become the centers of economic activities, and behind the decentralization of production process, manufacturing and patent rights are still highly concentrated in the hands of corporations; fourthly, production multi-nationalization is the source of unprecedented decentralization in the world; fifthly, for the first time in the history of capitalism, capitalist production mode has really become globally abstract and is divorced from its specific European historical origins[2].

Michele Albert, an academician of French Academy of Ethics and Political Science, has reviewed the history of capitalism. He thinks that in the past 200 years till present, the capitalism has experienced three stages. The first stage, starting in 1791, is a stage of "capitalism against state" and lasted about one century. In

1   Dorothy L. Sayers: 21st Century Socialist Vision, published in Foreign Theoretical Trends, 2000 (1), p. 12.
2   Arif Dirlik: World System Analysis and Global Capitalism: Review of Modernization Theory, published in Strategy and Management, 1993 (1).

this stage, state was barred behind laws and regulations, real civil institutions have appeared and civil servants were no longer badge hats. In this period, faced by the market forces, states have recoiled, undertaken the functions of gendarme states and dealt with the "dangerous class", i.e.: emerging industrial proletariat. The second stage, starting by 1891, is a stage of capitalism regulated by state. In this stage, all reforms were aimed to correct market deviations and defects and alleviated capitalist violence. State seemed to become a stronghold opposing autarchy and unfairness in the free market and a guardian angel of the poor. In the second stage, under the pressure of workers' struggle, states have tried —by means of laws, decrees or collective agreements — to make the rigorous capitalism humanly. But the third stage, starting in 1991, is a new stage of "capitalism superseding state". State is no longer considered a guardian angel or a regulator but a parasite, a brake and a heavy burden. In nearly half a century in the second stage the power of democracy and state has decorated and forged capitalism. At present, their roles are swapped mainly due to the economic globalization. Economic globalization prefers powerless states. Therefore, at least from 1991, we have entered the stage of "capitalism superseding state".

Taking the example of France, Albert enumerates the changes in the capitalist society: firstly, the guilty feeling towards money disappears. This symbolizes a fundamental transformation from the old society with Catholic tradition to the Anglo-Saxon model; secondly, egoism –"everyone for himself" has become a trend, and meanwhile collective organizations, like trade unions and associations, suffer a shocking decline; thirdly, the society is in a hard time. Particularly laborers, their new burden related to competition and worries due to unemployment has increased; fourthly, human behaviors are being vulgarized, particularly under the monopoly of TV control. Albert has asserted that the changes in these four aspects reveal that France is developing towards the direction of Americanization.

Albert is a member of the Monetary Policy Commission in France and an academician of French Academy of Ethics and Political Science. He is a Europe-wide even world-famous economist. His perspective on capitalist changes is authoritative and representative. He has concluded that this trend rather is world Americanization or capitalist Americanization than economic globalization. This "Americanization" is a kind of retrogression of capitalism, so it is "capitalism against capitalism", and is also "declining capitalism"[3].

---

3   In October 1990, Albert has published an article titled "Capitalism against Capitalist" in magazine "L'Expansion". A reader named Jacques wrote an article titled "declining capitalism" as a response. Later on, this article was included into the appendix of Capitalism against Capitalism.

2. NEW VISIONS ON FUTURE SOCIALISM

In his article "New Vision of Socialism in the 21st Century", Japanese scholar Yoshihiko Saito has argued that the development of capitalism and the establishment and later collapse of socialism in the 20th century, all have gone beyond the predictions of socialists in the 19th century. At present, the states restricting civil societies and public sector have been engulfed and shaken by the waves of globalization. Civil society has transcended national boundaries. The focal problems in current society – environmental problem, ethnic and religious conflicts, cultural frictions, violence and exclusionism cannot be explained by the theory of non-production mode. The concept of counterbalance between socialism and capitalism predicted in the 19th century is already outdated[4].

Therefore, Saito thinks that socialism should no longer limit itself with such aspects as autonomous management of labor and production, socialization of production relations and equal distribution of labor products. Socialism should focus on the "politics of identity" centering on the development of individual subject. Besides, not only the issue of distribution should be reviewed but socialists should not neglect the existent way of consumption and consumption attitudes. Not only material production should be emphasized but also the existence of space cannot be neglected, in other words, the issue of space development in the social order should be reviewed.

Saito has further explored the development model of future socialism:

Firstly, the issue of radical democracy and socialism: We should redefine Marxist democracy concept based on the interpretation of radical democracy approach. Theory of freedom and equality advocated by Radical democracy can be extended to economic and production realms. In production, it may guarantee the decision-making power of producers and the equal distribution of products. More than that, the powers of decision on what the enterprise produces, how to dispose social surplus products, and so on could all be endowed to producers. The principles of radical democracy offer the theoretical basis for the resistance against subjection and suppression. It not only indicates that people's resistance is originated from the will of economic exploitation of class rule but also reflects people's demand for fighting against sexual discrimination and racial discrimination to establish the equal relations and common sense of democracy.

Secondly, socialism should transform to a "citizenship doctrine". In capitalist society, citizenship is an important motive for capital accumulation. In modern times, citizenship is closely integrated with state and it is a unified and equal right. Today,

---

4   Saito: New Vision of Socialism in the 21st Century, published in the Journal of Foreign Book Information, 2004 (9).

citizenship has the following four characteristics: (1) The access to information and knowledge has become more important and the information-related citizenship (technical citizenship) emerges. (2) Cross-border economic activities waver original citizenship which was previously linked to states. (3) Video, audio and numerous new contents promote the aesthetics of people's daily life. Citizenship is no longer regarded as an equal and abstract personal right but shows diversified concrete forms. (4) Economic development causes diversity and individualization of people's lifestyles. The social movements after 1970s have chosen to accept the subjectivity of individuals as their basis and these movements are developing steadily. All in all, under globalization today, we cannot limit ourselves to the concept of abstract equality and unified citizenship. Instead, we should establish a diversified citizenship concept.

Thirdly, socialism and space production: It seems that space has nothing to do with the social system. However, the space in the current sense is not the position people obtain during economic, social and political practice, but instead it refers to the products/results created through all kinds of practical activities. For a state, space is the object and it promotes political strategy. For capital, same as labor products, space refers to the production object. The whole social space is integrated into a unified body through communication network and information network. Human, material, currency and information keep flowing and they change sharply. The inherent things in regions, rural and urban areas are bereaved. In the flowing space, many rights are stolen from the spaces of people's everyday life and extended to the world. People gradually become self closed and lonely. The contradiction between the spaces where such rights are bereaved (stolen) and the spaces lacking such rights should be the basic struggle content of socialism.

Fourthly, socialism with emancipated non-labor time: In the organization of time and free time, socialism should adopt a method different from that adopted by capitalism and socialism should hold an antagonist approach to this capitalist approach. In the current society, less and less labor can create more and more wealth. Not only the management of the labor time is exceptionally important, but also how to distribute and manage the free non-labor time should not be ignored. If this problem is ignored, the gap between the poorer classes excluded by the society and the privileged class enjoying larger free time will be widened with each passing day. When free time exceeds the necessary labor time people spend in order to obtain their wages, how to fairly distribute free time and guarantee its effective use will become one of the basic issues of socialism.

During the establishment and development of socialist society, it is necessary to formulate a policy related to the systematization of social time. The time policy here is not based on the economic principle of reduction of labor time and improvement of social productive forces but should be established on the principles of social justice. When social average labor time is being shortened and everybody participates in the labor process, necessary time policy will enable everybody to play and develop his personal capacity, thus promoting social subjectivity. Under this new time policy, the extension of the labor time of a certain person will cause a shortening of the labor time of another individual and thus s/he is partially excluded from labor and employment.

In a word, Saito asserts that the socialism in the 21st century should employ radical democracy approaches, such as free-flowing citizenship, spaces occupied by groups, and organization of free time, thus socialism will be endowed with brand-new connotations[5].

3. AIMS OF FUTURE SOCIALISM

After the collapse of socialism in the Soviet Union and Eastern Europe, many communists and Marxists have reviewed socialism. The Bill of Rights in Socialism written by Gus Hall, National Chairman of the United States Communist Party is very representative.

In his article, Hall firstly confirms that socialism will certainly supersede capitalism. Hall has asserted that: "socialism is the best substitute for capitalist system because capitalism only serves its own purpose and cannot meet the demands of the majority. We believe that socialist United States of America will be established based on the tradition, history, and culture and according to the national circumstances of the United States." Hall has further expounded his ideas on the socialist future.

Firstly, about the goals of a socialist society:

(1) Wipe out insecurity and poverty; eliminate unemployment, starvation and homelessness.

(2) Eliminate racism, national oppression, anti-semitism, and all kinds of discriminations, prejudices and bigotries; put an end to women's unfair status.

(3) Improve and expand democracy; terminate the dominance of conglomerate American companies and the capitalist ownership by the state; try to establish a truly humane and reasonably planned society in which human's personality, creativity and talent can be fully played.

---

5   *Ibid.*

Secondly, foundations of socialism:

Political power will be in the hands of laboring people. Socialism should natio-nalize factories, agricultural enterprises and the production of social necessities at first. Large monopoly companies and large banks should also adopt public ownership. Socialism also means that all natural resources and energy industry adopt public ownership. Socialism will completely wipe out bourgeoisie's power of exploiting and oppressing the common people. However, socialism will not do away with all private business.

Socialist government plans the whole economy. Due to planned economy, pro-gress of science and technology and protection of natural resources and natural environment, the production of socialist society will be much superior to capita-list society.

Socialist government is based on total democracy. At first, it starts with econo-mic democracy. The more people involve in economic management, the more stable people's power will become and the more possible American socialism can succeed.

In socialist America, trade unions will ensure the fairness and balance between production and income of laborers. They will play a decisive role in promoting safety and health guarantee, preventing the raise of labor intensity and ensuring smooth traffic, good working conditions and sound factory equipment. Public utilities, such as: schools, hospitals, welfare, transport, parks and roads, can hardly be guaranteed in the capitalist society, while in the socialist society, public utilities and housing will be remarkably improved and extended.

In socialism, due to production expansion to meet people's demand, adequate employment will be quickly realized. The automation in labor and life will shorten the working times and further improve the living standard.

The goal of eliminating poverty will be realized in a short time, because the large amount of resources currently being consumed by military production, corpo-rate interest and luxurious lifestyle based on ill-gotten wealth will be returned to public.

All education will be free. Free education and training will finally realize indepen-dent job selection. Everybody will enjoy free and complete medical and health care.

Socialism will quickly wipe out racism and national oppression and bring comple-te equality for the people who suffer from racism and national oppression.

Thirdly, distribution according to work will be realized. A fundamental principle of socialism is: from each according to his ability, to each according to his work. Socialism provides an incentive mechanism to encourage people to work hard, but socialism does not adopt the policy of income equalitarianism. Socialism ensures everybody's income meets subsistence needs, but the remuneration will depend on occupation and efficiency. Socialism enables everybody to benefit from labor fruits. It will render more spiritual inspiration to the people. Nobody rakes profit from other people's labor. Once social goal is accepted by the public, all people will be willing to work in order to realize this goal. Work is no longer seen as a burden. Instead, it will be considered a creative activity. Everybody eyes others with solidarity rather than an opponent.

Fourthly, the socialist road:

The future of the United States is socialism, because socialism is the best substitute of capitalism in terms of logic and practicality. Capitalism will not exist forever, just like the previous social systems. More importantly, socialism will be the next inevitable step of human civilization ladder[6].

4. ISSUES OF SOCIALIST STRATEGY AND GOALS

How to realize future socialism is also an interesting issue for scholars. To summarize, there are the following views:

The first, socialism can be realized either by peaceful or violent means. For example, when talking of the realization of the socialist road in the United States, Gus Hall thinks that it is possible to achieve socialism in the United States through peaceful means, for example: voting. Clearly, socialism can be realized in the United States through peaceful means only when a majority of American people long for socialism. However, if ruling class is unwilling to peacefully surrender its power, revolution will have no choice but to evolve into violence.

The second, capitalism may freely and peacefully transform to socialism. This view is popular among some socialist scholars. Although these scholars think that socialism is the "substitute" for capitalism and claim that "another society is possible", they stop here at this "possibility" hypothesis and do not move ahead and talk about how to realize it. These socialist scholars rather propose learning from and preserving some major things of capitalism, for instance: capitalist market economy, multi-party politics and representative democracy. For example, a Western socialist scholar has ever called large capitalist enterprises to shift to

---

6   Refer to Huang Hongzhi: Bill of Rights of Socialism of the United States Communist Party, published in Foreign Theoretical Trends, 2000 (1).

socialism: "continue to do what you do under capitalist conditions."[7] This implies capitalism and socialism are mutually compatible and have no boundaries, and capitalism absolutely can enter and is entering socialism peacefully.

The third, in the future, socialism will demonstrate its obvious superior progressive role through three forms: (1) Through socialist revolution, and established socialist regimes which will fundamentally change the political and economic status of millions of laboring people in backward countries; (2) Through legal peaceful means, socialist parties in developed states assumes political power, promotes the policy of democratic socialism and remarkably improve the living condition of the masses; (3) In the states where socialist power is not yet established, international socialist movement forces bourgeoisie regime to make major concessions, they have no way but to adopt welfare state policies and obviously improve people's living standards[8].

The fourth, the concept of socialism should change with the changes of capitalism. Major changes have occurred in the political and economic structures of the developed capitalist states. These changes impose serious challenges to the traditional socialist theory. If we say that the foundation of traditional socialist movement is the industrial proletariat, the class/social foundation of the "new socialist" movement will change as the vast masses of the "white-collar working class". For this reason, we can rarely see the traditional socialist concepts among socialist scholars in the developed countries, such as: violent revolution, proletariat dictatorship, single-party leadership by the communist party, state-owned economy and democratic-centralism in organization.

5. ON THE PATTERNS OF FUTURE SOCIALISM

After the upheaval of the Soviet Union and Eastern Europe, many socialists, socialist scholars, socialist activists and politicians have reviewed the experiences and lessons and put forth their own visions and vistas for future socialism.

Adam Schaff, former member of the Central Committee of Polish United Workers' Party and an academician of Polish Academy of Sciences have several systematic ideas on future socialism. He has asserted that future socialism needs to clarify the following aspects:

---

7   Chen Xueming: Foreign Trend of Marxism after Collapse of Soviet Union and Eastern Europe, Beijing, China Renmin University Press, 2000, p. 133.
8   *Ibid.*, p. 134-135.

Firstly, economic forms of future socialism:

(1) Relation between social ownership and private ownership on the production means

(2) Relation between planned economy and market economy;

(3) Relation between centralized system and decentralized system

Secondly, social form of future socialism, particularly class structure:

(1) What social classes will appear in this structure?

(2) Is socialism without working class possible?

Thirdly, political forms of future socialism:

(1) Relation between state and democracy (with disappearance of working class, proletariat will also gradually disappear);

(2) Relation between political pluralism and single-party system.

Fourthly, cultivation of new socialist human and the role of "ethics" in socialism.

Fifthly, he has discussed the position and role of Marxism in future socialism.

Schaff and Ownership on Means of Production

As for the economic forms in future socialism, Schaff has argued that on the issue of ownership on the means of production, attention should be paid to the ideas different from traditional views. Firstly, a revolutionarily elimination of the private ownership on productive means is a necessary condition for a socialist re-volution, but not a sufficient condition. The acknowledgement of this point will clear confusion in our minds – including the revolutionists who devote their lives to the fight against "capital" as advocated by Marx. Secondly, practice has not pro-ved that the private ownership on the production means blocks the development of productive forces, and that social ownership accelerates their development. On the contrary, the results of the competition and comparison between these two ownership forms in the spheres of innovation of science and technology, labor productivity and development of productive forces are rather embarrassing. Thirdly, what is more, practice has not proved that market economy and its anar-chic nature under capitalist system causing crises of overproduction play a negati-ve role in social life. In all socialist states, economic crises have generated broader negative impacts than it does in capitalist states. Fourthly, practice indicates that the anarchic nature in the capitalist production causing economic crises does not stem from market economy. It is in fact caused by excessive centralization, excessive centralization also causes poorness in the spheres of ideology and theory and vision, and economic crises are also caused by the lack of sufficient technical foundation necessary for the implementation of economic plans. Here we can see that Schaff is in favor of preserving a certain portion of the private economy and also in favor of a certain degree of market economy.

Next, Schaff opposes excessive worship of market economy. He has asserted that, firstly, the traditional planned economy has lost its effect in practice, but socialist parties have not formed correct cognition on it. Secondly, the failure of planned economy has significantly confused Marxist theorists and activists. Consequently, some people regard market economy as the sole magic weapon and believe it can perfectly solve the economic problems of socialism in the best possible way. This is a very harmful thinking. Thirdly, the craze for market economy induces people's disappointment at socialist planned economy and they attribute all achievements of Western economy to market economy. In fact, the "market economy" pursued by the people does not exist at all. Fourthly, in the globalized world economy, it is the economic plan rather than free market that becomes more and more important. The normal development of economy today needs the cooperation of plan and market, these two driving tools. Eliminating market mechanisms in the name of planning and abolishing planned economy and substituting it with market both will cause negative consequences (likely even greater) on the economic life. Fifthly, currently the failure of planned economy has caused a hysterically frantic worship of market economy, but we cannot therefore say that plans do not work. The reason for the failure of planned economy was the absence of the technical infrastructure necessary for the implementation of modern economic plans. Therefore, in a technical sense, the implementation of planned economy is also possible, even globally.

Lastly, Schaff has argued that in future socialism, due attention should given to study the issue of "centralized system and decentralized system" in the economic structure. It is an inevitable trend to adopt decentralized system in the new industries brought by microelectronic and informatics technology and service industry. But the production part of micro-electronic technology industry necessitates huge investments and research and development investments thus centralization of investment and production becomes rational.

On the issue of social forms in future socialism, Schaff thinks it is mainly an issue of class structure. Whether a socialism without working class is possible in the future or not is a vital issue and also a new major "blank field" of socialist theory. Based on the class structure of the society he has personally experienced in Poland Marx's predictions have not proved correct. Marx had predicted that an even stronger two-pole social structure would be generated in capitalism and this polarization would cause a greater part of the middle class joining the ranks of proletariat. However, nearly 150 years has passed, the actual situation is quite the opposite. Proletariat and bourgeoisie are shrinking, while middle class expands and their effect is growing. This indicates that future socialism may become a society of middle class.

On the issue of the political forms in the future socialism, Schaff has explored the issue of relations between state and democracy and the relations between political pluralism and single-party system. First of all, Schaff has reviewed the history of socialist revolution. He thinks that in some of the socialist states, the concept of democracy is distorted, democracy is deemed as a contradictory concept that snuffs out its dictatorship, and this "blasphemy" constitutes a threat to democracy principle which is the natural form for social organizations. The existing socialist states and communist movements are paying huge price for it. However, after socialism as a new system is introduced and it is still in an immature stage, without proletariat dictatorship and compulsory measures, it will be unable to secure socialist power. Many Marxists believe that state will disappear in the future, but Schaff thinks that experience tells us that state is a very important tool and only utopists may believe a regime can exist without state. Schaff warns that if future socialism still practices collective ownership as its economic foundation, a "communist fascist system" might be generated. This issue is another "blank field" in the future socialism.

Schaff has also commented on the issue of relations between political pluralism and single-party system. He thinks that the disastrous consequences of the proletariat dictatorship experiments conducted according to the theories of Lenin and Stalin for 70 years fully indicates that socialist democracy should be plural (multi-party regime) quoting from Gorbachev. The democracy of future socialism should adopt this pattern of democracy[9].

As for the issue of cultivation of new socialist humans and socialist ethics, Schaff has argued that in the past, in the experiments of socialism, the issue of cultivating new socialist humans had been introduced, but the result was disappointing. Not only the old men could not be reformed into new men, but these policies broke their spines and destroyed their ethical codes. If future socialism cannot seriously handle this issue, it will certainly end up with failure[10]. Schaff continues that at the turn of the 19th century and the 20th century, a merciless struggle opposing "ethical socialism" had emerged in Germany. Undoubtedly, this struggle was right, because the theory of "ethical socialism" was absurd.

9   Gorbachev, Brandt et al.: Future Socialism, Beijing, Central Compilation & Translation Press, 1994, p. 112.
10   *Ibid.*, p.113.

However, in this ideological struggle, the advocates of socialism have failed to see an extremely important thing—value of ethics. Schaff thinks that ethical value is absent in the current socialist movement, particularly in socialist states, so it is necessary to form a value system which can promote the building of socialism.

As for the position and role of Marxism in future socialism, Schaff thinks: (1) Marxism is a scientific theory, its soul is its practicality, and this also decides that it is an open theory; (2) Marxism is the traditional ideology of working class. In its development process, two wrong tendencies have appeared: one is the tendency of dogmatism and rigidity. The other is the tendency of abandonment; (3) some theoretical views of Marxism were refuted by history, so it is necessary to make thorough revision in Marxism; (4) Marxism needs modernization, so we should vigorously research Marxism; (5) Marxism (modernized Marxism) will play its role as an important theory and ideology in future socialism.

Alfonso Gellar's New Socialism

Further, the former deputy general secretary of Spanish Socialist Workers' Party and Spanish deputy prime minister Alfonso Gellar has introduced the concept "new socialism". The pattern of this "new socialism" will have the following characteristics:

(1) New socialism should optimize the forms and procedures of democracy, extend it to every aspect of life, enable citizens to actively participate in social affairs and ultimately improve the social self-regulation and self-management mechanisms;

(2) Arouse people's sense of freedom through equality and popularization of culture and education;

(3) Broaden social time and space, and enable that individuals can develop their creative abilities, beget healthier and better rewarded living conditions;

(4) Overcome those factors causing social marginalization and poverty among the population;

(5) Create better conditions for social balance and harmony, which can guarantee the necessary stability of the democratic political system, ensure the qualitative and quantitative improvement of citizens' living standards and determine comprehensive standards of a decent society life for each person;

(6) Establish peaceful and balanced relations in international relations which can provide a sense of security and might steer those huge resources for armament to

peoples' welfare and natural resources' protection[11].

In conclusion, Gellar thinks that future socialism should aim to eliminate all forms rule suppressing humans, including rule of economy, politics, culture and race. Future socialism thus should emancipate mankind.

Jose Felix Tezanos and Future Socialism

Studying on the issues of future socialism, Jose Felix Tezanos, Professor of Sociology and Secretary of National Executive Board of Spanish Socialist Workers' Party in charge of education has pointed out that socialism is not complete yet. Socialism had emerged at the moment when rationality and the possibility of human progress were strongly worshipped. In a sense, socialism has inherited the spirit of enlightenment and liberty. However, after decades' of socialist practice, the basic issues of socialism, like "what" (what is socialism), "who" (who is the socialist subject) and 'how" (how is socialist strategy like) could not be solved. We can neither advocate the future socialism as a road people explores aimlessly and do not know its destination nor suggest that socialism is the concrete and definite alternative social model with a clear profile. Tezanos has suggested the following ideas:

Firstly, today we cannot see socialism as a social and political phenomenon which is closely related to traditional industrial society thus we cannot design future socialism conforming to those conditions and vicissitudes of this bygone stage of human society.

Secondly, the socialist practices in the history should be perceived and evaluated as a positive stage of the deepening and development process of democracy.

Thirdly, the theoretical disputes on socialism should be treated with a long-term view and avoid any risk of rigidity.

Fourthly, when combining past socialism with future socialism we should guarantee that socialism continuously plays the important role as the motive force of social progress, because social progress is the key for the policies of freedom, equality and ecological balance.

Fifthly, if we want to design future socialism, we must try to obtain a new thinking mode at first. That is to say, the issue on future socialism should be re-illustrated on the basis of new coordinates.

Sixthly, socialism should be perceived as a process of driving social progress.

---

11   *Ibid.*, p. 50.

Seventhly, some expositions on socialism in history were based on the extreme simplification of the current society.

Eighthly, Tezanos has asserted that socialists should admit and fully bear in mind the complexity of the reality (society), adhere to theoretical pluralism in exploration and prove that they have the ability to employ new views to understand future socialism.

The new views should include: (1) From a single-aspect theory to multi-aspect theory; (2) From seeking to establish great, comprehensive and all-inclusive theories to focus on several middle-range theories such as dominance and suppression in human relations, ecological balance, problems of lower classes and democratization of labor relations. Meanwhile socialists should make some special efforts in theoretical level and consider their limitations in effecting those spheres which are not yet completely studied. (3) From the notion of adopting socialism by state support to plural supports for socialism; (4) From the theory of single revolutionary subject to plural socialist subjects; (5) From the closed and absolute notion of socialism to the open and composite notion.

The above three socialist theorists have analyzed, produced their forecasts and have envisaged the future socialism. This plays an important heuristic role for Marxist researches on the present and future of socialism. For example, Alfonso Gellar's vision on "new socialism" insists that future new socialism should perfect the forms and procedures of democracy, make citizens actively participate in social affairs and ultimately improve the social self-regulation and self-management mechanisms; broaden social time and space ; establish peace and balance in international relations. All these views provide food of thought for us. Among the above three theorists, particular attention should be paid to the views of Adam Schaff, for he had lived under socialist system for a long time, has personal experiences in all aspects of socialism and had fought for a long time against the wrong approaches in the former Polish ruling party.

In his book "Blank Fields" of Contemporary Socialism, Schaff has centrally expounded the issues in the following aspects:

Firstly, on the economic form of future socialism: Schaff expounds the issue of the relation between social ownership and private ownership of the means of production and the relation between planned economy and market economy in future socialism. Schaff proposes that future socialism may preserve a certain portion of private ownership, but should not excessively worship market economy. Planned economy is feasible and should not be completely negated. His view is absolutely right.

Secondly, on the social forms in future socialism: Schaff explores the issue of what social classes will appear in future socialism and whether socialism without working class is possible in the future. Schaff thinks that future socialism will have no working class, because working class possibly will become the middle class and the future socialism will be a socialism of middle class. This issue is really worth discussing. Following the improvement and development of productive forces, great changes have occurred in the status of working class, the working class existent in the days of Marx is not there today and more and more of them have become members of the middle class. Particularly, in a socialist society, working class and other classes are jointly getting richer and their quantity is decreasing, and they have not only become propriety class but also become middle class. Therefore, the debate on the leading class in future socialism deserves further study.

Thirdly, political forms in future socialist society: Schaff expounds his ideas on the relation between state and democracy and the relation between political pluralism and single-party system. He asserts that future socialism still needs state, while the democracy of future socialism should be "plural" democracy, i.e.: multiparty democracy. Obviously, in this issue, Schaff adopts the democratic view of democratic socialism. Here there are many doubts: firstly, it is an issue related to the nature of each party in multiparty system some parties in some countries will rigidly oppose and desire to cause political crises and a stable socialist society could not be achieved but in some others parties in other regions of the world could easily form a consensus on a socialist development. If the bourgeois party exists, proletariat will be unable to firmly control power all the time; secondly, is the democracy of future socialism is "plural" democracy? How to understand "pluralism"? What is the essence of democracy in future socialism? These questions still need our further study.

Fourthly, on the cultivation of new socialist men and socialist ethics: Schaff thinks that in the late 19th century and early 20th century, Marxism ever criticized German "ethical socialism". This approach was right, but it had abandoned the ethical code of socialism. Future socialism must succeed in cultivating new socialist men. Otherwise it will fail. Without doubt, Schaff's view is completely right.

Fifthly, the role of Marxism in future socialism: Schaff asserts that Marxism will still play a role as an important theory and ideology in future socialism, but Marxism needs modernization and intensive revision, for many of its theoretical concepts have become outdated.

In conclusion, Schaff's attitude towards Marxism is in the main is appropriate. Marxism needs constant modernization, enrichment and needs to keep pace with the times. However, I should say that Schaff's vision of future socialism has also

several severe mistakes, for example: he envisages the democracy of future socialism as "plural" – "multi-party" democracy. Apparently, Schaff, at this point
cannot resist his temptation for the democracy view of democratic socialism. If
we imagine, under the circumstance of multipartite system, how can the status
of proletariat and working class be assured all the time? That is to say, when
multiple parties co-exist legally, how can we shatter the bourgeois state machine
and establish the political power of the proletariat and laboring people? Historical
facts indicate that control of power by the proletariat and laboring people under
the circumstance of multi-party system is only an empty talk. The problems of
socialist practice by the social democratic socialist party in today's Western society
can fully prove this point.

REFERENCES

• Gorbachev, Brandt et al.: Future Socialism, Beijing, Central Compilation &
Translation Press, 1994.
• Michel Albert: Capitalism against Capitalism. Beijing, Social Sciences Academic
Press, 1999.
• Chen Xueming: Foreign Trend of Marxism after Collapse of Soviet Union and
Eastern Europe, p. 133, Beijing, China Renmin University Press, 2000.

CHAPTER IV

CAPITALIST CRISIS THEORIES BY ECOLOGICAL MARXISM

1 *A Review on Ecological Marxism*
2 *Leiss' and Ben Agger' s Theories*
3 *James O'Connor on Capitalist Crisis*

1. A REVIEW ON ECOLOGICAL MARXISM

Developed in 1970s, ecological Marxism is both the product green political movement and a brand new form of Western Marxism School. It is one of the most influential Western Marxist schools in the late 20th century. Just as Italian theorist Luciana said, ecological Marxism undoubtedly represents a new development stage in Marxism in the last years of this century.

The emergence of ecological Marxism has a complex social and historical background. After the Second World War, the developed states in the West have greatly promoted the development of productive forces with the help of scientific and technological revolution and alleviated class contradictions through welfare state policies. However, their economic development model was established on the basis of predatory development of natural resources, thus capitalist contradictions have become increasingly obvious and prominent, the contradiction between bourgeoisie's infinite pursuit of economic growth and the finite natural resources was intensified and ecological imbalance has worsened. Meanwhile, capitalism's essence of pursuit of extra profits has caused an expansive economy. They have externally pursued ecological colonialism and mercilessly exploited underdeveloped states, resulting in deterioration of ecological environment in underdeveloped states and regions. By 1960s-1970s, the global ecological crisis has aroused a universal concern and has pushed the emergence of the green political movement. Ecological Marxism was generated in this movement during the exposure, critique and retrospect of the inevitable ecological crisis resulting in capitalism. In the beginning it has represented a left wing trend in the green movement which can be termed as radical eco-socialism.

Ecological Marxism, just as its name implies, is a school formed through the combination of ecological ideology and Marxism. Ecological Marxists have asserted that the marriage of Marxism and ecology is possible. The two are organically related rather than mutually repulsive. The attacks made against Marx and Engels' anthropocentrism is groundless. In fact, Marx's view on society embodies the thought that humans should avoid alienation from nature and human's utilization of the nature should not based on capital and capitalist accumulation needs but should be based on individual and social needs shortly keenly caring on the ecological rational productive forces (as called today)[1]. Therefore, the allegation that Marx's theory on man-nature relationship is nothing but the objective reflection of capital's blind continuous expansion of production, and productivity is unreasonable.

Ecological Marxism asserts that although there are still some theoretical blanks Marx and Engels' theories , in their vision the history of human and the history of the nature are undoubtedly considered in a dialectic interactive relation; they were aware of anti-ecological essence of capitalism and have expressed a preliminary theoretical vision for eco-socialism. In addition, ecological Marxism has also argued that Marx had put the main emphasis on the human system, while reserving an extremely scanty theoretical space for the natural system. In Marx's historical materialism and Marx's classical works, what decides the relation between material production and nature is mainly the means of production or in other words, the way of exploitation on laborers rather than the status of natural environment and the process of ecological development. Marx's theory successfully demonstrates that the nature encounters different social formations under different modes of production, but the authentic independency of nature as a force which can either help or restrict human activities is forgotten and marginal in this theory.

For this reason, they have argued that it is imperative to reform Marxist theory with ecology. While stressing natural humanization, we should also pay attention to the naturalization of human history. Marxism needs to extend its connotation outwardly to the material nature, because the history of the nature, regardless of "the first" nature or "the second" nature, will exert more influence on human history. In the same time, Marxism also needs to extend its connotation inwardly, because human changes in the dimension of biology and socialized reproduction process of human itself will affect human history and the history of the nature no matter how extensively these two processes can be regulated or managed by the society.

As for the generation and development of ecological Marxism, I can divide them into two stages.

---

1   James O'Connor: Natural Causes: Essays in Ecological Marxism, Nanjing, Nanjing University Press, 2002, p. 3-4.

The first stage is the emerging stage in 1970s-1980s. Polish Adam Schaff, communist Rudolf Bahro from Democratic Republic of Germany and Frankfurt School are the pioneers of ecological Marxism. Adam Schaff is the first communist who has engaged in the ecological movement. He was ever appointed as the chairman of the executive board of "Club of Rome" and is an ecological Marxist in a real sense. Rudolf Bahro is a representative figure of the Left wing in the ecological movement and European peace movement. In theory, he has advocated ecological humanitarianism and democratic socialism, and sought for the convergence of "red" (communist movement) and "green" (ecological movement) political forces and is the first Marxist who put the views of ecological Marxism into practice. His masterpiece book is *From Red to Green*. Herbert Marcuse from Frankfurt School is the earliest founder of the theory of ecological Marxism. He thinks the "compulsory consumption" promoted by modern industrial society infinitely stimulates material demands and enjoyment which are not the real natures of human, this confuses people mistakenly observe this "false demand" as "real demand" and pursue for endless consumption, and turns individuals into vassals of commodities in the spheres of economy, politics and culture. Thus humans become increasingly one-dimensional and distorted, completely controlled by commodity fetishism. Capitalism is the root cause of ecological and natural crises. Nevertheless, it is Ben Agger who has first put forth the concept of "ecological Marxism". He is a sociological professor of the University of Waterloo in Canada. He has started with the studies of the contemporary development of Marxist crisis theory and applied the ecological crisis theory to contemporary capitalism. His masterpiece is *Western Marxism: An Introduction*. In this book, there is a thought provoking chapter about "towards ecological Marxism". The influential ecological Marxists in this stage also include William Leiss and André Gorz. William Leiss is also a Canadian leftist scholar. Proceeding from the analysis of Frankfurt School on capitalist alienation, he has criticized alienated in consumption and proposed the establishment of "steady-state growth" economy. His masterpieces are *Domination of Nature* and *Limits of Satisfaction*. André Gorz is an important leftist theorist in France. In his book Capitalism, Socialism and Ecology, he centrally expounds the relations between capitalism, socialism and ecology, expresses his basic ideas on the future of socialism and its development road, and opposes monopoly capitalism. His works including *Division of Labour, Ecology as Politics* and *Critique of Economic Reason* are influential, too. In this emergence stage, ecological Marxists have made intensive and meticulous studies on the root causes of ecological crisis, on the social forces who can check the global ecological crisis, the means and methods that should be adopted in this struggle, and new conceptions for future society. Particularly, they have explicitly put forth the requirements of eco-socialist view on politics, economy, culture and social life. All these were important symbols marking the systematization of ecological Marxism.

The second stage is development stage starting from late 1980s. In this stage, the theory of ecological Marxism was established and systematically criticized capitalism from the perspective of the linkages between the capitalist mode of production and ecological crisis; and comprehensively put forth the conception of eco-socialism and completely improved its situation in 1970s-1980s creating a complete political program and social ideal for ecological movement. Following the establishment of ecological Marxism, it has gained a certain influence on the green ecological movement, the phenomenon of "reddening of greens" has become the key political characteristic in this period, the status of "red" in ecological movement was further strengthened, and there occurred a trend that "red" as a later comer was surpassing the former. In this period, in addition to some original ecological Marxists who were active, some new ecological Marxists have joined the movement with representatives like George Labica, Rainer Grundmann, David Pepper and James O'Connor. George Labica had joined the French communist party at his early age. Later on he has become one of the key theorists of the French left-wing movement. After the upheaval of Soviet Union and Eastern Europe in late 1980s, he has continually published many theses including *Ecology and Class Struggle*, and studied on the relations between global ecological crisis and eco-socialism and has also argued that the workers' movement has entered a new stage – "the cultural revolution stage of workers' movement". Rainer Grundmann, a German left-wing scholar, has proposed to employ Marxist historical materialism as a guide to solve the global ecological crisis. He has asserted that Marx was a profound "anthropocentrist". He has defended Marx's theories on man-nature relationship and further developed the Marxist tradition; the theory of artificial nature as termed by several Marxist thinkers. David Pepper was an important representative figure in the theoretical development of ecological Marxism in 1990s. His masterpieces are *Roots of Modern Environmentalism and Eco-Socialism: From Deep Ecology to Social Justice*. He has claimed himself a "Marxist Leftist" in the ecological movement. His major theoretical contribution is that he outlined the political profile of the "red green party" and "green green party" in the ecological movement, and deepened the argument on the relation between eco-socialism and ecologism, and he has greatly contributed to the establishment of the basic principles of eco-socialism. James O'Connor is the editor in chief of the book *Capitalism, Nature and Socialism*. His masterpiece is *Natural Causes: Essays in Ecological Marxism*. In this book, he has tried to explain the ecological crisis of capitalism from the vantage point of the stance of historical materialism, and proposed strategies to overcome the ecological crisis. Apart from them, there are also many influential ecological Marxists. Their theories constitute the most dynamic achievements in the Western Marxism School after 1990s.

Analyses on the capitalist crisis are one of the focuses of ecological Marxism. The focal points of the first stage and second stage in the theory of ecological Marxism both explore the issue of capitalist crises, but the two stages have differences in their approaches. The first stage stresses that the capitalist ecological crisis has superseded the economic crisis; the second stage emphasizes that in the capitalism exists both an ecological crisis and an economic crisis at the same time, and the two are closely related. Although the ecological Marxism in these two stages both advocate that the root cause of capitalist ecological crisis is capitalism's endless pursuit for surplus value, the first stage mainly follows the tradition of Western humanitarian Marxism, particularly influenced by the Frankfurt School which regards alienation as a core concept to analyze capitalist crises. The second stage strives to establish this analysis on the basis of Marxist historical materialism and its crisis theory, so this stage is more intensive and theoretically more convincing.

2. LEISS' AND BEN AGGER'S THEORIES

Marx's theory on capitalist crisis is established on the basis of the analysis on the immanent contradictions of capitalism. The contradiction between the sociality of production and the private possession of productive means determines the contradiction between the organized production in particular enterprises and the anarchic production of the whole society under the capitalist system, and also the second contradiction : between continuous expansion of production and relative reduction in laborers' payment capacity. When developing to a certain extent, these contradictions trigger economic crises and finally cause to the proletarian revolution. However, with the continuous adjustment of capitalist production relations—particularly the adoption of Keynesian policies in 1930s, the increasing state intervention and regulation in capitalist economy and the adoption of welfare state policies, the immanent contradictions of capitalism were alleviated to some extent. Some theorists therefore have started to believe that Marx's theory on economic crisis was out of date. They introduced new concepts such as "legitimacy crisis", "fiscal crisis of the state", "ecological crisis" and other theories to replace Marxist crisis theory.

The "ecological crisis" theory was first introduced by William Leiss, Ben Agger et al. in 1970s. They have asserted that the ecological crisis has substituted the economic crisis and has become the principle problem in capitalism. "Today's crisis theory should stress both the inherent structural contradictions in capitalism (the contradiction caused by the decline of profit rates as called by Marx) and the trend that developed capitalism deepens alienation, separation of human existence, environmental pollution and plunder of natural resources."[2] Under the drive of interest, capitalists keep enlarging production scales and madly exploit the nature by means of science and technology, thus creating irrecoverable destruction on the living environment. Particularly, through the policy of "ecologi-

---

2   Ben Agger: Western Marxism: An Introduction, California, Goodyear Publisher, 1979, p. 269.

cal colonialism, developed capitalist states turn underdeveloped states into their warehouses of raw materials, refuse depots and places to which they move their industries with serious pollution.

William Leiss, Ben Agger and other early ecological Marxists have generally followed the tradition of Western Marxist humanitarianism; particularly, Frankfurt School which regards alienation as the core concept to analyze the capitalist crisis. Frankfurt School has argued that through constantly luring people to pursue "false demands", capitalism thus realizes control on humans and maintains the interests of capital. Ecological Marxists have also employed a similar theory —the theory of alienated consumption— to analyze the ecological crisis of capitalism. The logic of this theory proposes that ecological crisis is caused by the "excessive consumption" pushed by capitalism. "Excessive consumption" is closely linked with "excessive production". Excessive production will inevitably surpass the bearing capacity of the nature and create environmental and ecological problems. Therefore, the ever-increasing blind consumption constitutes the real harm factors against environment.

In *Limits of Satisfaction*, Leiss discloses modern industrial society is leading people to such a lifestyle: people live in high-rise buildings in the cities, their energy supply, food and other necessities even the disposal of waste all rely on a colossal and complex system, meanwhile people mistake that it seems that the ever-increasing consumption can make up the sufferings faced by them in other living spaces, especially their sufferings in their working life , so people frantically pursue consumption to give vent to the discontent towards laboring, thus equaling consumption with contentment and happiness. In other words, they regard the quantity of consumption and money spending as the only yardstick for their happiness. Leiss has pointed out that equaling consumption with contentment and happiness is a typical characteristic that shows modern industrial society creates enormous alienation.

André Gorz has also opposed to capitalist consumption: "the economic rules of productive forces are thoroughly different from the ecological rules of resource protection. Ecological rationality aims to employ the best way to meet (people's) idiosyncratic demands: try the best to provide minimum and most durable things with highest use values, and produce them with little consumption of labor, capital and resources. On the contrary, the maximum pursuit of economic productive forces aims to sell maximum quantity of things produced at the highest efficiency in order to make the most profit. However, all these attitudes are based on maximum consumption and demand. Only through such maximum consumption and demand, is that possible to get rewards: "the reward of capital appreciation and accumulation". The maximum development of productive forces at the enterprise level results in the deterioration of economic waste. From an ecological point of view, it is the waste and destruction of resources. But from the economic view, it is the source of growth[3]. Therefore, the "excessive production" and "excessive consumption" caused by the anarchic character of capitalist production based on private ownership and its aim to pursue maximum profits will inevitably cause the predatory exploitation of natural resources. Under capitalist conditions, it is impossible that the individual companies could carry their production and operation in an ecological way which goes against their own interests and caters for collective and long-term interest, so global ecological crisis is unavoidable. This contradiction is inherent and determines the impossibility of sustainable and green capitalism: the ecological contradiction of capitalism makes sustainable and green capitalism merely an unrealizable dream, a self-deceiving trick[4]. He has argued that one of the most important traits of economic rationality is that the whole society closely focuses on consumption and tries its best to push people to the road of consumption, i.e.: produce things as much as possible for people's endless consumption. André Gorz criticizes the harms of economic rationality: "on the one hand, it transforms inter-personal relations into money relations; on the other hand, it turns the relation between human and the nature into a instrumentalist/tool relation and the core problem is that laborers lose humanly natures. For Gorz, capitalism is a society pursuing economic rationality, its market economy, maximization of capitalist production and the continuous expansion of market and consumption certainly destroy the basic elements of life and life quality, and the cause for ecological crisis rests with the logic of capitalist accumulation.

Just because the ecological crisis of capitalism results from "alienated consumption", ecological Marxists try to expose and criticize the "alienated consumption" in order to eliminate ecological crisis. Agger pins the hope of solving ecological crisis by the dialectics of expectation-shattering effect. He said, the crisis of capitalist society represented by the phenomenon of "alienated consumption" is pregnant with expectation-shattering, and this will wake people up from the delusion on capitalist production and consumption. Agger has concretely described the process of expectation-shattering effect: (1) Contemporary capitalist society obtains its legacy from people's expectation of endless commodity consumption. In other words, the legacy of contemporary capitalist society is established on the basis of stimulating people's expectation for endless consumption; (2) As the ecological system is unable to support this unlimited growth, the ecological crisis will inevitably cause a supply crisis; (3) People get used to regard the affluent material life they expect as the compensation for their alienated labor life, while supply crisis will shatter their expectations. Their confidence that capitalism can infinitely meet their material demands gets lost, and consequently they will dramatically doubt on the entire capitalist system, so they start to re-think what on earth human really needs; (4) In the process of expectation shattering and this process

---

3   André Gorz: Capitalism, Socialism and Ecology, London, 1984, p. 32-33.
4   *Ibid.*

of rethinking, many obsolete demand concepts and value concepts are destroyed and new expectations and the ways to meet these expectations will be generated. In a word, the expectation-shattering shock will trigger the revolution in people's demand structure, break the connection between "more" and "better" and enable the combination of "better" and "less". Leiss calls this transformation as the transition from quantitative standard to qualitative standard, while in the sense of Gorz, this will directly promote the society to move to equality and promote the ideal of socialist equality.

Accordingly, ecological Marxists direct their utmost effort to promote a concept of happiness different from the concept of "consumption for consumption" as advocated in contemporary capitalism, and point out that people's satisfaction ultimately lies in production activities rather than consumption activities. Leiss insists that the alienation concept which equals consumption with satisfaction should be changed. He said: there is such cognition which goes through the works of some scholars like Fourier, Marx and Marcuse: People should look for contentment in the activities they do. That means people's contentment ultimately is determined by production activities, this is because: (1) Through participation in direct production activities, people can realize self-fulfillment and live in a truly creative way. Moreover, this life is rich and colorful. People obtain enjoyment from this kind of productive activities; (2) As this life is not a productive activity directed to support malicious consumption, it will cut off the direct link between production and consumption and will reduce the production capacity of capitalism, the result of this kind of production will not increase the antagonism with the nature but will cause a harmonious co-existence with the nature. In this brand new relation, men can feel enormous contentment and happiness. Criticizing capitalist economic rationality, Gorz advocates "ecological rationality" that tallies with humanity. In his sense, the process of realizing the transition from economic rationality to ecological rationality is also a process in which people continuously shift themselves from consumption field to production field to obtain contentment. He thinks that only after the fetters of economic rationality is smashed and the whole society is transformed to the track on which people can obtain contentment from production field, can a sufficient free space be opened for modern people.

Shifting people's attention from consumption field to the production field is not to make people completely give up consumption but to have the people make a major change on their current consumption mode. According to this new concept, spurn the concept of "the more consumption the better" and combine "better" with "less" rather than "more". Gorz suggests: "as long as we produce more durable products and more products not damaging environment, it is possible that we consume less, and the better our life will be". He also asserts that when people discover the more is not necessarily the better, the more money and more consumption do not necessarily lead to a better life, and there are demands more from those money can buy, they will emancipate from the fetters of economic rationality. […] When people realize that not all values can be quantized, and money cannot buy everything, and the things not bought with money are the most important, or the most indispensable, the "market-based order" will be shaken from its fundaments. Gorz further believes that as long as the link between 'more" and "better" is really broken in consumption field, and the combination between "more" and "less" is realized, mankind will ascend to the realm of "less production and better life". "Less production" is the production guided according to "ecological rationality". In this realm, market disappears, everybody feel contented and everybody realizes their own value.

3. JAMES O'CONNOR ON CAPITALIST CRISIS

"The Second Contradiction" Theory

After the late 1980s, the most influential analysis by ecological Marxism on crisis is the "dual crisis theory" of capitalism. In his Natural Causes: Essays on Ecological Marxism, James O'Connor has systematically expounded this theory. As mentioned before, William Leiss and Ben Agger have argued that the ecological crisis has substituted the economic crisis and has become the principle problem of capitalism. However, O'Connor holds a different view: capitalism suffers from both economic crisis and ecological crisis. Therefore, in his sense, Marx's historical materialism and capital accumulation theory as well as economic crisis theory are not only not outdated but also constitute the starting point of the analysis of ecological Marxism.

O'Connor thinks neither Marx nor Engels is an "ecological economist", although they have both acknowledged clearly that the destruction of capitalism on resources, ecological and human nature, and have warned that the production, distribution, exchange and consumption processes in capitalism cause resource consumption and exhaustion, enormous waste and serious pollution, and warned against capital's world-wide level destruction on the nature. It is true that they have not considered the issue of ecological destruction as the central problem of capitalist accumulation and not included this contradiction in their social and economic transformation theory. They have under-estimated the extent of resource exhaustion and degeneration of the nature caused by the development of capitalism. Therefore they have only left a plain legacy for ecological economics. Their explanations on ecological system and energy issues was not in their historical materialism theories and the theory of capitalist accumulation and theory of economic crisis and they did not offer a systematic analysis on the "causes" of ecological destruction as a whole. Meanwhile, Today's Marxists and other people have exposed and illustrated capitalism's destruction on the nature, but they all lack systematic analysis on global environmental degeneration and they often rigidly perceive the "causes" as: common greed, pursuit for profits, unrestricted competition on resources in the market, and the economic development pattern established on the basis of shifting the costs to natural system and some consider the problem areas as the production department of means of livelihood, and IMF-World Bank anti-ecological loans and investments. Similarly, this narrow approach also cannot give a systematic theoretical analysis on the causes of ecological destruction.

Therefore, in the sense of **O'Connor** although historical materialism constitutes the starting point of the theory of ecological Marxism, if we want to systematically analyze the reasons for ecological crisis, we should rebuild historical materialism and particularly re-interpret the connotation of productive forces and production relations. O'Connor thinks that in traditional historical materialism, productive forces denote the technical relations between human and the materials provided by the nature, also includes the technical relations between man and industrial technology, machines, tools.

This connotation of productive forces is in the "narrow sense" and does not include the "cultural" and "natural" productive forces. Likewise, the production relations in traditional Marxism refer to property forms and power seizure form including the ownership of social products and also lack "cultural" and "natural" aspects. In fact, both productive forces and production relations are cultural and natural. These two elements are embodied in social labor. Therefore, historical materialism should not only study the productive forces and production relations in a "narrow sense" but also study the relationship in which social labor acts upon nature and culture, i.e.: we should establish a new methodology incorporating cultural and natural themes into the category of traditional Marxist laboring or material production process.

O'Connor thinks that both productive forces and production relations are incorporated with the issue of cultural norms. Laboring is both material practice and cultural practice. Therefore, productive forces and production relations both contain the dimension of objectivity and the dimension of subjectivity. In addition, O'Connor thinks that historical materialism does not include (or has a very weak sense of) the natural theory which studies the autonomous process of ecology and the nature during labor. In fact, while man reforms the nature through his labor activities, the nature also changes and re-constructs itself. It is a development process in which human power and the power of the nature are united during production. O'Connor points out that as Marx has neglected the cultural dimension and natural dimension of productive forces and production relations, his historical materialism does not have sufficient cultural attribute and embodies a limited materialist approach. In Marx's theoretical exposition about capitalist accumulation, competition, economic crisis, centralization of capital and formation of monopoly, and other relevant issues, although the ecological and material links inside natural system as well as their impacts on the cooperative modes in labor process are not completely omitted, they are relatively underestimated indeed[5].

On the basis of reconstructing historical materialism, O'Connor introduced the concept of "the second contradiction" in capitalism. In his sense, the introduction of the second contradiction in capitalism analysis will be an important train of thought which enables us to clearly grasp the issue of global environmental destruction. He said that in capitalism exists "the first contradiction", i.e.: the contradiction between productive forces and production relations as described by Marx, but also exists "the second contradiction", i.e.: the contradiction between productive forces and production relations against production conditions. In O'Connor's concept of "the second contradiction", the concept of "production conditions" is crucial. If we say "the first contradiction" is the "intrinsic obstacle" for capitalism, "the second contradiction" will be the "extrinsic obstacle" for capitalism, while this extrinsic obstacle is the result of capitalized production conditions. O'Connor analyzes that production conditions are those things which are not the commodities produced according to market law, but are treated as commodities and are virtual commodities with virtual values. O'Connor reviews the three types of production conditions described by Marx: the first is external material conditions, or the natural elements entering between invariable capital and variable capital; the second is the "personal conditions of production" and refers to the "labor force" of laborer; the third is the "communal and general conditions of social production" as mentioned by Marx, for example: infrastructure and space.

Focusing on Production Conditions

O'Connor thinks that although traditional Marxist historical materialism and the Marxist theory of capitalist accumulation and crisis constitute the starting point of the theory of ecological Marxism, they are not enough to study "the second contradiction", because he thinks, Marx had rarely dealt with those issues such as : the damages of capital on the society and environmental condition which causes an increase in capitalists' costs and further threatens the capability of capitalists' profits. i.e.: this also creates a potential threat for economic crisis. Meanwhile, Marx also does not talk or talks little on the impacts of higher capital costs caused by social, economic and political struggles which revolve around: acquiring or protecting production conditions. O'Connor points out that Marx had not clarified that capital could cause increases in "the natural obstructive elements" and trigger an ecological crisis closely related with economic crisis.

---

5 James O'Connor: Natural Causes: Essays in Ecological Marxism, p.73.

O'Connor expresses through comparison that the starting point of traditional Marxist economic crisis and the Marxist theory of transformation to socialism is the capitalist contradiction between productive forces and production relations. When this contradiction reaches a specific form, it becomes a contradiction between the production and realization of value and surplus value. The motive power of socialist revolution comes from the proletariat. The production relations in capitalism constitute the most direct target of social transformation. This social transformation embodies the transformation of political system, state and the old exchange system. On the contrary, on the issues of economic crisis and socialist transformation, the starting point of "ecological Marxism" is to solve the contradiction between capitalist production relations (as well as productive forces) against capitalist production conditions. This specific contradiction between capitalist production relations (as well as productive forces) against capitalist production conditions also exists in the production and realization of value and surplus value. "New social movements" and the old social struggles targeting the "intrinsic obstacles" of capitalism are both important forces for social transformation. Thus, social relations in the reproduction of production conditions become the direct target of social transformation.

O'Connor analyzes that in traditional Marxist theory, capital is the most formidable enemy of its own. Due to the contradiction between increasing socialized mass production and private ownership, capitalist production for pursuit of surplus values can meet difficulties because capitalist production is not only the production of values but also the production of surplus value. The firmer the political power of capital over labor, the higher the degree of exploitation on labor will be, or in other words, the higher the rate of surplus value, the more the produced exploitation profit will be. Just for this reason, it may become difficult to realize these potential profits in the market and sell these products at a price of production cost plus average profit rate. Under the drive of interest, particular capital groups will raise the labor productivity, increase labor tempo , reduce wages and use some other methods to enrich the labor time content and obtain more output from fewer workers thus meanwhile the remuneration for them will be reduced. Particular capital groups attempts to safeguard their profits by these methods, but "the first contradiction" of capitalism indicates when they do it in this way, there will be an unexpected consequence – the ultimate demand of consumers will decline. If all other conditions are fixed, then the more the profit is generated, or the higher the degree of exploitation on labor is, the less the profit will be realized and the less the market demand will become. In conclusion, the production of any kind of surplus value will cause -to some extent- insufficiency of demand in the commodity market; or conversely, any insufficiency of demand in the commodity market is based on the creation of a certain amount of surplus value or a pre-defined exploitation rate. The more the created surplus value is, or the higher the exploitation rate is, the more difficult becomes the realization of value and surplus value in the market. This contradiction between overproduction and inadequate purchasing power in the market leads to economic crisis.

O'Connor further analyzes: according to traditional Marxist theory, capitalism not only is full of crises but also relies on crises to survive. Capital is accumulated through crises, crises provide an opportunity for capital to re-integrate and rationalize/adjust itself so that it can regain/reform its ability of labor exploitation and capital accumulation. Capital usually solves crises in those ways favorable to its own interest. One method is to adjust productive forces and the other is to adjust production relations. No matter what aspect of adjustment, the premise is new direct or indirect collaboration inside and between individual capital, inside state, and between capital and state. The higher (radical) the degree of these collaborations or adjustment project is, the higher the socialization of production process will be and the more complete and deep will be the commodity and capital fetishism, or the "original" characteristics of capital and capitalist economy will be sublated (Aufhebung, *Germ.*). Hence, according to Marx's theory on crises, they in essence create the possibility and conditions for transformation to socialism.

O'Connor said, in the sense of ecological Marxism, although traditional analysis on capitalist crisis is effective, it is one-sided and limited, because traditional model assumes the supply of "production conditions" as infinite, and assume that capitalism can overcome the bottleneck in the supply of production conditions, and assume growth is only restricted by demand, whereas if the cost of labor, nature, infrastructure and social space increases radically, capital will be faced by its "second contradiction" – economic crisis stemming from cost levels, for example: the "cotton crisis" occurred during American civil war; or the higher growth of labor wages than that of productive forces in 1960s; and the "oil crisis" in 1970s.

O'Connor points out that two reasons contribute to the crisis at cost levels. The first reason is the strategy adopted by particular capitalist groups to safeguard and revive their profits. They ruin or are unable to maintain the long-term material and social conditions for their own production, for example: ignore labor condition (thus increasing health costs), damage soil (thus reducing the productive forces of land), or neglect the degradation related to local city infrastructure (worsening traffic congestion or increasing police costs or others). O'Connor analyzes, in the early period of capitalism, labor force and undeveloped resources and space were sufficient, so the prices of labor force, natural resources and space could be controlled. Over time, capital transformed everything and everybody into capital and everything was potentially included into the cost accounting of capital operations. For example, nature is priced and meanwhile degenerated; the situation in the labor markets became less desirable, followed by increases in all economic and social costs and problems; raw materials and unpolluted public resources have become sparse. This lifts the "cost of capital factor" as mentioned by Marx; local city infrastructure and space became sparse, too. This raises the costs on alleviating traffic congestion, land rent and the cost of pollution control. The second reason is some social movements from below, such as: labor and women's movements, environmental protection movements and city movements. They demand that capital should more properly maintain and preserve these production conditions, for example: they demand better medical and health care, protection of soil from destruction and maintenance of urban municipal facilities. All these will increase capital costs and reduce capital flexibility. In a word, due to these two reasons, the capitalization of production conditions, particularly the capitalization of environment and nature decreases the adaptability and flexibility of capital.

O'Connor points out, in capitalist society, the impact of the "first contradiction" on profit rate changes and the impact of the "second contradiction" interact with each other rather than counteract. In the "first contradiction", the rate of exploitation reflects the social and political power of capitalism over labor forces as well as the trend of crisis in capital overproduction. This contradiction is inherent in the system and has nothing to do with production conditions. The "second contradiction" is inherent in the category of "use values", such as: the distribution of consumption and its value content, amount of fixed assets and their intrinsic values, the price caused by the inclusion of natural factors into invariable capital and variable capital calculations , land rent decrease reducing surplus value and other all kinds of extrinsic factors. In the 'second contradiction", no factor plays a core role as the rate of exploitation (profit rate) does in the "first contradiction". O'Connor points out that the "first contradiction" exerts impact on capital from the perspective of demand. When an individual capitalist enterprise reduces cost in order to maintain or revive its profit, the unexpected result will be the decrease of market demand on the commodities. But the "second contradiction" exerts impact on capital from the perspective of costs. When an individual capitalist enterprise reduces cost in order to maintain or revive profit—for example, when they externalize (transfer) their costs to production conditions (the nature, labor force or city), the unexpected result will be the increase of the costs of other capitalist enterprises (at least the costs of the whole capitalist class). Hence, profit will decrease. In the first case, there is no problem with the production of surplus value, while problems appear only in the realization of value and surplus value; in the second case, there is no problem with the realization of value and surplus value, problems appear only in the production of surplus value. O'Connor thinks that today, capital faces both the weakening market demands and the rising production costs, in other words, capital faces both the "first contradiction" and the "second contradiction". O'Connor thinks that this situation means both the collapse of the macro-control theory of Keynesianism and the failure of neo-classical/neo-liberal economic policy.

O'Connor on the Root Causes of Ecological Crisis

Different from Leiss and Agger who attribute ecological crisis to excessive consumption, O'Connor looks for the root causes of capitalist ecological crisis from inside of capitalism, and tries to find the internal links of capitalist accumulation, economic crisis and ecological crisis. O'Connor thinks that there are two types of ecological crises in capitalism: one is the ecological crisis triggered by the general accumulation of capitalism; the other is the ecological crisis connected with economic crisis, or the ecological crisis triggered by economic crisis. These two types of economic crises must be differentiated carefully.

As for the ecological crisis triggered by the general accumulation of capitalism, O'Connor demonstrates that capitalist accumulation is established on the basis of continuously increasing productivity or continuously decreased costs of the reproduction of working class ("relative surplus value"). The growth of productivity means that a certain amount of hired labor can process more raw materials than before. If the economy keeps growing, the demand on raw materials will keep increasing (assuming other conditions remain the same). The result: raw material costs takes up a bigger share in the expenditure of invariable capital, thus calculates a bigger part in the value commodities (in other words, this capitalist enterprise must use a bigger portion of its profit to buy more raw material). O'Connor analyzes, in this case, the increase of resource demand and increasing costs of resource development will raise average costs, thus inhibiting the growth of the profit rate and capital accumulation. Therewith, through investment in equipment, technology and infrastructure, individual capital is forced to discover new minerals and mineral fuel reserves as well as arable land, and tries to overcome the above mentioned "bottlenecks". The relative high price of raw material and energy can also stimulate individual capital groups to re-utilize them or use substitutes or raise efficiency in using raw materials and fuels. On the contrary, if reverse development trend in raw material (lower average cost than before on the precondition of more effective production and use level) appears, cost and price will go down and the average profit rate will go up and the development of raw materials and capital accumulation will rapidly increase. The lower price of raw materials results in the risk of faster consumption and loss of resources. When raw materials are relatively cheap, the profit rate will increase and the process of resource demand and accumulation will be quickened. A vicious circle is thus formed: high profit rate results in high accumulation rate, but in return, high accumulation rate will result in greater demand on raw materials; higher-level development of raw material results in the reduction of production costs, while the reduction of production cost will make the high profit and accumulation rates even higher. In short, if raw material is very cheap, accumulation rate and resource consumption and exhaustion rates of resources will be relatively high; if raw material is expensive, capital investment will be used to bring down cost or develop a method to increase their use efficiency.

Whether the cost of raw material, energy and other "invariable capital and variable capital factors" is high and keeps increasing or low and keeps decreasing, capital accumulation and economic growth both rely on the enlargement of the category-1 investment as mentioned in Marx's Capital. The faster the first category grows, the higher the average growth rate of productivity, profit and economic aggregate will be. On the contrary, supposing other conditions are not changed, the higher the growth rate of the economy is, the higher the resource consumption and exhaustion rates will be, and meanwhile the more possibly the excessive by-products (pollution) will be generated.

O'Connor further points out that in fact a given economic growth rate may also cause a higher consumption rate and pollution rate. The global warming, biodiversity, disappearance of ozone sphere, acid rain, marine pollution, deforestation, exhaustion of energy and mineral reserves, soil loss and other major ecological changes are all the result of the fast economic growth of industrial capitalism (as well as former state socialism model) in the last two or more than two centuries, while to a great extent, this fast growth is also the result of the development and expansion of the category-1 industry.

Second Type of Ecological Crisis

As for the ecological crisis triggered by economic crisis, O'Connor thinks that it is not all the same as the "standard" ecological deterioration accompanying capital accumulation. As a whole, economic crisis is related to excessive competition, efficiency infatuation and cost reduction. Therefore, it is also related to the intensification of economic and physiological oppression on the workers, the increases in cost externalization and exacerbation of environmental deterioration. Economic crisis and cost reduction will also stimulate the resurrection of the technologies which are harmful to environment and which are forbidden, and causes the emergence of more advanced modern technologies. This will create a high-tech pollution. In addition, economic crisis is also related to the efforts of reducing capital circulation time, and this will make enterprises pay even less attention to workers' health, the environmental and sanitary impact of the sold commodities, urban conditions and the sustainability of infrastructure. O'Connor thinks that the ecological problems resulting from capitalist accumulation is quite different from the ecological problems caused by the economic crises, but at any moment, they are both integrated and co-exist. In order to save money, the enterprises or industry branches in difficulty will disregard environmental cleanliness and protection, while during their exploitation of nature, it will be more impossible for them to care about the problems of technical and land use from an approach of ecology during exploration, exploitation and operation. On the other hand, the fast-growing enterprises or industry branches, in order to cater for the ever-expanding market, will consume resources more quickly and will not think much of the use efficiency of energy and raw materials and they will not care the issue of environmental protection.

O'Connor thinks that ecological crisis may also trigger economic crises. The ecological problems from capital per se—shortage of raw material due to market force, high land rents, cost from traffic congestion, rise of energy cost and other factors, will decrease profits or trigger the risk of inflation, for example: the negative economic impact of the "oil crisis" in 1970s. At the same time, the environmental movement can influence the economic crisis. This is because social movements, political struggles and state policies play a role in intervening ecological and economic changes and transformation. The environmental movement as well as labor, city and other types of social movements may cause flexibility in cost increases and capital reduction, thus may endanger or impair capitalist accumulation.

All in all, generally speaking, capitalist accumulation will result in economic crises; economic crisis and ecological problems are connected; the extrinsic obstacle for capital is manifested as rare resources, urban space, health, well-trained hired laborers and some other production conditions. They increase costs, thus constituting a threat to profits; lastly, the environmental movement aiming to protect living condition, forest, soil quality, environmental comfort, sanitary condition and urban space, as well as other social movements may also result in cost increases and capital loses its flexibility.

O'Connor concludes that capitalist accumulation and crisis may cause ecological problems, while ecological problems (including the response by environmental and social movements to this kind of problems) in return will cause economic problems. This is a mutually determining interactive relation between economic crisis and ecological crisis—in the dimensions of production, market relations, social movement and politics. While damaging or destroying its own production conditions, capital moves towards self negation (Aufhebung, *Germ.*). In this sense, ecological crisis and economic crisis are both caused by themselves, and moreover, the movements from below are two different aspects of this general process.

Changes in Production Conditions and Eco-socialism

O'Connor strives to derive the prospects for eco-socialism from "the second contradiction of capitalism". He claims neither Marx himself nor other Marxists have developed a theory to explain the relation between crisis-triggering changes in the capitalist production conditions and thus the emerging conditions for eco-socialism; he has indeed devoted himself to overcome this deficiency.

O'Connor said after comparison, in traditional Marxism, crisis-triggering changes in productive forces and production relations are determined by the need for cost cuts, raise of labor intensity and re-adjustment of capital structure. Productive forces and production relations have a trend of transformation towards more socialized forms. Same as traditional Marxist theory, ecological Marxism thinks that capitalism is not only full of crises but also dependent on crises for further development. Similarly, crisis-triggering changes in production conditions are also determined by the need for cost cuts, reduction of land rent, increase of flexibility and reorganization of production conditions. O'Connor analyzes that capitalism always tries to solve crises in ways favorable to capital interests: one way is reforming the conditions of productive forces, one example can be: more direct collaborative relations in the field of production conditions. The other is reforming the social relations in the conditions of reproduction, one example can be: more forceful control or more effective plans for production conditions. No matter what adjustment is made, the premise is new direct or indirect collaboration inside and between individual capital, inside state, and between capital and state, or in other words, the premise of reform is a more socialized management/operation form related to the metabolism between human and nature, and between man and man and thirdly between natural and social environment. This deeper/higher collaboration will make the politicized production conditions more political, collaborative or planned. The higher the degree of collaboration or plan is, the greater the socialization of production process will be and the more complete the fetishism of commodities and fetishism of capital, and the "natural/original" characteristics of capital and capitalist economy will be sublated (as also indicated by Marx as negative sublation). Hence, crises in essence create a possibility and conditions for transformation to socialism.

However, O'Connor thinks that this trend of more socialized production conditions is only the initial/basic condition of socialism and does not mean certain advent of socialism. He said: it is impossible that the advent of socialism has any transcendental basis. Reforming the production conditions (from the dimension of productive forces) more suitable for the higher socialized production forms does not in the least mean that capitalism has a "natural" trend of self-transformation towards socialism. The reason is that when capitalism transforms to a more socialized form in the supply of production conditions through political and ideological intervention, then it is self-deconstructive or/and self-subversive. O'Connor explains the premises of this view as follows: any kind of given technical and labor relations as part of the production conditions can be consistent (fit) with more than one kind of social relations which can reproduces these conditions; likewise, any given form of these social relations can (fit) also be consistent with more than one form of technical and labor relations as part of the production conditions. Therefore, the "conformity" between social relations and the reproduction of production conditions is rather loose and volatile. In a crisis, two-way struggles exist. Not only the new production conditions in the dimension of productive forces should be suited to the new production conditions in the dimension of production relations, but also the latter should be suited to the former. O'Connor thinks, in contemporary capitalism, the new social and political forms for reproduction of production conditions are diverse, and it seems that today's worldwide crisis will cause various types of social and political forms. Therefore, the roads to socialism are not only one. He said, possibly, we are on a long journey, and on the way, there are many different roads all opening to socialism. Therefore, seemingly traditional "socialist construction" model is giving way to a new-type "socialist construction" process, which is the reconstruction of human per se and the production conditions including social environment — a political view which values that condition is the foremost. His conclusion is that the construction of socialism is firstly desired and secondly necessary in the "first world"; also firstly desired and secondly necessary in the "second world"; but firstly necessary and secondly desired in the "third world".

O'Connor further demonstrates that today's environmental movement, feminism and other new social movements are "driving" capital and state to a more socialized reproduction form of production conditions. He points out that labor exploitation – "the primary contradiction of capitalism" as the foundation of Marx's crisis theory triggers the labor movement which becomes a "social obstacle" for capital. The cruel utilization of the nature will cause the environmental movement which may also become the "social obstacle" for capital.

O'Connor concludes that the changes of production conditions caused by crises will inevitably bring about more state control, more planning inside large capital groups and a capitalism which is more socialized and more politicized in management and organization, i.e.: a capitalism with less indifference to the nature. In such a capitalism the changes in production conditions will be more and more political and legally regulated. By these changes capital will be forced to externalize more cost. The unscrupulous utilization of technology and nature in order to realize (exchange) value in the circulation sphere of the economy and the combination of other similar negative factors will one day cause a huge "natural resistance", i.e.: more powerful social movements aiming to stop destruction of ecology. Particularly, in today's crisis era, no matter what theoretical interpretation is given on its reasons, capital constantly tries to shorten production and circulation cycle. This undoubtedly will worsen environmental, health and safety regulations. Therefore, the adjustment needs of capital will deepen rather than solve ecological dilemma.

O'Connor claims, just like the destruction of capital in the commodity market front, in the second front: the larger the production of surplus value is, the greater will be the harm of capital on its own production profit, and the more definitely will be the production of surplus value established on the basis of destructive utilization of the nature (in a broad sense). Just as the crisis of overproduction pushes the reconstruction (adjustment) of productive forces and production relations, the crisis of underproduction pushes the reconstruction (adjustment) of production conditions. Likewise, just as the adjustments of productive forces means more socialized production relations to fit their development (and vice versa), the adjustment of production conditions means a two-aspect movement – a more socialized form in production conditions, and a more socialized form in social relations and new production conditions can only be reproduced in such new social relations. In short, for O'Connor the combination of a more socialized form of production relations, productive forces and plus production conditions prepares the conditions for transformation to socialism. These developments are brought by crises.

Therefore, O'Connor thinks that in capitalism, there are two types rather than one type of contradictions and crises; similarly, in capitalism, there are two types rather than one type of adjustments and reconstruction caused by crises. This is O'Connor's important view on ecological Marxism.

REFERENCES

• Ben Agger: Western Marxism: An Introduction. Beijing, China Renmin University Press, 1991.
• James O'Connor: Natural Causes: Essays in Ecological Marxism. Nanjing, Nanjing University Press, 2003.

CHAPTER V

BAUDRILLARD'S CRITIQUE ON MARXIST ECONOMICS

1 *Critique against Political Economy of the Sign*
2 *Premises for Political Economy of the Sign and Marxism*
3 *Rupture from Marxism: "The Mirror of Production"*
4 *Journey to Post-Modernism: Termination of General Political Economy*

Jean Baudrillard (1929-) is one of the most important and controversial contemporary thinkers in France. Since 1980s, Baudrillard has gradually become a central figure in the academic circle and a core figure of almost all Post-modernist periodicals. He is considered on par with Deleuze and Lyotard. What is more, his influence has rapidly spread to the English and German speaking regions of the globe, and many academic organizations, theoretical periodicals and symposia initiated by "post-modernism" consider Baudrillard a fashionable topic and a hot figure. For example, British Guardian has introduced Baudrillard at a whole page with the title of "who is Baudrillard" on September 21, 1988, and called him "a sociological professor, a prophet of future world and the most popular figure in the literary circle of New York; American New York Times called Baudrillard "a sharp-shooting Lone Ranger of the post-Marxist left"; in the Australian academic circle, some scholars simply put forth the concept and proposition of "Baudrillard Landscape"[1]. Some scholars have even directly compared Baudrillard's theory to the coming of storm (Nick Stevenson). In regard to this powerful influence, scholars unanimously believe that it is not because Baudrillard's thought is a cultural fashion, but because it has raised many doubts and challenges to modern life and opened many new research directions. Here we will mainly discuss Baudrillard's efforts on the critique on Marxist political economy.

---

1 Bao Yaming Editor in Chief: Postmodernity and Geopolitics, Shanghai, Shanghai Education Press, 2001, p. 43-44.

1. CRITIQUE AGAINST POLITICAL ECONOMY OF THE SIGN

In the sense of Baudrillard, Marx's overall logic is production and this logic can only explain the preliminary stage of capitalism. Following the transformation of Western society in 1955-1960s, consumption has assumed a dominant position in the West. Baudrillard insists that signs and commodities have appeared at the very beginning of capitalism, i.e.: everything has its existence basis only when it is converted into a sign value, and this conversion process is also an intensive construction of dominant ideology in contemporary capitalist society. Therefore, Baudrillard thinks that modern capitalist society is not an era in which traditional material production is dominant, but an era in which codes assume a dominant position. The significance of commodities is not stipulated by their uses. Instead, it is related to the mutual difference and order inside the sign system. Hence, Baudrillard has tried to integrate Marxism and semiotics and introduced a critique against the political economy of the sign in a novel way. Moreover, he thinks that the critique against the political economy of the sign is more radical than the critique against political economy by Marx.

Logic of Values in Consumer Society

Baudrillard has declared that one change has happened: we have entered from the political economy of commodity to the political economy of the sign, and commodity form has given way to sign form. At first, he analyzes and articulates the four logics of value and thinks that it is necessary to distinguish the logic of consumption (logic of signs or logic of difference) from other logics.

Here we will focus on his four logics:

(1) Functional logic of use values: such as: nail hammer (instrument);

(2) Economic logic of exchange values: such as: things for exchange or money (commodity);

(3) Logic of symbolic exchanges: such as: a diamond wedding ring (symbol);

(4) Logic of sign values: such as: an ordinary ring (sign).

Baudrillard thinks that the first is the logic of actual operation, the second embodies the logic of equivalents, the third embodies logic of ambivalence and the fourth is the logic of difference. Or they can be expressed as: functional logic, market logic, gift logic and status logic. The objects organized in consistence with the above four logics stand for instrument, commodity, symbol and sign, respectively[2].

---

2   See Jean Baudrillard: For a Critique of the Political Economy of the Sign, Telos Press, 1981, p. 66.

According to Baudrillard's early critiques on Marx, the force driving the progress of human society is neither need or shortage nor the commodities which can be transformed to direct "use values" (used to meet these needs) and "exchange value" (playing a role in fluctuating market price) in economy. Beyond use value and exchange value, Baudrillard adds two more "values": "sign value" and "symbolic exchange value". Baudrillard thinks that one kind of logic corresponds to one kind of value and symbolic exchange value corresponds to ambivalence-related things. In fact, symbolic exchange value is not real value but an economic level which must be ripped thus generating a "value" type and is a positive exchange relation. Baudrillard has asserted that this was the level to which any real revolutionary approach trying to overcome the contemporary consumer society should aim to go —back to this level—. The commodity system in the modern society is a sign system, while commodity is an abstract sign. It is both the signifier and the signified and has the properties of equity, substitute and exchangeable. In this system, one person or a commodity can substitute another person or commodity. In other words, commodities have been structured into a sign value system dominated by rules, codes and social logics.

Logic of Difference and Hierarchy

In the sense of Baudrillard, only the difference logic of sign value is the real consumption logic, because the reason why an object becomes an object of consumption is not that it is the symbol of spirit or soul, a functional tool or a commercial product but that it is a sign which complies with the logic of difference. This is sign consumption theory. Just as Baudrillard proposes in Consumer Society, a real consumption theory cannot be based on demand theory but on the theory of cultural sense, because the basic demand of human is defined by society, it is not natural and biological, human society is not decided by shortage as claimed by economists but by meanings, surplus or waste, and the standard of luxury decides the standard of basic demand. In other words, consumers give much higher regard to the meaning of commodity sign than the demand of basic functions. Therefore, consumption is defined by the meaning of commodity and people do not deem commodities as an object. Baudrillard follows the thought of Saussure and believes that the logic behind sign value is the logic of difference. If we that say exchange value has to do with balance (exchange of equivalents), and use value has to do with utility, then sign value will be a thing having to do with difference. However, sign value or object status as a definite sign is still related to the object status which possesses use value in everyday practice, as well as the exchange value in capitalist accumulation system. Cultural hegemony manifests itself as a process in which all objects are transformed to sign values, but it eliminates neither the everyday life practice established on use values nor the capital accumulation system based on exchange values. Just because of this reason, sign value and consumerist connotation or the object system as called by Baudrillard become more important in capitalist society. Just as the commercialization of everyday life, sign value dominates culture and through the hegemony of consumer culture, everyday life is commercialized. Initially, in fact Baudrillard had asserted that commodity form had developed to such a higher degree that use value and exchange value was substituted by sign value, and sign value redefined commodity as a sign to be consumed and exhibited3.

Therefore, in the sense of Baudrillard, the definition of consumption object is completely independent of objects and is the exclusive function of the logic of sign. An object is a consumption object only when it is freed from spiritual determinant like a symbol, from functional determinant like an instrument, and from economic determinant like a product, thus it is emancipated to a sign and represented by fashionable formal logic, i.e.: logic of difference. Therefore, in the sense of Baudrillard, the meaning of a sign is not extrinsic concrete truth but the difference between signs. The truth (i.e.: the signified) is the effect and ideology of sign and can be manipulated and controlled by the sign. This is the very reason why Baudrillard wants to develop a critique against the political economy of the sign.

Economic order aims to control accumulation and expropriate surplus value, while the sign (economic) order corresponding to the production of sign values aims to control luxury and the circulation process of meanings. Baudrillard thinks that in the modern capitalist society, the latter is decisive. Modern capitalism converts economic exchange values into the sign values established on the basis establishing the monopoly of codes. The basis for the legacy of the capitalist society has changed: it used to be the possession of means of productions but now it is the possession of sign meaning. This sign meaning reflects the difference(s) and hierarchy in real life. In the sense of Baudrillard, the past pure critique of political economy or the theory of material production is merely a kind of "commodity fetishism", and also semiotics or text production theory is a kind of "sign fetishism". Neither of these two theories combines the analysis of sign form with the analysis of commodity form. Only his "critique of the political economy of the sign" as a general theory fundamentally solves the issue of combining the analysis of sign form with the analysis of commodity form4. If we say that in the early capitalist society, social control was realized through capitalists' expropriation of the surplus values created by the workers' labor, Baudrillard tells us a consumer society achieves more effective social control through production of sign value. The sign value system in a consumer society not only transforms commodity into homogenous, interchangeable and substitutable value and meanwhile also transforms the subjects of consumption into a homogenous and rationalized demand system. That is to say, not only different commodities have same value for all consumers but also all consumers have the same needs. In such a society,

3   See Douglas Kellner (ed.), Baudrillard: A Critical Reader, Blackwell, 1994, p. 41.
4   Bao Yaming Editor in Chief: Postmodernity and Geopolitics, p. 66.

consumers are completely internalized into the capitalist system and there are no more so-called revolutionary subjects who are beyond the system.

Cultural Analysis and Critique on Consumer Society

According to Baudrillard, we are still in the "Holy Bible" of politics and living in the culture conquered and manipulated by ruling class. Ruling class pays great attention to culture, they are not content with the utilization of "manpower reserves" and also use sign reserves and value system; their purpose is nothing but confusing class antagonisms and mystify proletariat ideology. But where are these signs originate from? Baudrillard interrogates: if economy is really a decisive factor, why does ruling class still need culture?[5] Sign value is generated from a kind of social labor – the production of difference and the production of the hierarchical system of difference. It should not be confused with economic exploitation of surplus value. The former indeed not originates from the latter. In the sense of Baudrillard, between the two there is another kind of labor which converts economic value and surplus value into sign value: this is a luxurious operation, which swallows and surpasses economic value through a completely different exchange. However, Baudrillard asserts: in a sense this operation also generates surplus value; this is another rule not to be confused with economic privileges and profit. The latter (economic privileges and profit) is, to some extent, only the basic material condition and springboard for political operation, the political operation to strengthen power based on the sign. In this way, ruling power is related to economic power, but it does not automatically stem from economic power; on the contrary, it stems from economic power through transforming economic values[6]. In the sense of Baudrillard, in the old economic order, the control on accumulation and expropriation of surplus value is dominant. In the sign (cultural) order, the control on spending/consumption is decisive, i.e.: the control on the conversion from economic exchange value to sign exchange value on the basis of code monopoly is critical. From the very beginning (including ancient and traditional society), ruling class has ensured their dominance through sign values or tried to transcend and surpass their economic privileges and sanctify it in the sign privileges, this stage is recognized as the final ruling stage. Baudrillard thinks that this logic can be completely observed in an art auction and that it gradually substitutes hierarchical logic; it is no longer clarified through the (control) ownership of means of production but through the control on the sign(ification) process, and it constitutes a production model completely different from material production.

Sign value is generated through the hierarchical order of commodities. Baudrillard believes that the analysis of sign value provides an important view neglected by a majority of Marxists, i.e.: provides a way to establish the dominant value of

---

5   Jean Baudrillard: For a Critique of the Political Economy of the Sign, p. 114.
6   *Ibid.*, p. 115.

luxury so as to obtain class status. Sign value is organized by the codes of political economy. It symbolizes differences and the hierarchy of values. According to Baudrillard, the analysis of sign value and fetishism provides a new solution for the emergence of a social rule system. He asserts that these phenomena were neglected by Marx, and confuse the understanding on how capitalism obtains the power and control over individuals[7]. Indeed, the theory of sign value provides a very sharp explanation on the motives of consumption in a consumer society. For Baudrillard, consumption exists through the possession and exhibition of sign values rather than their uses and enjoyment by these products. Through comparison, Baudrillard thinks that capitalism establishes its social rule through forced establishment of a sign value system, so individuals are in a consumer society and surrender to its rule through consumption activities.

Baudrillard thus establishes a critique of the political economy of the sign, and converts commodity market into a sign consumption system. In fact, this approach is also a shift from traditional critique of political economy to the critique by culture. It transcends the relations between human and object and between human and human, and extended to all the levels of history and culture. Consumption exactly explains a development stage in which commodity is completely regarded as sign and sign value, while sign (culture) is regarded as commodity. At present, nothing (object, service, body, sex, culture, knowledge and so on) can be separately interpreted as sign during production and exchange process , or separately evaluated as commodity, in the context of general political economy, the thing playing a dominant role is neither commodity alone or culture alone but the inseparable combination of the two, and use value, exchange value and sign value all join in a complex system , thus presenting the most universal form of political economy[8].

Baudrillard's "critique against the political economy of the sign" is the result of combining the analysis of sign form and the analysis of commodity form. This combination in the final analysis is to introduce cultural analysis into the field of the analysis and critique of political economy, so the "critique of the political economy of the sign" in fact is also cultural analysis, cultural theory or cultural strategy[9]. Here Baudrillard in fact has developed the thought of Henri Lefebvre in Everyday Life in the Modern World: if sign again forms the foundation of dominance in modern society, economic dominance will give way to the cultural dominance of the sign, so the critique and reform of actual society must be shifted from previous economic perspective to the perspective of cultural revolution. In other words, Baudrillard thinks that people's symbolic desire to products is much more stronger than their functional demand on the products, and traditional

---

7   See Douglas Kellner, Jean Baudrillard: From Marxism to Postmodernismand Beyond, Stanford University Press, 1989, p. 24.
8   Jean Baudrillard: For a Critique of the Political Economy of the Sign, p. 148.
9   Bao Yaming Editor in Chief: Postmodernity and Geopolitics, p. 67.

Marxist research on production and economic structure should be shifted to level cultural research on the sign.

Douglas Kellner speaks highly of Baudrillard's theory and thinks that Baudrillard's emphasis on the consumption can be regarded as a supplement to Marx's production analysis, while his explanation of culture and sign can be regarded as the development of Marxist political economy. It means that Baudrillard adds the levels of culture and sign to Marxism. By contrast, Gunn criticizes Baudrillard's "critique against the political economy of the sign". Gunn thinks that the mechanism of social reputation is the result of the development of social practice and historical culture, British workers like beer, French workers like grape wine, and wine is produced both for market and for non-market (these two processes are totally inseparable). This indicates that wine may possess sign value and exchange value and may also gain values as gift and social reputation, so Baudrillard's view of combining the use value of "objects" to the sign system is apparently narrow. The analysis on use values must be carried by combining it with other social practices and cultural process outside the sign system[10]. Since advertisement, fashion, mass media and other new means were not as dominant in Marx's era as in contemporary society, therefore sign value and its function and the process of rationalization and systematization did not become the core of observation in Marx's theory, Baudrillard's naturalist or economist interpretation on Marxism aiming to raise the value of his own sign theory is a single-dimension approach and completely ignores the emphasis of Marxist historical materialism on social-cultural practice and social-historical course[11].

I can say that Baudrillard's thought proceeds from the neo-Marxist critical theory, and employs structuralist semiotics approach to analyze modernity and he later performs a kind of rupture and variation. Although Baudrillard has since long challenged the social system based on political economy (capitalism), he still stands on the segment of history, and develops his thought on the background of the dialectic relation between object and subject. Interestingly, he has developed the above theory on the sign; only after he has discovered that the critical theory was also an adjustment –concession- to sign order within a kind of logic.

2. PREMISES FOR POLITICAL ECONOMY OF SIGN AND MARXISM

If we analyze culture, consumption and sign as ideology, this effect will not be obtained through eliminating them or achieved by refuting them. On the contrary, we must integrate them into the structure of political economy. Baudrillard says:

---

10   See Mike Gane, Baudrillard: Critical and Fatal Theory, London and New York, 1991, p. 84.
11   Bao Yaming Editor in Chief: Postmodernity and Geopolitics, p. 68.

"this means we do not have to pay attention to the traditional boundaries of the traditional political economy which is worshiped as a "Holy Bible" by both bourgeois economics and Marxism. To criticize Marxist political economy and the political economy of the sign, the theory of general political economy must be constructed. Only a complete critique against this general political economy can clarify revolutionary theory and practice".

Three Stages of General Political Economy by Baudrillard

Stage 1: Baudrillard does not want to give a theoretical representation on different logics of value and only tries to explain the transformation of each field and from one field to another, i.e.: the conversion among use value (Uv), economic exchange value (EcEv), sign exchange value (SgEv) and symbolic exchange (SbE), for example: (1) Uv-EcEv, (2) Uv-SgEv, (3) Uv-SbE, (4) EcEv-Uv, (5) EcEv-SgEv, (6) EcEv-SbE, (7) SgEv-Uv, (8) SgEv-EcEv, (9) SgEv-SbE, (10) SbE-Uv, (11) SbE-EcEv, (12) SbE-SgEv.

(1) denotes the conversion from use value to exchange value. Baudrillard thinks that it is the field of exchange value production process and the commodity form as described by political economy and belongs to productive consumption.

(2) is the conversion from use value to sign value. Baudrillard claims that it is the field of sign production triggered by destructive usage and belongs to non-productive consumption. It is the conversion from commodity form to sign form and transformation from commodity system to sign system.

(3) is the transcendence from use value to symbolic exchange.

In the sense of Baudrillard, it is the field of consumption[12] -destructing use value. Symbolic exchange is restored in economic transcendence, as manifested by gift, celebration and so on.

(4) is the conversion from exchange value to use value. It is a 'consumption" process in the sense of traditional economics and aims to acquire use value.

(5) stands for the conversion from exchange value to sign value. The consumption process here is re-defined according to political economy of the sign. Here Baudrillard expresses commodity form rises to sign form, economic system is transformed into sign system and economic power is transformed into social hierarchical privilege.

---

12   In English, consumption has two meanings. The "consumption" used here is equivalent to French "consommation". Its meaning is burning up and exhaustion. The meaning of consumption corresponds to "consommation" in French. The French title of Baudrillard's Consumer Society is La société de consommation.

(6) is the transcendence from exchange value to symbolic exchange.

Wholly speaking, (1) and (4) are two factors of the circulation sphere in the classical (and Marxist) political economy. Baudrillard thinks that they do not consider political economy of the sign. It is also a field where exchange value is sanctified through use value and commodity form is transformed into object form. (2) and (5) describe the transformation from use value and exchange value to sign value (or from object form and commodity form to sign form). (3) and (6) symbolize the transcendence of object form and commodity form through a symbolic exchange.

(7) is the conversion from sign value to use value. Baudrillard claims that same as commodity, sign has both use value and exchange value.

(8) is the conversion from sign value to exchange value. This involves the re-transformation of cultural privilege and sign monopoly into economic privilege.

(9) is the transcendence from sign value to symbolic exchange. Baudrillard claims that the deconstruction and transcendence of sign form lead to symbolic exchange.

(10), (11) and (12) denotes symbolic exchange is converted into use value, exchange value and sign value, respectively. Baudrillard claims that these three describe the same process: reversion of the transcendence described in (3), (6) and (9)—destruction and restoration of symbolic exchange and establishment of economics. These three processes jointly analyze the "cost" of symbolic exchange. This exchange is under multiple abstract and rational value codes (use value, exchange value and sign value). Baudrillard has commented that political economy might explicitly mention every code, but these codes were integrated into a simple form and opposite to symbolic exchange as a whole[13]. For Baudrillard in order to establish symbolic exchange, all value forms must be negated (object, commodity or sign). There should be a fundamental rupture from value field.

Stage 2: Baudrillard extracts some important presentations from the overall transformation process of in production, reproduction, conversion, transcendence and transformation of values. These presentations constitute the second stage. The first presentation is: SgEv/SbE=EcEv/Uv. In other words, just like between the multiple "concrete" use value and abstract exchange value of commodity, a same process of transformation, abstraction and rationalization also exists between symbolic exchange and sign value. Baudrillard has claimed: "if people accept this equation, it means a same process works on the two sides of the equation. This process is political economy. This means that political economy of the

---

13   See Jean Baudrillard: For a Critique of the Political Economy of the Sign, pp. 123-125.

sign is applied to analyze the first relation and it is represented in the political economy of material production and reflects itself in the ideological process[14]. In the sense of Baudrillard, the political economy of the sign is roughly manifested as the form of theoretical linguistics, and exists in the form of semiotics in most time, but the latter avoids the analysis under the framework of political economy (this means the critique against the political economy of the sign follows same theoretical steps as Marx does). This circumstance is formed unconsciously: in the fields of sign and meaning, it is same as the classical bourgeois political economy before Marx's critique. Therefore, Baudrillard points out that, the reason the political economy of the sign is as susceptible to critique as classical political economy, this is because their form is the same—sign form and commodity form, but not their content[15].

The second stage shifts from the mechanical combination of values to form relation and to overall homology. Baudrillard has commented that it was a huge progress, but not decisive. In fact, this form relation expresses all kinds of value logics, but to make this homology completely consistent, it must be horizontal relation that strengthens vertical relation. Sign value/symbolic exchange=exchange value/use value (the relation presupposed above), and besides, sign value/exchange value=symbolic exchange/use value, i.e.: $SgEv/EcEv=SbE/Uv$. Now, if in the framework of general political economy, sign value and exchange value (sign form and commodity form) are in fact linked due to the relation of logical form, we have not found any analogous order that links the symbolic exchange value and the use value – Baudrillard points out : "on the contrary, as the former is the transcendence to the latter and the latter is the restoration of the former; then this equation will be inconsistent, strictly speaking, symbolic exchange is fundamentally opposite to all values[16].

Stage 3: Baudrillard claims that these inconsistencies ultimately will break this equation and cause a general reconstruction. He summarizes as follows:

Firstly, sign as overall value is substituted by the signifier and the signified, the latter two are elements constituting sign and it is very necessary to display them.

Secondly, in this way, a definite relation is established between the sign form and the commodity form: $EcEv/Uv=Sr/Sd$, say in words: the ratio of exchange value to use value is equal to the ratio of the signified to the signifier. On this basis, we will say that this homology (time consistency) describes the whole sphere of political economy.

---

14   *Ibid.*, p. 126.
15   *Ibid.*
16   *Ibid.*, p. 127.

Thirdly, as homology contains the symbolic exchange, it is repulsed by the value sphere (or the sphere of general political economy). Baudrillard claims it is equivalent to substitute and transcend the basic definition of value.

Fourthly, it is alleged that the "/" bar indicating restoration process or rational abstraction process separates the use value from the exchange value, and separates the signified separated from the signifier. "/" is substituted. Baudrillard claims that basic transformation no longer occurs between the use value and the exchange value, or between the signified and the signifier, but between the overall system and symbolic exchange[17].

In the sense of Baudrillard, "/" that separates the use value from the exchange value, and separates the signified from the signifier is a dividing line in the sense of formal logic. However, this line does not fundamentally make these items separated; on the contrary, it establishes structural relations between these items. In fact, all these relations form a system in the structure of political economy. The logical organization of the whole system negates, suppresses and transforms symbolic exchange[18]. According to Baudrillard, what makes all items separated from symbolic exchange is not "/" in structural sense but the line of fundamental elimination. Hence we obtain the general distribution of the items, concretely: $EcEv/Uv = (Sr/Sd)/SbE$. As such, Baudrillard thinks that this is the sole major antagonism between the whole value sphere and non-value sphere -symbolic exchange sphere, i.e.: general political economy/symbolic exchange.

In the value sphere, the process of material production (commodity form) and the process of the sign production (sign form) are expressed with same system logic. Therefore, Baudrillard has commented, the critical theory against general political economy (or the critical theory against value) is same as the theory of symbolic exchange. It is the foundation of Baudrillard's revolutionary anthropology.

Critical Theory against General Political Economy and Symbolic Exchange

Gary Genosko believes that For a Critique of the Political Economy of the Sign is so far the most systematic works of Baudrillard, because in this book, Baudrillard introduces his theory of general political economy, and sums up a series of conversions between Marxist political economy and semiotics. This conversion process basically consists of three parts: production, consumption and transcendence, while transcendence is the most important. The first part indicates the interdependence of the production and consumption processes in the classical political economy and Marxist political economy; the second part systemizes

---

17   Ibid., pp. 127-128.
18   Ibid., p. 128.

and unifies material production and sign production based on Baudrillard's commodity and sign equation (i.e.: the structural relation between exchange value and use value is equal to the structural relation between signifier and the signified); the transcendence in the third part indicates the transformation from the fields of economic value and sign value to symbolic field, whereas this re-conversion describes the reductive re-evaluation of symbolic exchange. This is fulfilled through re-instrumenting symbolic exchange into commodity or sign. Although symbolic exchange surpasses all other values, in order to explain his general political economy, Baudrillard also involves symbolic exchange in other value theories. Therefore, Genosko emphasizes in the end that symbolic exchange is extremely anti-semiotics, it advocates a revolutionary and consumptive (see consommation in French) practice – "sign must burn", it blows a serious destruction on value system[19].

The so-called political economy is general, and expresses the logical correlation between commodity form and sign form and describes the whole value system. Moreover, sign form is always definitely related to special sign order and theory. According to Baudrillard, these transcending conversions (Uv-SbE; EcEv-SbE; SgEv-SbE) indicate the transformation from value field to symbolic field, so symbolic exchange is the another side of political economy. Through symbolic consumptive mode, the conversion from one side of use value, exchange value and sign value to another side eliminates value. In this way, Baudrillard transforms and defines the order of contemporary society according to the semiotics of symbolic relation, while symbolic relation is established on the basis of transparent, concrete, antagonistic and obligatory contracts. The relations between humans are decided by the absolutely unitary symbol (such as: wedding ring and other tokens). When the symbol is materialized into a sign, the value of the symbol will be freed from this system and its contradictoriness will become the equivalent of structure and make the social relations of production and consumption abstract and opaque[20].

In brief, "the critique against general political economy (or the critical theory against value) and the theory of symbolic exchange are an integrated same thing, which is the foundation of revolutionary anthropology[21]. Baudrillard has asserted that Marxism has analyzed some elements of this anthropology, and proved that it could not be developed to the separation point of critique. The critique against political economy here refers to Marx's critique against political economy, and also includes Baudrillard's critique against the political economy of the sign. Its aims are: firstly, to criticize Marxist political economy. In order to restore the idealist anthropology that even Marxist political economy still has to face, Baudrillard

---

19   See Gary Genosko, Baudrillard and Signs, p. 4.
20   *Ibid.*, p. 5.
21   Jean Baudrillard: For a Critique of the Political Economy of the Sign, p. 128.

has commented: "we need to extend the critique against political economy to the fundamental critique of use values". The critique of use value fetishism is necessary — analyze the relation between object form and commodity form. Secondly, Baudrillard aims to criticize political economy of the sign. "In order to clarify how the logic, free operation and circulation of the signifier are organized like the logic of exchange value system, and to explain how the logic of the signified belongs to the logic of the signifier in strategy, just like the logic of use value belongs to the logic of exchange value, we need to extend the critique of political economy to signs and sign system"; Baudrillard has claimed that in the end we need a critique of signifier-fetishism – analyze the relation between sign form and commodity form ; "Marx only criticizes exchange value, so the critical theory against use value, the signifier and the signified needs further development". Thirdly, Baudrillard aims to put forth the theory of symbolic exchange. Through a critique of Marxist political economy and the political economy of the sign, Baudrillard tries to exterminate and transcend all value forms, thus establish the theory of symbolic exchange[22]. Through above considerations, Baudrillard extends his critique to sign field, and thinks the critique of sign must proceed from the signifier and the signified, corresponding to sign value and sign form. Therefore, Baudrillard's final aim is to establish a theory of symbolic exchange and eradicate all value forms (including the forms of economic value and sign value). This is the original intention when he re-constructs the theory of general political economy.

In the sense of Baudrillard, classical political economy is the first stage. This stage is the emphasis of the classical bourgeois political economy and Marx. The political economy of the sign is the second stage. In this stage, nothing has a true value before it is converted into sign. In the sense of Marx's political economy, the core is "production mode", and the concepts of use value, surplus value, exchange value, labor, exploitation and so on all revolves around this core; while in the sense of political economy of the sign, the core is "mode of signification", and sign value and the translation of sign consumption become key topics for discussion. Baudrillard thinks that only symbolic exchange can offer the real transcendence of the capitalist society and this is embodied in his general political economy of the third stage. Only in this stage, all forms of political economy are no longer important and all are transcended. In the sense of Baudrillard, the first two forms has no relation with the form of symbolic exchange, on the contrary, the latter is the rupture and transcendence from the former and is the ultimate deconstruction of the former. Baudrillard thinks that these former two are in an isomorphic relation. Therefore, it is necessary to criticize the theories of use value, the signified and the signifier, and construct a theory of symbolic exchange.

---

22 *Ibid.*, pp. 128-129.

3. RUPTURE FROM MARXISM: "THE MIRROR OF PRODUCTION"

In his early works, Baudrillard had mainly enunciated ideas on consumption. He did try to supplement and develop Marxist political economy from the perspective of semiotics, but in the end he still thought production was the benchmark. But after he published his book The Mirror of Production, Baudrillard has started a new journey completely departing from Marxism, "production was the basic concept dominating Marx's thought and was a difficult problem or blind spot in Marx's thought" and thus introduced the theory of symbolic exchange. This symbolizes Baudrillard's radical rupture from Marxism and indicates his decision to embrace post-Marxism.

Antagonism between Symbolic Exchange and Commodity Exchange

In his book For a Critique of the Political Economy of the Sign, Baudrillard points out that there is a fundamental antagonism between political economy and symbolic exchange, and the critique against political economy is equal to the recognition of symbolic exchange theory, so it is necessary to criticize the theories of use value, the signified and the signifier and construct a base for an all-round critique against capitalism. This base could be the theory of symbolic exchange. He has claimed that symbolic exchange is the waste of remainder and an anti-production exchange mode, only in symbolic exchange, the law of value, here accumulation and exploitation will disappear, and there will be no more capitalist spirit as in protestant ethics. In The Mirror of Production, he further enunciates his ideas on the antagonism between symbolic exchange and commodity exchange, and thinks that only symbolic exchange can be the antithesis of capitalist society established on the basis of commodity exchange. In the sense of Baudrillard, Marx's analysis is not complete, because the opposite of exchange value should not be the use value but the symbolic exchange value. This also indicates that the symbolic order is superior to sign order. According to Baudrillard, the start of modern times announces the death of "symbolic exchange", the modern exchange that had emerged with the development of capitalism is an abstract exchange, political economy makes a systematic construction of its own, but the exchange value of commodity still cannot leave use value, cannot free itself from this foundation. The use value of the commodity in fact is constructed by political economy in order to support the exchange value system. Under the conditions of modern society, the use value of commodity is a natural and non-alienated function or need. Use value also contains the social status, power and other aspects penetrated by objects. Baudrillard thinks that the exchange after since modern society is sign or linguistic exchange rather than commodity exchange, the political economy of the sign should be used to substitute traditional political economy of commodity.

Baudrillard uses the "mirror of production" to summarize Marxist political economy, and illustrates that Marxist political economy is still deeply stuck in the production logic of capitalist society and is unable to undertake the mission of revolutionary theory. Concretely speaking, Marxist political economy uses commodity production and exchange as research objects, tries to disclose the logic of production and reproduction processes in the capitalist society, points out to defects in the capitalist society – alienated labor, and on this basis provides us with an ideal picture – overall overcoming alienation[23]. In the sense of Baudrillard, Marxism's illusory understanding on capitalist society still stays as the inherent logic of capitalist society, it only re-forges the priority of production in theory, while in fact, the priority of production is exactly the product of capitalism itself, and this is mainly reflected in Baudrillard's critique of Marxist labor anthropology. Baudrillard thinks that the core content of Marxist political economy is "anthropology" of labor, i.e.: labor is the most fundamental activity of human, through labor, human needs are satisfied and human potential is displayed; or in other words, labor is the essence of human, and human constantly creates itself through labor. Marx criticizes the alienated labor process under capitalist condition but this critique is not for cancelling labor priority but aims to emancipate labor. The overcoming of alienated labor and laborers' possession on the means of production and possession on their labor fruits as mentioned by Marx are all for enabling labor to realize sufficient and unlimited development. As for this labor anthropology of Marxism, Baudrillard points out that it is also a typical capitalist value, i.e.: it is for the development of the production without any restriction and limitation[24]. "Through the concepts of historical materialism, dialectics, mode of production and labor force, Marxist theory always tries to smash the abstract universality of bourgeoisie ideas (nature and progress, human and rationality, formal logic, labor and exchange, and so on). Marxism on the contrary generalizes these concepts through the critique of imperialism, just as other theories do. At the same time, Baudrillard admits that through radicalizing the concepts of production and production mode, Marx has broken the social myth of exchange value. From this rupture, this concept obtains its all strategic power. Just through this concept, Marx has broken the illusory universality of political economy.

Baudrillard insists that the true rupture is not between "abstract" labor and "concrete" labor, but between symbolic exchange and labor (production and economics)[25]. The abstract social form of labor and exchange is only the form to complete reasonable evaluation and production model determined by capitalist political economy. This model has existed long before. It breaks away from the symbolic organization of any kind of exchange. In the process of production,

23 Yu Wujin et al.: Dialogues of Modern Phenomenology and Western Marxism, Shanghai, Press of Shanghai Academy of Social Sciences, 2002, p. 261.
24 Yu Wujin et al: Dialogues of Modern Phenomenology and Western Marxist, p. 261.
25 *Ibid.*, p. 45.

accumulation and possession, productive lust suppresses the nature of all other meanings and suppresses exchanges in symbolic release. In order to interrogate the restriction of political economy and the violence of value, and rethink release and symbolic exchange, Baudrillard asserts that the concepts of production and labor introduced by Marx (not to mention political economy) must be explained and analyzed as ideological concepts relating to the general value system. Marx makes a radical critique against political economy, but its form is still political economy. He employs tricks of dialectics which is undoubtedly the limitation of all critiques. Dialectics cannot get away from the fate of critique[26]. In the sense of Baudrillard, materialist dialectics has used up its content during reproduction of its form. At this level, it is no longer the case of critique and unavoidable. Marx has launched the same revolutionary movement. After him, we must go up to a completely different level, transcend his critique and make it possible to clearly explain political economy. This level is the level of the symbolic exchange theory. Baudrillard expresses that he —just like Marx —thinks that it is necessary to use the critique of law and physiology to open a road to critique of political economy, and in the range of all current ideologies, the fundament of this change is metaphysical critique of signifiers and codes. As there is no better word, we call it critique against the political economy of the sign[27].

According to Baudrillard, the concepts of "shortage", "necessity", "production" and so on must be broken, because they all support political economy. For this reason, in The Mirror of Production, Baudrillard starts to take leave from Marxism, and believes that the categories of Marxism reflects the capitalist mode of production , these categories depend on bourgeois political economy without critique and cannot be used to explain any society outside capitalism. Therefore, Baudrillard claims using symbolic exchange to substitute commodity exchange. Symbolic exchange is manifested as gift giving, celebration, consumption and waste. It terminates the linkages with any political economy and any recognized semiotic science and provides a heterogeneous activity mode.

Repulsing "Mirror of Production"

Baudrillard points out that in order to thoroughly criticize political economy, disclosing only the things behind consumption concept –disclosing the anthropology of use value— is not enough. We must disclose all the things behind the concepts of production, production mode, productive forces and production relations. Meanwhile, we must interrogate all basic concepts of Marxist doctrines. This interrogation should start with Marx's thorough critique and the requirements of transcending the political economy[28]. In the sense of Baudrillard, if

26   *Ibid.*, p. 50.
27   *Ibid.*, p. 51.
28   *Ibid.*, p. 21.

we say that Freud's psychoanalysis is the mirror of desires, then Marx's political economy will be the mirror of production. The "mirror of production" mainly refers to: in Marx's theory, the labor or production as interaction between human and nature is decisive – it is the source of value, and the foundation of human society and the motive of historical development. Since human is defined as laborer or producer, the emancipation of productive forces will mean the freedom of human; but the freedom of human does not result in the disappearance of production – it is still based on production, this necessary field. Baudrillard thinks that Marx explains everything with production – imagines production as a mirror, thus society, history and human are all reflected in this mirror. Through establishing everything on the concept of production, traditional Marxism subordinates the behaviors of culture and meaning to economic activities; what supports each social and economic system and forms its secret is its "production mode", i.e.: produce what products, by whom and by what method. Marx and classical political economy do not have much difference – the two both proceed from labor value theory. Therefore, Baudrillard said, like Feuerbach who criticizes religious content in the form of religion, Marx has criticized political economy in form of political economy. Baudrillard thinks that Marxism evades both the analysis that economics regards production as the ultimate goal and universal and realistic principle, and the analysis of the generation of production principle, because Marxism only enters the structural field of production. As economic law is assumed, Marxist critique perhaps can articulate the operation of political economy system, and meanwhile it reproduces this system as a model[29].

It needs to be noted that apparently, Baudrillard neglects an important difference between Marxist doctrine and classical political economy: Marx's labor value theory and surplus value theory are inseparable from his analysis of capitalist private ownership. Of course, what Baudrillard is interested in is not the form of ownership. He wants to enunciate that Marx has gone astray from the starting point – human is producer or laborer, and production or labor is decisive. "Marxism assists the cunning of capital. It convinces men that they are alienated by the sale of their labor power, thus censoring the much more radical hypothesis that they might be alienated as labor power, as the 'inalienable' power of creating value by their labor[30]. He thinks that in the era of Marx, political economy system had not sufficiently developed all of its contradictions, so it was impossible for Marx to give fundamental critique and to understand capitalism in its early stage. Marx himself was unable to intrude into the overall logic of this system. Only when this system comes to its mature stage, the critique can reach the groundwork. According to Baudrillard, particularly the fundamental determinism of economy will lead to the road of rupture from symbolic exchange and avoid fundamental revolution in social relations. Only after political economy has intruded into all

---

29   *Ibid.*, p. 66.
30   *Ibid.*, p. 31.

fields of social and individual practices of humans rather than only the field of material production, can it be depicted and understood. Of course, Baudrillard admits that it is useless to accuse Marx of these problems. Only a stage of universal development process has been analyzed, thus Marx's critique could only reach this step because at this stage other issues could only be speculated.

In fact, the title of the book The Mirror of Production is a metaphor. In the sense of Baudrillard, Marx regards labor as human's basic demand and the primary activity through which human displays its potential, the contradiction between productive forces and production relations constitutes the basic contradiction which has dominated the whole history of human society up till present, all other phenomena in the human society can be explained and described according to the relations between productive forces and production relations, and this "productive logic" "re-writes" the nature from the perspective of production and "re-writes" history from the perspective of production relations[31]. Baudrillard expresses that in fact, it is a mirror image of capitalism in which production assumes a dominant role and is the top principle: the discourse of production and discourse of symbol are both a kind of mirror image, through which the system of political economy is reflected in imagination and regenerated as a decisive factor[32]. For this, Douglas Kellner thinks that Baudrillard only uses another imagination to replace Marx's imagination. Kellner disagrees with such a dogmatic proposition. He proposes that to truly understand the ongoing social process and social changes, we need many theories, and it seems that production theory and the sign theory are both important. Baudrillard's critique on Marx's use value and demand theory is unfair to Marx, because in the critique of bourgeois political economy, Marx also foresees many ideas put forth by Baudrillard. Marxism is economism or reductionism as alleged by Baudrillard. Like Lefebvre, De Poitiers and the critical theorists of Frankfurt School, this means many Marxists have also foreseen many ideas of Baudrillard – although many scholars admit that it is not against Marxism in an extreme form[33].

Baudrillard puts forth symbolic exchange as an antithesis of commodity exchange. Its important meaning is that symbolic exchange is considered to represent a thing truly heterogeneous to capitalist society, and Others. From this angle, we discover that, when Baudrillard makes semiotic critique on modern society, he regards modern society as a system and even suggests the death of subject, but he does not completely give up the search for Others nor give up participating in the revolutionary road. He only wants to emphasize that it is impossible and useless for us to seek Others in the capitalist system, and particularly impossible to find

---

31   Bao Yaming Editor in Chief: Postmodernity and Geopolitics, p.70.
32   Jean Baudrillard: The Mirror of Production, p. 20.
33   Douglas Kellner, Jean Baudrillard: From Marxism to Postmodernism and Beyond, pp. 51-52.

out a way to reform capitalist society from the production process of capitalism. To really jump out of capitalist system, we should only focus our attention on the special behaviors with the meaning of symbolic exchange[34]. Baudrillard believes that only through symbolic exchange, can we break through the system of modern society and move to Others different from it. In The Mirror of Production, although Baudrillard offers an all-round critique on Marx's political economy of commodity, he still considers his "political economy of the sign" as its "dialectic continuation". In his next book Symbolic Exchange and Death, Baudrillard no longer limits himself with the critique of the framework of political economy – he claims "the political economy of the sign" is just "an expedient", and advocates the termination of general political economy.

4. JOURNEY TO POST-MODERNISM: "TERMINATION OF GENERAL POLITICAL ECONOMY"

Baudrillard thinks that Marxism uses the category of economic foundation to explain superstructure and uses labor and production to explain the relations between human and nature and between human and human, which is a component of the semiotic culture, while Marxist revolution is only an adjustment to the sign order and does not go beyond the sign logic. Opposite to this traditional revolutionary concept, Baudrillard wants to find an articulation mode and critique basis to reach to the wholly Other. The theory of symbolic exchange is just an attempt for this purpose. Later on, he has started comprehensively observing the contemporary semiotic culture, and has substituted simulation with the sign system, replaced his symbolic exchange theory with temptation and reviewed it by a method similar to reduction to absurdity. While challenging his French fellow Foucault (Baudrillard published Forget Foucault), Baudrillard has also challenged his early theories, i.e.: his own critical theory against the consumer society, thus gradually shifting himself from the theory of critique against the political economy of the sign to radical Post-modernist theory. This change is mainly reflected in his most influential masterpieces Symbolic Exchange and Death and Simulacra and Simulation.

Rise of Simulacrum Culture

Baudrillard's symbolic exchange theory was based on participation in the exchange process in a rational sense by mutual response and non-economic expectations, and was also participation in process which departs from the rationalism of political economy, but this participation is feasible only at the level of utopia, and cannot solve the realistic problems. It was impossible to realize this delusion,

---

34 Yu Wujin et al.: Dialogues of Modern Phenomenology and Western Marxism, p. 264-265.

so later Baudrillard has decided to introduce his theories of "simulation" and "hyper-reality" and so on to enter the Post-modernism register. When talking on the above theme of his previous participation ideas, Baudrillard has commented that he had published a series of works in 1960s, although they were critique on various kinds of cultural products existing as objects and the critique directed towards all kinds of explicit and implicit signs in the object structure, these objects and the signs still had certain significance. From 1980s on, he more profoundly exposed the senseless and uncertain signs popular in the cultural life of the contemporary society, as well as their anti-logical operation process . "This is the rise of simulacrum culture".

In his book, Baudrillard describes a series of changes from "production mode" to "code", from "production" to "reproduction", from "ideology" to "simulacrum", from "sign" to "simulation" and so on to summarize the development and changes in the current society. The core concepts are "simulation" and "simulacrum". The concept of simulacrum was mentioned many times in Baudrillard's early works. In The Consumer Society, Baudrillard had used the concept of simulacrum to explain the difference between the pre-modern society and the modern society, and asserted that the objects in the modern society are "simulacrum objects" and "illusive objects". For example, when describing the attitude of aborigines towards consumer society, Baudrillard has mentioned that people receiving divine presence through consumption also arrange a set of simulacra and a set of symbols with the characteristics of happiness and then look forward for the advent of happiness[35]. In For a Critique of the Political Economy of the Sign and The Mirror of Production, he has also used same or similar concept. Only in the book Symbolic Exchange and Death, Baudrillard has departed away from the topics of political economy and its critique, and begins to establish a relatively complete theoretical framework centering on the two core concepts "simulation" and "simulacra". In this book, Baudrillard has also further combined the research of simulacra with the research of sign culture and the research of modernity, and points out that the breakthrough by modernity against feudal order starts with order of simulacra, while the establishment of the order of simulacra also means the establishment of the dominant position of sign culture. Baudrillard states that today we are in the era of simulation, and the wide existence of simulation is a key factor resulting in the disappearance of the boundaries between reality and imagination and between true and false. It is getting more difficult to distinguish the genuine from the fake. Every contemporary event is the mixture of reality and imagination. In fact, according to Baudrillard, neither truth nor reality exists, they have vanished in snow-sliding simulations, people live in a huge simulacrum – not a non-reality but a simulacrum, an endless circulation in a reference system or on a circumference, a simulacrum absolutely not exchanging with reality and only

---

35   Jean Baudrillard: The Consumer Society, London, 1998, p. 31.

exchanging with itself[36]. As a result, except particular things, simulation absolutely eliminates the existence of the meaning.

Baudrillard singles out simulacra as a special topic when he studies the sign culture in the contemporary society, mainly because of his strong feeling towards the changes in actual life. In his early works, he has theoretically described these changes from the perspective of sign culture's dominant position. Here he wants to make more concrete analysis on the historical form of the sign culture, particularly on the new forms of the sign culture emerging after 1980s. Baudrillard summarizes in a concise way the three development stages of human history in relation to "simulacra". These stages are divided according to the codes constituted by the relations between signs and external references, and the occurrence, development and evolution process of simulative operation. Baudrillard thinks that simulacra have three sequences, corresponding to the change stages of the value of law since Renaissance: firstly, "counterfeit" is the dominant framework in the "classical" era from Renaissance to Industrial Revolution; secondly, "production" is the dominant framework in industrial era; thirdly, "simulation" is the dominant framework in current era controlled by the "codes". The simulacra in the first sequence follow the law of natural value, the simulacra in the second sequence follows the law of market value and the simulacra in the third sequence follows the law of structure[37].

Baudrillard centrally analyzes the artificial sign systems which are senseless but pretended to be something in contemporary society. Baudrillard calls these artificial sign systems "simulacra" and regards these simulacra and their operations as the basic characteristics of contemporary society. Simulacra here refer to the regeneration or reproduction of objects or events, so Baudrillard's observation on the orders of simulacra focuses on the relation between the sign and the reality. In brief, the simulacra at the first level are obviously the duplicate of reality. The simulacra at the second level are so vivid that they blur the boundary between reality and token. The simulacra at the third level generates their own reality, but are not established in any real world. It is a world generated by computer's codified language. This mathematic model is an abstract and independent entity. This is the third level of simulacra, which is called hyper-reality by Baudrillard. The third order of simulacra is originates from the rise of mass media and the revolution in exchange. Signs cover the absence of basic reality. Baudrillard has commented that the stage of mass production is transient and thus we will find ourselves in the third order. The imitation of original objects in the first order and the pure series in the second order disappear. In the third order, according to the difference adjustment principle, all forms are derived from models and meaning can be generated and expressed only on the precondition of loyalty to

---

36   Jean Baudrillard: Simulations, Semiotext (e), 1983, p. 11.
37   See Jean Baudrillard: Symbolic Exchange and Death, London, 1993, p. 50.

the models. All functions have no ultimate goal and start with models, and like the ultimacy mentioned above, only the signifier of model reference can provide a credible result. This is the simulation in contemporary sense. Industrialization is only its elementary form. What decides simulation order is "model" itself. Now it is independent of any purpose and function originated from utility world. This is the world in which "law of structural value" has become dominant. In a sense, reproduction takes a ruling role, it is different from simple mass production, this simulation substitutes "truth", and referent becomes "signifier of the reference". Hyper-reality is a dominant simulation form and in terms of its accurate meaning, it defines itself during the connection with the things which have always been reproduced. Simulacrum is no longer the simulation of a field, a referent or an entity, it does not need original object or entity and instead it produces reality through models: a kind of hyper-reality.

"Termination" of the Political Economy

Baudrillard expresses that today we live in the third order of simulacra, and the relation between the imitation and reality is that simulation constitutes reality, or in other words, the constructed imitation is reality and there is no another real world to surpass it. All the "real" content represented by the sign has no longer exists, the current simulation fully complies with the principles of structure and random matching, and there is no value equivalence but the binary opposition that maintains structure; the political economy of production and commodity should be changed into the political economy of sign and simulation. What is more, Baudrillard even commented that political economy of the sign was only a temporary word, because: firstly, it still cares about value and the law of value. Only its care is different from before and it profoundly influences political economy — its content has been changed even removed, "political economy" is only a pure implicit term, which gives more emphasis on "politics", because what it cares for is to destroy the social relations regulated by value, although it is not a pure issue of economics. Secondly, sign per se is only an implicit term. As the structural value of law also affects signification, it is not manifested as a form of common sign but an organization form of code, whereas codes do not organize all signs. Commodity law of value is not an instance of material production in a specific time. Conversely, structural law of value does not indicate the superiority of any sign[38], not only irrelevant with extrinsic reality, but also the signifier of a sign is completely separated from the signified, and signifier freely swims, plays, multiplies and reproduces during floating.

All in all, Baudrillard thinks that political economy, "production" myth and labor all have been terminated and become members of signs, because wage is not reasonable remuneration of work or the actual value of production labor, while

---

38   See Jean Baudrillard: Symbolic Exchange and Death, p. 7.

it is decided by the differential relation in the system structure. Hence the era of "reproduction" and the era of simulation have started. The "origins of simulacra" are everywhere: in fashion the beauty and ugliness are exchangeable, in the media the true and false are exchangeable, the usefulness and the uselessness of objects are exchangeable, and the nature and culture at all levels of meaning are exchangeable. All great humanistic value criteria and all civilization values of morality, aesthetics and practice judgment disappear in our image and sign system. It is a typical result of code dominance over everything and in all issues. It is based on the principles of neutralization and no utility. In this order, "law of structural value" dominates everything. In other words, in the relations of code/model and object, the former obtains priority, decides the constitution of object and constitutes reality. According to Baudrillard, the law of structural value refers to the uncertain relation between each field and its specific content (the result is the transition from the certain realm of sign to the non-determinacy of code). It is not enough to say that production field and sign field exchange content. They disappear indeed and lose their specificity and determinacy. The form of value gains advantage. It is the more common organization form which eliminates certain relation and production. Baudrillard has written: the concept of political economy of the sign still expresses commodity law of value and the result of expansion of its authenticity at the level of sign, whereas the structural combination of value terminates production system, political economy, token, sign and other regimes in an extremely simple way. All these enter simulation kingdom together with code[39]. Strictly speaking, "classical" economics and the political economy of the sign no longer exist: both result in dependent existence and become illusory exhortation principles.

As for the first order and the second order, reality still exists. Our success in measuring simulation opposes reality. Baudrillard's worry about the third order of simulacra is that model generates "hyper-reality" – a world without real origin. Hyper-reality is a major way to experience and perceive the world[40]. Through descriptions on the three orders, Baudrillard articulates how simulacra gradually rule social life. Accordingly, the order of simulacra should be deemed as "depiction of history", i.e.: the clear depiction of the phenomena in historical simulation process. According to Baudrillard, after the alienated society of landscape (the second order of simulacra)[41], and the frantic society of exchange (the third order of simulacra), we now have moved to a new stage (the fourth order of simulacra). In the first stage, the reference of value is nature and it is based on the natural use and development of the world. In the second stage, value is determined according to the principle of equivalent exchange, and its development refers to

39   *Ibid.*, p. 8.
40   See Richard J. Lane, Jean Baudrillard, London and New York, Routledge, 2000, pp. 86-87.
41   Mike Gane (ed.), Jean Baudrillard, Vol.I, Sage, 2000, p. xv.

the logic of commodity. The third stage is dominated by sign system. In this stage, the development of value refers to a sign model. At the fourth stage – the fractal (or virus or radiative) stage, there is no point of reference at all, and value radiates in all directions, occupying all interstices, exactly speaking, there is no law of value, merely a sort of epidemic of value, a sort of general metastasis of value, a haphazard proliferation and dispersal of value. In fact, we should not talk of "value" any more, for such infinite proliferation and chain reaction make all valuation impossible [...] it is as impossible to make estimations between beautiful and ugly, true and false, or good and evil as it is simultaneously to calculate a particle's speed and position[42]. If we combine The Transparency of Evil with Baudrillard's early works, we can easily see his fourth order of simulacra – fractal stage of value –is to a large extent the natural extension of the third order: the value in these two orders does not use any external thing as reference – it is either structural (in the third order of simulacra) or has no structure at all (in the fourth order of simulacra), and has no substantial content; therefore, the value in these two orders is situated in the mutual imitation of values (manifested as infinite reproduction of sign/model) and is the neutralization of value – in other words, is in pure imitation.

From the perspective of hyper-reality, political economy (including "political economy of commodity" and "political economy of the sign") has died: in this period, exchange is conducted between sign and sign rather than sign and reality, while value is determined by the structure specified by the differentiation and relativity of all kinds of signs. In this way, value – signified commodity and com-modified sign value – no longer has any external reference system: referential value is cancelled, and structuralist rules take the upper hand. As a result, demand, labor, value, currency and other categories of political economy all flow as signs in sign structure without restriction by "reality". Thus the termination of labor, termination of production and termination of political economy as described by Baudrillard occur. Nevertheless, termination does not mean disappearance. In other words, political economy per se also becomes pure sign or model in the order of simulacra[43]. When Baudrillard wrote on the termination of political economy, his academic career also realized transformation from the early period to the late period. For Baudrillard, the core of modern society is commodity pro-duction and consumption, while Post-modern society is organized centered on the simulation and use of signs and images. The dominant rule of Post-modern society is simulation. In this simulation order, personal identity is established dur-ing the use of signs, and codes and models decide personal self-consciousness and inter-personal relations. Economy, politics, social life and culture are ruled by the logic of simulation. Commodity consumption, political operation, cultural production and everyday life operation are all full of codes and models.

---

42   Jean Baudrillard, The Transparency of Evil, Verso, 1993, pp.5-6.
43   Xia Guang: Post-structuralist Thought and Theory of Post-modern Society, Beijing, Social Sciences Academic Press, 2003, p. 293.

REFERENCES

- Jean Baudrillard: For a Critique of the Political Economy of the Sign, Telos Press, 1981.
- Jean Baudrillard: Symbolic Exchange and Death, London, 1993.
- Bao Yaming Editor in Chief: Post-modernism and Geopolitics. Shanghai, Shanghai Education Press, 2001.
- Xia Guang: Post-structuralist Thought and Theory of Post-modern Society. Beijing, Social Sciences Academic Press, 2003.
- Gao Xuanyang: Post-modernism. Beijing, China Renmin University Press, 2005.

CHAPTER VI

POST-MODERN FEMINISM AND MARXISM

Feminism is both a social thought which consists of relevant ideologies and views, and a social movement guided by this thought. As a social movement, it has attracted great attention all over the world; as an international thought, it has developed into an influential ideology.

Feminist movement has experienced three waves: the first wave has lasted from late 19th century to 1920s. Under the influence of bourgeoisie's early Enlightenment thought, the women in Western Europe have launched the feminist movement. This stage is represented by liberal feminism. In this movement, the women in major capitalist states have obtained suffrage; the second wave has occurred as women rights movement in the late 1960s and early 1970s; aiming equal pay for equal work irrespective of sex, gender equality in morality, and several other demands. This stage is represented by socialist feminism and radical feminism; the third wave was the feminist movement in 1980s-1990s under the influence of Post-modernism thought in the West. It was mainly represented by Post-modernism feminism.

Here it is necessary to distinguish two concepts: Post-modern feminism and post-feminism. They are completely different. In the realm of theory, post-feminism is a wide concept and category. Existentialist feminism, Post-modernism feminism and psychoanalytic feminism all belong to the category of post-feminism[1]. Post-feminism is mainly influenced by post-structuralism, post-modernism, post-colonial theory, psychoanalysis theory and other thoughts in the 20th century. On the one hand, it has started to interrogate the terms used by feminism and involves society, culture and psychological structure, as well as the terms and expressions

1   Sophia Phoca and Rebecca Wright: Postfeminism, translated by Wang Li, p. 1, Beijing, Culture and Art Publishing House, 2003.

indicating physiology and gender identity. On the other hand, it has developed through deconstructing the discourse of patriarchy. In comparison, Post-modern feminism is a relatively narrow concept and category. It refers to the new feminist theory and thought formed and developed under the influence of Post-modernism thought when feminism has evolved to 1980s-1990s.

Post-modernism feminism is a feminist theory and thought formed on the basis of traditional feminism through absorbing and integrating the thoughts of Post-modern thinker –French great thinker Foucault, psychoanalyst Lacan and deconstructionist Derrida. It adopts a new view on gender inequality and provides a new train of thought for women's emancipation.

Post-modern feminism is a feminist theory developed under the background when abrupt changes has occurred in Soviet Union and Eastern Europe, two sharp political blocs in the world were dissolved, international socialist political movement had retrogressed to a low tide and feminist theory was in full retrospect. It has absorbed the essence of traditional feminist theory and traditional classical theories and meanwhile was heavily influenced by Post-modern theory. It shows distinctive theoretical features as reviewing and criticizing feminist theories. Post-modern feminism has generated an extremely important influence in the contemporary era; therefore research on post-modern feminism has theoretical and practical significance for Marxists. Post-modern feminism and post-Marxism are both theoretical thoughts which have developed under the influence of Post-modern theory in 1980s; and between the two are many theoretical connections and similar theoretical features. Post-Marxism is the Marxism which integrates Marxist spirit of critique with post-modernism, post-structuralism, feminism and other contemporary theories in an attempt to deconstruct and transcend Marxism. In a sense, Post-modernism feminism has enriched and contributed to the theory of post-Marxism, so it is also necessary to summarize and compare these two theories. Post-modernism and Marxism both have a strong spirit of critique. This makes them attractive in theoretical circles. The theory of Post-modern feminism generated on the basis of post-modernism has also established ties with Marxism during its development. It interrogates historical materialism and meanwhile has its limitations and one-sidedness in the overall evaluation on Marxism, so our research on the relation between Post-modern feminism and Marxism should not be just a fashionable topic. It is an issue we, Marxists, must study seriously and understand clearly. In the end, although the theory of Post-modern feminism lacks correct and comprehensive understanding on Marxist theory of women's emancipation and has obviously smaller effect compared with Marxist theory of women's emancipation, it has unique theoretical advantages in guiding the practice of women's emancipation and its own development when compared with other feminist theories. In this sense, we should give full affirmation on it. Nevertheless, the theory of Post-modern feminism also has some limitations and defects which can hardly be overcome. We should not neglect them, either. Above aspects has practical significance for our concrete understanding on the theory of Post-modern feminism and current development trend of feminist theory and the development of women's emancipation.

1. POST- MODERN FEMINISM

The generation of Post-modernism feminism as the newest school of feminism was inevitable since it has distinctive theoretical views and characteristics. It has generated extremely important influence in contemporary era which needs a deeper research.

1.1. DEVELOPMENT OF POST-MODERN FEMINISM

Post-modern feminism is a feminist theory and trend which rose in 1980s-1990s which is theoretically product of feminism and post-modernism. I can explain the objective reasons for its generation as follows, of course there were both internal and external causes:

The theoretical and practical requirements in the development process of feminism have constituted the internal causes for the formation of Post-modern feminist theories.

Traditional feminism is the predecessor of Post-modern feminism. The three traditional feminist theories were greatly diverted and have seriously disputed during their development. This has laid a theoretical and practical basis for the generation of Post-modernism feminism.

The three traditional feminist theories are liberal feminism, socialist feminism (including Marxist feminism, these two theories are too close and hard to distinguish in practice) and radical feminism. In general, none of the three traditional feminist theories have satisfactorily explained the reasons for the subjection of women, due to their common limitations: firstly, they have all insisted there is one most fundamental even sole reason for the subjection of women; secondly, they all directly apply the logic of patriarchic culture to feminism which attacks patriarchy. These limitations not only hamper the development of feminist theories but also put feminist theories' to an awkward state in the real practice. I think feminist theories need to be developed from a new visual angle. This has provided both a theoretical foundation for Post-modern feminism and an opportunity for the generation of its theories.

On the other hand, Post-modern feminism is a product of the integral shift of feminism towards "Post-modernism" under the influence of external cause - post-modernism.

Post-modernism is a thought rose in 1960s after developed capitalism has entered the process of post industrialization. It has reached its prime peak in around
1980s and declined and fell apart after 1990s. Post-modernism is the critique
and reflection against modern developed capitalist society, it is the critique and
heritage of Western contemporary and modern philosophies, and a cultural
thought formed during the critique and reflection against Western society, philosophy, science, technology and rationality. Its main theoretical characteristics are
anti-glotto-centrism, anti-foundationalism and essentialism, anti-grand narratives,
anti-center, difference and indeterminacy, anti-rationality, deconstruction of modernity and deconstruction of subjectivity. Post-modern feminism has absorbed
a great deal from Post-modern thought when developing its theory. Concretely
speaking, French great thinker Foucault's theories on power and discourse have
made a great influence on the thought of Post-modern feminism. Foucault has
interrogated the determinacy and robustness of all existent regimes. This has
provided a new visual angle for Post-modern feminists' re-contemplation on the
issues of women's rights and status. Psychoanalyst Lacan's "symbolic order theory" has undoubtedly provided new ideas for Post-modern feminism on the issue
of the root causes for gender inequality. Deconstructionist Derrida's thought of
"emancipation from basic binary opposition and existence—vanity has also served as a revelation for Post-modern feminists[2]. The purpose for the generation
of Post-modern feminism was to reflect and criticize the limitations which had
become quite apparent in the traditional feminism. Of course Post-modern feminism has inherited several important characteristics of traditional feminism but
has aimed to surpass.

Just due to the above two reasons, the theory of Post-modern feminism with new
theoretical method and perspective could develop and enrich itself, inject a new
energy and vitality to the previous feminist theory and trigger the third wave of
feminism. By now, Post-modern feminism includes two major theoretical camps.
One is the essentialists which have inherited and revised the theory of traditional
feminism. They use deconstructionism as methodology to re-debate the possibility of women's emancipation. As they largely admit men and women are two
opposite categories, they are called essentialists. Their representative figures are
Gayle Rubin – founder of social gender system, and Catherine Mackinnon who
advocates establishing a legal system on the basis of feminist principle[3].

The other camp is the constructionalist. They aim de-construction, deny the concepts of "men" and "women", believe gender equality concept is the continuation of the thinking logic of male chauvinism, and cannot fundamentally clearly

2   Rosemarie Putnam Tong: Feminist Thought: A More Comprehensive Introduction,
translated by Ai Xiaoming et al., Wuhan, Central China Normal University Press, 2002, p.
289-292.
3   Bao Xiaolan Editor in Chief: Review on Western Feminist Studies, Beijing, Sanlian
Bookstore, 1995, p.4-5.

identify the root cause for women's oppression. The representative figures are Denise Riley and Judith Butler. They have widely absorbed various kinds of Post-modernist concepts, abandoned the pursuit for concrete goals in women's emancipation and strive to de-construct the feminist impact of social consciousness, thinking habit, human subjectivity and chauvinist ideology. Both essentialists and constructionalists have enriched and developed feminism through social and cultural levels.

While absorbing the unique perspectives and mode of post-modernism, Post-modern feminism has formed and kept improving and developing feminist theory with a new theoretical perspective. It manifests itself in the following aspects[4]: oppose grandes théories and advocate that only decentralized, local and small theories are more effective; oppose women's oppression by traditional discourse reflecting male hegemony and advocate the establishment of a discourse for women; oppose traditional metaphysical binary oppositions and advocate plural models; oppose essentialism and universalism, stress the differences between women and women, and women and men caused by the difference in nation, race, class and religion, and call on paying attention to women's internal diverse experiences; advocate using a new gender equality concept based on gender difference to substitute traditional abstract gender equality concept, and demand carrying out all-round cooperation with men and establishing harmonious partnership, pursue equality in difference and reflect individuality and independence in equality.

1.2. THE RISE OF POST-MODERN FEMINISM

In the first two waves of feminist movements, the women in the United States and European developed capitalist states have achieved successful results in women's freedom and rights and highly increased the hopes for the future practice of women's emancipation all throughout the whole world. But following the great upheaval in the Soviet Union and Eastern Europe, and the disappearance of the confrontation between the two international blocs, international communist and leftist political movement has declined, this was also true for the feminist movement .Under the effect of this general change the inherent existent difficulties of the traditional feminist movement have worsened both in theoretical and practical aspects. Due to inherent existent limitations its leadership position has also weakened. This has offered an opportunity for the Post-modernist feminism and they have started to enlarge their effects by a critical review on the three traditional feminist theories; this was also an opportunity for them to enrich and develop their own feminist theories. Thus their influence has steadily developed in this new period both in theory and practice.

---

4   Li Yinhe: Rise of Women Rights, Beijing, China Social Sciences Press, 1997, p. 122-130.

Theoretical Critique by Post-modern Feminism

Post-modern feminism has developed its theoretical critic to transcend previous feminist movements. Post-modern feminists have argued that the view of natural rights (legalist aspect) and view of social justice embodied in liberal feminism ignores the capitalist patriarchic culture. It means liberal feminism bears the effects of patriarchy in their ideas, and they unconsciously inject the logic of patriarchic culture into feminist camp and this is the most serious problem of liberal feminism, but patriarchal ideology and institutions should be the primary target of feminist movement. On the other hand socialist feminism has long advocated that the men's dominance over women should be regarded as the inevitable result of capitalists' domination over working classes. Post-modern feminism has attacked socialist feminism arguing that socialist feminists only consider the economic and class relations in the society .Post-feminists have argued that class theory could only be applicable in the capitalist society, and this theory cannot reveal the long historical root causes for women's oppression and cannot offer a clear strategy against this oppression. But division of labor based on gender and subjection of women have existed long before capitalism. Radical feminism has advocated that women's oppression is caused by patriarchy. Under this patriarchal system, male group possesses the power to rule female group. With regard to the issue of power, radical feminism has argued that power is authority, power is the right to rule and exploit all individuals and it is a unified and perpetual force.

But Post-modern feminism has raised the idea that power should be decentralized and dispersive and should not concentrate on any institution or group ; for them "transformation" should be started inside women themselves, and the attention in the struggle should be shifted from historical status to more concrete things like women's education opportunities, employment opportunities, inner family violence and etc[5]. Post-modern feminism has criticized that all traditional feminist theories to a degree advocate the versions of enlightenment thought and are still male-centered, so they cannot overcome the thinking mode of androcentrism, while the struggle of new feminism should be deconstruct androcentrism and patriarchy. One of the most effective strategies to realize this goal is the Post-modern theory on deconstructionism which as mentioned above largely influenced Post-modernist feminism.

Advantages of Post-modern Feminism in Practice

Post-modern Feminism has also gained some obvious advantages in leading women struggle during the aforesaid period. In the first two feminist waves guided by previous feminist schools, the women in developed capitalist states have

---

5   Zhuang Yuxia: Confrontation of Postmodernism and Feminism, published in Jiangxi Social Sciences, 2002 (7), p. 93.

won equal rights as men in the aspects of politics, economy, law, social status, education, employment and suffrage. As another observation I can say that the previous feminist theories developed in Western developed capitalist states rather reflect the will and attitudes of the middle-class white women in developed capitalist societies and opposed sexual discrimination. Therefore previous feminist ideas have reflected the European and American middle-class white women and simply generalized their ideas and experiences for all the women in the world, this approach has inevitably concealed the huge differences among various women groups and strata, their different demands, and caused certain prejudice on the women belonging to other races and ethnical groups, and neglected different forms of sexual discrimination among different women groups or classes.

The new theory of Post-modern feminism has exactly attached importance to approach equality on the basis of "differences". Post-modern feminism has sharply raised its ideas criticizing previous feminist schools for neglecting different women approaches caused by their differences in class, race, location, culture and prospect. "Universalizing the ideological and behavioral patterns of the middle-class white women in the United States and European developed states is impractical to embrace all the women demands and struggles". Women's rights should be the rights of the women in the whole world, including the rights of the women in the Third World and should not be the privilege of the middle-class women in developed states. This raises feminism to a height of politics. Feminism is no longer limited to a conflict between two genders and also contains the cognition and critique of colonialism and imperialism. Thus, the battlefields and scope of feminist struggle are enlarged and more women in the world may join feminist ranks for equal and free development.

From the above aspects, we can see that Post-modern feminism has made a profound theoretical influence in developing and enriching feminist theory, and meanwhile has made a far-reaching effect in the practice of women's emancipation and development in the world.

1.3. POST-MODERN FEMINISM AND WOMEN'S MOVEMENT IN CHINA

Post-modernism is still an influential theoretical trend though it has declined in 90ies. It has created great impact on many spheres like culture, art and philosophy. Post-modern feminism as the product of the combination of feminism and post-modernism has a distinctive stance and view and has enriched and developed feminist theory.

At the same time, women's emancipation and development has become an irresistible global tide and trend in today's world. From being the struggle of women covering limited strata or classes and only several developed regions of the world it has now spread world-wide and developed into a worldwide movement covering vast women from all classes. Through the unremitting effort by several generations, women's movement has become an in-negligible part of the international political movement, and a powerful component of the human emancipation and development cause. The impressive feminist theory and discourse have become an increasingly important part of the comprehensive human freedom cause and has aroused worldwide attention.

At present, in Chinese academic circles the research on feminist theories, especially Post-modern feminism studies lag behind. Since the founding of the People's Republic of China and the establishment of the socialist system, Chinese women have gained new opportunities for emancipation and free development, and their current degree of emancipation and free development enjoys several advantages compared to the women in other states in the world, but it is noteworthy that in the real social life, sexual discrimination still commonly exists, for example: men have obvious advantages in economy, politics, employment and education. Family violence, sexual harassment and other social problems also occur. At present, China is in a period of peacefully developing the socialist economy. I think these problems in China cannot be solved by hard political struggles or social movements as advocated by traditional feminist theories. Women's movement in China needs to find a development mode which should include the living and cultural spheres related to the majority of the women masses. Post-modern feminism is exactly a feminist theory which aims to oppose sexual discrimination occurring in social, cultural and ideological spheres. I think it will serve as an important guidance and reference for Chinese women's search for a way of further emancipation and development.

Besides, the development status of women in China varies with regions and nationality. For some minority women and the women living in remote mountainous areas, as the economic conditions in these areas are backward, their development is radically limited. Chinese theoretical community should give more attention to and make more effort to solve this problem. The theory of Post-modern feminism is a theory advocating pursuit of equality in difference. It attaches more importance to realize women development from the vantage point of the experiences of different women groups. It does not simply regard all men as enemies who oppress women and thus strives to obtain equal status with them. Instead, it pushes women to find the most suitable way from numerous ways while they behave like women. Comprehensive understanding of difference is a very complex process. Women should not restrict themselves on the descriptions of experiences, identity and recognition but pay more attention to study the links of the parties with difference, observing their mutual relations, divergences and conflicts in women's special living environment and find out a theoretical solution for the problems occurring in practice.

While absorbing the content of Post-modern feminism theory, which is favorable for women's emancipation and development in China, we should more clearly consider that every coin has two sides. The theory of Post-modern feminism also has certain limitation and one-sidedness. More importantly, as a feminist theory established at ideological level, Post-modern feminism holds a contradictive and conflictive attitude towards Marxism by and large, while Marxism is the mainstream ideology in mainland. When we draw on the theory of Post-modern feminism to solve the problems of women in China, we should also take that into consideration.

In a word, strengthening understanding and research of Post-modern feminist theory is a matter of theoretical significance for Chinese women's effort to solve the theoretical problems with women's development and promote feminist theories; a matter of practical significance for Chinese women to solve the problems of today's women, improve women's living and working conditions, eliminate sexual discrimination in social culture and people's ideology, and strive for women's free and comprehensive development.

2. RELATIONS BETWEEN POST-MODERN FEMINISM AND POST-MARXISM

The two theories: Post-modern feminism and post-Marxism were both generated under the powerful influence and impact of the Post-modern theories in 1980s-1990s. They both have aroused great attention and caused hot debates in theoretical circles. I would like to introduce the relations between two.

Post-modernism as the Origin

What is "post-Marxism"? Post-Marxism is generally a derivative of post-modernism. It was still vogue in 1960s. If we compare "post-modernism" to a long rattan, then "post-Marxism" will be one of the "melons"[6]. Therefore, we think "Post-modernism feminism" is another "melon" on the rattan of "post-modernism". The theory of post-Marxism and the theory of Post-modern feminism have a common theoretical origin — the theory of post-modernism.

Feminism is a theoretical school bearing revolutionary meanings and has important influence in many cultural thoughts. It was unavoidable for feminism to converge post-modernism, and once they meet, they have naturally joined hands and go ahead together. In this sense, the theory of Post-modern feminism was jointly formed.

---

6   Zeng Zhisheng: Domain of Post-Marxism, published in Academic Research, 2004(7), p. 53.

Post-modern feminism draws its nourishment sources from Post-modern thoughts. They have many similarities: both of them are the theoretical thoughts intending to overcome current established traditions and have the practical common aim, trying to change the current society according to an ideal plan. In this sphere, Post-modern feminism does not only has a harmonious relation with the positive and constructive dimension of post-modernism and it completely absorbs and makes use of the diversity, pluralism and differentiation among objects as advocated by Foucault, Lyotard and Derrida, but Post-modern feminism also finds those wholesome ideas totally consistent with its own main aim inspired by the negative and destructive dimension of post-modernism. That is to say, post-modern feminist critique of traditional ideology is to destroy the existent thinking mode of "androcentrism". Foucault shook the position of rationality in the traditional ideology, brushed off the deconstruction of rational subjectivity or subjectivity concept and destroyed the concept of "man" as the symbol of male rights and traditional metaphysics established on male dominance excluding female; Lyotard has attacked traditional metaphysical system, imposed certain threat to "grand narratives" or general theories and criticized the ideological system established on men's thinking mode and norms which fetter and oppress women. Although their thoughts also have great negative impacts on feminism's endeavor to wake up women's subject consciousness and guide women in changing their passive position in social history through establishing a general theory, they could also act as powerful theoretical weapons of feminism to fight against androcentrism and eliminate gender inequality. Derrida deconstructed the binary opposition between essence and image, speaking and writing, and men and women in Western tradition, he overthrew traditional plural structure, thus directly destroyed the tradition of "androcentrism" which reflects men's limited insight", attacked traditional gender model that men rule women and women are submitted to men, and pushed gender relation to zero-degree equal position. This has provided a favorable condition for the theoretical construction and political practice of feminism.

These theories and thoughts have deconstructed current thinking habits, moral conventions and value stereotypes from different perspectives. This trend completely tallies with the spiritual values of feminism which rebels against patriarchic domination and has inborn subversive character. The Post-modern feminists in Britain, France, the United States and other countries have all obtained important theoretical basis, critical spirit and support from above theoretical discourses. For example, Cixous' "body writing", Kristeva's "sign language" and Irigaray's "feminine" all were influenced by Derrida, Lacan and other Post-modern thinkers. Therefore, we may conclude that Post-modern feminism is the product of feminism and post-modernism when they meet, and is another "melon" on the rattan of post-modernism.

2.1. RELATIONS BETWEEN POST-MARXISM AND POST-MODERNISM

Post-Marxism is a contemporary concept developed in the recent decades. Many people have misconceptions about it and also the ideas on it are not very consistent and clear. Nevertheless, it can be roughly studied from two aspects: broad and narrow[7].

The "post-Marxism" in a broad sense includes three versions: in the first version, all the Marxisms after Marx and Engels are deemed as "post-Marxism". This classification has a wider content, including the Marxism of "the Second International" led by Bernstein and Kautsky in late 19th century and early 20th century, the "Oriental Marxism" led by Lenin and Stalin, and "Western Marxism" opposite to the "Oriental Marxism". David McLellan's book *Marxism after Marx* adopts this classification method. Another classification considers all the heterodox Marxisms after the Second World War as "post-Marxism". For example, German scholar H. Fleischers calls all the Marxisms which were being pluralized after the Second World War as "post-Marxism". Another version of definition considers all kinds of Marxisms emerging after the great upheaval in the Soviet Union and Eastern Europe belong to "post-Marxism".

The "post-Marxism" in a narrow sense refers to the Marxist school, which has appeared after 1960s, particularly after 1973 when American scholar Daniel Bell published The Coming of Post-Industrial Society, and a Marxism which has the leading spirit as "post-modernism". After the publication of *The Coming of Post-Industrial Society*, many concepts and terms with prefix "post" were created, like "post- socialism", "post-communism" and "post-structuralism". However, in this book, Daniel Bell has not mentioned the term "post-Marxism". It was after the publication of Ernesto Laclau and Chantal Mouffe's book *Hegemony and Socialist Strategy: Towards a Radical Democratic Politics* in 1985 that the concept of "post-Marxism" has become widely known and debated by more people and was really established as a more complete trend of thought. In this work, through their genealogical reflections on the issue of "hegemony", Laclau and Mouffe have tried to reconstruct a "plural, radical and democratic" left-wing political theory on the basis of criticizing traditional Marxism, and explicitly called their new interpretation on Marxism as "post-Marxism".

International academic community classifies "post-Marxism" in a narrow sense as I have mentioned above. Its representative works and branches are Laclau and Mouffe's "post-Marxism of radical politics", Jacques Derrida's "de-constructionist Marxism", Jameson's "Marxism based on cultural critique", and Habermas' "post-hermeneutic Marxism".

---

7 Zeng Zhisheng: Review on Post-Marxist Thought, published in Teaching and Research, 2003 (7), p. 65.

Interaction between Post-Modern Feminism and Post-Marxism

Their Common Spirit as "Critique and Rebellion"

Post-modern feminism and post-Marxism have some similar theoretical characteristics and are interwoven.

Critical and rebellious spirit is the most distinctive and prominent characteristic adopted by Post-modern feminism on the basis of absorbing traditional feminist theories besides Post-modern theories. It is the theoretical basis of post-modernism that created conditions for Post-modernism feminism to enrich and develop its own theory.

Concretely speaking, from 1980s on, the goal of Post-modernism feminism was no longer a blind pursuit to build a theoretical edifice according to a unified and grand conception, but rather a common "project" on the precondition of admitting the differences among women, or as a large project composed of many sub-projects. In this way, it has broadened its traditional theoretical orientation based on the middle-class white women and tried theoretical studies with a pattern of diversified themes, absorbing ideas from many schools and co-opting widely different views. On the other hand, Post-modern feminism has substituted traditional abstract view of gender equality with a new view of gender equality based on gender difference.

Many theoretical schools of post-Marxism include the spirit and characteristics of critique and rebellion against traditional theories. This can be also observed for Post-modern feminism. Jameson's "post-Marxism" incorporates Marxism and post-modernism aiming to revitalize and develop Marxism, his theory also shows that rebellious spirit and style of post-modernism. Derrida and Habermas' "post-Marxism" seems an unrealistic "deconstructive interpretation" on Marxism. Derrida's "post-Marxism" applies "deconstructionist" spirit to re-interpret Marx's texts, review Marx's critical spirit and form a rebellious spirit against holism, against logocentrism and grand narratives. The "post-Marxism of radical democracy politics" advocated by Laclau and Mouffe more concretely reflects that rebellious spirit and characteristics. This post-Marxism is radical Marxism based on anti-centrism and anti-essentialism and is quite inconsistent with traditional Marxism. They propose developing Marxism as a "theory" rather than a religious doctrine, and suggest people should never rigidly stick to the argumentations and theories of traditional Marxism.

Thus we can see without difficulty that post-Marxism and Post-modern feminism – the two major theories rising in 1980s-1990s both have "critical and rebellious" spirit and characteristic.

Between these two theories, there are many overlapping ideas should be noted. For example Mouffe as the famous representative figure of post-Marxism; has also made contribution to the theory of Post-modern feminism.

In 1985, Mouffe and Laclau have jointly published *Hegemony and Socialist Strategy: Towards a Radical Democratic Politics*. This attracted universal attention from academic circles and received both critique and praise. From 1970s, Mouffe as a women had began to pay attention to feminist movement and its theoretical development. She has greatly developed and enriched the theories of Post-modern feminism. She has written many articles and short essays commentaries on neo-feminism. The most representative one was the article "Feminism, Citizenship and Radical Democratic Politics" published in 1995.

In the article, Mouffe has criticized both liberal feminism and socialist feminism. In her comments on liberal feminism, she points out that liberal movement has a political demand guided by certain values. This value set includes love, care, friendship and an identity caring for others. In the meantime, she has also criticized socialist feminism commenting that it has rather established a female identity stressing maternity and private family life. Many feminists have supported this new critical view arguing that liberal feminism and socialist feminism has tried to re-construct the duality of female identity from the perspective of natural female characteristics. This approach has excludes some women groups rather than join them altogether. Some people have expressed disagreement against new ideas arguing that every woman has a certain kind of family experience, as they are born to be some people's daughters. But I can also say that to a certain degree the views of liberal feminism and socialist feminism indeed are exclusive.

Thus view of "radical democracy" by "post-Marxism" has made a great influence on Mouffe's feminist theory.

2.2. CONTRIBUTION OF POST-MODERN FEMINISM TO POST-MARXISM

Post-Marxism is a new thought influenced by Post-modern theory criticizing capitalism. Its main representatives Laclau and Mouffe try to deconstruct and transcend Marxism. Mouffe's post-Marxist theory also inherits some critical spirit of Marxism, it has maintained the Marxist spirit of pursuing human emancipation, and even also has a kind of socialist orientation. But their Post-Marxism also openly criticizes the basic theories and political practices of Marxist socialism.

Mouffe's theories and ideas on Post-modern feminism also provide theoretical support and articulation of post-Marxist theory. She has tried to combine the critical spirit of Marxism with post-modernism, post-structuralism, feminism and other contemporary theories to establish a kind of radical and plural democratic theory. Radical and plural democracy theory is the core of Mouffe's post-Marxist theory. This theory insists on the stance of critique on capitalism, tries to explore a new anti-capitalist socialist road, and has become a new hope in the contemporary Western leftist thought and has generated great influence[8].

Mouffe deconstructs the class and class interest concept of traditional Marxism and substitutes that concept with the recognition of identity/ies; thus she also refutes the unified concept of working class. She argues that that there is no longer any common objective interest in our current world and it is no longer possible to form a unified and united working class. There is an increasingly plural society, and a society full of diversity and differences, in which social contradictions and conflicts cannot be simplified into the conflicts based on class's objective interests and class struggles. Therefore, she proposes substituting working class with randomly constructed plural subjects with different identities and explores to employ them as socialist subjects.

Mouffe and Her Contribution

Mouffe's articulation on female identity in her book *Feminism, Citizenship and Radical Democratic Politics* in fact is a very good example for her deconstruction of Marxism's class concept. In this article, she tries to expound such her view as: "an anti-essentialist standpoint may bring up the establishment of feminist politics. Such politics also contains the aims of radical democracy". Of course, she does not argue that essentialism in the left will inevitably lead to reactionary politics. Moreover, she also admits that essentialism can be constructed in a progressive way. She has argued that to develop a democracy strategy that aims to synthesize the struggles against different types of oppressions, essentialism will be certainly inadequate. The identity generated by essentialist view will be incompatible with the radical and plural democracy view, and does not allow us to establish any new view as required by politics[9].

Many traditional feminists have argued that if women's socio-historical identity is neglected it will be impossible for the feminist political movement to gain a strong foothold. Therefore in order to set and pursue a specific feminist program, women should be united as women. Opposing this view, Mouffe has argued: "the deconstruction of the female essential identity should be regarded as a necessary condition for a thorough understanding of the diversity of social relations, and

---

8   Chen Binghui: Mouffe's Post-Marxist Theory, published in Marxism and Reality, 2003(2), p. 122.
9   Chantal Mouffe: Return of the Political, p. 85.

the principles of freedom and equality should run all through these diversified social relations. There is not any unified homogenized entity, instead it is plural and should include all kinds of subject positions, and the ranks of radical democracy will be formed by all these subject positions -through random combination.

Mouffe has argued that after the Second World War, in the society, various kinds of new resistance forms and antagonisms were generated, feminist movement and other new social movements have shaped, and all these cannot be simply reduced to class contradictions or class struggles. She has thus proposed to substitute Marxist class concept with the temporary, diversified, heterogeneous, variable and an open post-Marxist identity and subject concept by re-interpreting new social relations, substitute class politics with identity politics, provide theoretical basis for contemporary new social movements and establish the radical and plural democracy strategy for change[10].

In addition, Mouffe has further emphasized the relation between feminist politics and radical democracy politics. Different from traditional feminists, Mouffe has argued that as believed by many "the foundation for feminist political struggle will not be eroded, if the view "which considers the existence of women as woman" is rejected. The loss of female essential identity will not block the struggle unity or common action; instead the radical democracy strategy aiming to synthesize and combine various/plural kinds of struggles against oppression will have farther deeper prospect. The radical and plural democratic feminist politics aims to resist various dependency forms occurring in many social relations.

These oppressive forms do not all manifest themselves as gender-related relations or problems. This new view helps us understand how a progressive subject can be constructed through different discourses. Moreover, compared with the view which reduces women identity to a unitary position as — class, race or gender — obviously these plural subject positions are more appropriate for forming a force for change.

We can see that while developing her theory of Post-modernism feminism, Mouffe has also makes further articulation and explanation of her post-Marxist theory.

In addition, there are also some feminist theories which have criticized Postmodern subject theory but still somehow can be deemed as the enrichment of post-Marxist theory. For example, Rosemary Hennessy's "materialist feminism" concept is formed based on the critique of Lacan, Mouffe, Foucault and other Post-modern theorists. In her famous book Materialist Feminism and the Politics of Discourse published in 1992 , she has offered her critique that the material

---

10   *Ibid.*, p. 87

links between women lives and their knowledge often cannot be explained by
post-modern approach. To demonstrate her ideas I will quote two paragraphs
from her where she describes her "materialist feminism": "Reading sexuality under capitalism as an ensemble of discourses whose hegemonic articulation relies
on a pre-constructed patriarchal and heterosexual organization has several implications. One of them is the insistence that totalities like patriarchy, heterosexuality, or imperialism continue to organize people's lives in systematic and oppressive
ways. Implicit in this assertion is the argument advanced by recent feminist work,
like that of Sylvia Walbie which argues that the reconfiguration of relations of
production under the late capitalism, for all of its atomizing effects on social
arrangements has not eroded these systems of domination so much as it has
re-scripted them. We see this modification now in new household arrangements
among the middle class households. As gender hierarchies become less rigid in
middle-class households, many women spend fewer hours of their day as housewives and are given more permission to leave their husbands, re-marry, or have
children without marrying. In comparison with men of a generation ago, many
middle class husbands and fathers are given less permission to take up the traditional position of master of the house and are encouraged to be more "involved"
type fathers. But even though patriarchal divisions of labor and controls over
reproduction are being more flexibly managed in the domestic family sphere, this
does not mean that patriarchy is disappearing. Household labor and child care are
still devalued. Although many middle-class women may spend less time as housewives, they still perform many more hours of housework and child care than men
and earn lower wages in the sex-segregated capitalist market. As the recruitment
of more and more middle-class women into the labor market re-formulates the
ideology of separate spheres and as the boundaries between public and private
become more porous, one effect has been the production of new frontiers for capitalist and patriarchal colonization. Electronic media and the advertising industry
are prime technologies for disciplining the unconscious and the body through the
sexual saturation of the subject. In the informatics of domination that increasingly define our everyday lives, patriarchy is alive and well and continues to rely on a
pre-constructed heterosexual norm even as it helps configure the "postcolonial"
boundaries of neo- imperialism.

Materialist feminism's oppositional practice is critique. As a feminist practice,
critique has historical affinities with consciousness-raising. However unlike the
empiricist notion of the subject as experiencing self that served as the frame
of intelligibility for much feminist consciousness-raising, critique understands
consciousness as ideologically produced subjectivity. This framework breaks out
of the empiricist dilemma of the self's mediated relationship to the world by
opening consciousness up to discourse and history. Derived from a Marxian theory of ideology, critique is bound to crisis and to ideology in a definitive way.
In that the dominant ideology continually works to seal over the cracks in the

social imaginary generated by the contradictions of patriarchal and capitalist social arrangements, it is continually engaged in crisis management. As an ideological
practice, critique issues from these cracks, historicizes them and claims them as
the basis for an alternative narrative. Together the operations of critique "work
on" the subject-form of discourse by continually historicizing the contradictions
in which it is inscribed."

She tries to establish a link between the plural subjects and their subjectivity constructed by discourse which she thinks can substitute the concept of "common
women", and the hierarchy which exploits and oppresses women. The results
which can be achieved by discourse and knowledge is physical. One of the effects
of this discourse is the construction of subject, but this subject is severed by
the difference rooted in unequal hierarchy, thus difference is not only diversified but also unequal. She thinks that the material relation between language/dis-
course and society can be solved by theorizing it into a kind of ideology through
discourse building, because every ideological theory is a theory about society.
Hennessy's "materialist feminism" combines post-Marxism and Post-modernism
subject theory which also reflects Hennessy's critique on Post-modern subject,
discourse and language. As she seeks help from plural political, economic and
cultural practices, we can say that her standpoint is close to post-Marxism.[11]

2.3. RELATION BETWEEN POST-MODERN FEMINISM AND MARXISM

Like post-modernism, by its critique on tradition, Post-modern feminism generates a bright and effective impression and influences people's ideology, consciousness, culture, life and many other aspects, but its inevitable theoretical limitations
puts it in an awkward situation which I can define as "abundant theories, little
action". Besides, Post-modern feminism underlines opposing grand narratives –
theories, laws–on the development of human society. This inevitably causes a
sharp contradiction and conflict between it and Marxist theory. The overall understanding and attitude by Post-modernism feminism on historical materialism
and Marxism are incomplete and misreading. I think it is necessary to fully analyze
and understand the relation between Post-modern feminism and Marxism. This
comparison has certain significance for a deeper understanding on Marxist theory and its development through withstanding critique raised by contemporary
trends.

11 Huang Jifeng: Materialist Feminism, published in Foreign Theoretical Trends,
2004(3), p. 24.

Its Attack on Historical Materialism

Same as post-modernism, Post-modern feminism criticizes and deconstructs the core theory (social-formation theory) and basic views of historical materialism and considers it as a doctrine defected by essentialism, determinism and reductionism, and interrogates many concepts of historical materialism[12]:

Thus, Post-modern feminism refutes the view of historical materialism "which reduces oppression structure into class exploitation". In general, post-modernism tries to explore the situation in the historical era of post-industrial society or post-capitalist society. According to post-modernism, the production relations in this era are no longer manifest universality and clear, but messy without a system, and traditional class analysis method and class struggle concept both have lost their effect and also ignores historical continuities (both inheritance/negation) in the development of capitalist social formation. The scholars of Post-modern feminism think that historical materialism reduces oppressive structures into class exploitation, thus neglecting sexual discrimination, racial discrimination and other concrete oppression forms. They agree with the Post-modern analyses approach and its radical critique on post-industrial society or post-capitalist society. In this new period, consumerism is prevalent, class struggle has become an abstract concept and individuals/groups no longer express their identity based on class positions; because the groups they belong are not determined by their economic position in social production process in such examples as: female sex (bigger group) and homosexual group. For post-modern feminists, it is hard to say if the most outrageous sexual discrimination is caused by capitalists or by unprivileged ordinary workers. In fact, some men in working class are obviously sexists. Therefore, Post-modern feminists think that in the post-capitalist society, people no longer suffer economic miseries caused by capitalist control and exploitation, and sexual discrimination and racial discrimination no longer differ strictly according to class boundaries, the theory of absolute class boundaries seem too simple, rigid and inflexible, thus contradictions pushing feminist movement and other new antagonisms causing other type of struggles should not be reduced to class issue or class struggle issue.

Obviously this refutation does not hold water. Though Post-modernism feminists accuse historical materialism as being "reductive" which ignores sexual discrimination, racial discrimination and others, exactly it is they themselves who cannot point to the root cause of women's oppression. In fact, the oppression forms — sexual discrimination and racial discrimination are caused by the capitalist system rather than by "men", to say nothing by men belonging to lower classes.

---

12 Excerpted and edited by Yi Jihong: American Scholars' Comments on Postmodern Feminism's Attitude towards Marxism, published in Foreign Theoretical Trends, 1996 (7), p. 54.

Meanwhile, the women in a superior position are also involved in this discrimination and benefit from it. Therefore, if we depart from production relations and the class relations determined by them, this will inevitably lead to explanations and solutions on the issues like sexual discrimination and racial discrimination astray[13].

Secondly, Post-modern feminism attacks the generalization of class analysis methodology in historical materialism. Post-modern feminism assimilates post-modern theoretical approach which interrogates "grand narratives". Thus the political theories inspired by historical materialism ignore the difference and diversity in human practice. Post-modern feminism emphasizes the differences, complexity and variations among women thus divides women into many scattered and various small groups. This means post-modern feminism goes one step closer to the blind spot of post-modernism – only see the differences among things and not see their universal connection, to say nothing grasp the common essence in the universally connected things. Unlike post-modernism, Post-modern feminism has not declared the termination of politics and underline alliances with political advocates/organizations, however they still insist on the emancipation of women themselves, and carries a strong tendency of opposing ideological systems and dislikes politics.

Refutation of "generalization" by Post-modern feminism often causes fatal theoretical problems in their theories. Firstly, without a universal stand, it is impossible for Post-modern feminists to base their struggle on a common support or common foundation. This point often exposes post-modern feminists to severe critics. In addition, as Post-modern feminists argue that there are relative, local and transient common interests among individuals and groups, to develop politics around the most unique and unitary resistance forms are never possible. This unique post-modern tendency makes their feminism lose the power of their resistance to oppression. Socialist feminism particularly criticizes the non-political tendency of post-modern feminism and argues that feminist movement should link itself with the social objectives of traditional Marxism.

Thirdly, Post-modern feminism holds that the social-historical development theory of historical materialism is simple determinism. Post-modern feminists argue that Marxism sums up the development of human society into the development of social productive forces and it is a simple technical determinism. In history, some theorists of the Second International have indeed interpreted historical materialism as simple technical determinism, but this is not Marx and Engels' historical materialism. Post-modern feminists think that social history is only a randomly constructed non-deterministic process full of non-determinative random and

13   Huang Jifeng: Comments on Postmodern Feminism and Its Accusation of Historical Materialism, published in Theoretical Frontier, 1998(22), p. 23.

occasional acts and is only the aggregate of discrete acts/choices, random situations and contingencies thus development of human history is non-deterministic. It is not that the basic contradictions between productive forces and production relations and between the economic foundation and superstructure which determine the development of social history. Moreover, the process of social history cannot be reduced to the progress of productive forces and the development of economic base. In their eyes, there is not any decisive motive force deciding social historical development, or any essential factor or fundamental factor deciding social and historical development or any objective and certain logic in the process of social and historical development, so the truthful grand narratives like historical materialism should only be repulsed and deconstructed. They think social progress and development can only be ultimately pushed forward by relying on righteous-discourse and its power (subject construction), and the emancipation and free development of women can be achieved only through establishing a true feminist discourse and approval and cognition of this discourse by women groups.

Overall Evaluation by Post-modern Feminism on Marxism

The Marxism generated in mid 19th century shares a common characteristic with post-modernism generated in mid 20th century; that is they both criticize the current society. Therefore, during its development, the theory of Post-modernism feminism inevitably faces identity, connection, competition and contradiction with Marxist theory.

The similarities between Post-modern feminism and Marxist theory are mainly manifested as both their concern on the current world and their reflection and critique of traditional theories. However, in essence, they differ greatly. Marxism attaches importance to the critique on the macro conditions of capitalism, while Post-modern feminism attaches importance to the analysis of the concrete and micro fields and focuses on gender inequality in the current society; Marxism attaches importance to the critique of the economic foundation and complete social system of capitalism and aims to fundamentally overthrow the capitalist social system, thus opening the broad avenue for the emancipation and freedom of the whole mankind, while Post-modern feminism aims to achieve women's emancipation mainly from the levels of ideology and culture critique ; both Marxism and Post-modernism feminism subvert the traditional subject concept, while in the sense of Marxism, subject no longer refers to (self-consciousness) ego-consciousness or ego, instead it permeates with historicity – he is a real man in specific historical circumstances—his essence is a unity of free and conscious activity , plus ensemble of social relations . For Marx, man's most decisive activity is productive activity besides theoretical and communicative activity, thus he recognizes three activities by man which distinguishes both man/woman. While post-modern feminism deconstructs the concept of "woman" by micro approach, and points out that "woman" identity is a relative and plural concept, this woman identity is the contrast of man — in this way, post-modern feminism aims to de-construct the subjectivity of men in the current chauvinist society and also strives to construct the subjectivity of female subject.

From the above aspects, we can see that although Post-modern feminism and Marxism are similar on the external outset, at the same time Post-modern feminism aims to radicalize and draws on –to a degree–Marxism's critical spirit. But the critique of Post-modern feminism targets a constructed ideal and an abstract object in an abstract manner; whereas Marxist critique targets real subjects in the real life-world-in their concrete practice in a revolutionary and practical sense. Since Post-modern feminists focus opposing all grand theoretical narratives related to the development human society, they are unable to give a correct evaluation on Marxism. Their overall evaluation on Marxism can be summed up as follows:

Firstly, Post-modern feminists think that the Marxist theory is a "grand narrative", so criticize it. An important theoretical concept of Post-modern feminism is to "negate all grand narratives". They are dedicated to criticize all the grand and all-inclusive modern theories and try to establish a community theory – they aim to transform the subjectivity of smaller size special communities, based on their experiences, re-build their moral and political subjectivity, and they also deny cause-effect relations and macro social concepts. They think only decentralized, local and small theories can be effective. After the developed capitalist countries have entered into the post-industrial society, the general discourses on the development of human society were interrogated, including Marxist theory. Post-modern feminism opposes macro analyses on gender, race and class and argues that all these analyses will be are too rough. As the things inside each social group could differ numerously, all suppositions will be non-practical. For the above reasons, the feminist struggle advocated by Post-modernism feminist theorists cannot achieve much in practice and contribute substantially to the theory of women's emancipation. Consequently, the feminists who used to struggle for women's common rights become the feminists who only care for sexual roles.

Secondly, same as post-modernism, Post-modern feminists argue that Marx's several key theories have lost their validity after changes occurring in capitalism. This one-sided view contends that every grand narrative exists in a form of "truth" worshipped as the starting point people view the world although science develops in leaps and people easily observe that grand narratives are not absolute truth, therefore Marxism cannot be considered as the world-view to lead people. For post-modern feminists, Marxism is a theory which is not tested and proved, since it is not proved experientially it cannot be recognized as truth.However, recently many Post-modern theorists declare on the merits and impassability of Marxism.

In his book *The Coming of Post-Industrial Society*, Daniel Bell has commented that "although Marx had lived in the early industrial society, he has provided us "accurate predictions" on "several important characteristics" of the post-industrial society. Foucault has written that nowadays it is impossible to write history beyond the horizon of the ideology defined and described by Marx and without using a series of thoughts directly or indirectly relating to Marx's ideology[14]. In his book *Spectres of Marx*, Derrida writes that there will be no future without Marx and his heritage[15]. In the sense of Post-modernist thinkers, due to the decentralization and heterogeneity in systems, contemporary society can hardly be understood as an integral body, so there can be no central point to be opposed. For instance, capitalism cannot be understood as an integral system, because there is no axis to base our cognition on it. Some Post-modern thinkers have argued that as contemporary Marxism adopts universal categories such as production and class, but those oppressions which are closely related to economic reason by Marxism, such as: oppression on women, the blacks, homosexuals and other oppressions cannot be explained as such.

Thirdly, Post-modern feminism simply labels Marx's theories as economic determinism but Marx's theory on social formations as crucial part of historical materialism regards economic base as the real foundation of society, but it does not simply reduce and simply link all oppression forms with the economic base and presupposes complex links and interaction between the economic base and the superstructures of the society. As a matter of fact, different from Post-modern feminism which focuses on specific oppression forms like sexual discrimination and racial prejudice or colonialist prejudice, Marxism explores and studies the respective forms of these oppressions and their manifestations forms, observing their complex interaction with major class domination forms and class contradictions. For example, take the workers who are at the lower level of social ladder, generally their practices and understanding related to sexual discrimination and racial discrimination (in ideology and practice) manifests itself quite different from that of the upper classes. It does not mean that the former group does no way involve in oppression or its oppression is insignificant but in the socio-political process to overcome these oppressions under the conditions of capitalist society it is obvious that main obstacle becomes the power of the dominant classes —not the ruled and subordinate— when we closely study their respective material conditions and historical practices. Therefore, Post-modernist feminist prejudice against Marxism as economic reductionism becomes highly doubted.

---

14   Michel Foucault: The Order of Things: Archaeology of the Human Sciences [M]. New York, Pantheon Books, 1970, p. 21.
15   Jacques Derrida: Specters of Marx, Beijing, China Renmin University Press, 1999, p. 21.

2.4. DEBATES ON POST-MODERN FEMINISM

In his letter to Ludwig Kugelmann in 1868, Marx wrote: "Everyone who knows anything on history also knows that great social revolutions are impossible without the feminine ferment. Social progress may be measured precisely by the social position of the fair sex (plain ones included)."[16] Thus it can be seen that without women's contribution, the social revolutions would be impossible, and without them, human would not exist. Feminist theory is the summary of the progressive practice and struggle for gender equality and also a beacon and guide for women's emancipation and their development. The efforts by post-modern feminism are a matter of significance to overcome the problems facing today's women and it promotes the development of feminism.

Comparison between Post-modern Feminism and Marxism

Not all the Post-modern feminists hold the same theoretical view, their view and attitude towards Marxist theory on women's emancipation differ greatly. Nevertheless we still may roughly study their approach into two categories.

Firstly, most Post-modern feminists deny that original Marxism contains a feminist theory. They think that although Marx and Engels had discussed the issue of gender based on division of labor and women's unpaid housework, this issue was not studied in the framework of historical materialism, so Marx and Engels have surrendered "androcentrism" have focused their attention on economic and political fields and paid little attention to the issue of women's oppression.

At this point, it is necessary to further re-read Marxist works and remarks on women issues and evaluate them. Marx indeed did not specifically analyze the issue of women's oppression, but his works provide powerful insights to understand the structural relation hidden in the phenomenon of women' oppression and the works of Marx, Engels and other Marxists also contain rich thoughts on women's emancipation[17]. They regard women's emancipation as a part of human emancipation. German socialist leader August Bebel had published *Woman in the Past, Present and Future* in 1879 and reviewed this book in 1883. The book was well received, but it partly contains the colors of utopian socialism and reflects certain approaches socialist reformism in the socialist movement. It is well known that in his work *Origin of the Family, Private Ownership and State*, Engels had indirectly targeted several important immature and erroneous ideas in Bebel's book, and Engels had explicitly expressed that the support of socialist movement to the emancipation of women also urgently needs a well-established theoretical basis.

---

16   Collected Works of Karl Marx and Frederick Engels, Chinese edition 1, Vol.32, Beijing, People's Publishing House, 1975, p. 571.
17   See Martha Gimenez. Lisa Vogel: Introduction of Marxist Feminist Thought Today. Science & Society, New York, The Guilford Press, 2005(1), p. 6.

In the sense of Engels, the subjection of women, emergence of private owner-ship and transformation towards the patrilineal society are closely related with the formation of monogamous nuclear families. The only purpose for the formation of monogamous families is to protect the social continuity of private property ownership. Male dominance, firstly in patrilineal form and then in patriarchic form, is the result of **"class" separation between men with property and women without property.** Engels had pointed out: Monogamy form was not based on natural conditions but on economic conditions. "It was not in any way the fruit of individual sexual-love". Monogamy had "remained as before marri-ages of convenience"[18]. For Engels, sexual relations can be established on the basis of equality and "true" love only when women's economic dependence on men disappears. Therefore, Engels said: "the first premise for the emancipation of women is the re-introduction of the entire female sex into social production–industry[19]- so that women no longer depend on men economically; the second premise for the emancipation of women is related with the further development of modern large industry. The dawn of real emancipation process of women can only appears with a highly developed industrial society; the third premise is the socialization of housework, i.e. incorporating private housework as part of general social production. In the pre-class society housework was a kind of "pu-blic work", while after the formation of monogamous families, housework [...] is irrelevant with the society. It becomes a private service; wives become principal maids and are excluded from social productive labor process[20]. Ultimately, the fundamental condition for the emancipation of women is to eliminate the capi-talist system and establish the socialist system. Engels thinks that social progress in a country can be measured with women's social status. Meanwhile, Engels also regards women's entry to labor market and participation in social labor process as a progress in human history.

Secondly, although a smaller part of Post-modern feminists admit that Marxism contains thoughts and views for the emancipation of women, they interrogate these views or subjectively reform Marxist thoughts on women's emancipation. They do not agree that the generation of private ownership and class was the fundamental condition for the generation of gender oppression, but they do not totally deny the role of these factors in gender oppression. Meanwhile they have made utmost efforts to explore other factors to find out the root cause for women's oppression.

Famous Post-modern feminist Gayle Rubin has critically applied Marx-Engels' view that the emergence of social division of labor is the root cause for women's oppression, and from the vantage point of Marxist political economy, has argued

---

18   Marx and Engels Selected Works, Edition 2, Vol. 4, p. 62.

19   *Ibid.*, p. 72.

20   *Ibid.*

that women's oppression exists in social relations. In her article *The Traffic in Women* in 1975, she has emphatically discussed the root cause of gender inequality – gender system as well as the derived social gender division of labor. During her concrete studies on these issues, she has compared and made use of Marx-Engels' view that the emergence of private ownership and class is the source of women's oppression, as well as structural anthropologist Levi-Strauss' theory on pledge exchange and incest taboo and Freud's view on "Oedipus complex", and has developed her own "sex/gender system" theory as a primary site of female oppression (as opposed to labor)[21]. But her theory —except gender conflict— neglects the differences of class, race, ethnic groups and national conflicts.

Rubin, arguing that sex and gender are socially produced and constructed, contends that the subordination of women is the result of the situational relationship by which sex and gender are socially organized and reproduced. What counts as sex...is culturally determined [...] Every society...has a sex/ gender system—a set of arrangements by which the biological raw material of human sex and procreation is shaped by human, social intervention and satisfied in a conventional manner [...].

Rubin uses two metaphorical terms as, the "erotic pyramid" and "the charmed circle", to describe the stratification of sexual populations and sexual practices according to a hierarchical system of sexual values that structures modern capitalist society. At the climax of the erotic pyramid, inside the charmed circle, is heterosexual, marital, monogamous, reproductive, non-commercial sex; at the bottom of the pyramid and outside the charmed circle, is homosexual, unmarried, promiscuous, non-procreative, commercial sex.

Rubin has not made much effort to seek the ultimate reason of oppression on women – but has focused on the sex/gender system, and hoped to overcome gender based discrimination outside labor process. And every woman though oppressed by patriarchy, their actual situation differs in numerous ways. Therefore, for Rubin to seek the main reason for the occurrence of gender oppression and seek a common strategy to overcome gender inequality will not bring a significant benefit in the struggle of women's emancipation. Obviously, the theory of sex/gender system and the similar theories which deny capitalist private ownership as the root cause of women's oppression are all practically doubtful; we can say that these theories only notice the shadow and omit the substance. Marxist theory on women's emancipation is a theory developed on the basis of practice and is the natural aim followed by socialist states as the only correct guiding ideology and theory which lead the people including women to emancipation and free all-round development. Only after getting rid of capitalist fetters, can women obtain real freedom.

21   Bao Xiaolan Editor in Chief: Review on Feminist Studies, Beijing, Sanlian Bookstore, 1995, p. 4-5.

Although capitalist society develops and changes, there is no fundamental change on its essence and women's status is not fundamentally improved, so Marxism's inference to the fate of capitalism and the emancipation of women will not lose effect. In the Science and Society[22] journal published in the United States in 2006, the debate on today's Marxist feminism was reflected. The magazine has collected the theses of several feminists on the current status of Marxist feminism and its prospects. They have unanimously expressed such a thought: to achieve real progress, feminist thought and feminist movement should absorb the current mainstream theories and combine them with theoretical ideas in Marx-Engels' works. The development of contemporary capitalism has made it more possible to achieve substantial progress on the issue of women's housework burden as proposed by Marxist classics. Following the convergence of social/public sphere and private field; the commercialization of the housework is more and more possible which weakens the burden on women. The unpaid household labor carried by women, such as: looking after old people and children, cooking and cleaning could possibly lose its effect through women awareness and further adjustments in capitalist production relations ; these relations also pushes more and more middle-class women join the labor force market. Thus it becomes more obvious that the condition of women is decided by production relations as advocated by Marxism; since in regard to its economic system capitalism is bound to constantly develop the productive forces. This inevitably causes adjustments in the production relations.

Post-modern Feminist Theory and Women's Emancipation and Development

Although Post-modern feminist practice seems "abundant theories and little action" and manifests certain theoretical narrowness, as a theoretical product of the contemporary era termed as post industrial society in developed capitalist countries, it has its own advantages and plays a significant role in promoting women's emancipation and development.

In the history of international women's movement and theoretical development, no doubt the women's movement and feminist theories in the developed capitalist states have always played a dominant position, since the feminists in these states are not only the initial introducers of feminist concepts and theories but also dedicated practitioners. But if we make a general evaluation, women's emancipation and free development in the world show radical imbalances and unevenness. The women's movement in the United States and European states pay great attention to women movements and issue of women emancipation in the Third World and those women from minority ethnic groups and races in the United States and west European countries. In my opinion Post-modern feminist theories have

---

22   Please refer to "Editorial Perspectives" of this magazine, p. 3.

certain advantages when dealing with women issues related to ethnic groups and races' in developed countries and also suits to the demands and desires of the women in the Third World. This is manifested mainly in the following aspects[23]:

Firstly, Post-modernism feminism criticizes the blind modernization and encourages development planners to pay attention to the actual living conditions of the women in the Third World and the women of minority races in the United States and European states. Their economic poverty and lower status are the very reasons why their emancipation and development status is at a poorer level when compared with other women groups in the world. Therefore, these disadvantaged groups receive more and more attention from women theoretical circles. After the Second World War, the thinkers and policy makers in the Western states have highlighted "helping" and supporting "development" in the Third World still blended with imperialist ideological prejudices, they have generally regarded "enlightened" Western society as the only yardstick, and have humiliated the cultures of the people in the Third World, and meanwhile simply equaled the concept of modernization with development. Development would automatically lead to modernization in the 'backward" Third World. The only problem was how to proceed and how fast could the goal of development be possibly achieved, but the essence and content of the goal of modernization was neglected. The economic and political role of the women in the Third World was also greatly neglected. Since the late 1960s, some economists began to admit that development and modernization was not as easy as expected and the social status of the women in developing countries was not improved with economic development as expected; but on the contrary, it had declined. Some feminist scholars have begun to focus on this reality —the role of the women in the Third World in economic development- and asserted women could play a key role in the development of Third World. Post-modern feminists have played leading roles in this regard and tried to understand the desires and demands of the women in the Third World. They have played active roles being the voice of those disadvantageous silent women groups and have particularly focused to reveal and publish life experiences of these groups. For post-modern feminists the strategy for improvement of their lives should be based on their vivid experiences and desires.

Secondly, the post-modern feminists remind the women in the United States and European developed countries that the women in the Third World cannot be generally defined in one category without differentiation. Generally the women and feminists in the Third World consider feminism as a movement suited for the developed countries, so some scholars have labeled it as white women's feminism: "Western feminism or North American feminism to refer to the ideologies/ movement of the middle-class women in the capitalist society opposing sexual

23   Edited by Xu Baoqiang and Wang Hui: Illusion of Development, Beijing, Central Compilation & Translation Press, 2001, p. 352-355.

discrimination and oppression. Feminist scholars in the Third World including Trinh T. Minha have argued that "Western feminists often complain about the uncivilized and backward nature of the women in the Third World. What is more, as colonialism lords over the world, their inappropriate description is consecrated as invariable rules[24].

The idea of homogenizing the Third World women, omitting the differences among women in these regions- is the approach which is generally raised by "women development" experts in international organizations, but I think it could restrict our understanding on women in the Third World. Post-modern feminism has urged people to pay attention to the differences between women and women, and between men and men in classes, nations and races. It has changed the outstanding tendency in the traditional feminist movement which centers on middle-class white women, and has revealed the complexity and diversity of women's life practices, also extended the concept of gender difference.

Thirdly, Post-modern feminism attaches importance to construct women's struggle (power) discourse based on the spheres of social culture and ideology. Those experts working for "women development" generally do not involve the issue of class; instead they focus on poverty prevalent among women in the developing countries. On the other side traditional feminists focus on materialist analysis and neglect the importance of ideology and discourse aspects when building women's gender consciousness. By contrast, Post-modern feminism pays attention to these aspects; adding discourse analysis, consciousness/power relation and differences into materialist analysis which is vital for women movements in the Third World. Analyzing the formation of gender ideology helps the experts and scholars to understand how gender ideology shapes and restricts women from acquiring consciousness and power in the society and also provides possibility to understand and transcend patriarchic ideology.

All in all, Post-modernism feminism not only interrogates and criticizes the mainstream thoughts on modernization, but also criticizes how the society or patriarchy defines the feminine ego, and the restrictions on the feminine ego in the process of social development.

Limitations of Post-modern Feminist Theories

Although post-modern feminist theories offer a positive guidance to women's emancipation and development by a different perspective than traditional feminism, and enrich feminist theories, they also have several shortcomings. They are manifested in the following:

---

24   Bao Xiaolan Editor in Chief: Review on Western Feminist Studies, Beijing, Sanlian Bookstore, 1995, p. 24.

Firstly, the non-political or post-political tendency in Post-modern feminism makes feminist struggles lose common goals. The divergence between traditional feminism and Post-modernism feminism lies in their different views on identity recognition and subject. When women just become the subjects struggling for their own rights, they are to a certain degree separated from the struggle universal human rights and man's holistic emancipation cause. Post-modern feminism applies "deconstruction" approach and methodology, and considers women subjects as flow-able and changeable characters and opposes the use of such more general concepts like "feminine" because they are "essentialist"; thus the goal of feminist struggle is considered as building a new women subject according to post-modern feminist discourse and ideology. Therefore, in a sense, Post-modern feminism has also de-constructed the political activities of feminists[25].

Secondly, Post-modern feminism ignores the common features the women's movement in the world shared by them. Some theoretical aspects of Post-modern feminism completely adopt the stance and view of post-modernism. During the application of deconstructionist methodology, they deny and criticize things blindly, and cannot properly handle the relation between deconstruction and construction, spare no effort to attack essentialism and universalism, trying to substitute them with plural and particularistic theories, all these cause certain negative effects in the feminist practice. But women's actual particular practices have many converging and common aspects; therefore I think it is quite necessary to develop some trans-cultural macro theories which appropriately include commonalities and universality.

Thirdly, the theories of post-modern feminism give an excessive emphasis on "differences". This is their great defect. In reality, although women differ greatly due to the differences of nationality, ethnic group and class or stratum, their status and situations under the oppression of patriarchy bear remarkable resemblances. Just on the basis of these resemblances, they can have common struggle goals as proven by feminist movement's long history. Feminism should encourage a united and plural women struggle in the world raising common demands. Post-modern feminism's excessive emphasis on the differences among women generally cause internal separations in feminist ranks and endangers cohesion and solidarity among them.

Fourthly, Post-modern feminists are inclined to academism which weakens their practical capacities and political role of feminism. Many people call their ideas as "academic feminism" and criticize them as indulging themselves in obscure terminology, escaping from real revolutionary practice and practical activities like demonstrations and protests , enjoy the pleasures of thinking in a spiritual garden, they are narcissistic and seldom leave their paradise and sacrifice their free time,

25   Li Yinhe: Feminism, Jinan, Shandong People's Publishing House, 2005, p. 72.

their discourse becomes increasingly irrelevant for most women[26]. Post-modern feminists dedicate themselves to invent or discover feminine discourses and regard all concrete oppressions women suffer in reality (for example: violence in the family and sexual harassment) as pure discourses. As a result, they reduce the issue of changing the current social system which oppresses women to discourse construction which narrows practice and practical activity to change the actual direction of development.

Post-modern feminism indeed explores a way to eliminate sexual discrimination, achieve gender equality and realize women's emancipation and development through the levels of social culture and ideology. This is an important step forward when compared with traditional feminism which has approached women issues from the level of concrete social issues. I think faced by the critique of post-modern feminism Marxist feminists should insist to evaluate sexual discrimination and all forms of oppressions on women interwoven with the main aspect social reality and combine particularity with universal social reality of capitalist class society. Marxism drafts the universal route to complete human emancipation which includes many aspects and many contents such as the emancipation of oppressed women, oppressed working classes and oppressed nations. It is also necessary to integrate theory with practice, enrich Marxist theories which guide feminist practice thus draw a more comprehensive strategy for women movements.

REFERENCES

• Bao Xiaolan Editor in Chief: Review on Western Feminist Studies, Beijing, Sanlian Bookstore, 1995.
• Xu Baoqiang and Wang Hui: Illusion of Development, Beijing, Central Compilation & Translation Press, 2001
• Sophia Phoca and Rebecca Wright: Postfeminism, translated by Wang Li, Beijing, Culture and Art Publishing House, 2003
• Rosemarie Putnam Tong: Feminist Thought: A More Comprehensive Introduction, translated by Ai Xiaoming et al., Wuhan, Central China Normal University Press, 2002.

---

26   Rosemarie Putnam Tong: Feminist Thought: A More Comprehensive Introduction, translated by Ai Xiaoming et al., Wuhan, Central China Normal University Press, 2002, p. 302.

CHAPTER VII

SOCIALIST FEMINISM

Socialist feminism is a quite influential trend of thought in the contemporary world. It came into being between the end of the 1960s and the beginning of the 1970s, as the integration of two schools: Marxist feminism and socialist feminism, which have emerged one after the other. As the outcome of combination of feminist ideology and socialist thoughts in the contemporary Western countries, these trends of thoughts reflect not only the Marxist influence on feminism, but also the interaction of feminist movements with socialist movements. The study of these thoughts is of great significance to understand the current feminist movements in our era as well as the curreent trends in related social thoughts, especially socialist thoughts and their development in those countries.

1. THE RISE OF SOCIALIST FEMINISM

The emergence of socialist feminism has its own social background and origins in theory and ideology. The oppressed workers, including large numbers of women in the class society, particularly in the capitalist society, suffer oppression and exploitation. Socialist feminism has emerged under such historical settings. Socialist feminism came into being in the 1960s, when Western capitalist society met several social crises and turbulences, especially when the new social movements rose. The rise and evolution of feminist movements, particularly the climax of the second feminist movement between the end of the 1960s and beginning of the 1970s, were the direct causes for the emergence of socialist feminism. It was indeed based on the outcome of women's emancipation and rising self awareness in both socialist movements and the feminist movements, and has united them to form their own theory and ideology.

1.1. EMERGENCE OF SOCIALIST FEMINISM

Thoughts of socialist feminism, as the outcome of the integration of feminist and socialist thoughts, were not only related to social settings of the feminist thought and movements, but also to social settings of socialist thoughts and movements. As a matter of fact, these two backgrounds were interrelated, making up social and historical settings for socialist feminist thoughts.

Exploitation and oppression in the capitalist society can be seen as the social source for the rise of socialist feminism. On the one hand, women being oppressed in the capitalist society, has created conditions for new feminist thoughts and movements. On the other hand, workers are being exploited and oppressed in the capitalist society, which produce conditions for socialist thoughts and movements. All these conditions are interrelated. For example, female workers suffer oppression not only from males but also from capitalists. Therefore, the exploitation and oppression in the capitalist society has not only brought about feminist thoughts and socialist thoughts respectively, but also the combination of these two as the socialist-feminist theory and practice.

The rise of socialist feminism was set in the background where the oppressed and exploited women in the capitalist society fought for their own emancipation (feminist movements and socialist movements). Though women's oppression is a long and deep rooted historical phenomenon, there had not appeared feminist movements and thoughts for women's emancipation prior to the capitalist society. Similarly, socialist movements and socialist thoughts as well, in a real sense, have emerged in the capitalist society to some extent on the prerequisite of capitalist development. Both feminist and socialist movements have emerged in large scale in the middle of the 19th century. From then on, they both have gone through a history of rises and falls. Additionally, they have shared the similar or same miseries in many eras. They have influenced each other and tended to approach to each other in the process of their development.

First feminist movements have started in the middle of the 19th century. This movement was known as the first-wave of the feminist movement, or first great leap in women's emancipation and women's development. This period had lasted until the end of the 1920. In this great movement, women have fought for equal political and legal rights with men. Their criticism has directly aimed against capitalist states and those laws that excluded women from the rights of education, employment, participation in government and political affairs etc. The initiation of the U.S. feminist movements was marked by The Declaration of Sentiments, which was issued in July 1848. From 1890 on, feminists in the United States have made great efforts to organize women to participate in suffrage movements. In 1917, two women's emancipation organizations "National American Woman Suffrage Association" and "National Womens' Party" have jointly organized a 24-hour demonstration against the White House. In 1919, the U.S. Parliament was forced to issue The 19th Amendment on the U.S. Constitution, clearly prescribing that women had the right of suffrage. This feminist movement in USA has gained fruitful achievements. Till the end of the First World War, women in several European and American countries have obtained rights of suffrage, property and inherätance rights and rights for higher education. It is noticeable that the peak period of the first feminist movement was as well the time when socialist movements in capitalist countries were vigorously ascending. For example, in the middle of the 19th century the scientific socialism had emerged; Marx and Engels' Communist Manifesto was issued in February 1848, which was just a little bit earlier than The Declaration of Sentiments by feminists in the United States. Later on, the Paris Commune and the founding of proletarian political parties and their unions, particularly the Russian October Revolution in 1917, all have marked the climax and great achievements of socialist movements.

In the beginning of the 1930s, Western women's emancipation movement was at a low ebb. With the outbreak of the capitalist economic depression, prejudices against women's employment have sharply risen in the European and American countries. In 1920ies, although the success of the Russian October Revolution has encouraged proletarian revolutions in several European capitalist countries, they had little success and failed to seize power. Thereafter, capitalist states have brutally suppressed the proletarian movements. And afterwards in 1933 Hitler came to power in Germany, he launched the War policy , crazily expanding fascism globally, and the world war has greatly destroyed women's organizations in some of the European countries. After the end of the Second World War, capitalist countries with the leadership of the United States have launched the policy of "Cold War" against communist parties and communism, suppressing feminist movements as well as labor movements. Particularly in the 1950s, movements against feminism have reached a crescendo in the United States, strongly restricting women's participation in public life and working life. In this period a younger generation of American female intellectuals were forced to abandon their studies and their career one after another, regressing to the dream of "happy housewives" and aiming that as their top life goal. From then on, the momentum of feminist movements has completely descended. At the same time, in this era the labor and unionist movements in capitalist countries as well receded towards a low ebb.

Especially after the Second World War, great changes have occurred in capitalism.Promoting the new scientific revolution, the Western countries have adjusted their policies in many spheres, particularly in economy and politics, which have not only alleviated class contradictions but has also greatly promoted economic development. Consequently, traditional labor movements in the Western capitalist countries generally fell into a decline.

By the end of the 1950s and beginning of the 1960s, Western capitalist countries have begun to enter another turbulent period, causing the emergence of the New-Left movement against capitalist reality and as well the second rising period of the feminist movement. Reforms in capitalism during the postwar years could not eliminate the inherent contradictions of capitalism and capitalist states could not overcome their drawbacks and evils, such as long-term economic stagnation, militarization of economies, government's financial deficits and high state debts, intensifying social bipolarization, distorted social development, increase in crime rates, drug trading and use, widespread venereal diseases, prevalent superstition, deep-rooted racial discrimination, increasing destruction on the ecological system,environmental pollution, rampant bureaucracy, ceaseless escalation of nuclear and conventional armament race, all of which have trigerred great discontent among broad masses. It was with the intensification of these social contradictions and crises that the struggle against capitalist reality was fueled again. These struggles and oppositions have attained different forms compared with the struggles of traditional labor movement. For instance, they were based on a wider and intricate social basis, which was loose, decentralized and unsteady. There was no common political ideology, and their organization forms were also amorphous, unsystematic and instable; there was no long-term objective, neither was there a clear class orientation. Those participated in the movements belonged to different classes, stratums or parties, and rather aimed or united for the realization of a specific social goal; thus, did not appear as a movement stamped by a certain class or stratum. The movement of racial civil rights of blacks, the anti-war and peace movement, the New Left movement, new feminist movement and ecological movement have all supported each other. They have widely and increasingly spread in Western countries in the form of "movement for a New Society", one wave after another.

Among those movements for a new society, the new feminist movement was a very important one. It has in fact originated from the "New Left" movement. In the large-scale mass movements exploding in the United States, the "New Left" which was based on the mainstay of university students and young intellectuals, had become an attractive political and cultural movement in the United States in the 1960s. They have supported blacks' movement against racism, actively participated in movements for civil rights, opposed the Vietnam War and criticized the established system of schooling and education institutions, and fiercely attacked the U.S. social system. These left-wing student movements have also inspired women to struggle for their own emancipation. Many women who had actively participated in these movements had hoped that they could find positions in the New-Left movements. However, they were disappointed by the reality they had faced, and soon observed a strong andro-centrism in these organizations. The leaders of the New Left groups have viewed women as a vase, or assigned them do odds and ends, like serving tea. They went so far as to express their backward ideas publicly, "In the anti-war student committee, women could only be placed in such secondary positions, or, in other words, they should behave obsequiously." This kind of attitudes have indeed irritated women in the "New Left". They have keenly realized and expressed: "It is more urgent and vital for women to emancipate themselves than struggle for blacks or for other aims"and have cognized that it was necessary for women to push for their own emancipative movement.

During the "National New Politics Conference" organized by the "New Left" in the United States in August 1967, a female member was refused to read her article on women issues by those men in charge of the meeting organization. A week later, women have decided to hold an independent meeting in Chicago, releasing "A Letter to Left Women", calling for them to unite in order to initiate a new "women's liberation movement". Thus the second feminist movement had emerged in the United States in the middle of the 1960s, and then spread to Western Europe and to the entire capitalist world. Between 1968 and 1970, the new feminist movement has spread all over Britain, and has reached a new tide in France in 1968 due to the baptism of "Revolutionary May Storm". At the same time, in Northern Europe, like Denmark and Norway, the new feminist movements have also shown a vigorous development, women's organizations were being organized one after the other. The aims and scopes of this new feminist movement included all aspects of women rights and demands, which has far surpassed the first wave feminist movement both in depth and width. If the first feminist movement can be regarded as the one for political and legal rights such as universal suffrage, then we can say that the second feminist struggle was characterized as an all-round and multi aspect movement, including political, economic, educational and cultural spheres, and covering a range of problem areas in the society, family and schooling. Furthermore, the second feminist movement was even more radical. It has advocated a complete change in the social system to create necessary emancipative conditions for women, rather than reforming the current society on the basis of the existing system through parliamentary legislation.

It was also in the second feminist movement that socialist feminism has emerged. In this second wave of feminist movement, a variety of theories or schools could be distinguished such as, liberal feminism, radical feminism, Marxist feminism and socialist feminism. We will introduce in this chapter the latter two, Marxist feminism and socialist feminism which are subsumed as "Socialist Feminism".

1.2. IDEOLOGICAL ORIGINS OF SOCIALIST FEMINISM

The ideological origin of socialist thoughts for women's emancipation is intricate. To sum it up, there were two aspects: one is the thoughts on women's emancipation advocated by traditional socialism; the other is the ideas rooted in traditional feminism.

1.2.1. WOMEN'S EMANCIPATION THOUGHTS

In the 19th century and beginning of 20th century, two utopian socialists Charles Fourier and Robert Owen, and existentialist activist and thinker Simone de Beauvoir were the first to definitely link women's emancipation with socialism. In the process of criticizing the capitalist reality and advocating the socialist ideal, they have clearly raised the idea of women's emancipation. De Beauvoir has pointed out that capitalism should be stamped as an unreasonable society if it did not care for the future and emancipation of women, who covered half of the population in the society. In Fourier's view, the development quality of a certain historical era could be judged by the degree of women's liberty; "The degree of women's emancipation is the natural criterion to measure the universal emancipation level." Owen had criticized the marriage in the capitalist society and advocated men-women equality , demanded realizing equality in practice. To set an example of alleviating women's housework, he was the first to establish a kindergarten in the world. The exploration by utopian socialists on women's emancipation was not only an important source for Marxist theory on this problem, but also for later socialist feminists.

Marx's and Engels' theories on women's emancipation also constitute an important source for socialist feminism. Most women's thoughts were more or less affected by Marxism. Some of them were true Marxists, who had committed themselves to apply Marxist theory to analyze women's emancipation problem in the capitalist society. Some of them did not declare themselves as Marxist when studying feminist issues, and had even criticized the Marxist viewpoint on women's emancipation. However, whether they inherited or learned from or not and approved or disapproved Marxism, we cannot ignore that the feminist socialist concepts, thread and ideology was partly inspired by traditional Marxism.

What feminist socialists adopted and developed from Marxism mainly involves two aspects: The first aspect includes some basic standpoints and methods expounded in Marx's social and historical viewpoints or works- Marxist historical materialism, critics against bourgeoisie political economic theories and his analytical methods, class theory and also his early theories related to human nature and alienation. Though these theories and methods did not directly involve feminist problems, we can say they can serve that purpose as well. The second aspect includes direct Marxist thoughts on women problem and emancipation. Builders of classic Marxism have paid much attention to women's emancipation issues. This can be seen in Marx's *Economic and Philosophical Manuscripts of 1844* and in Engels' *The Condition of the Working Class in England in 1844* and their co-authored works *The German Ideology* and *The Communist Manifesto*, also in Marx's *Capital* and Engels' *Origin of the Family, Private Property and the State*, all of which have to a degree dealt with issue of women's emancipation. They have revealed women's conditions in the capitalist society, specifically focusing on laboring women being exploited and their body and health ruined under heaviest working conditions. For instance, in his book *Origin of the Family, Private Property and the State*, Engels had systematically demonstrated Marx's thoughts on women's emancipation. He had definitely pointed out, "As long as women are excluded from broad participation in social productive labor process and restricted to private labor in the family, it is, or will be impossible for them to be liberated or equal with men. Women's emancipation will not be possible unless they can participate in production and unless housework occupies only a small part of their time ; this can be achieved on the basis of nothing but modern industry."[1]

German socialists have also developed important ideas on women's emancipation. Bebel, one of the outstanding leaders of the German Social Democratic Party, was the first to systematically explore the relationship between women's emancipation and socialism in his book *Women and Socialism*. This book reveals why and how women were enslaved in human history, with a systematic analysis on women's enslaved position in different historical periods from numerous aspects, such as physiology, psychology, culture and education, marriage and family, profession and morality. He has pointed out that in the capitalist society, especially in families of the propertied class, women are degraded to nothing but machines to produce legal children, as housewives or female wards of exhausted husbands. As long as the capitalist society remains, evils, such as money based marriage, infanticide, abortion, increasing divorce rate and prostitution will continue to exist and will even worsen. However, "women's complete emancipation and gender equality are one of the developing objectives of human civilization; there is nothing on earth that can prevent the practice for such a goal." As a movement aiming to eliminate the capitalist system and establish a new social system, socialism

---

1 *Selected Works of Marx and Engels*, Second Edition, Volume 4, p. 162. Beijing: People's Press, 1995.

is directly linked with women's emancipation. "The future belongs to socialism, and first of all, it belongs to workers and women."[2] Clara Zetkin, an influential socialist as well as German politician, was the first to raise the proletarian flag for women's emancipation, and has devoted herself to socialist movement. She has pointed out that the reason why women had an inferior position for thousands of years is not related with the laws "formulated by men", but in their economic status and property relations. To emancipate themselves, women should step out of their houses, and participate in social production, and join workers' movements and socialist movements. As an important part of human emancipation, women's emancipation will inevitably push the cause for the emancipation of labor from capital. It will be impossible for the proletariat to get liberated unless they unite regardless of gender distinction. It is the same with the socialist cause; it cannot be victorious unless it unites vast number of women in the struggle for the future new society.

1.2.2. FEMINIST THOUGHTS ON WOMEN'S EMANCIPATION

Feminism is a quite influential trend of thought in contemporary society. It firmly expounds the theoretical aspects on how and why women suffer oppression, and their problems of freedom and equality, and guides the struggle for women's rights and emancipation. Socialist feminists have also adopted a lot from several feminist thoughts prior or contemporaneous to them. Liberal feminism, Beauvoir's feminist thoughts and radical feminism all have inspired socialist feminism.

Liberal Feminism:

Liberal feminism is the thought based on the theories of bourgeois liberalism. This feminist school can be traced back to the book *In Defense of Women's Rights* by Mary Wollstonecraft in the 18th century. In the 1960s, the book *The Subjection of Women* co-authored by John Stuart Mill, and his wife Harriot Taylor Mill a British feminist in 1869, is a classic of liberal feminism. Representatives of this school were mainly well-known feminists in the United States, like Betty Friedan. Friedan's book *The Feminine Mystique*, which was first published in 1963, is another classic of feminist movements after *The Second Sex* by Simone de Beauvoir. Liberal feminism generally worships the liberal principles of the European Enlightenment Movement and evaluates women's emancipation in line with individual liberties, self-independence, natural rights and emphasizes rationality. It asserts that women are born into rationality and have limitless potentials to develop and improve themselves, just as men do; if equal opportunities are provided, women can also exert their wisdom and talent as men do. The disparity of roles and status between men and women mainly lay in legal and political regulations. This kind of

---

2   Bebel, August: *Women and Socialism*, p. 471. Beijing: Central Compilation and Translation Press.

inequality is unfair. It is necessary for women to organize and struggle for equal political and legal rights to overcome that disparity. Once women obtain equal political and legal rights, they can emancipate themselves on the basis of everyone's joint effort. Liberal feminism was the mainstream thought in the first feminist wave, and has also influenced the second wave to a certain degree. Although socialist feminists have adopted several ideas and practices from liberal feminism, generally they have a critical and oppositional attitude towards it.

Beauvoir's book *The Second Sex* can be regarded as the feminist "Bible", which has made a great influence on feminist movement and established its theoretical base. Socialist feminists were also more or less influenced by this book. In the book, Beauvoir has made a profound analysis on women's living conditions, fiercely attacked the deep oppression over women by the bourgeoisie. She has sharply explored women's actual conditions from women's physiological, psychological, economic and historical aspects, and boldly revealed women's social and life problems. Her sharp comment reading as follows: "one is not born, but rather becomes a woman" has made an unprecedented effect in the feminist movement history. According to Beauvoir, it is the society that produces the difference between men and women, which is the major source for women's subordinate position. If women should strive for freedom and human dignity, it is necessary to eliminate this artificial distinction. The book *The Second Sex* was published in 1949, when the feminist movement faced a decline; in the period between the first and second feminist movements. As a result, this book has become an epitome in theory of the first movement, and offered a theoretical preparation for the second wave. When analyzing the feminist problem, we can see that Beauvoir was apparently inspired by Marxist thoughts and methods. Her critical attitude and perspective based on social history has shed much light on the development of contemporary feminist theories. Her approach includes similar characteristics with socialist feminism, thus we can easily regard Beauvoir as the pioneer of socialist feminism.

Radical Feminism:

Radical feminism is a "current" that has emerged in the second feminist movement at the end of the 1960s. This current has almost co-existed with socialist feminism, and they have largely impacted each other. Representative works of this school were Kate Millett's Sexual Politics and Shulasmith Firestone's *The Dialectic of Sex*. Radical feminists have argued that women constitute a separate class, and this class is under several deep oppressions, among which men's oppression is the most primary one, and it is the basis and core of other oppressions on women. They have strongly rejectwd the liberal feminist view that the source of women's oppression lies in their lack of political and civil rights; neither do they agree with the Marxist feminist view that the source of women's oppression lies mainly in class oppression. They argue that its source is nothing but patriarchy and patriarchy is an institution advocating men's rule over women. This patriarchal system is characterized by power, rule and hierarchy. Patriarchal system has emerged prior to capitalist society and continued to exist and play its role in social history. Radical feminists assert that patriarchy primarily originates from division of labor based on sex. And it is the biological cause that leads to women's oppression and unfortunate fate. Thus, radical feminists suggest that women should reject the "task of giving birth to and bringing up children". They, with the aid of science and technology — artificial reproductive technologies— women should aim to share this "task" to the whole society so as to emancipate women. Some radical feminists go so far as to advocate blurring up sexual distinction, pursue to establish a hermaphrodite culture, advocate sexual separatism, reject heterosexuality and support lesbianism.Since radical feminism has gone to extremes, generally enjoys a minor impact among women. However, its criticism on patriarchy has offered an inspiration on socialist feminism.

Additionally, socialist feminism as well has adopted some thoughts from the trend of "Western Marxism" -Horkheimer, Adorno and Marcuse, and from Gramsci's thoughts on "cultural hegemony".

1.3. DEVELOPMENT STAGES OF SOCIALIST FEMINISM

As a trend of thought, socialist feminism has gone through two stages, which also demonstrate themselves in the form of two theoretical schools, the former as Marxist feminism and the latter as socialist feminism. Though differences in their forms and evolution, they are usually considered as two different schools. They are both influenced by Marxism, employing Marxist terms and its analytical methods when exploring women's problems. In their view, it is necessary to combine feminism with socialism, and seek ways for women's emancipation on the road to socialism. Diachronically, they are in a sequential order. Marxist feminism has emerged in the beginning of the 1970s, while socialist feminism rose in the middle of the 1970s. The former has promoted and has given much enlightenment to the latter, while the latter has absorbed some ideas from the former to some extent and continued its exploration on this basis. Therefore, it is reasonable to study them together as two integrated thoughts.

Members of Marxist feminism are mainly female scholars who believe and study Marxism, and apply Marxist viewpoints to illustrate the feminist problem. Representatives of them are reknown scholars, such as Heidi Hartmann, Lisa Vogel and Lin James. They have openly declared that they regard Marxist theory on women emancipation as the source of their thoughts. They believe Marx and Engels' illustrations on women's social position offer a valuable source and choose to follow the Marxist tradition emphasizing economic and class analysis, especially focusing on women's economic position and interests, and study problems related with women's working conditions. Above all, they apply Marx's method, he used when analyzing the capitalist commodity economy in his work *Capital*. Marxist feminists have also adopted many ideas from Engels' work *Origin of the Family, Private Property and the State* when studying family issues and women problems including studies related to domestic housework carried by women. On the basis of their analyses on housework, they have revealed from another aspect how oppression and restriction occurs in this kind of work and have included this problem in their strategy for women's emancipation.

Socialist Feminism:

Socialist feminists, besides adopting some viewpoints and methods of Marxist feminism, have as well absorbed the patriarchy hypothesis from radical feminism, and have strived to integrate those two sources when interpreting women's conditions and emancipation. Its representatives are mainly those from Britain like Juliet Mitchell, Zillah R. Eisenstein, Ann Ferguson, Nancy Folbor, Barbara Ehrenreich and Alice Jagger. Compared with Marxist feminism, the source of socialist feminism is a little more intricate; and its theoretical orientation vaguer, and does not have a clear linkage with Marxism as the former.

Between the late 1980s and early 1990s, the feminist movement has entered a new stage, and socialist feminism was faced by new changes and developments. In this new period Post-modernism has started to influence feminist thoughts including socialist feminism. It was a dual relationship; on the one hand socialist feminism has gained some similarities with post-modern feminism in some aspects; thus has occurred a tendency of convergence and further alliance between the two. On the other hand, post-modernism has caused a shocking effect in socialist feminism. This was because post-modern feminism negates macro analysis in theory or rejects general concepts, such as "society", "feminism" and "women". Their approach has caused a great confusion and dynamism in the existing feminist movements. Under such a mutual interaction socialist feminism has chosen to develop a new approach. In the 1970s or 1980s, socialist feminists had applied general methods in the analysis of women's social reality but later they have thus started to put more emphasis on researches related to women's self-experiences and emotions in daily life and their rebellion to current reality.

1.4. BASIC FEATURES OF SOCIALIST FEMINISM

First, the majority of socialist feminists are female persons. As a trend based on female thoughts, feminism supports the ideas for women's interests and actively struggle for them. Feminist ideas are easily supported by most females. Therefore, feminism is still a kind of women's self thought and self-movement. Although there are male writers and social activists who advocate gender equality and women's emancipation and contribute to it, some feminists view them as only supporters of the feminist movements, and not regard them as feminists. In fact, the most renowned figures of feminism, including socialist feminism, are female writers, scholars and activists.

Second, socialist feminism is a trend or "current" in reality, and also a feminist movement in reality. Socialist feminism has emerged in the new feminist movement, and turned out to be a theory actively participating in the feminist movement. Most of the renowned members of socialist feminism are female intellectuals making academic researches on women's problems from different aspects, and make an important contribution for the contemporary women's studies. Meanwhile, they are active public figures and activists who advocate and undertake practical positions in the movement, thus women struggle for their own rights. Most of them are in the front ranks of the struggle as leaders. Thus, it is not right to study this trend of thought merely focusing on its theories, but necessary to expand our research into its practices.

Finally, socialist feminism is different from those comparatively homogenous schools. It integrates feminist thoughts with socialist thoughts, and strives to combine various feminist movements and their demands with socialist movement. Socialist feminism bears a duality, it can be regarded as either a kind of feminism or a kind of socialism which receives its theoretical nutrition from different sources and attempts to integrate the analytical methods and achievements of both. Thus, in the illustrations or theories of socialist feminism, we can observe some parts inconsistent with each other. Some put more emphasis on Marxism and socialism, while others highlight feminism. Or it is related with the subject's practice, on certain occasions, and its analyses on a certain problems lean to Marxism, while at other times it is close to feminism.

2. VIEWS OF SOCIALIST FEMINISM

There are various different trends among socialist feminists; for instance, early socialist feminism has paid attention to analyses on political-economy, while late socialist feminism places more stress on non-economic spheres, like ideology and culture; the U.S. feminists rather incline to make macro explorations, while British feminists usually follow Marxist tradition. In spite of these differences, they share commonality and consistency on their basic stand and viewpoints. Generally speaking, socialist feminists have mainly conduct their researches around on problems, we shall demonstrate below.

2.1. WOMEN AND OPPRESSION

2.1.1. WOMEN IN MODERN CAPITALIST SOCIETY

Socialist feminist researchers usually start their studies on women problems from the analysis of women's conditions. They try to offer a diachronic review on women's social status and conditions in history, especially in modern capitalist society.Though women make up half of the humankind, and their role are irreplaceable, the role they play in economy, politics and society is greatly undermined, and were judged as inferior compared to men for a long time in history. Though the development of capitalist new industry and technology provides solid conditions for women's emancipation and women have gained equal legal and political rights through women movements, they have not yet freed themselves from the severe oppression in the capitalist society. Oppressed women masses still exist extensively in capitalist society and this oppression is comprehensive, tangible and intangible prevalent in all walks of social life. In her book *Capitalism, Patriarchy and Job Segregation by Sex*, Heidi Hartmann makes a vigorous demonstration on these problems.

First, women's activity scope in the family is still limited and restricted. Socialist feminists argue that human society is for a long time in the segregation of two spheres: one is social production and public life which are regarded as men's world; the other is family and private life, which are assumed to be under women's mandate. Social public sphere is regarded as vitally important, while the sphere of family and private life is considered as secondary or even marginal. Men and women seem to live in two separate worlds with disparate social positions. Men engage in what is regarded as more important and brilliant by the society, and they not only earn more , but also enjoy higher social reputations, while women merely undertake trivial domestic family labor thus women's activity scope is restricted in a quite narrow range. Women have little opportunity to break away from the familial restrictions and are isolated form a broader social world; neither can they have good chances to undertake important positions related to those social public affairs with higher reputation. Though women can have more access to jobs with the development of market economy, no essential improvement have occurred in the range of their activities, and most of them still remain in the familial sphere, which is considered as their sole or basic activity space. Though some women have gained majority in certain social professions, they are still not free from or cannot give up family labor. As a matter of fact, women still shoulder dual burdens of family labor and social labor.

Second, women are in a subordinate status in the family. In depiction of women's family role, socialist feminists hold the view that men are still masters in the family, who demand or even order women to do the family labor. Returning home after work, men pose themselves as the emperor of the family, expecting that they are bestowed with manly privileges; wives should provide considerate family service for them. Though some husbands also share some family labor at home, they do not regard it as their duty, but as a temporary fad. Even wife herself considers family labor as part of her natural duty. In some families, wives even suffer from their husbands' violence. In Juliet Mitchell's view, there is a fallacy that is popular in the society for a long time: a "genuine woman" and family are symbols of peace and wealth; amidst the atomized and chaotic world, the family life presents a piece of clean indestructible land, where couples love each other and enjoy a safer and a more harmonious life. In fact, women are both sufferers of violence and depression in the family.

Additionally, women lead an alienated life in the family. Alice Jagger suggests employing Marx's alienation concept in the analysis of women's condition under oppression. She has argued that alienation not only occurs in the sphere of laboring as traditional Marxists have asserted; and it falsely seems that the family labor that women undertake does not bear alienation. But actually, observed by Marxist spirit, one can easily find that alienation also emerges in all aspects of women's life. For instance, when analyzing the love life of a woman, just as the worker is aleniated from the product he produces, she as well is alienated from her body. Although usually many women say that their diet, exercise and make-up are all for herself; but in fact, they do them just for men. When a woman trims her eyebrows, dyes her nails and has esthetical plastic surgery, her body becomes an object both to men and her. Additionally, just as workers compete among colleagues for a higher pay, women as well become rivals in pleasing men. Jagger, comments that motherhood also includes an alienated practice for women. This is because number of kids a woman should have is not decided by herself, but by others or the society. Let alone gynecologists' using complex technological means to manipulate women's parturition.Bringing up children as well turns out to be an alienated experience ; mothers work day and night merely to bring up their children following advices of alleged women experts', rather than choosing their own ways.

Finally, even though women have the opportunity to participate in social work, they remain still disadvantageous in labor markets. Socialist feminists have made comprehensive analyses on the conditions of women who participate in social work, and have concluded that though large numbers of women have already entered the ranks of labor force in capitalist society, they still remain at the margin of social economy; their status and conditions are not much better than housewives. This is because there is also discrimination based on gender in labor markets; thus women are just forced to step into a particular segmnet :"female labor market". They mainly join those professions that are viewed to be typically fit for females, like nursing, primary school teacher, and secretary and shop sales assistant. What they usually do is in fact is the extension of their family roles. For instance, to be a primary school teacher actually reflects women's role as caring for children in the family. They are paid less for their work compared to men, and some earn just the half what men earn. Hartmann points out, "in labor markets, men's dominance remains to be a discrimation : labor division based on gender. Woman labor is considered as non-skilled, including no technology, which can use less power in exertion and supervision, thus she should be paid low. [...] Women's inferiority in labor markets also intensifies their subordinate role in the family. In turn, their subordinate role in the family as well reinforces their inferior position in the labor market."[3]

2.1.2. OPRESSION FORMS ON WOMEN

Socialist feminists have not only depicted the status of oppressed women in the capitalist society, but have also made further inquiries to grasp other sources of oppressions.

2.1.2.1. Physiological and Social Oppression

Socialist feminists completely disagree that the source for women's oppression lies in their physical weakness. Mitchell has pointed out, "Most of the classic theories are all based on the supposition that women are too weak to shoulder heavy physical labor, and argue that this is the essential factor that leads to women's subordinate position. But in fact, this supposition is highly insufficient."[4] This is because it ignores the interaction between social oppression and labor division on the basis of physiological power. As a matter of fact, it is not a natural phenomenon, but the consequence of culture and result of social oppression, namely women being restricted in the family. "It is not because of her physical weakness that she is excluded from social production activity, but due to her social

---

3   Li Yinhe (compiler): *Women: Longest Revolution - Selection of Contemporary Western Feminist Theories*, p. 61. Beijing: SDX Joint Publishing Company, 1999.
4   *Ibid.*

inferiority that she is degraded to a slave in the society."[5] Though the laborer's muscle strength has become less important under the new conditions of capitalist machinery production, and modern new science and technology has diminished the role of direct live physical labor; women are not yet emancipated as some had expected.

Socialist feminists as well disagree with the view that women's special physiological structure is the source for oppression. In the view of radical feminists, the reason why women are in subordinate position in the last analysis lies in their physiological structure, because they shoulder the responsibility of having a child, and are sexually different from men. For their emancipation, it is necessary for them to reject bearing children by the help of modern biological techniques, and even eliminate their sexual distinctions. Socialist feminists have criticized the above view arguing that although women undertake different roles in the division of labor compared to men; this does not necessarily mean that women are oppressed because of this very reason. As a matter of fact, women's physiological features cause their subordinate position but only as a part of oppressive social structure and oppresive social relations.

2.1.2.2. Debate on the Sources of Women's Oppression

Influenced by traditional Marxism, nearly all socialist feminists have put emphasis on the analyses of the economic sources for women's oppression, and argued that women's dependence on men in economy is the key factor for their inferior position in the society. However, they do not regard the economic factor as the sole source for women's oppression. Apart from emphasizing economic reasons, feminists have as well analyzed sources of women's oppression from other aspects, like political, cultural, and ideological factors as well as daily social life. Some have focused on the political analysis of private life, like family, revealing power relations in those spheres that result in women's oppression; some have focused on cultural and ideological aspects, and consider traditional patriarchical or capitalist ideology as the key factor leading to women's oppression; others have offered a holistic analysis which combines family relations and relations in social production. Mitchell for example, has put forth the concept of "general social structure" in her discussion on the sources of women's oppression, assuming that women's oppression in the capitalist society is comprehensive. The social oppression includes four aspects: production, having child, sex and children's socialization. Among them, production occurs in the economic sphere outside the family, while the other three, having child, sex and responsibility for children's socialization, are components of family life. To reveal the sources for women's oppression, one should make an in-depth analysis on the family structure, and examine the relationships and relationship modes among those above three components in

---

5   *Ibid.*

the family structure, apart from researching oppression occurring in the social production sphere.

2.1.2.3 Labor in the Family and Reproduction Labor

Park Quick was the first to raise the proposition: "reproduction of labor force is the source for women's oppression." She has argued that in the reproduction of labor force, namely, in the period of women's reproduction, like pregnancy, child-bearing, lactation and later fosterage, the labor division based on gender intensifies women's oppression and discrimination. In the view of some feminists like Vogel, the material foundation of women's oppression lies in social reproduction; it is the very reason that women are oppressed in the class society. The physiological role women play in giving birth to a child results as their dependence on men in economic sphere, which cause the division of labor in the familial sphere and also the discrimination in the sphere of social labor.

Employing the basic theories and methods Marx had applied in his work Capital, socialist feminists have made an analysis on the reproduction of labor force in capitalist society. They have studied the conditions and function of family labor as part of the capitalist production mode in order to reveal the economic reasons for women's oppression. They have concluded that the value of women's reproduction is not properly acknowledged and appreciated in the capitalist society.

In their views, under the conditions of capitalism it is necessary to divide social life into two halves: "public sphere" and "private sphere"; since it is necessary for the labor force to go through the process of childbearing, fosterage and socialization. However, these processes still cannot be effectively and completely realized in the public sphere, but in the family. Meanwhile, the process of basic labor is as well divided into non-related two halves: industrial labor and family labor. Properties of these two are fundamentally different. Family labor reproduces the labor forces for the labor market, while industrial labor produces commodities and services for commodity markets. This difference between the two labor processes lead to a division in labor forces which is generally based on gender. Women undertake the labor process in the familial sphere, while men lead industrial labor. Labor process in the latter is capitalist production, while the former belongs to labor force reproduction. Women's labor in the familial sphere plays a vitally important role in the reproduction of capitalist labor force.

In their view, the family labor of housewives' which reproduces labor force is as well a kind of labor which creates value. Commodities, like houses, food and clothing, which are exchanged against industrial labor wages, do not directly affect the process of reproduction of labor force (familial labor) and cannot directly reproduce labor forces. Thus another kind of labor, namely family labor is necessary to reproduce labor forces. When a housewife directly uses wages to buy commodities, their familial labor becomes part of the universal necessary labor in the society (the term was also studied by Marx in Capital). And when the labor force is exchanged as a commodity in the labor market, the value it creates is realized. However, in real life appearance, wages appear as the pay against the labor that is solely completed in the industrial labor process. As a matter of fact, in reality wages are not paid solely against that industrial labor, but for the labor that reproduces all the labor force in capitalist society. The reason why this illusive phenomenon occurs lies in that industrial workers appear as independent agents directly dealing with the capitalist employer, while familial labor which reproduce the whole labor force in the society is hidden behind the curtain. Socialist feminists hold the view that Marx had indeed revealed the deceiving secret of labor wages, but had ignored another aspect of its secret; namelyhe had neglected housewives' contribution to the whole process of capitalist production. In capitalism, housewives' labor is excluded from those deals occurring in the labor market between laborers and capitalists, and is completely ignored. Their labor is not considered as genuine labor which produces value. The labor of housewives is concealed, and she cannot prove her existence through wages. Therefore, she has no ways to demonstrate her labor and herself. Consequently, she utterly relies on her husband materially who provides her necessary money for living, and loses her independence.

2.1.2.4. Combination of Capitalism with Patriarchy

Marxists argue that the source reason for women's oppression lies in capitalism, while radical feminists think that it lies in the patriarchy. Taking the two sides into consideration, socialist feminists hold the view that the source reason for women's oppression does neither lie in capitalism nor in the patriarchy alone, but in the combination of the two. As for such "combination", socialist feminists generally hold two different views. One regards capitalism and the patriarchy are in a correlative relation, and argue that combination of the two factors result in women's intensified oppression. This view is known as the "binary theory". The other approach holds that capitalism and patriarchy are integrated in a unity of one, and form the "capitalist patriarchy" or "patriarchal capitalism". This view is called "unitary theory".

Binary Approach:

Socialist feminists who advocate "binary theory" hold the view that patriarchy and capitalism as two different systems embody different forms of social relations and interest patterns. They coexist in modern capitalist society, and play their respective roles. Patriarchy has emerged in the very early history, and continues to exist and exerts its influence in capitalist society. It is the overlapping effect of capitalism and patriarchy that intensifies women's oppression. Socialist

feminists with this view advocate that it is necessary to treat patriarchy and capitalism as distinctive and correlative phenomena in the analysis of the source
reason for women's oppression. Heidi Hartmann and Juliet Mitchell insist on this
binary assumption. In fact, they regard the patriarchy and capitalism as systems
that function in two different spheres: patriarchy exists in the family and plays
its role there, while capitalism functions outside the family and exerts its impact
therein. Concretely speaking, in the family, occurs the sexual oppression, namely,
male oppressing female; while in the social sphere outside the family, particularly
in the economic sphere, occurs the class oppression, namely capitalist oppression and exploitation over laborers. By this differentiation they offer a unique
approach and analysis on the patriarchy and its relation with capitalism. Heidi
Hartmann views patriarchy as a structure in social relations system which has a
certain material base, arguing that patriarchy is materially based on men's control
over women's labor force. Men limit women's economic sources and control their
reproduction. Men's control over women's labor capability or capacity varies in
different social formations and at the different stages of human society. In the capitalist society, their control is exerted in the specific social institution like monogamy. In this institution, women are responsible for childbearing, bringing them
up and undertaking housework, which results in their economic dependence on
men. Different from Heidi Hartmann, Juliet Mitchell evaluates patriarchy mainly from two aspects as women's bio-sociology and ideological criticism. In her
opinion, in some aspects family life is undoubtedly the result of changes in the
economic base of the social formation and production mode. However, family
is as well the outcome of women's bio-sociological concept and social ideology
(particularly concept of sex in the society). No matter in which direction the
production mode changes, bio-social perspective of the family and sex concept
will remain unchanged. Thus, Mitchell puts more emphasis on the ideological criticism of the current family concept, assuming that incomplete family awareness
is an important reason for women's being tamed. She suggests employing Freud's
psychological analysis when studying the issue of male-female relationship and
the ideologies related to this relationship. As it is, Mitchell's view on patriarchy
focuses on ideology, which transcends or by-passes history and time, and is not
affected due to the changes in the production mode.

The Unitary Approach:

Lisa Vogel and Alice Young advocate the "unitary" theory. They oppose evaluating capitalism and patriarchy as two different things, but suggest to view them as
an integrated unity of "capitalist patriarchy" or "patriarchal capitalism". In their
view, capitalism and patriarchy are inseparably integrated. This concept in essence
is non- "class" approach because for them "class" is a concept which could discard sex differences, but "labor division based on gender" reflects the truth much
better. In the view of Alice Young, the analysis method based on labor division

is better than that of class to explain why women usually are obedient and undertake dull jobs with lower pay, while men give orders and undertake more lucrative jobs with higher rewards.

In their eyes, there is a close correlation between patriarchy and capitalism. In order to keep their traditional patriarchal privilege and maintain their position as males who "shoulder the existence of the family" financially, men also join hands to protect their interests and support the status which restricts women's employment. Consequently, labor division based on gender difference and restrictions on women's employment guarantee women's economic dependence on men, and force them to opt for housework as their career. Meanwhile, capitalism benefits from this arrangement in which women undertake housework because this is an efficient scheme for the reproduction of labor force. The "bargains" between capitalism and men mainly include how to divide the time between two parties, but those two finally agree to keep women laboring at home for capitalist reproduction of labor force; women are forced to serve men,doing housework and bringing up children; in return, capitalist rulers offer men the privilege to enter into the social production sphere. Capitalism and patriarchy support and fit best to promote each other. Therefore, they have argued that women's subordinate position neither can be simply viewed as the outcome of capitalism, nor can it be separated from the capitalist system.

2.1.2.5. Ideological Aspects of Women's Oppression

In the view of socialist feminists, the combination of patriarchal ideology and the capitalist ideology has existed for a long historical period, and has turned out to be a mighty power. It pervasively penetrates all walks of social life, people's mind and spirit, to maintain men's rule over women in the society. This combined ideology supports the current status in which women are oppressed, and provides some "rational evidence" for gender inequality. In this combined ideology, the concept propagated as "woman's temperament" is an important item. As division of roles between men and women; people have always considered men should possess "male temperament", while women "female temperament". This is the Godly truth. In the view of socialist feminists, men and women are not born into alleged "male temperament" and "female temperament", but acquire them later. Children are cultivated in the society with "male temperament" and "female temperament; boys are taught to be independent, brave, persistent and successful, while girls are told to be gentle, quiet and obedient. This ideology pervades the whole society, and is universally accepted. Not only males hold such a view, but also females themselves are deeply influenced by it. It is such an education as "female temperament" and ideological influence that counteracts women's ambitions and independence, weakens their self-awareness, and makes them unconsciously appendages of men.

Aleniated consumption by women

Additionally, the dominant ideology in the capitalist society also fully misleads women's consumption; that is to say, it actually indoctrinates women with the notion of alienated consumption. The culture humiliating and discriminating against women pervades in the commodity consumption, and misleads women by all kinds of means. Commodities, such as costumes, shoes and stockings to hairstyle and cosmetics, are designed with no exception to orient women as a sexual object and target. Advertisements are full of exaggerated marketing tricks promoting luxury commodities, and seduce women to follow the current fashion. With "ideal woman" and "ideal family", ideology capitalists lure a large mass of women to seek unnecessary consumption. This kind of consumption is not only a direct economic exploitation but also a measure to oppress women from awakening.

2.1.3. WOMEN'S EMANCIPATION AND ECONOMIC EMANCIPATION

Women's emancipation as advocated by socialist feminists includes many aspects, rather than just few aims. Women in the first wave feminist movement have mainly strived for political emancipation; they have struggled for and won political rights, like universal suffrage and other advantages. Then, in the second wave of feminist movement, feminists, especially socialist feminists have realized that women's emancipation is not merely having political rights, but an overall comprehensive liberation, including economic emancipation.

Four aspects of women's emancipation

Mitchell has focused her studies on the holistic nature of women's emancipation highlighting its four aspects. In her eyes, women's oppression is caused by four factors:in the spheres of production, childbearing, sex and children's socialization. These four factors (structures) are closely related and jointly determine women's status and plight. "If one of the structures changes, another will be strengthened and counteract to that the effect, but what only will change is the form of oppression or exploitation."[6] Thus, "ultimate solution can only be found by a strategy targeting all the structures that impact oppression and exploitation of women."[7] "It is necessary to do the revolutionary struggle based on the analysis of those structures; and these structures develop in an unbalanced pattern, we should attack the weakest structure in that combination. Only in this way, can this integrated system can be fundamentally destructed and we can accomplish a real great transformation in women's conditions."[8] Mitchell believes that sex is

6 Li Yinhe (compiler): *Women: Longest Revolution - Selection of Contemporary Western Feminist Theories*, p. 31. Beijing: SDX Joint Publishing Company, 1999.
7 *Ibid.*
8 *Ibid.*

the most vulnerable and the weakest link in the chain of those four structures, and is the key to solve other the contradictions; it is necessary to focus our attack against this structure. However, problems cannot be completely settled when we merely focus the struggle against the sex structure. As a matter of fact, if the revolution goes too far in this aspect of sex sphere , it may also cause several negative results too.

Women's overall and comprehensive emancipation includes such aspects as economic, political and ideological emancipation. In the economic emancipation, women should liberate from their dependence on men, and women working in the factory and family should be freed from overt or covert exploitation and be economically independent. In terms of political emancipation, women should not only obtain equal legal political rights as men and strive for the realization of those rights in practice, but apart from socio-political sphere, the struggle for emancipation should cover the private spheres, like family, which is under the control of patriarchy. As for the ideological emancipation, women should transcend patriarchy in their minds which had restricted and dominated their awareness for a long time in history, women should be confident of their self-capability and powers, and develop their consciousness for self-esteem, self-confidence and self-reliance.

In women's overall emancipation, economic emancipation bears a special significance. Mitchell acknowledges that economic structure is ultimately determinative in the integrated societal structure. Thus, any emancipation movement, including women's emancipation movement, should focus on the economic aspect. Women's economic emancipation concept proposed by socialist feminists is generally linked with women's economic independence from men. They offer several approaches to realize this aim. I can summarize them as follows.

1. Women in labor force market: In the view of Marxists, it is an important aim for women to break away from the familial restrictions and participate in social production for their emancipation. Some socialist feminists have inherited this view of Marxism, -the advocacy of women entering labor markets and participating social production-.By the development of capitalism, demand for woman labor force increases, and women start to enter labor market one after the other. Women's access to employment rights becomes an important aspect and a symbol in their struggle for emancipation. Women's access to employment indeed raises their position to some extent: on the one hand, some professions bring them an independent income, thus economically they no more completely depend on their husbands as before; hence the their position in the family rise; on the other hand, their participation in social work as well opens them a new horizon, and enables them to think beyond the traditional family affairs. However, some socialist feminists have argued that women are not really emancipated by participating in social

production because women are still remain in a disadvantageous position in the labor markets, and they are paid unequally compared with men.

2. Housework should be paid: Some socialist feminists propose that housework should be paid as wages. Housework itself is an indispensable part of social labor, and it is impossible to exclude this labor from social production. There is no distinction in regard to their relative importance; housework and the labor outside the family are both vital. Solution to this problem does not lie in whether women should give up housework and participate in social labor; it means their struggle should aim gaining payment solution for their housework and make people acknowledge the value of housework.

Dalla Kosta and Selma James, British socialist feminists, advocate that women's housework should be paid, public should adequately understand the difference between house labor and wage labor and support those women who struggle for housework pay. In their view, women should not be paid by individual men (husbands, fathers or boyfriends) but by capitalists.This is because women's housework, as it is the process of reproduction of labor force, does not benefit (men) their husbands, but capitalists who own all the production means used in social production. If capitalists do not pay them, the state should. This is because in the final analysis, the capitalist state benefits from women's housework. When calculating the pay for housework, equal criteria should be used with the labor outside the family; it is not right to view the housework as cheap labor and pay it symbolically. Some feminists have evaluated and developed standards to calculate the labor in the family, some calculations have shown that housework of a woman with two children equals to nearly ten thousand pounds a year in 2003. As the first step the pay for housework should not necesarrily take the form of monetary wages; it could also be paid as welfare allowances or as other services for example overburdened mothers could be offered free childcare. Socialist feminists also insist that women should have the right to "strike" and stop the reproduction of labor force, and the struggle methods they could employ could be divorcing, contraception and abortion if the state refuses to pay them.

There are also some socialist feminists who question the feasibility of the struggle for housework pay. They have argued that this struggle could legitimate women work in the family; and as a result, women will continue to remain at home, isolated from the outside world, their opportunities for other better jobs will decrease and this will consequently damage their struggle against labor division based sex in labor markets.

3. Housework should be socialized. In the view of Margaret Benston, British socialist feminist, the socialization of housework is a much more effective approach for women emancipation than women's participation in social work. Socialization

of housework should precede women's participation in social affairs. She also admits that socialization of housework will mean that women will continue to undertake the housework they are already engaged in. However, even so, this could offer a kind of progress forward. The struggle may not free women completely from this kind of familial labor, but its significance lies in that everyone in the society will grasp the vital contribution of this kind of labor for the society. Once people see how hard and important the housework is, they will not undermine women's labor in the family. Vogel points out "a main solution to alleviate housework is to socialize family affairs. For instance, it is possible to transfer such kinds of housework related with clothing and home textile care or dining or preparation and storage of food, to social production sphere, and those kind of services can also provide new businesses for capitalist enterprises. Public education and healthcare services can be expanded to include those functions which today are part of the housework and housework related to these works could be reduced and state can take the lead in this step. As another step the cost of labor for reproduction assumed by mothers can be widely shared by the members of the whole society through a taxing system[9].

2.1.4. STRUGGLES AGAINST CAPITALISM AND PATRIARCHY

Socialist feminists hold that the society is actually divided into two halves: inside the family and outside it; thus, women's struggle as well falls into these two spheres accordingly. Struggle in these two spheres have different features and requirements. Women's activity is mainly limited in the familial sphere; as a result, the family is the major battlefield for the self-emancipation of women.

Struggle in the family should be realized by each woman individually against patriarchy. In their co-authored book, *Contemporary Marxist Theory and Practice: A Feminist Critique*, Heidi Hartmann and Ann Markusen, have written; "women are in isolation, this is the same in their struggle against patriarchy, it is necessary for them to apply strategies different from those strategies employed against capitalists. The essential feature of this strategy is that each woman should fight against their men who command the patriarchal rule in the house; the struggle should take one-to-one form. Just as Gilman Grille has once mentioned, "all over the country, a revolution is taking place in the bedroom"[10] Women's struggle against patriarchy should mainly aim to take the control of the production means that are necessary for population reproduction, it is just similar to workers' struggle which aims to take the control of the production means. "Inside the family, the woman should strive for the right of abortion and contraception, and fight

---

9   Vogel, Lise: *Marxism and the Oppression of Women: Toward a unitary theory, Rutgers* University Press. New Brunswick. New Jersey, 1983, p. 74-75.
10   China Women Publishing House: *Anthology of Feminist Movements Abroad.* p. 28. Beijing: China Women Publishing House, 1998.

against her husband's will; in the sphere of local neighborhood communities, they should strive to transform community healthcare centers and control their operation aims thus oppose and change the medical healthcare system which operates under the rule of patriarchal institutions."[11]

Socialist feminists have also argued that it is necessary for women to establish a common strategy though it is necessary to fight individually against patriarchy in the family. Patriarchy has linkages and is part of the whole social system and its superstructure; thus, it is impossible for women to win the struggle against it separately without forming a common broad strategy. The goals of the common strategy should not be isolated from each other, but they should be properly combined. For instance, when a wife slaps her husband, it is possible for the husband to set up a new family with another woman to maintain his privilege, which equals to "firing" a worker and "hiring" another. This possibility could hinder the success of individual struggles in the family. In such a case, women will need other women to help, just as workers striking in a factory need to get the support of those in other factories.

The housewives' struggle needs support and help from women's groups and organizations. "The main style in women's political organizations should be different from that of workers. The tenet of women's political organizations is supposed to form and guide a strategy with consensus, give support to those women who are struggling in the family, and oppose both non-governmental and state departments with the aim of isolating and weakening patriarchy."[12]

Struggles against Capitalism outside the Family

Socialist feminists hold the view that the factory and state should only be secondary battlefields where women fight, but they should also pay attention to the whole battlefield in the society and engage in political struggles. Women should struggle in three spheres: economic, political and cultural.

As for the economic struggle, they should mainly strive for equal rights in economy. For instance, they fight for the equal pay for the same work as men do, and for maternity leave and flexible working hours before and after the maternity leave in the workplaces. And they also fight against discrimination in the labor markets. Socialist feminists fight for equal access in the actual realization of right of work to avoid discrimination and strive to break down the system of wage bracket. Women are treated as a second-class labor force after they enter the labor markets. Even if they are employed by a job that demands the same qualifications

11 Ibid.
12 China Women Publishing House: *Anthology of Feminist Movements Abroad.* p. 29. Beijing: China Women Publishing House, 1998.

in techniques and responsibilities required from men, mostly they only get the half pay compared with male workers. Advocates of this wage system claim that the market determines who will earn higher pay or the reverse according to their value contribution. Socialist feminists retort to this view, and argue that it is hard to observe whether the market really determines higher pay to those who contribute more. Additionally, no one can measure if the work one performs embodies more value than another work made by another individual. Furthermore, even if the work women perform embodies less value from the work men do, it should not hinder women from earning a decent pay, just because of this. This is because women cannot live a decent life without a decent pay. For socialist feminists, the movement against wage bracket system and its elimination in fact targets capitalism because this wage bracket system is a feature of capitalism.

As to political struggles, they both aim social reforms and lead some radical revolutionary attitudes and activities. Some socialist feminists are rather strive for social reforms, such as wage increases, more social benefits, bestowing childbirth liberty and free abortion, and advocate legal and ethical demands related to same sex marriages. Some socialist feminists rather choose to participate in the broader movement of working class, and also criticize male workers' androcentrism in labour unions. Some groups lead women to demonstrate their critics in their daily life, namely they support micro political movements in a localized pattern. They usually organize women in a struggle community/troop to take part in these micro movements, and struggle is generally restricted by the individual fighting capacity of that community organization. Some socialist feminists sharply oppose to those who pool women struggles to social reformist aims, and advocate radical changes. Mitchell points out "Contemporary left reformists prefer the mildest attitude in their criticism, such mild which is far behind compared with the level of development of women's movement and demands; as a result, there is no progressive content in it."[13] Based on such a viewpoint, these socialist feminists advocate more active and deeper political struggles, and advocate both rigid organizational forms and also struggles without any organization. The struggle within the family needs no organization, but it is necessary to have a rigid and efficient organization to mobilize and lead women to fight against the capitalist system and its state machinery, and here specialized type of organizations are anecessary. They propose to set up a united revolutionary women front and establish a broader alliance with other oppressed groups, organizations and even political parties. Women's emancipation cannot be realized unless they organize and ally with organizations of other oppressed classes and stratums. Of course, women's organizations should be different from trade unions or political parties, and so it is with their movements. As a matter of fact, most women organizations are usually restricted, which foster communication among women or promote friendly

---

13   Li Yinhe (compiler). *Women: Longest Revolution - Selection of Contemporary Western Feminist Theories*, p. 3 Beijing: SDX Joint Publishing Company, 1998.

ties among them, transmit and share information on women's movement and exchange new ideas and viewpoints. Thus their current activities are far behind from being so revolutionary.

As for cultural struggles, socialist feminists strive to criticize capitalist and patriarchal ideologies. In their view, women's political and economic emancipation are external, while their ideological emancipation is an internal and a more profound aim. This involves an in-depth ideological reform, which is a more difficult task. They insist on criticizing capitalist culture, the deep rooted old cultural concepts which humiliates and undermine women as the second-class sex, prevalent since old times, and against the concept of alienated consumption that confuses and destructs women's awareness. They advocate and strive to lead a critical daily life; and emphasize to sublate or correct current old concepts on equality, liberty, solidarity and political responsibility with socialist feminist values. They promote and support those women working in the spheres of culture and education to write books and their ideas which criticize capitalist culture and advocate women's values.

3. EVALUATION OF SOCIALIST FEMINISM

As a left trend of thought in the contemporary society, socialist feminism plays an important role in the struggle for women's emancipation and struggle against capitalism. Its theoretical exploration adds considerably both to the scientific analysis of woman issues and to the application of Marxism to women's emancipation practice.

3.1. ITS SOCIAL PROPERTEIS AND EFFECTS

Socialist feminism has emerged in the movements which struggle for a new society. These movements are left-wing social movements launched by the petty bourgeoisie and masses of lower strata who oppose the capitalist system. Among the movements for a new society, the new feminist movement has kept a certain distance from the traditional left organizations and "New Left", and has openly criticized the male chauvinism in these organizations. However, it still shares a similar political stance with other left wing movements, but behaves slightly more radical compared to them. New feminist movement of the left-wing is the outcome of combining socialist thoughts with feminism, and bears strong features of socialism; this is particularly true for socialist feminism.

Socialist feminists have to a certain degree enriched and also expanded the influence sphere of Marxism, and exerts an extensive influence in those movements seeking for a new society; this includes the new feminist movement in the left wing. A number of radical intellectuals and young students enthusiastically keep seeking ideological inspiration and theoretical support from Marxism. It is also in such a background that some pioneers of female intellectuals have accepted the Marxist analytical method, and employed it in the analysis of women's issues. Leaving aside whether they actually grasp the essence of Marxism or their ides are in line with Marxist spirit, we can easily say that they expand the Marxist influence among the contemporary progressive trend of thoughts.

Socialist feminists play an active role in revealing and fighting against capitalism. They, from numerous aspects disclose women's oppressed conditions that exist universally in capitalist countries. They demonstrate the realistic fact that capitalists do not only exploit the surplus value created by the workers, but also exploit the labor of housewives without compensation for reproduction of labor force. Consequently, the socialist feminists have drawn the conclusion that the important source of women's oppression lies in the capitalist exploitation. Socialist feminists as well demonstrate the role, the dominant ideology in capitalist society plays in controlling and oppressing women. Among various trends of thoughts in the developed countries, socialist feminism is prominent in politics, and features a relatively strong mass and militant character, and the role it plays in women's emancipation is unique compared to other schools.

Socialist feminism combines both the struggle for women's emancipation and for a socialist future. In its historical development, it was inevitable for feminism to combine with socialism. Socialism aims the emancipation of proletariat and that of the whole humankind, including women's emancipation. Beginning from its inception, the socialist movement, including women's emancipation movement, has ceaselessly explored approaches to women's emancipation in its development process. The new feminist movement with its left leaning orientation is greatly associated with the socialist movement. In their view, "Marxism is remarkably consistent with feminism in both concept and aims. This provides a strong possibility and opportunity to establish an alliance between the new feminist movement and the left movement". Sheila Benhabib, a socialist feminist, has once commented; "feminist movement presents some brand new approaches to re-launch a powerful socialist movement participated by masses", I think this reflects the right direction of the feminist development.

Of course, socialist feminists pay great efforts in their attempt to integrate feminism with socialism. However, observing their theoretical basis and practice, they actually fail to realize it. They still remain vague about the socialist aim and in their approaches on socialism.

3.2. EVALUATION OF SOCIALIST FEMINIST THEORIES

Inspired by Marxism, socialist feminists apply Marxism in the analysis women issues. Mitchell has underlined that it is necessary to analyze women emancipation issues with the approach of scientific socialism, and she has also employed this approach in her researches. It is true that socialist feminism inspired by Marxism offers more reasonable solutions on the women issues and brings more profound and systematic ideas on the problems of women's emancipation. By a general comparison we can see that they have broader social vision, and give due emphasis on the economic aspect when analyzing problems, also develop specific views on various women issues and have a deeper understanding on the effect of ideology. Feminists of other schools when criticizing the current family only offer a general approach; however, socialist feminists hold the view that this "general family", actually refers to the white families of middle class -mainstream bourgeoisie family – namely those white families that are comparatively well-off, bi-parental and heterosexual. It is improper to restrict critical studies on such families; but it is necessary to take into account the class differences, races and nationalities. For instance, in the working class and in most black families mothers do not feel that they have become housewives under oppression; on the contrary, mothers who work two shifts to earn a living, realistically long to be housewives -an unattainable dream for them-. However, for black women, it is more urgent to overcome racial discrimination than sexual segregation. For unmarried or divorced women, it is more urgent for them to alleviate poverty or lack of free time than overcoming labor division based on gender. Additionally, families formed by homosexuals have similar different problems. Some socialist feminists have also fairly questioned the concept of "female temperament". For example, Greens as one of them has argued that the concept of "female temperament" is absolutely inapplicable for women belonging to certain ethnic people. "They first orient themselves towards social production, and their familial role is certainly secondary. The fact is that in most cases men-and-women relations in black families are cooperative rather than being contradictory, which may be regarded as guarding against social, political and ideological oppressions.

The active theoretical exploration by socialist feminists provides Marxists a positive enlightenment. This trend of thought explores women's oppressed status in modern times and the new problems they face. Their studies cover women's oppression from the perspectives of economy, politics, history, culture and physiology, practical strategies for women's emancipation, and in-depth analysis on certain woman issues. For instance, they apply Marxist theories on production and reproduction in the analysis of housewives' roles, which offer a mechanism to capitalists for the reproduction of new labor forces at the lowest cost and housewives also offer them cheap flexible labor force as reserve. Socialist feminists argue that this mechanism works on the basis that women rely on men's wages for their living, and this causes their dependence on men. As it is, this is a creative exploration to push forward Marxist theories. They lay emphasis on the study of culture and ideology, regard ideology as the important reason for women's oppression, and advocate fighting against that "invisible enslavement", which is also a creative and important idea.

However, socialist feminists have several grave problems in dealing with Marxism and when combining Marxism and feminism. As to treating Marxism, feminists quote Marxist phrases out of their context to serve their purposes. Some just borrow Marxist terms to decorate feminism, while some reverse Marxist research approach; others even go so far as to openly criticize Marxism, especially the Marxist views on women. They pay painstaking "efforts" to supplement and rectify socialist theories with feminism. Lisa Vogel has also commented on this point: "Generally speaking, in the view of socialist feminists, it is necessary to widen or completely change socialist theories with the insight provided by feminism in theory and practice."[14] In Alice Young's opinion, socialist feminism is featured as a "marriage" between the essence of feminist fashion trends of thoughts developed between 1960s and 1970s and Marxist theories which aims to rebuild it."[15] On one hand, socialist feminists attempt to deepen feminism with Marxist theories to analyze specific forms of women's oppression; on the other hand, they borrow a series of theories on patriarchy from radical feminists in analyzing these problems, in order to "supplement" and even leaving aside Marxist approach. Thus several conclusions in their studies on patriarchy are unsystematic and insufficient in many basic aspects which cannot clearly illustrate the basic characteristics of patriarchy in the capitalist society. They really cannot organically integrate these two theoretical systems-Marxism and feminism— and combine them in their researches. Just as remarked by a representative socialist feminist, contemporary socialist feminism is "combination of traditional Marxism with neo-feminism, combines class differences with gender/sex differences, production with reproduction, and the public with the kingdom, which is its duality."[16]

---

14   Vogel, Lise: *Marxism and Women's Oppression*, p. 13.

15   Young, Alice: *Transcending Unhappy Marriage: Criticism of Binary System*, p. 85. Boston: Southern Press, 1981.

16   China Women Publishing House (compilation): *Anthology of Feminist Movements Abroad.* p. 14-15. Beijing: China Women Publishing House, 1998.

REFERENCES

• China Women Publishing House (compilation): *Anthology of Feminist Movements Abroad.* p. 29. Beijing: China Women Publishing House, 2004.

• Alison Giger: *Political and Human Nature of Feminism.* New Jersey: Rowman & Littlefield Publishing Group, 1988.

• Yu Keping: *"Socialism" in the Era of Globalization.* Beijing: Central Compilation and Translation Press, 1998.

• Lise Vogel: *Marxism and the Oppression of Women:* Toward a Unitary Theory, Rutgers University Press. New Brunswick. New Jersey,1983.

• Xiao Wei: *Ethics of Feminist Concern.* Beijing: Beijing Publishing House, 1999.

• Wang Wei, Pang Junjing: *Western Marxist Thoughts in the 20th Century.* Beijing: Capital Normal University Press, 1999.

• Zhang Xiaoling: *Women and Human Rights.* Beijing: Xinhua Publishing House, 1998.

• Li Yinhe (compilation): *Women: Longest Revolution - Selection of Contemporary Western Feminist Theories.* Beijing: SDX Joint Publishing Company, 1999.

CHAPTER VIII

MODERNITY, POST-MODERNITY AND MARXISM

1. MODERN AND MODERNITY

"Modern" is a quite familiar term to people, but perhaps many people cannot tell correctly what on earth "modern" is. Then, what is "modern"? Some scholars think "modern" is an ancient concept and it has first appeared in the late fifth century as "modernus" (modern) in Latin language[1]. Some other scholars assert that the term "modern" had first appeared in late 16th century. In that time, "modern" and "contemporary" were synonymous and both referred to the period of departure from middle and ancient ages. In the 18th century Jane Austen had defined "modern" as a state of change, perhaps a state of improvement". People in the same era with Austen had used "modernization", "modernism" and "modernist school" to mean updating and improvement. By mid 19th century, the term "modern" rather implied promotion and progress. For example, Ruskin's *Modern Painters* published in 1846 demonstrated a modern style which was faithful to the nature and different from tradition. However, for a very long period, people have always regarded the term "modern" linked to the past which forms a contrast with the term "contemporary" which denotes the present[2].

Some scholars consider the Age of Enlightenment in Europe in the 18th century as the start of "modern". Naturally, they also consider the first industrial revolution of capitalism (1750-1830) as the start of "modern age". In 1750, British James Watt had invented spinning machine. In 1751, the "Encyclopedia" written by French Diderot et al. was published. This means it was time for bourgeoisie

1   Yao Dazhi: Post-modern–Western Philosophy in Late 20th Century, Beijing, Orient Press, 2000, p. 456.
2   Raymond Williams: The Politics of Modernism: Against the New Conformists, Translator Yan Jia, Beijing, Commercial Press, 2002, p. 48.

to climb to the historical arena. By then, capitalist "modernism" started in a real sense. This stage has lasted till 1973 when American Scholar Daniel Bell published *The Coming of Post-Industrial Society*. Of course, if we choose a tool as a symbol for post-industrial society, it can well be the first electronic computer invented by American scientist Wiener in 1946.

"Modernity" and "modern" have very close links. "Modern" only has the boundary of time, indicating the "era" we are in, while "modernity" not only indicates the boundaries of an era but also indicates its characteristics, styles and common characteristics of this era. Famous German scholar Habermas has suggested that modernity, once established, certainly breaks the restrictions of all outdated and obsolete norms. Therefore, as a kind of aesthetic consciousness, "modernity" expresses the rebellious experience against all normative things, but the establishment of "modernity" will certainly erect new norms and form its own new tradition, thus contradict with new "modernity"[3]. French scholar Lyotard defines "modernity" as a way of thinking, a way of expression and a way of feeling[4]. American scholar Jameson has proposed that "modernity" has four maxims:

Maxim 1: We cannot periodize modernity.

Maxim 2: Modernity is not a concept, a philosophy or similar, but a narrative category.

Maxim 3: The narration of modernity cannot be based around categories of subjectivity; because consciousness and subjectivity are non-representable; what we can narrate are only the multiple situations of modernity.

Maxim 4: No theory of modernity makes sense today unless it comes to terms with the hypothesis of a postmodern break with the modern[5].

Jameson's understanding on "modernity" is a post-modernist' approach to modernity, because he also considers "modernity" as a "narrative category" (consciousness and subjectivity are non-representable) and he points to the "rupture" between "postmodern" and "modern".

Related to "modern" and "modernity", there is another concept as "modernization" which implies generalization and further deepening of modernity. "Modernization" is an effort to make everything around us meet the requirements

---

3   Jürgen Habermas: Modernity versus Post-modernity, please refer to New German Critique, New York, Winter Publishing House, 1981, p. 2-5.
4   Jean-Francois Lyotard: Universal History and Cultural Differences, please refer to The Lyotard Reader, London and Cambridge, Andrew Benjamin Press, 1989, p. 314.
5   Frederic Jameson: Modernity, Post-modernity and Globalization, Beijing, China Renmin University Press, 2004, p. 74-75.

and needs of the "modern", discard all obsolete and backward things and universally achieve every condition required by "modern". For example, in China we often say we should achieve the modernization of the "three spheres": material production, spiritual production and human re-production. In China this includes realizing "four modernizations" in material production sphere; realizing ideological and cultural progress in the spiritual sphere; and realizing good pre-natal and post-natal care and family planning in human re-production. Naturally these are all new things. "Modernization" is a quite complex and a dynamic process. The depth and width of "modernization" reflect the civilization and development degree of a society. "Modernization" itself is closely related to social system. Generally speaking, a backward and conservative social system will certainly fetter or weaken the development process of "modernization", while a progressive and an advanced social system will certainly promote and develop "modernization". Of course, some backward and conservative or even reactionary societies may also be forced to push on "modernization" when they are faced by a crisis of survival, but in the final analysis, it will be a limited "modernization".

Another concept in relation to "modern", "modernity" and "modernization" is "modernism". "Modernism" generally means to appreciate or respect "modernity", promote "modernization" and advocate a "modern" spirit/approach. American scholar Michael Bell has suggested that the period from the last decade of the 19th century to before the Second World War (1890-1939) was a period of strong modernism. The prime era of modernism in the USA and UK was from 1910 to 1925, and its knowledge structure has compromised with the ideological lines of Marx, Freud and Nietzsche. These three ideological "giants" have fundamentally transformed the meaning of human life. Marx has analyzed the external kingdom of social and economic processes, and disclosed the "false consciousness" supported by the dominant class. Freud has explored the internal kingdom of human soul, demonstrated how consciousness becomes a complex obstacle through sublimation and blocks the cognition of the real essence of instinctive desires. Nietzsche has diagnosed the entire metaphysical tradition in the West since Socrates as an obscure form of falsehood which reflects the internal depression and external control.

After the Second World War, modernism seems to "decline" and it was gradually superseded by "post-modernism". Post-modernism has violently criticized modernism and thoroughly negated it. I can say that this cannot be the attitude of historical materialism but rather historical nihilism. Realistically observing, mankind has indeed made great achievements in the era of modernism, which should not be denied easily. In the Age of Enlightenment in the 18th century, the great curtain of "modern" was opened. For the enlightenment thinkers, modernity was a great and glory cause. They have propelled science and culture and wanted to popularize them among the whole mankind; they have asserted that everybody is born equal; they have strived to establish a democratic, liberal, equal, human caring and progressive society; they wished to replace dictatorships with the rule of law; they have hoped to establish a society in which economy is advanced and all citizens are happy. [...] The history of more than 200 years has proved that most of the great ideals of those thinkers have been realized: After the bourgeoisie revolutions, autocratic monarchy was abolished in most countries and humans have entered into the era of "civil society" which has replaced the society of dependent subjects ; and they have realized the three great "industrial revolutions", creating huge leaps in human economy; Marxism – a great theory seeking the thorough emancipation of mankind was created causing fundamental changes in the landscape of human world and it had later inspired the establishment of the first batch of socialist countries; unprecedented scientific and technological inventions were created, which has carried mankind into the era of advanced modern science, thus all these have significantly improved the quality of people's life and health .

However, post-modernists have assertively evaluated the modernization cause since the Age of Enlightenment as a huge irrecoverable failure, thus adopting a repulsive attitude towards it. The main essence of the critique by post-modernism on modernism is that modernism has not yet realized the ideals of enlightenment thinkers on the contrary today still many dark and violent negative factors and phenomena continues to exist, such as: two world wars, nuclear threat, drug trafficking, radical polarization between the rich and the poor, child-work, woman trafficking and trade and many other evils in human life. [...] This attitude by post-modernism has aroused wide attention; while some people agree and some not.

How should we evaluate modernism? Habermas has ever given an appropriate comment. He said modernity is an unfinished cause, although modernity has encountered many problems, it is not yet at its dead end and still has much available potentials. Modern is not over, so what is the sense of "postmodern"? Habermas has argued that enlightenment movement has left a dual legacy – progress and retrogression thus "modern" embodies: rationality, democracy, freedom, equality, science, morality, law and art which are progressive, while international world invasion and subsequent "colonization of "life-world" which are retrogressive. Meanwhile, Habermas has criticized that the post-modernisms have only observed the problems in the process of modernization and those things retrogressive, while they have failed to comprehensively and justly judge enlightenment its rationality and modernity, and they cannot evaluate retrogression and progress in a holistic approach. The views of Habermas are comparatively fair. Post-modernists only reflect the evil problems of modernity and completely deny its contributions. People may ask: without modernization, could there be such an advanced economy and advanced society of today? If all the things of modernity are ignored, we could only go back to superstructure of the middle ages sublated by the

Age of Enlightenment. Therefore, some post-modernisms who oppose modernization inevitably harbor the ideas of revivalism and conservatism. No wonder Habermas has once called them "old conservatives", "neo-conservatives" and "young conservatives". It is true that modernization has also generated many negative things, but this is a normal phenomenon in the development process of the history of human society. Was there any era or period which had developed on a straight line? Was not there any negative thing in the feudal society? There were too many. In the feudal society, modern economy and population explosion had not yet existed, and humans were still surrounded by the primitive natural environment. Is not there any negative thing in the "postmodern" society as defined by Post-modernisms? The answer is yes. From 1960s on, (post-modernists assert it is the beginning of the "postmodern age"), "postmodern" society could eliminate none of the "10 plagues" criticized in Derrida's book Spectres of Marx.

Of course, the greatest critique of post-modernisms on modernity is their critique against capitalism. They disclose and criticize the defects and plagues of the capitalist society. This has nothing wrong, but their attitude of total negation is the approach of the extreme left anarchism. Although Marx and Engels have pungently criticized capitalism in Communist Manifesto, they have also given due affirmation on the historical role of capitalism: "The bourgeoisie, historically, has played a most revolutionary part." "The bourgeoisie, during its rule of scarce one hundred years, has created more massive and more colossal productive forces than those all preceding generations together."[6] In comparison, post-modernist attitude on modernity is obviously unilateral. What is worse, some post-modernists, like Lyotard and Baudrillard, also evaluate and include Marxism as one of the representative product of modernism- as a "meta- narrative" and discard it, which is obviously doubtful.

2. POST-MODERNISM

The term "postmodern" has existed for a long time. Some scholars (such as: American scholar Ihab Hassan) suggest the term "post-modernism" was first used by an editor named Federico de Onis in early 1930s in the book *Anthology of Spanish and Spanish-American Literature*; and Trotanoy used it in early 1940s in *Contemporary Latin American Anthology* edited by him; D.C. Sommerville also used it in 1947 when he extracted the first volume of the historian Arnold Toynbee's Study of History; by 1950s, Charles Olson has frequently used the term "post-modernism". American scholars Douglas Kellner and Steven Best have observed post-modernism from an even longer history. They suggest that around 1870, British painter John Watkins Chapman had introduced the idea of "postmodern painting" to refer to the painting works which were more modern and avant-garde than the French impressionist paintings. In the book *Crisis of European Culture*

---

6   Marx and Engels Selected Works, Edition 2, Vol. 1, p. 274; 277.

published by Rudolf Pannowitz in 1917, the term "postmodern" was used to describe the nihilism and value crisis in the European culture. This book also describes the emerging of numerous militarist, nationalist and elite "postmodern" figures in the society during those days. In 1950s, cultural historian Bonnard Luxemburg has used the term "postmodern" in the introduction of his collected works *Popular Culture* (1957) to describe a new living condition in the mass society and predicted that a kind of fundamental change was occurring in social and cultural fields. In the same year, economist Peter Ferdinand Drucker has described a kind of postmodern society in his works *Landmarks of Tomorrow: A Report on the New 'Post-Modern' World*. Drucker was positive and optimistic to this kind of postmodern society and asserted that in the postmodern world, poverty and ignorance could be terminated, nation states would decline and modernization could be promoted worldwide. In 1964, British historian Geoffrey Barraclough has released his book *An Introduction to Contemporary History*. Compared with the previous books, this book has more systematically and more elaborately exposes the views on post-modernism. In this book, Barraclough explicitly proposes using the term "postmodern" to describe the period following modern history. He has accurately forecasted the characteristics of this new era: revolutionary progress in science and technology, new-type of imperialism and the resistance by the revolutions in the Third World, transformation from individualism to mass society, and a new world view and a new cultural forms.

The above brief introduction indicates that it has taken a fairly long time between the appearance of the concept of "postmodern" and its application in philosophical and sociological studies. This also indicates that the publication of American Scholar Daniel Bell's *The Coming of Post-Industrial Society* in 1973 is by no means accidental. After this book concepts with "post" were spread to many disciplines and studies including philosophy, politics and sociology.

Just as its name implies, "post-modern" refers to "after modern", but this perception is not very complete in fact. Lyotard – one of the "fathers of postmodernity" ever said: "this is an extreme simplification; I define post-modern as incredulity towards meta-narratives." The "meta-narratives" (or "grand narratives"[7]) mentioned by Lyotard here refer to all theories formed under the influence of those concepts in the thought trends which were dominant in the modern age. For example, the "grand narratives" formed in modern period mainly include: (1) Christian narrative of redemption through love of Adam's fault; (2) Enlightenment narrative on the emancipation from ignorance and servitude through knowledge and equalitarianism; (3) Speculative narrative on the realization of the universal idea through dialectics of the concrete; (4) Marxist narrative

---

7   Jean-Francois Lyotard: The Postmodern Condition: A Report on Knowledge (Excerpt), please refer to Wang Min'an et al.: Postmodern Philosophical Discourse- From Foucault to Said , Hangzhou, Zhejiang People's Publishing House, 2000, p. 252.

on the elimination of exploitation and alienation through socialization of work; (5) Capitalist narrative to overcome poverty through technical progress and industrial development[8]. Lyotard argues that all these narratives are "narratives of emancipation", their common content is to place the materials provided by an event into a historical process, and the end point of this historical process is defined as liberty. Thus it can be seen that Lyotard criticizes "meta-narratives", i.e.: "narratives of emancipation". In fact, he criticizes "modernism". After "modernism" is criticized, "post-modernism" will be erected, therefore he has written: "I define postmodern as incredulity towards meta-narratives."[9] To sum up, "postmodern" has initially referred to describe the features and styles in literature, art and also to define a new historical era , but later the one which has become popular was not the concept used by literary/art critics or artists and historians. Instead, the concept was used by some philosophers in their critical theories during 1970s-1980s.

The core of "post-modernity" is the critique of "modern". Why criticize "modern"? In the sense of post-modernists including Lyotard, the sins which "modernity" possess include at least the following aspects.

Firstly, modern narratives of emancipation proceed from the "we" as called by Kant, i.e.: defining universal human history in the name of "we". This means the rest "they" (others) should accept "our way of thinking and behavior". In this way, the narratives of emancipation in the name of "we" have to adopt "terror" and "dictatorship".

Secondly, the numerous events occurring in the 50 years after World War II indicate that "grand narratives" are becoming more and more incredible. This is an obvious sign of the failure of modernity. For example, Berlin in 1953, Budapest in 1956, Prague in 1968, Poland in 1980, the youth revolutionary movement in Paris in 1968 and the economic crisis during 1974-1979 have all rebutted the "grand narratives" of historical materialism and liberal democracy.

Thirdly, "grand narratives" have fabricated the "white terror of truth", because "grand narratives" always speak in the name of truth, and since Enlightenment this discourse of truth has become the "meta-discourse", i.e.: thus truth has assumed a priority and a privileged position among all discourses, truth is fostered as a standard, and all other discourses must keep up and consult with it to obtain their meanings. This kind of meta-discourses repulses other weak discourses, so the pluralistic discourses should be promoted.

---

8   Jean-Francois Lyotard: Universal History and Cultural Differences, please refer to The Lyotard Reader, p. 314.
9   Jean-Francois Lyotard: Postmodern Condition, please refer to Lyotard et al: Postmodernism, translator Zhao Yifan, Beijing, Social Sciences Academic Press, 1999, p. 3.

Fourthly, the one who endows "grand narratives" with legacy is the subject and the one who raises "truth" to a priority position is also the subject, but human does not exist as a subject, in fact this approach on the subject was just a late invention and was determined by a specific culture (modern culture), whereas subject per se is the product of a specific discourse (modern discourse). Therefore, in the sense of "post-modernism", "the human as subject has died"[10].

From the above descriptions, we can observe that "post-modernism" is a philosophical, sociological and political thought growing from the matrix of "modernism" and rebels against "modernism". Based on its various attitudes, scholars classify it into different categories: Ben Agger classifies it into contributive post-modernism and extreme critical post-modernism; Todd Gitlin classifies it into warm post-modernism and cold post-modernism; David Griffin classifies it into constructive post-modernism and de-constructive post-modernism" or "perishing post-modernism and revised post-modernism; G. Graff classifies it into cynical and pessimistic post-modernism and visionary and unrestrained post-modernism; Hal Foster classifies it into reactive post-modernism and resistive post-modernism—the former praises the current status, while the latter resists the current status. For this reason, Foster calls the former as "neo-conservative post-modernism", and the latter "post structural post-modernism".

2.1. POST-MODERNISM AND POST-MARXISM

Post-modernist Marxism ("Post-Marxism" for short) reflects the integration of philosophy, sociology, politics and other disciplines with Marxism by post-modern thinkers. Meanwhile, it also offers different interpretations on Marxism influenced by those diverse standpoints developed by post-modernist thinkers. Below we will review different representatives of "post-Marxism".

2.1.1 FREDERIC JAMESON AND POST-MARXISM

Fredric Jameson is one of the most influential contemporary Marxist critics who focuses on culture in the United States and also a philosopher deeply influenced by the "Western Marxism" trend in the European continent. In 1971, in his book *Marxism and Form*, he has introduced the Frankfurt School, Lukacs, Adorno and other Western critical theorists of Marxism to American ideological circles, thus he has introduced Marxist critical methodology to American ideological and cultural circles. In this book, Jameson's another important contribution was his appeal for the establishment of "post-industrial Marxism" which should strive to explain current "post-industrial monopoly capitalism" in the United States.

---

10   Jean-Francois Lyotard: Universal History and Cultural Differences, please refer to The Lyotard Reader, p. 315.

In 1975, Jameson has fully affirmed the argumentation of "termination of modernity". In early 1980s, he has explicitly started to use of the concept of "post-modernism", and tried to develop a new theory of "post-modernism". In The *Political Unconscious*, he has explained post-modernist trend integrating it with the background of capitalist development process and has attempted to review several Marxist theories and Marxist politics in the current era. This book reflects Jameson's first attempt to integrate Marxism with post-modernism.

Jameson's theory of post-modernism was influenced to a great extent by Ernest Mandel's book *Late Capitalism*. In this book, Mandel attempts to use the mode of thinking in Marx's Capital to analyze the new features of contemporary capitalism, and has argued that the new developments in contemporary capitalism has proved the movement law of capitalist mode of production as discovered by Marx's in *Capital*. The failure of fascism and changes in the conditions of working class revolutions has caused basic changes in the movement of capital, this new capital accumulation has ushered the "late period" of capitalism. In this so called "late period", the capitalism has gained more purer, advanced and self-sufficient characteristics when compared with Marx's analyses in his age. This capitalism has extended the power of commodities to almost all fields of social life and personal life and also penetrates to all knowledge and information fields, even effects human sub-consciousness. Possessing parallel views Jameson has argued that each development stage of capitalism corresponds to a particular kind of culture. For example, the cultures corresponding to free market capitalism, monopoly capitalism and transnational/international capitalism are realism, modernism and post-modernism, respectively.

In his some works, Jameson has also severely criticized "post-modernism" and has argued that its first feature is a new "insipid feeling" and superficiality without depth, but as a whole, he definitely agrees and advocates "post-modernism". He has refuted those views which oppose using the concept of "postmodern" and commented: "as the characteristics which are embodied in "postmodern" have now changed from a subordinate position to a dominant position and the degree of this change is very remarkable, we have every reason to define it as a new era so as to underline its discontinuity with the previous form and style. Furthermore, he also believes that post-modernism offers a significant framework[11].

In his two articles "Five Theses for Post-Marxism" and "Marxism in Reality", Jameson has profoundly expounded his thinking system which integrates Marxism with post-modernism.

---

11 Douglas Kellner and Steven Best: Postmodern Theory: Critical Interrogations, Beijing, Central Compilation & Translation Press, 2001, p. 243.

Firstly, Jameson affirms the significance of Marxism in reality. In "Marxism in Reality", Jameson has given positive remarks on Marxism and has commented that Marxism is a science dealing with capitalism, or more appropriately, a science on the immanent contradictions of capitalism. He asserts that the approach which celebrates the "death of Marxism" and declares the decisive victory of capitalism and market system is illogical . It is far more paradoxical if they celebrate the death of Marxism in the same breath when they praise the ultimate victory of capitalism. Marxism is the only science on capitalism. Its mission in cognition rests with its infinite power in describing the historical origin of capitalism[12]. In "Five Theses of Post-Marxism", Jameson has also expressed the same ideas. For example, he has again written that Marxism is a science on the immanent contradictions of capitalism, Marxism enjoys a theoretical superiority by offering a more universal mode, and the core concept of Marxism is "integration of theory and practice", i.e.: theory and revolution per se. Jameson opposes the "post-Marxist" view that negates the "theory of class" and argues that in the whole social sphere, nothing is more complex than the meaning of class, particularly today. It will be a great mistake by Marxists to think the category of class is more or less out of date and treat Marxism as a kind of Stalinism, thus it will mean to ignore this extremely rich analysis sphere which is yet to be explored[13].

Secondly, Jameson argues that no fundamental change has occurred in capitalism. Jameson has argued that "post-Marxist" analysis on capitalism has the following defects: (1) Their perception: The capitalism as a class society no longer exists and has transformed to "post capitalism" and its characteristics exposed by Marx no longer exist in the "post capitalist" society, either. (2) Their compromising approach : Although several structures similar to that of capitalism still exist, these, due to several reasons have been improved and has become more suitable to people's wishes and collective needs .Therefore they conclude that a thorough institutional reform is possible and revolution is bygone. (3) Capitalism indeed exists indeed, but its ability to create prosperity and at the same time its capability to solve and correct its problems is greatly underestimated by Marxists. Therefore they conclude that capitalism is the only visible road to modernization and universal reform. Jameson has sharply refuted above ideas and commented: "my core idea is that no fundamental changes have occurred in today's capitalism, and these "changes" do not exceed the range of illusions raised by the people in the times of Bernstein[14].

Thirdly, Jameson regards post-modernity as a new stage of capitalism. Jameson thinks that by now, capitalism has experienced three stages: the first stage is the stage of domestic capitalism; the second stage is the stage of modern capitalism

---

12   *Ibid.*
13   *Ibid.*
14   *Ibid.*

or imperialism; the third stage is the post-modern stage. The development of the third stage or post-modern stage of capitalism- the multinational capitalism- is neither geographically restricted nor a regional development; instead it constitutes in itself a super-geographical realm and is a rapid acceleration of colonization targeting original capitalist areas and additionally includes post-modernization of the new areas and post-modern capitalism penetrates with commodities and super-geographical and hyper-space information technology[15]. The degree of globalization in the third stage of capitalism is much higher than that that in the imperialist period. The intrusion and expansion range of capital and markets are much broader than previous stages of capitalism. Jameson also agrees with the view of Mandel that the nuclear energy and control theory of capitalism are compatible with present multinational capitalism and globalization. These tech-nologies are both the productive forces which create new types of commodities, and tools for developing new world space. They have made the world "smaller" and expanded capitalism to a new scale. Therefore, it is appropriate to summarize and understand the characteristics of late capitalism with information theory or control theory[16].

Fourthly, Jameson emphasizes the role of Marxism in the late capitalist stage: "Contemporary post-Marxism has appeared in the era when the modern stage of capitalism gave away to post-modern stage."[17] Jameson thinks that the Marxism in the post-modern era of capitalism (as all kinds of political movements and all forms of knowledge and theory-based resistance movements) should certainly di-stinguish itself from all kinds of Marxism developed in modern era, in the second stage of capitalism, i.e.: the stage of imperialism. Marxism should generate an ex-tremely different relation with globalization. Comparing with previous Marxism, it should bear more obvious features of cultural critics and radically oppose those phenomena such as consumerism and consumer society.

Jameson claims himself to be a Marxist intellectual. In many aspects, he is devo-ted to Marxist critical researches on culture. He has attempted Marx's theories to analyze capitalism and define the new development stage of contemporary capi-talism as the third stage of capitalism, late capitalism or Post-modernism stage. At the same time, Jameson supports and sticks to the key views of Marxism, such as: the view on class, and the view on revolution to thoroughly change capitalist system. But on the other hand, Jameson is bewitched by many "post-modernist" views, and exaggerates some cultural trends. He orients "post-modernism" as a new cultural logic of capitalism, adopts post-modernist views and theories when analyzing the culture of late capitalism thus he merely understands it as a visu-al, segmented, mosaic and dissociated culture. I think Jameson's standpoints of

15 Ibid.
16 Ibid.
17 Ibid.

post-modernism are not fully compatible with his own Marxist views, and even damage the Marxist views he sticks to. Just as Douglas Kellner and also Bernard have commented in their works that Jameson has sometimes placed the post-modern "culturist"approach superior to Marxist political-economic analysis, thus neglecting the decisive effect of economy and class on the culture, but his works describe a balanced multiple angles of view in a very good way; the potential danger of his theory is: it tries to integrate a great many views, but some views are mutually incompatible and in a tense state. The difficult alliance he establishes between classical Marxism and post-modernism is an outstanding example[18].

2.1.2. LACLAU AND MOUFFE'S POST-MARXISM

Laclau and Mouffe are famous for their book Hegemony and Socialist Strategy: Towards a Radical Democratic Politics. In this book, Laclau and Mouffe have applied both post-structuralism and post-modernist view to almost negate the socialist movements in the 20th century. They have advocated breaking with the Marxist tradition of "universality" and put forth the theory of "new hegemony" and their new socialist strategy as "radical and plural democracy".

Laclau and Mouffe in fact have attempted to develop a "new Gramscian thought" through their theory on hegemony, thus establishing a theory of "radical and plural democracy"—a theory of "post-Marxism". Inspired by Gramsci's theory of "hegemony", Laclau and Mouffe have established their theory of "new hege-mony", including the following four main points:

(1) The imbalance of power is constructive.

(2) Hegemony exists only because universality/particularity-dichotomy is elimina-ted; universality exists only because it is reflected in a particularity and overthrows it. On the contrary, if a particularity cannot have or express itself where/when universality makes its effect, it cannot become politics.

(3) Hegemony is inclined to produce a void signifier. When the incommensurabi-lity between universality and particularity is achieved, this signifier will enable the latter to become a representative of the former.

(4) The field in which hegemony can be expanded can be described as such a field: The generalization of representative relations should be the condition for the structure of social order[19].

---

18   Douglas Kellner and Steven Best: Postmodern Theory: Critical Interrogations, p. 250.
19   Ernesto Laclau: Structure, History and Politics, please refer to Judith Butler et al.: Contingency, Hegemony, Universality: Contemporary Dialogues on the Left, p. 218-219.

According to Laclau's explanation, the first dimension in the above framework emphasizes the dependency of universality on particularity. Whereas Marx's political emancipation model is: the conditions of universality -in advance- set a fundamental repulsion. This is the first dimension of power. The second dimension of power is the unbalanced distribution of power in organizations and social spheres of life. These two dimensions of power hypothesize the dependency of universality on particularity: no universality takes effect through pure universality, while only relative universality which is generated from the expansion of equivalent chain and which surrounds the core of central particularity can exist. The second point in the framework of "new hegemony theory" emphasizes universalized effect. Different from the category of "class struggle", this aspect anchors the elements of struggle and antagonism to the partial identity of a group, and meanwhile any meaningful struggle will surpass all partial identities and will become a kind of comprehensively illustrated "collective will". The third point in the framework of "new hegemony theory" emphasizes the significance of an equivalent (egalitarian) discourse which can create and form the modern new collective-will. The front of masses indicates a kind of alliance among political powers. Except that emancipation exists in the discourses with empty anchorage terms, no real emancipation exists. The fourth point in the "new hegemony" theory emphasizes the issue of representatives. The discourse of a representative can become the discourse of his constituency. He can universalize his experience. Therefore, the relationship of representative becomes a tool for universalization, while universalization becomes the premise of emancipation, it can itself also become the road of emancipation, too.

Below, I will try to summarize the essence of Laclau and Mouffe's theory on "new hegemony" as follows:

(1) Laclau and Mouffe have asserted that the "zero degree" (starting point) of their "new hegemony" is inspired by Marx's *Critique of Hegel's Philosophy of Right* – Introduction. In this book, Marx for the first time uses the term "proletariat", and claims that the proletariat announces the collapse of existent world system and Marx asserts that once proletariat masters philosophy, this spiritual weapon, German people will be emancipated. In addition, here Marx also analyzes the foundation for a political revolution as follows: a part of people in the civil society emancipates themselves and obtains an universal position; and by this approach emancipation from a particular social domain is manifested as universal self-emancipation[20].

(2) "Hegemony" in the sense of Gramsci is authority and influence, and it is a power which controls and dominates. This power is not realized through coercion and military-bureaucratic apparatus. Instead, the hegemony in philosophy and

---

20   Marx and Engels Selected Works, Edition 2, Vol.1, p. 14; 15.

ethics sphere is assumed and obtained by the method of "consent" and persua-sion. By reviewing and reforming Gramsci's theory of "hegemony", Laclau and Mouffe have thus developed their theory of "radical and plural democracy".

(3) The theory of "radical and plural democracy" is a "reflective" criticism on the struggles of the social democratic parties of the Second International and the communist parties of the Third International in the 20th century, and offers a new research on the "political topography" of the current world, i.e.: attach importance to the forces of new social movements in contemporary Western society and the change of the subject in revolution. Thus they have shifted from "hegemony" theory to "radical and plural democracy"- "new hegemony" theory. This "new hegemony" theory has spurned the "theory of class", by highlighting autonomy and underlining radical and plural democracy.

(4) Laclau and Mouffe's "new hegemony" theory is a response to the new chan-ges in the socialist movements at the turn of the century and possesses quite reasonable ideas when analyzing and criticizing the "leftist" mistakes made by the Third International when this International handled some major issues of the revolutionary movements in the 20th century. They have defined their strategic goals as "radical and plural democracy". This gives the impression that they are "radical left", but in view of the fact that they negate Marx's theory of class – and the great achievements by proletarian revolutions in the 20th century, and their socialist fruits, they are "radical right" in fact. Their "new hegemony" theory is a new doctrine which is quite abstract and illusory, contains merely ethical values and is divorced from reality. No wonder even their "pen pal" Slavoj Zizek has also commented that they are secret Kantists. Butler has made another comment: "they hypothesize an (hegemonic, sexually performative, [...]) abstract, transcen-dental and formal model [...] they are indulged in a logic of "falsified infinity": no final decision but an endless and complex process of partial displacements. In the sense of providing a transcendental form of matrix of social space, is Laclau's hegemony theory not formalistic?[21] The right-wing theorists of the Second International, i.e.: the first-generation revisionists were just "Kantists". It is no accident that Zizek called some people including Laclau "secret Kantists". No wonder some people call them "the second-generation of revisionists".

In their works, Laclau and Mouffe have expounded their socialist strategy of radi-cal and plural democracy. Firstly, "radical" refers to radically break with traditional Marxist revolutionary views. It manifests itself in two aspects: (1) Spurn the "nar-row" and "worker-ist" concepts of socialism and oppose to evaluate socialism as a movement led by working class for a classless society and a new mode of pro-duction; (2) Spurn the revolutionary concept of socialism and oppose to evaluate socialism as the grand rupture of the bygone millennium. Secondly, "radical"

21   Judith Butler et al.: Contingency, Hegemony, Universality: Contemporary Dialogues on the Left, p. 112.

refs to advocate "post-modern philosophy" and radically transcend modern philosophy and also take post-modern philosophy as an indispensable tool for the completion of radical political goals. "Plural democracy" is no different from traditional Western liberal democracy and the democracy after the abolishment of the theory of class. Laclau and Mouffe's new socialist strategy mainly includes the following content:

(1)   Reviewing Socialist Aims

As Mouffe says in *Return of the Political*, the term of "radical and plural democracy" is introduced in *Hegemony and Socialist Strategy: Towards a Radical Democratic Politics* in order to redefine the socialist cause, and visualized as the extension of democracy to the vast spheres of social relations. Our aim is to bring the aims of socialism into the framework of plural democracy again and insist that these aims and political liberal system must be integrated into an organic body[22]. Obviously, Laclau and Mouffe's strategy for future socialism is primarily "radical and plural democracy". This is not only the aim of socialism but also a substantial content of socialism. Secondly, future socialism is perceived as a process of economic democratization. Lastly, a "liberal socialism" is advocated. They agree with the view of Bobbio and Rossellini: socialism can be and only be realized in a liberal democratic system. Therefore, liberalism and democracy is not a pair of contradictory terms at all. On the contrary, they should be integrated. The aim of socialist movement is to integrate socialist tenets with liberal democratic principles: constitutional system, parliamentary system and a multi-party competition system.

(2)   The Subject of Social Reform

As mentioned above, Laclau and Mouffe have evaluated the socialist movements in the 20th century as movements guided by "narrow theory of class". In other words, these movements have only emphasized class interests and "hegemony" of the proletariat. In the process of striving for "hegemony", the subject of the struggle is working class. Laclau and Mouffe assume that Marxism gives an ontological priority to working class, and turns them from social foundation of the revolution and puts them as the leaders of mass movements. In the sense of Leninism, working class and its vanguard do not change their class identity when integrating diversified democratic demands, and these diversified demands realize a political re-organization through "hegemonic" practice. Proletariat regards these demands as conditions and necessary short-term steps for the pursuit of their own interest. But for Laclau and Mouffe under these circumstances, the relation between "vanguard" and the "masses" can only be extrinsic and manipulative. Therefore, when democratic requirements become more diversified and the mass struggle becomes more complicated, the vanguard (political party) because it continues to be consistent with the objective interests of proletariat will

---

22   Chantal Mouffe: Return of the Political. p.103

certainly enlarge the crack between its own identity and those social groups it tries to lead[23]. Therefore, Laclau and Mouffe believe that the idea of class theory [...] blocks the road of linking various democratic requirements and contradicts with the collective-will among the large group of mass hegemony[24]. They also rebuke that Marxism regards "people" as an in-organized and imprecise category[25]. In the face of the new challenges of the contemporary democratic revolution, who are the subjects of struggle for "hegemony"? Laclau and Mouffe believe that "new social movements" include all kinds of struggles, such as: urban struggle, ecologist struggle, anti-authoritarian struggle, anti-institutionalization struggle, feminist struggle, anti-racist struggle, power struggle by minorities, or struggles by sexual minorities [...], these diversified struggles indicate more and more re-lations have become important in highly developed industrial society, and new political subject is constructed and formed within these antagonistic relations. Therefore, Laclau and Mouffe have asserted that they were considering the emer-gence of this new subject diversification, and "only after we can give up the ca-tegory of unified or unifying subject, can we think on its new structure and ways of its decentralization[26].

(3)   Socialist aims of "radical and plural democracy"

Mouffe has written in *Return of the Political* that in *Hegemony and Socialist Strategy: Towards a Radical Democratic Politics*, Laclau and she ever attempted to describe the significance of such theoretical view on radical and plural democracy[27]. Laclau and Mouffe have asserted that the "re-construction of the category of subject as a non-unitary, transparent and sutured entity opens the way to the recognition of the particularities of the antagonisms arising on the basis of different subject positions, and hence, it will be possible to deepen plural and democratic concepts. Democratic revolution has crossed a certain threshold. Diversity induces anta-gonisms. This gives us a theoretical terrain on the basis of the notion of radical and plural democracy – which will be central in our arguments from this point on – finds the first conditions under which it can be apprehended. Only if it is accepted that the subject positions cannot be led back to a positive and unitary founding principle–only then can pluralism be considered radical. Pluralism is radical only to the extent that each term of this plurality of group identities finds within itself the principle of its own validity. This radical pluralism is democratic to the extent that the auto-constitutivity of each one of its terms is the result of displacements of the egalitarian vision. Hence, the strategy (project) for a radical and plural democracy, in a primary sense, is nothing but the struggle for

---

23   Ernesto Laclau and Chantal Mouffe: Hegemony and Socialist Strategy: Towards a Radical Democratic Politics, p. 59.
24   *Ibid.*, p. 80.
25   *Ibid.*, p. 68.
26   *Ibid.*, p. 204.
27   Chantal Mouffe: Return of the Political, p. 88.

maximum autonomy of spheres on the basis of the generalization of the equiva-lential-egalitarian logic[28].

From the above descriptions, we can see that Laclau and Mouffe's so called "transcendence" of Marxism in fact is to set Marxism aside without a deep analysis, while they have themselves established a "new" theory to substitute Marxism. As Wood and Glass point out, Laclau and Mouffe have holistically misread Marx and Marxism[29].

2.2. POST-MODERN MARXISM

2.2.1 JACQUES DERRIDA AND DECONSTRUCTING MARXISM

The concept of "deconstruction" was invented by Derrida. What is "deconstruction"? Derrida has reiterated that deconstruction was neither demolition nor destruction but to superficially disclose a simple and harmonious hierarchy behind metaphysics as well as its internal tense situation, and internally break and overthrow the complex of hierarchical structure. Deconstructive movement first of all is a positive activity, not certain but positive[30]. It can best be described as a theory of reading which aims to undermine the logic of opposition within Texts. For Derrida this requires a scrutiny of the essential distinctions and conceptual orderings (hierarchy) which have been constructed by the dominant traditions of Western philosophy.

For Derrida, deconstruction was conceived not as a negative operation aimed at tearing down, but rather as a kind of close analysis that seeks "to understand how an 'ensemble' was constituted and to reconstruct it to this end". It is in the process of reading closely, with an eye for how a discourse is constructed, that a thinker also comes to see the points of potential instability within the structure. Deconstruction is the event that happens within a close reading. In one of many statements in which Derrida asserts that deconstruction is not a method of analysis or a critique, he has said: "Deconstruction takes place; it is an event that does not await the deliberation, consciousness, or organization of a subject, or even of modernity. It deconstructs it–self. It can be deconstructed." Deconstruction happens to both the text at hand, the one being closely read, and to the interpretation itself.

During the lectures of Derrida at Peking University, Chinese Academy of Social Sciences, Nanjing University, Fudan University, Chinese University of Hong

---

28 Ernesto Laclau and Chantal Mouffe: Hegemony and Socialist Strategy: Towards a Radical Democratic Politics, p. 186-187.
29 Douglas Kellner and Steven Best: Postmodern Theory: Critical Interrogations, p. 261.
30 Jacques Derrida: A Madness Must Watch over Thinking, Shanghai, Shanghai People's Publishing House, 1997, p. 21.

Kong, "Reading" magazine and other academic institutions in 2001, scholars have mostly debated with him on his "deconstruction" approach. This has indicated that scholars (at least Chinese readers) still knew little on this concept.

According to Derrida's explanation on his concept of "deconstruction" in the past, as well as his explanations to Chinese scholars' questions during his lectures in China in 2001, we can summarize his explanations on the concept of "deconstruction" as follows:

Firstly, "de-construction" is not equal to "post-structuralism" and is prior to "structuralism"; "deconstruction" refers to focus on the structure. Engaging in deconstruction is also a stance of structuralism, but meanwhile it is a stance of anti-structuralism, too.

Secondly, "de-constructivism" is not "post-modernism". There is much difference between "de-constructivism" and "post-modernism".

Thirdly, "deconstruction" is not destruction or critique. Deconstruction is a kind of ideological work and the work which is still going on or will go on through upcoming things. Deconstruction is not negative but positive. It is the affirmation to "impossibility".

Fourthly, "deconstruction" requires not only paying attention to history but also proceeds from history and treats each thing part by part. Such deconstruction is history. Deconstruction certainly is not non-historical. It is to think over the history in a special way and neutralize history by this deconstructive method.

Fifthly, "deconstruction" is not as simple as philosophy. It tries to surpass philosophical thinking and realize de-construction inside philosophy itself. Deconstruction is neither philosophy nor a methodology. The occurrence of deconstruction is an event, an organizational event not subject to deliberation, consciousness, or subject and even modernity[31]. Therefore, Derrida calls it "ideology".

Sixthly, "deconstruction" will at least avoid negative determination of its connotation or implicate meaning. In this case, our question in fact is: deconstruction is not what, or might as well say: should not be what.

After reading the above content, readers may still be unclear of what "deconstruction" is. Let's have a look at Karrer's analysis on "deconstructive study strategy in his book *Deconstruction*. Perhaps, it can give us a deeper insight into Derrida's

---

31   Editors in Chief Du Xiaozhen et al.: Lectures of Jacques Derrida in China , Beijing, Central Compilation & Translation Press, 2003, p. 233.

concept of "deconstruction". Karrer thinks "deconstructive strategy" contains four aspects:

Firstly, deconstructing the propositions which have binary oppositions in traditional philosophy; it means deconstructive study turns over its hierarchical order in a specific time.

Secondly, overthrow the classic propositions containing binary oppositions in practice and completely convert their system. Therefore, deconstruction activity operates inside this system, aiming to break this system.

Thirdly, it means employing the most prudent and immanent method to holistically examine the structural pedigree of a concept, meanwhile from an un-identified or indescribable angle, corroborate what this period of history has covered, has repulsed and forgotten when it built its own historical process through this crucial inhibition.

Fourthly, through identifying the rhetorical activities of argumentations, central concepts or premises in a text and using the logic of discourses to push them to the extreme, we will be able to see the so-called argumentations, central concepts or premises are a kind of very ambiguous and self-contradictory things and do not have any integrity. In this way, binary oppositions can be cleared up[32].

In his book *Post-modernism and the Social Sciences*, American scholar Pauline Marie Rosenau has summarized the view of "deconstruction" by Post-modernists with different attitudes: (1) Deconstruction is explanation or explanation of an explanation. Deconstruction emphasizes the critical power of negation, while explanation expresses an active view. (2) Deconstruction is a kind of interpretation. Deconstruction both implies disclosing the mystery of a text and disintegrates the text to disclose the meaning of its immanent and any hierarchy and its premises. (3) Deconstruction is critical, left and revolutionary. It opens a revolutionary road, shakes current status, and challenges the ruling discourse and attacks hierarchy and bureaucracy.

Let's analyze the French word "déconstruction" (de-construction). It consists of prefix "dé" and postfix "construction". The prefix "dé" means "separation", "dismantlement" and "opposition"; the postfix "construction" means "building", "construction" and "structure". Derrida in many occasions has denied that "deconstruction" had the meaning of destruction, opposition and critique, but in view of its origins, it inevitably contains the meaning of destruction, opposition and critique, let alone he himself also admitted "deconstruction" was a stance of anti-structuralism. Since it can treat structuralism from the stance of opposition,

---

32   Chantal Mouffe: Return of the Political, p.88.

it may also treat all other philosophies by the same stance. The fact is so inde-ed. Derrida regards traditional Western philosophies as propositions containing binary oppositions with strict hierarchies, so it is necessary to overthrow these classic propositions containing binary opposition by using the strategy of "de-construction". This strategy includes two stages: The first stage is the stage of "overturn"; the second stage is the stage of "change". He thinks that in the first stage, one rules out "the other" in the binary opposition, and takes a higher po-sition with senses of value and logic. In order to resolve this opposition, people must turn over this hierarchy in a specific time. The overturn of this hierarchy must be realized through neutralization. It is not enough to explicitly negate this binary hierarchy. The strategic stage of resolution, i.e.: the second stage – change stage- is necessary. The purpose of this second stage is to introduce a new con-cept through the concept itself.

From the above descriptions, we can see that Derrida's definition on "deconst-ruction" is still obscure and confusing, so we would like to sum up his ideas into the following points:

Understanding Deconstruction

Firstly, "deconstruction" is an activity of criticism. Derrida has ever said that de-construction was not an activity of criticism and criticism was its aim, but he has also commented that deconstruction has always influenced from time to time the self-righteous criticism and critical theories. [...] Deconstruction is the destruc-tion of critical doctrines. It is obvious that the activity which influences criticism and critical theories and eliminates critical doctrines can be nothing but criticism.

Secondly, "deconstruction" is an activity of overturning. In the sense of Derrida, the main task of "deconstruction" is to overturn the state of binary oppositions containing strict hierarchies we can see in the traditional philosophies, i.e.: oppose to logo-centrism–the combination of "metaphysics of presence" and "phono-centrism". This is the major task of "deconstruction" as understood by Derrida.

Thirdly, "deconstruction" is a kind of "ideology" or "thinking". Derrida has ever said that deconstruction was not philosophy but literature, so he called it "ideology"[33]. He also said deconstruction certainly is not non-historical. Deconstruction thinks over the history in a special way[34]. He points out that the histories of ideology, Marxism and the Enlightenment Thought all should accept deconstruction. Thus it can be seen that "deconstruction" is nothing different than chewing and pondering on politics, ideologies, cultures and other super-structures which were generated in modern times and then raise new remarks and views.

---

33   Editors in Chief Du Xiaozhen et al: Lectures of Jacques Derrida in China, p. 70.
34   *Ibid.*, p. 68.

After Derrida introduced the concept of "deconstruction", inevitably it is associated with Marxism, as he suggested that the histories of ideology, Marxism, the
Enlightenment Thought and so on all should accept deconstruction. Scholars
call the Marxism involved by Derrida "de-constructivist Marxism". What does
Derrida's "de-constructivist Marxism" view contain?

Firstly, Marx is a "pre-deconstructivist". Derrida thinks that "deconstruction"
has appeared in Marx's early works such as *German Ideology,* and in this works, it
is revealed in a way of inadequate theories and thoughts. Behind Marx's stern
criticism on the German ideology, the recognition of its illusoriness was hidden.
Marx's critique on Max Stirner is a game of "circular hunting". This game has
started before Plato and runs through the entire history of Western philosophy.
In this game, Marx has tried in vain to determine the potential of material reality. However, Marx has opened a correct road, although containing "paradoxes".
German Ideology in fact is only the unfolded presentations of a table of spectres.
The new table is presented also as a tableau, the ironic tabularization, the fictive
taxonomy or the statistics of ghosts, and a table of the categories of the objects
or of being as specter in general. And yet, despite the stasis (a state of stability, in
which all forces are equal and opposing), that is appropriate for the exhibition of
a tableau or picture, this one knows no rest in any stability[35].

Secondly, Marx has not finished his work, so it is needed to incorporate his texts
into the range of deconstruction and apply deconstructivism to re-interpret these
texts. For Derrida, Marx, Engels and Lenin has only opened a road, but have
not finished their works. What work had Marx, Engels and Lenin done? Derrida
thinks that it is the work of humane, and "good deeds" in all kind of forms.
Derrida evaluates Marx as a "pre-deconstructivist". That is to say, although Marx
has criticized German ideology (it is also Western traditional ideology to some
extent), he also had some "reluctance", because while he made these criticisms, he
had to hide covert recognition of the criticized objects. Therefore, his critique on
German ideology is a game of "circular hunting". This game has started before
Plato and runs through the entire history of Western philosophy. According to
Derrida, Marx also belongs to this tradition of the entire Western philosophy. Just
as "father of post-modernism", Lyotard has asserted that Marxism also belongs
to "grand narratives" or "meta-narratives", so incredulity on it is also necessary.
In this sense, Derrida and Lyotard are consistent. Derrida ultimately thinks the
approach of trying to radicalize Marxism is a kind of "deconstruction".

Thirdly, Derrida in his book *Specters of Marx* has created a "theory of specters"
for Marx. In fact, the "specters" in the sense of Derrida are same as "ghosts"
and "spirits". His reason to deal on the specters of Marx is disclose the real spirit

---

35   Jacques Derrida: Specters of Marx, Beijing, China Renmin University Press, 1999, p.
199.

of Marx. Derrida has argued that Marx has talked on a Decalogue of specters in *German Ideology*. They are: existence of the supreme being (das höchste Wesen), God; being or essence; the vanity of the world; good and evil beings (die guten und bösen Wesen); being and its realm (das Wesen und sein Reich); the Man-God (der Gottmensch); man; the spirit of the people (Volksgeist); everything, transmuting everything, the All itself, into a ghost, as described by Saint Max. In the most critical and most ontological disclosure, same as Saint Max, Marx has inherited the tradition of Plato, more exactly, Plato's tradition of strictly combining image with specter, idolum, hallucination. Derrida thinks that the issue of Holy Spirit is a central issue in Marx's legacy[36], because he deems Marx's legacy as the spirit lingering in all fields of our daily life, like the description given in Communist Manifesto: "a specter of communism" is haunting. No matter how the reactionary powers exorcise it, it still exists eternally.

Fourthly, his critique on capitalism: Derrida applies Marx's spirit of critique to incisively criticize capitalism, and points out to the "ten plagues" (ten problems) of capitalist "new world": (1) Unemployment determined based on the new concept of "jobless", and various types of unemployment; (2) Massive homeless citizens even non-citizens who are excluded; (3) Ruthless economic wars, occurring among the countries in European Union , between Europe and the United States and between Europe and Japan; (4) Capitalism fails to control the contradictions in the free market economy in the senses of concept and norms; (5) Increasing burden of foreign debts and other issues arising from it in the developing countries have made a large part of the people desperate; (6) The arms trade. The inability to control in any meaningful extent the arms trade occurring in the 'black market'; (7) The spread of nuclear weapons cannot be controlled; (8) The highly technologic wars are steered by phantom and ancient ideas, or triggered by groups ,nation states based on sovereignty, border, land issues and phantom of primitive ideas (racism, religious fundamentalism) based on blood and flesh are widespread (9) The behaviors of ever-increasing secret societies and secret organizations are not restricted; (10) A serious infringement of the current international laws and international institutions[37].

The above descriptions indicate that the deconstructivist Marxism" in the sense of Derrida is not Marxism. It only indicates a kind of deconstructivist intellectuals' understanding on Marxism and an intellectual voice, and an attitude towards Marxism. Derrida has claimed on many occasions that he was not a Marxist and not a traditional Marxist. Of course, Derrida is a righteous Western intellectual. In the era when Marxism was vilified and buried, he dared to speak out from a sense of justice and advocated inheriting the spiritual legacy of Marxism. His brave act should be highly appreciated. However, that is all for Derrida's attitude towards Marxism.

---

36   Editors in Chief Du Xiaozhen et al.: Lectures of Jacques Derrida in China, p. 86.
37   *Ibid.*, p. 115-119.

2.2.2 HABERMAS' CRITICAL HERMENEUTIC MARXISM

Habermas has made very wide academic research. He is greatly influenced by the social critical theory of Frankfurt School, Gadamer's new hermeneutics, Structuralist School of Paris and British and American schools of linguistics. All these schools have contributed to his very complex theoretic thought. His works cover all disciplines of humanities –those disciplines which are part of different systems. These systems transfix the critical spirit of sociology and that of herme- neutics. Just as stated by American scholar Douglas Kellner and Best, Lyotard's critique on "meta-narratives" is similar to the ideological critique of Frankfurt School. Both Habermas and Lyotard have criticized the principles of legacy which assumes a dominant role in contemporary capitalist society. Therefore, on many occasions, the aim of Lyotard is very close to the aim of the critical theory of Frankfurt School. The two do not have essential difference in their critics against contemporary social structures. In addition, Habermas and Lyotard both express "rational critique on function" and they both oppose restoring ra- tionality and make it a tool of social reproduction. As Habermas' ideological theory is the combination of the social critical theory of Frankfurt School and Gadamer's new hermeneutics, and because he has also incorporated ideological critique into hermeneutics, his theory can be called "critical hermeneutic theory". Habermas' hermeneutic view can be roughly summarized by its three aspects: Firstly, Habermas' hermeneutics smashes the superficial objectivity and accuracy of traditional social science (including critical theory). Secondly, Habermas' her- meneutics strives to make the theories of natural science more rational. Thirdly, Habermas' hermeneutics facilitates better communication between natural sci- ence and the world of social life. Many works of Habermas largely deals with Marxism, so his theory can also be called "critical hermeneutic Marxism". After 1970s, the thought of "post-modernism" had become vogue in the West. In the beginning, Habermas has taken a stern critical attitude towards this thought. He has argued that modern was not yet over, so why "Post-modernism"? For this reason, he had considered "Post-modernists" as "conservatives" or "pre- conservatives". However, after the stronger rise of post-modernism, he has con- sciously or unconsciously influenced by it. Therefore, some scholars evaluate him together with Post-modernist theorists. For example, American scholars Kellner and Best think that the thoughts of Habermas are very close to the thoughts of Post-modernist theorist Lyotard. Although a dispute had happened between Habermas and Lyotard, it was a "dispute between brothers". They both advocate left wing liberal democratic discourse politics, both uphold justice and discourse politics and both show sympathy for all kinds of new social movements. In his book *Post- Metaphysical Thinking*, Habermas has criticized metaphysical thinking mode, as post-structuralist and Post-modernist theories have done[38]. Therefore,

---

38   Douglas Kellner and Steven Best: Postmodern Theory: Critical Interrogations, p. 301-327. In their book, they have classified Habermas among "postmodernists".

we can classify Habermas' theories, particularly his Marxism-related theories in his later period, as "post-Marxism".

Habermas' Post-Marxist Views

I can summarize his views as follows:

(1) Habermas thinks that many categories in Marx's historical materialism are to-day out of date, so it needs to be "reconstructed". Habermas thinks many of the basic categories of Marx's historical materialism, such as: the development trend of capitalism and fate of capitalism, productive forces and production relations, economic base and superstructure, social labor, and human history, have become out of date, and all need new interpretations. And many social realities, such as: class relations, science and technology becoming key productive forces, ways to exploit surplus value, and crisis of capitalism, have changed a lot. Therefore, Habermas thinks that reconstruction of historical materialism is inevitable. The method should be firstly, to introduce the concept of "communicative action" to historical materialism, making it a science truly about human. Secondly, we should substitute the contradiction between labor and communicative action instead of the contradiction between productive forces and production relations, because "labor rationalization" and "communication rationalization" have become most important problems, and mediation of this contradiction can promote social development. Thirdly, substitute communicative utopian society instead of so-cialism. He thinks that the desired human societies, such as: socialist and com-munist society envisaged by Marx, all are about the exploration on whether the rationalization of interpersonal communications can be realized, so a society with "rationalized communications" should be established to supersede socialism and communism.

(2) Habermas has argued that Marxist democracy theory is insufficient and needs additions. He thinks that the main value of Marxism is its functionalist analysis and but Marx has analyzed democracy as only a ruling tool of a class disguised under ideological forms, so this is obviously insufficient. Therefore to some extent, Marxism may be alleged as copying previous theories. Habermas' views on democracy can be summarized as follows: Democratic principle only accepts the legacy of the laws approved by all the people attending the discussion. Democratic principle originates from discourse principle and crisscrossed with judicial form; Habermas interprets judicial forms as an intermediary for medi-ation, so judicial forms are the institutionalization of discourse principle in the form of "legal system". Legal system guarantees the equal participation in the discussion when laws are produced as well as guarantees the participation in the formulation of communicative premises of these laws. The core of Habermas' democratic principle is discourse principle and legal system as the intermediary.

Discourse principle may generate legal laws, because laws are established on the basis of discourse. On this basis, Habermas has suggested the concepts of "deliberative democracy" and "mass democracy". As for "deliberative democracy", he thinks that if people want facticity, validity and sincerity to be guaranteed, they need to be re-determined through "democratic deliberation". Only when "deliberative democracy" is really implemented, can real democracy be generated. As for "mass democracy", he thinks it cannot be seen as the enlargement of the scope of democracy —the easily applicable scope of universal suffrage— but should be seen as a change in the nature of democracy. Mass democracy attaches importance to the tool value of democratic legacy rather being the foundation of the norms for democratic validity.

(3) Marx's economic analysis is out of date, too, because contemporary economy is quite different from the economy in the days of Marx, and even classical economics cannot predict an autonomous and re-generative economic system. Habermas has argued that Marx's economic theory is only applicable to the era of "liberal capitalism", whereas contemporary capitalism has entered into a new era of "late capitalism", the economic conditions of capitalism described by Marx in *Capital* will never appear and particularly fundamental changes have emerged related to the economic crisis of capitalism: the economic crisis in late capitalism is shifted from economic sphere to political, social, cultural and other spheres and becomes political crises, social crises (which contains integrated economic crisis, legacy crisis, rationality crisis and motive crisis), cultural crises and ideological crises. Even the crisis remaining in the economic field is completely different from the economic crisis envisaged by Marx and is an economic crisis in a brand new form. This economic crisis no longer assumes the nature of regime crisis and causes class struggles and no longer endangers the dominion of capitalism. Capitalist states have gained new functions to balance various social forces. Class reconciliations have become the essential characteristic in the social structure of contemporary capitalism, while the class consciousness of proletariat has become mutilated.

(4) Habermas suggests taking a radical stance and making use of the aims declared by the former bourgeois emancipation movement and supporting the potential demands of bourgeois citizens to realize social changes. Habermas has argued that according to the view of Marx, the realization of social change should have two conditions: firstly, the struggle between proletariat and bourgeoisie is intensified and proletariat consciously realizes the existence of this struggle, in other words they should have the consciousness for revolution. Secondly, capitalist crisis should be severe. For Marx, this crisis arises from the contradiction between the socialization of production and the private ownership of capitalism. Its main characteristic is the crisis of "over-production". But neither of these conditions exists in late capitalism, because in the society of late capitalism, two development

trends of "intensification of government intervention" and "increasing dependency between scientific research and technology" has appeared. These two new
trends have destroyed the original layout and status of the characteristics of the
capitalism which it could previously develop freely. In addition, proletariat's revolutionary consciousness has disappeared, because they have benefited from the
welfare policy of capitalism and lost the reason to stand up and resist capitalism.
Capitalists has combined workers' various interests with enterprises, and working class and bourgeoisie are inter-assimilated in their demand and desires, living
standards, leisure, ideologies [...]. Therefore, the conditions for social revolution
as described by Marx have all disappeared. Hence, Habermas no longer regards
developing productive forces and increasing social material wealth as the aim of
change. Instead, he considers realizing rationalization of "communicative action"
as the aim of social change. Language is a decisive factor for the rationalization of
"communicative action" and the promotion of social progress.

The above schools of Post-modern Marxism have developed different attitudes
towards Marxism. By attitude, they can be roughly classified into three schools:
left, neutral and right. Regardless of their differences, they basically agree with
Post-modernist stance and methodology, and use this stance and methodology to
criticize capitalism and treat Marxism. As a result, when we analyze these carefully
we can see that the decent and the erroneous are interwoven.

REFERENCES

• Michael Levitin: Modernism. Shenyang, Liaoning Education Press, 2002.
• Jean-Francois Lyotard: Post-modernism. Beijing, Social Sciences Academic
Press, 1999.
• Douglas Kellner and Steven Best: Post-modernism Theory: Critical
Interrogations. Beijing, Central Compilation & Translation Press, 2001.
• Judith Butler et al.: Contingency, Hegemony, Universality: Contemporary
Dialogues on the Left. Nanjing, Jiangsu People's Publishing House, 2004.
• Jürgen Habermas: Reconstruction of Historical Materialism. Beijing, Social
Sciences Academic Press, 2000.
• Chen Xueming: Comments on Habermas' Dissertations of Late Capitalism.
Chongqing, Chongqing Publishing House, 1993.

CHAPTER IX

MARKET SOCIALISM BY U.S. AND BRITISH MARXISTS

Market socialism is a theory which attempts to realize socialism by combining public ownership of the means of production with market economy. It has emerged in 1930s and was first proposed by a Polish economist Oskar Lange. During the reform of economic system in Soviet Union and the socialist countries in Eastern Europe during 1950s~1980s, the theory of market socialism was further developed by the economists in these countries and has become one of the important theoretical basis for the reform of economic system in these countries. In early 1980s, some leftist scholars in Western countries have studied the issue from the aspect of developed capitalist countries so that they can move to socialism. Influenced by the ongoing market-oriented reforms in the Soviet Union and Eastern Europe, they have also shifted their attention to the theory of market socialism and put forth some theories or models for market socialism, which could adapt to the situation in the developed capitalist countries.

In mid and late 1980s, the Soviet Union and the socialist countries in Eastern Europe have collapsed one after another, but the research of the leftist scholars in Western countries on market socialism has continued. On the contrary, after intensively reflecting on the failure of socialism in the Soviet Union and Eastern Europe, some leftist scholars who advocate market socialism, the leftist scholars in the USA and UK in particular, have suggested that market socialism is the only feasible solution to lead developed capitalism to socialism. Since 1980s, they have published many books and put forth various kinds of theories and models on market socialism, such as: British David Miller's "Cooperative Market Socialism", American John Roemer's "Coupon Socialism", American David Schweickart's "Economic Democracy" and American Thomas Weiskopf's "Democratic Autonomy".

The current theories or models on market socialism can be roughly divided into two types. One is the theory of market socialism represented by leftist scholars American John Roemer and British David Miller. Its features are: (1) The integration of mainstream Western economics and Marxist theory is its theoretical basis; (2) To be efficient, a complex society must have markets. Market is a perpetual phenomenon; (3) Socialism is a society which is fairer than capitalism. Market socialism is an efficient and fair social system; (4) Market socialism can be gradually realized in the current capitalist society.

The other is the theory of market socialism represented by Marxists like American David Schweickart and James Lawler. Its features are: (1) The relevant theories of Marx and Engels are its basis; (2) It believes that although market has insurmountable defects, it will be still needed in the transition period from capitalism to socialism and in the stage of socialism (first phase of communism), and market will be finally abolished only after the realization of communism; (3) Socialism is a society based on public ownership, in which cooperative enterprises are dominant and workers can democratically manage production; (4) The premise for the realization of market socialism is that proletariat assumes power in a democratic manner.

The theory of market socialism is hailed by some leftists, but it also receives opposition from the people who claim to be firmer Marxists. The representatives of the opponents are American Bertell Ollman and British Hillel Ticktin. They think that the first type market socialism in fact has no difference from the proposition of mainstream bourgeois scholars who safeguard capitalism, so there is no need to argue with them. In a sense, the second type market socialism is the proposition of Marxists, but their scheme is quite unrealizable and utopist. Nevertheless, since the advocates of these schemes all claim to proceed from Marxism, it is necessary to discuss with them.

To clear out the problems, Ollman has published a collection of essays which is titled "Market Socialism: The Debate among Socialists"[1]. This collection of essays collects controversial articles on market socialism from four self-claimed Marxists. Among them, Schweickart and Lawler agree with market socialism, while Ticktin and Ollman oppose market socialism.

---

1   It was published by American Routledge in 1998. Xinhua Publishing House published its Chinese version in 2000.

1. DAVID SCHWEICKERT

David Schweickart currently is a professor of philosophy at the Loyola University. Since mid 1980s, he has been researching the issue on how developed countries can realize socialism and argues that market is the only way for them to realize socialism. In his book *Against Capitalism*[2] published in 1993, he has utmost advocated market socialism and introduced a model of "market socialism with economic democracy". In the book *Market Socialism: The Debate among Socialists*, he has demonstrated market socialism from the following aspects:

Market Socialism Is Not Equal to Capitalism

In order to explain this issue, Schweickart firstly compares market socialism with capitalism. He thinks capitalist economy is a market economy characterized by private ownership of the means of production and hiring of labor[3]. Concretely speaking, overwhelming majority of the means of production in the society is owned by the private sector; and overwhelming majority of people are the hired laborers who work for wages; and overwhelming majority of economic transactions in the society are performed in the market. Different from the capitalist economy, market socialist economy, although still retains the market mechanism that regulates the overwhelming majority of economic activities (but more restrictions will be imposed on it than capitalism does), replaces capitalist private ownership with a version of state ownership or to workers' collective ownership, that is to say, the main assets of a nation will become the assets owned by collectives and will be controlled by the laborers who use them. Accordingly, what workers obtain is no longer contracted wage, but a specific share of an enterprise's net income, so the labor of the workers no longer possesses the nature of hired labor. Schweickart stresses that the difference between socialism and capitalism is not the practice of planned economy or market economy, but the adoption of public ownership or private ownership. Therefore, market socialism cannot be considered capitalism.

Proceeding from the above view, Schweickart criticizes the two types of people who equal capitalism with market. The first type people are the rightist scholars who attempt to defend capitalism through defending market, such as: Friedman and Hayek. When they defend capitalism, they often underline the strong points of market and also criticize the defects of central planning to conceal the issues related to hired labor and private ownership on the means of production. This is an effective strategy for them, because the defending market is much easier than

---

2   The Chinese version of this book is available and was published by China Renmin University Press in 2002.

3   Edited by Bertell Ollman: Market Socialism: The Debate among Socialists, translated by Duan Zhongqiao, Beijing, Xinhua Publishing House, 2000, p. 6.

to argue against the problems of hired labor and private ownership on the means of production. The second type people are the leftist scholars who oppose market socialism. Their critique on market socialism also focuses on market, more exactly, on market's defects and unreasonableness. Schweickart points out that in fact, attacking market abstractly is as easy as defending it, because market has both strong points and defects. The defenders of capitalism stress the strong points of market and insist that the opposite of market can only be central planning, so they ignore all criticisms against it. The left critiques on market socialism are worried by market defects and its demerits and insist that the model of market socialism is similar to the model of capitalism, so they condemn it totally. The argument strategy of the latter is quite convenient, because it excludes the need for carefully researching how market will run when it is transplanted to a property relation different from capitalism. Although this approach can be judged as convenient, it is too reckless.

Centrally Planned Economy and Its Four Hard Problems

Schweickart believes that an important reason for the collapse of socialism in the Soviet Union and Eastern Europe is their practice of the non-market centrally planned economy. For him, centrally planned economy is an economy in which a central planning department decides what should be produced and instructs enterprises to produce a specified amount of commodities with specified qualities. This economy faces four distinct problems: information input problems, incentive problems, authoritarian tendencies, and entrepreneurial problems[4].

As for information input problems, Schweickart points out that many people believe that modern industrial economy is too complicated to be planned in detail. This view is more or less exaggerated. In fact, the planners are able to plan an integrated economy. In the former Soviet Union, Eastern Europe, China and other socialist countries, planners have practiced that for decades. Through concentrating the production of specific products in a minority of enterprises (often large enterprises), issuing aggregate production targets and allowing a decision flexibility for enterprise managers in non-aggregate forms, products are produced and the fulfillment of demand – especially quantity oriented — often gives people a good impression for economic growth. Therefore, asserting that centrally planned socialism is "impossible" is ridiculous. Let's take the Soviet Union for example: under the grim situation of international hostilities and surrender and German invasion, it has survived for nearly 80 years, managed to build industrialization in a huge semi-feudal and peasant society, solved people's basic needs like clothing, food, accommodation and education and created world-class scientific institutions. Such an economic system cannot be considered as "impossible". However, Schweickart stresses that the opposite of "impossible" is not the "ideal". The

---

4   *Ibid.*, p. 8-9.

Soviet economy and those economies which has adapted Soviet model have always suffered from efficiency problems, and these problems have become increasingly worse as their economies have developed. Information input problems that were tractable when relatively fewer goods were being produced, and when quantity was more important than quality, later became intractable when more and quality goods were required. It is not without reason that centrally planned economies were compelled to introduce market reforms once reaching a certain level of development.

As for incentive problems, Schweickart has pointed out, centrally planned economy has many incentive problems inherently[5], which includes four theoretical aspects and usually faced practices : if the varieties and quotas for products are determined by the planning agency, enterprises will not have any enthusiasm to make full use of resources or try to study what consumers really need; when both production inputs and outputs are determined by the planning agency, enterprises will tend to hide their capacities and overstate their demands so that they can more easily fulfill tasks assigned to them by the planning agency. Besides, they will also try their best to persuade the planning agency to assign them lower production quotas and more advantageous allocation of raw materials. When workers' employment is guaranteed and their income has nothing to do and not related with enterprise performance, they will lose their motivation for work; if the planning agency is responsible for the success of the entire economy, they will have no motivation to shut down the inefficient enterprises, bankruptcy of an enterprise will cause a challenge for them as to arrange new jobs for the workers who lose their jobs.

As for authoritarian tendencies, Schweickart thinks that the planning agency possesses the sole and undivided authority and hard to be supervised, while the decision of production quotas (or prices) has great bearing on enterprises' performances. Thus corruption will be highly likely, because any bribery which can reduce enterprise quotas or raise their sales prices will enable an enterprise get more easy profit than it does by quality and efficiency improvement, or development of a new production line or introduction of a new production technology. What is more, even if the planning agency works prudently and honestly, they might still regulate production efforts by focusing on bigger production units although generally extensive large-scale mass production adapts to low efficiency, because the fewer production and decision units they have to deal with, the easier their work will be. Furthermore, it is an extremely complex task to plan a large scale economy, so they often meet with criticisms and objections and have to frequently revise it. Therefore, no matter how seriously the planners declare that they support the participatory and democratic system, in fact they tend to dislike democracy.

---

5   *Ibid.*, p. 10.

As for entrepreneurial problems, Schweickart has argued that centrally planned economy lacks a strong spirit of innovation. This is generally manifested as fewer new products or new production technologies being developed in such an economy. It is not difficult to assess the structural reasons for this situation. As there is no threat of bankruptcy, enterprises do not have to compete with each other, do not worry whether they can catch up with the new developments in science and technology and do not worry whether their markets will be taken away by rival companies. All these make inner innovation unnecessary. In addition, there are not many effective incentive methods, either. The planners in a centrally planned economy or enterprise managers often tend to be "conservative", because all innovations include certain risks, and compared with the chance of success by innovation, the risk for failure seems higher and they may lose their posts in such a case.

The Superiority of "Market Socialism with Economic Democracy"

Schweickart argues that market socialism, or at least some versions of it, such as: his model as "market socialism with economic democracy" is highly superior compared to capitalist economic system.

What is "market socialism with economic democracy"? For Schweickart, market socialism with economic democracy can be considered as an economic system with three basic pillars: management of enterprises by workers, societal control on investments, and a market for goods and services[6]. He explains them more concretely.

Firstly, the main assets in the society will be owned collectively and jointly controlled by the laborers who use them. That means each enterprise is democratically managed and workers legally have the rights to elect the enterprise manager on the basis of one person-one vote. The enterprise belongs to the political sphere rather than civil society sphere. Enterprise is not an asset legally owned by its workers but an asset controlled by the association of their workers. The ultimate power in an enterprise belongs to all of its workers. In a small enterprise, a manager can be directly elected. In a large or medium size enterprise, workers may firstly elect their representatives to form a worker committee and then the worker committee will elect and supervise the enterprise manager.

Secondly, societal control on investments will be realized. In the market socialism with economic democracy, the funds for investments come from the taxes paid by enterprises. Every enterprise will pay a tax based on its capital assets[7].

---

6   *Ibid.*, p. 16.
7   *Ibid.*, p. 15.

This capital property tax is the source for investments supervised and controlled by the society. Basing investment fund sources on tax collection from enterprises instead of basing them on individual savings not only eliminates the main cause of inequality as in capitalism – which needs to pay fund interests to individuals, but also frees the economy from the dependence on depositors and investors. Schweickart stresses that the re-investment mechanism in his model is different from the capitalist re-investment mechanism, because markets will not control the direction of the investments but the society will determine it. In his model, the investment fund will yield a return to the communities which are formed by equal individuals having equal rights to earn that investment yield. In this way, the capital also flows back to each member of the society. People are not forced to follow the needs of capital. When the investment fund is received by the workers association (community) this fund will be "lent" to the enterprises controlled by the community or to a group of community members who plan to open a new enterprise. This kind of "lending" is performed through the public bank network and on the two major principles – planned benefits and preserving employment opportunities thus avoiding unemployment. Market principle takes effect only in this stage but is not the sole principle even in this stage, because the society may encourage or prevent some types of production lines regulating this aims through different capital tax rates.

Thirdly, there will be only commodity and service markets but no capital and labor markets. The model of market socialism with economic democracy does not allow enterprises directly to reinvest their "profits" instead "all profit" should return and distributed among workers. Since enterprises cannot directly make new investments with their profit, although "capital " still exists, i.e.: the production means and materials are controlled by enterprise workers, the "capital" as an abstract category which has a character of self- appreciation as described by Marx does not exist here . Certainly, no capital market exists. In the model of market socialism with economic democracy, also no labor market exists, either, because what workers obtain is not contracted wages but a portion of the profit from the enterprise they each control. Same as in the capitalist system, profit here also refers to the difference between sales revenues and costs, but in this model, workers' income cannot be calculated as a cost. It is just the surplus of the enterprise, the surplus after purchase of the materials needed for production, after deduction for depreciation costs and capital tax payment. As what workers obtain is a portion of enterprise's profit, it is not appropriate to say that workers sell or hire their labor power to enterprises, which means the non-existence of labor markets.

Schweickart advocates that the model of market socialism with economic democracy is economically feasible. From the perspective of a micro enterprise, an enterprise is in fact a cooperative character organization. This cooperative nature can guarantee its benefits, because plenty of experience has indicated that cooperative enterprises are almost always as efficient compared to similar capitalist enterprises, often even more efficient. In view of the relationships among enterprises in the whole economic system and relationships between enterprises and consumers, the competitive character of the economy guarantees that no information input problems or incentive problems will appear as generally practiced by planned socialism. From the perspective of long-term economic development orientation, the investment mechanism will be guided by a plan which conforms to the existing market and its requirements. The planning is certainly superior to an unrestricted market force. The problem of corporate innovation is solved, too, because the competition pressure will lead enterprises to keep pace with science and technology. In addition, income increment, laboring time reduction and improvements in labor conditions in an enterprise also provide active incentives for innovation.

Schweickart also emphasizes that the model of market socialism with economic democracy is not only economically feasible but also superior to capitalism in many aspects : it is more equal and just, because it eliminates the income from "capital" assets and eliminates capitalists; it is more democratic, because it extends democracy downwards to factories and upward because the formulation of the policies for macro-economic development will be controlled by the society ; it also eliminates the most devastating feature of contemporary capitalism – excessive global flow of capital.

Feasibility and Merits of the Market Socialism

Some scholars have expressed objections to Schweickart's model of market socialism with economic democracy. They have argued that competition, injustice, advertisements and potential unemployment risk still exist in this model and have raised their doubts: Is it the real socialism? Schweickart has answered them resolutely: It is very important to cite the differentiation made by Marx himself. Socialism is not the advanced form of communism. Socialism is born out of capitalism and bears the vestiges and birth marks of capitalism. It is not a perfect society but a non-capitalist economic system. It inherits the best achievements of capitalism and overcome the worst flaws of capitalism[8]. In his opinion, market socialism is socialism, since it firmly opposes capitalism. Market socialism is based on such an insight on the contemporary era, in today's world, the positive effect of bourgeoisie as a capitalist entrepreneur is bygone, and there is no need for capitalists who raise and accumulate capital, manage industry, create new products or develop new technologies, because now there has emerged other better ways to realize these functions. Market socialism not only resolutely opposes capitalism but also reflects the most desirable ideals and values of socialist tradition, i.e.: economy is controlled by producers rather than producers are controlled by

8   *Ibid.*, p. 19.

economy. Schweickart has also emphasized that market socialism is not an "utopist" socialism, because it acknowledges that the values we pursue as socialists will not be perfectly realized at least in the current societal development stage. Market socialism includes the notions of balancing against capitalism, partial acceptance and also opposition and rejection. This is just the common sense of Marxism. In comparison, non-market socialist models are either economically infeasible or disaccord with the values and principles of socialism.

2. JAMES LAWLER

James Lawler is a professor of philosophy at the State University of New York at Buffalo and the Chairman of American Research Association of Marxist Philosophy. He has pointed out that the collapse of socialism in Soviet Union and Eastern Europe has made more and more socialists completely abandon the thought of centrally planned economy and turned them to believe that socialism and further existence of market relations could be compatible. In the main he certainly agrees with the above new ideas and proposes his model which could be closest to the notions underlined by Marx and Engels as to the characteristics of the emerging post-capitalist society[9]. To demonstrate his model and approach, he has made careful historical studies on Marx and Engels' works and asserts that Marx and Engels had both believed that market economy will continue to exist during the transition period after proletariat seizes political power, and also in the subsequent first stage of communism, i.e.: socialism. He has even suggested, in some sense, Marx and Engels are both market socialists.

Market Economy after the Proletariat Seizes Power

Lawler points out that, in the *Communist Manifesto*, Marx and Engels had written: "The proletariat will use its political supremacy to gradually wrest, by degree, all capital from the bourgeoisie, centralize all instruments of production in the hands of the state, i.e., state meaning as the proletariat organized as the ruling class; and begin to increase the total productive forces as rapidly as possible."[10] This paragraph indicates that the centralization of all instruments of production in the hands of the proletarian state as envisaged by Marx and Engels is a gradual (by a degree) development process. The text emphasizes that it is realized "by degree". As it is impossible that all capital of bourgeoisie is centralized in the hands of proletariat states at one go, the society in a period after the victory of revolution will be a "mixed society"[11]. It will contain both the elements of socialist

---

9   *Ibid.*, p. 24.
10   Marx and Engels Selected Works, Edition 2, Vol. 1, Beijing, People's Publishing House, 1995, p. 293.
11   Edited by Bertell Ollman: Market Socialism: The Debate among Socialists, translated by Duan Zhongqiao, p. 26.

economy and the elements of capitalist economy, with the former gradually assuming a dominant position.

If the proletariat cannot wrest all the capital from the bourgeoisie immediately after assuming political power, then how will the proletarian state wrest the property still remaining in the hands of individuals, after one part of the total capital is socialized direct after the victory of revolution? Lawler asserts that Engels had elaborated this issue in the *Principles of Communism* a few months before he had drafted the *Communist Manifesto*. Engels wrote: "Gradual expropriation of landowners, industrialists, railroad magnates and ship owners' capital, partly through competition by state industry, partly directly through compensation in the form of government bonds."[12] That is to say, in addition to direct socialization through compensation in form of government bonds, the proletarian state will also increase state property through competition, organizing its enterprises to compete against capitalist enterprises. The latter method also implies that socialist property is more effective than capitalist property and can win over in a fair and market competition environment. In this case, the society in this period can only be a kind of market socialism. In this society, the enterprises controlled by the proletarian state will continue to operate according to market principles and realize the goal of reducing bourgeoisie property and increasing proletarian property through competing with non-state-owned private enterprises. As Marx and Engels had also advocated that state ownership will be the main form of proletariat property in this period, this economic system created by socialist revolution can also be called as "state market socialism".

Lawler emphasizes that this market created by proletariat state is no longer the capitalist market in the original sense. This is because this new market starts playing the role of opposing bourgeoisie and safeguarding proletariat based on the conscious administration by the proletariat state[13]; armed by reasonableness or consciousness of the proletariat state —planned intervention—, the market no longer possesses a blind spontaneous power. Of course, the market intervention by the proletariat state is not equal to macro-management of enterprise activities but instead intervention aims to formulate and regulate new operation rules in this market. These regulations will represent workers' interests rather than private owners'. Lawler has commented: "from then on, "socialist" market starts its existence and more or less rapidly changes the conditions in the labor markets. As a result, "doing one day's honest work to get one day's honest wage" will be realized as a first step.

---

12   Marx and Engels Selected Works, Edition 2, Vol.1, p. 240.
13   Edited by Bertell Ollman: Market Socialism: The Debate among Socialists, translated by Duan Zhongqiao, p. 33.

Communal Control Cannot Be Adopted Immediately

From the above description, the following question may arise: why should the state property after the proletarian revolution be controlled by the hands of proletarian state rather than directly by the workers of each enterprise? Lawler bases himself on Engels' relevant ideas: "the peasants and manufacture workers of the last century changed their whole way of life and became quite different people as they were drawn into big industry, in the same way, communal control over production by society as a whole, and the resulting new development, will both require an entirely different kind of human material. People will no longer be, as they are today, subordinated to a single branch of production, bound to it, exploited by it; they will no longer develop one of their faculties at the expense of all others; they will no longer know only one branch, or one part of a single branch of production as a whole. Even today's industry finds such people less and less useful. Industry controlled by society as a whole, and being operated according to a plan, presupposes well-rounded human beings, their faculties developed in balanced fashion, able to see the system of production in its entirety. The form of the division of labor which makes one a peasant, another a cobbler, a third a factory worker, a fourth a stock-market operator, has already been undermined by today's machinery production and will completely disappear in the future . Education will enable young people quickly to familiarize themselves with the whole system of production and to pass from one branch of production to another in response to the needs of society or their own inclinations. It will, therefore, free them from the one-sided character which the present-day division of labor impresses upon every individual. Communist society will, in this way, make it possible for its members to put their comprehensively developed faculties to full use [...]."[14] This long paragraph indicates that in Engels' point of view, the reason for the infeasibility of laboring people's "communal control over production" direct after the proletarian revolution is neither that the proletarian state does not have the right or enough political capacity to deprive all the property from the bourgeoisie, nor that it has not possess those technical cadres who can formulate a central plan of production. The main reason is that the laboring people, the direct producers, are yet to possess the comprehensive all-round education, culture and skills required by communist society. Lawler has also emphasized that Engels did not say that "communal control" can be exercised by those technical cadre elites employed in the state central planning agency. "Communal control" only and only means the control will be performed by the society as a whole, rather than by a special expert group as "central planning" authority.

All in all, Lawler points out that Engels' dissertation clarifies five issues: (1) Just after the victory of the proletarian revolution the "communal control" over production can be impossible. Therefore, market mechanism guiding production

---

14   Marx and Engels Selected Works, Edition 2, Vol. 1, p. 242-243.

will continue to exist, although property relations will change gradually. (2) The consciousness or regulation capacity of the society over this market guided production will gradually increase and will benefit working people. (3) Once industry can be communally operated according to a plan, this communal control over the whole industry and economy will be performed the whole society rather than by a central planning agency of elite experts. (4) Capitalist production itself also develops towards this direction because the modern machinery and computer led production has changed the hierarchical structures in the management of capitalist enterprises and other organizations, like strict division of labor has become outdated. (5) This means that the post-capitalist society will be divided into two stages. In the first stage, market relations including capitalist enterprises will continue to exist, whereas the property will be gradually transferred to the hands of proletariat state through economic means and through socialist enterprises' successful competition with capitalist enterprises; in the second stage, the communal control over the economy will be gradually realized by the laboring people themselves. As commented by Engels, currency – "market relations cease to play its important economic roles only in the latter stage".

Cooperative Enterprises as the Key Players

Through his studies on the works of Marx and Engels, Lawler has also introduced the following view: in the period from 1848 to 1864, Marx and Engels have amended their thoughts on the economic strategy of proletarian state, in this respect they have no longer suggested the state property as the main form in the transition period from the old society to the new society, instead considered the building of cooperative factories as the most promising form of the socialist economy and as the starting point of the new society.

Lawler has emphasized that, in the works of Marx and Engels, communism is deemed as the negation of moribund capitalism and as a thoroughly different society to replace capitalism. Communism is a kind of development which has existed in capitalism. As Marx put it, "the working class has no fixed ideals to realize, but only to set free the elements of the new society to which old collapsing bourgeois society itself is pregnant to"[15]. The ready elements needed to be set free as mentioned by Marx here are workers' cooperative enterprises. Marx had also devoted a dissertation in Volume 3 of *Capital* on this issue: "The co-operative factories of the laborers themselves represent within the old form the first sprouts of the new, although they naturally reproduce, and must reproduce, everywhere in their actual organization all the shortcomings of the prevailing system. But the anti-thesis between capital and labor is overcome within them, if at first only by way of transforming the associated laborers into their own capitalists, i.e.,

---

15   Marx and Engels Selected Works, Edition 2, Vol. 3, Beijing, People's Publishing House, 1995, p. 60.

by enabling them to use the means of production for the employment of their own labor. They show how a new mode of production naturally grows out of an old one, when the development of the material forces of production and the corresponding forms of social production have reached a particular stage. Without the factory system arising in the womb capitalist mode of production there could have been no co-operative factories. Nor could these have developed without the banking credit system arising in the same mode of production."[16] Obviously, the co-operative factories owned by the laborers themselves will exist and operate in market economy. As the first sprouts of the new society, they will be enterprises organizing production for the market. Marx had realized the limitations of these enterprises, but he had still regarded them as the initial structure of the new society. He did not reject them just because of their "bourgeois" shortcomings. Of course, although Marx had considered co-operative factories owned by laborers as the "first sprouts of the new" growing out of the old, he had still insisted the first crucial step was to establish the proletarian government. Otherwise the co-operative movement could inevitably suffer setbacks. Only when proletariat seizes political power, can the co-operative enterprises of laborers more thoroughly demonstrate their superiority over capitalist enterprises in the market competition.

Lawler believes that Marx and Engels had in fact advocated the thought of market socialism thereby putting more emphasis on the role of co-operative economy. This can also be clearly observed in Engels' article *The Peasant Question in France and Germany*: "As soon as our Party assumes possession of political power, it has simply to expropriate the big landed proprietors, just like the manufacturers in industry. [...] The big estates, thus restored to the community, are to be turned over by us to the rural workers who are already cultivating them and they are to be organized into co-operatives."[17] This paragraph indicates that after the possession of political power, the proletariat will adopt mixed state-cooperative ownership form, and the big estates will be turned over to rural workers and they will operate them in form of cooperatives, although the ownership of these estates will be legally in the hands of the society. The conversion of capitalist enterprises into "social" enterprises does not rest there with the establishment of the regulated market economic system, but requires further steps: e.g. the conversion of private ownership, into community ownership and under direct control of workers who directly work in these enterprises. In Marx's *Civil War in France* in which he studied the Paris Commune experience , there are more precise dissertations on this issue: "If co-operative production is not to remain a sham and a snare; if it is to supersede the capitalist system; if united co-operative societies are to regulate national production upon a common plan, thus taking it under their own control, and putting an end to the constant anarchy and periodical convulsions which are the

16 Capital, Vol. 3, Beijing, People's Publishing House, 1975, p. 497-498.
17 Marx and Engels Selected Works, Edition 2, Vol.4, Beijing, People's Publishing House, 1995, p. 503.

fatality of capitalist production — what else, gentlemen, would it be but communism, 'possible' communism?" "The working class did not expect miracles from the Commune. They have no ready-made utopias to introduce *par décret* du peuple. They know that in order to work out their own emancipation and along with it that higher form to which present society is irresistibly tending by its own economical agencies, they will have to pass through long struggles, through a series of historic processes, transforming circumstances and men. They have no ideals to realize, but to set free the elements of the new society with which old collapsing bourgeois society itself is pregnant."[18] Lawler has commented: "although Marx here wrote on the tasks of Paris Commune as the first proletariat government, in fact he means that the proletarian revolution opens a transitory period. The starting point of this transition period will contain the first sprouts of the new society, which had already partially developed in the old society, i.e.: co-operative factories. After smashing the coercion apparatus of the capitalist state and by the supportive measures taken by proletariat regime, they will grow even faster. The development direction after the revolution is to promote the co-operative factories of laborers — the sprouts of the new society growing out of the old society-. The above paragraph by Marx can be interpreted in a way, that they have no longer advocated the state market socialism they had once mentioned in the *Communist Manifesto* but instead "co-operative market socialism".

Lawler argues that from the dissertations of Marx and Engels in this period, the following conclusions can be drawn: the transition period as the "transformation from capitalism into communism" can be divided into two "stages". The first stage will be the "mixed socialist – capitalist society" and in this stage, capitalist enterprises will still remain to exist. The second stage will be "pure market socialism". In this stage, co-operative factories will be dominant, but this stage still possesses certain features of capitalism and still to a great extent relies on production guided by market.

A Restricted Market Still Existing in the First Stage of Communism

Do market relations still exist in the first stage of communism, i.e.: socialist society? Marx wrote in *Critique of the Gotha Program*: "Within the co-operative society based on common ownership of the means of production, the producers do not exchange their products"[19]. Lawler asserts that Marx obviously did not think that market relations will exist in the first stage of communism, but he pointed out: "*in Critique of the Gotha Programme*, it will be not difficult to see that Marx in fact describes a different exchange system". Here Lawler refers to Marx's remarks on the "voucher" exchange: "Concretely speaking, in the first stage of communism, laborers obtain a kind of "voucher" based on their labor and use these vouchers to buy their needed goods in a similar market. Although Marx insists that these

18   Marx and Engels Selected Works, Edition 2, Vol. 3, p. 59-60.
19   Marx and Engels Selected Works, Edition 2, Vol. 3, p. 303.

"vouchers are the same as theatre tickets but not currency[20]; "they still perform the functions of a real currency"[21]. This is because the "vouchers" which indicate that the laborers have realized a certain "equivalent number of labor hours" cannot be equaled to theatre tickets or the quantitative supply documents in the wartime indicating the right to purchase some particular commodities. Instead for Marx, they are more like a credit certificate (credit card) , indicating how many value units of equivalent a worker has earned through his labor and they , (vouchers) can be used in the exchange of all kinds of needed goods, thus for Lawler: "they still perform some functions of currency". Based on his interpretation on the "vouchers" which still performs some functions of real currency, Lawler has concluded that market, in the first stage of communism, no longer exists in its full sense, but there still remains a limited or restricted market[22].

All in all, Lawler believes that in the first stage of communism, the currency in the full sense no longer exists, and moreover, according to Marx's definition in the strict sense, nor exists the commodity exchange, but there still exists restricted currency form of exchange and restricted market. They both will continue to play an active role in the newborn communist society[23]. Market will finally disappear only in the fully mature stage of communism.

3. HILLEL TICKTIN

Hillel Ticktin is a professor of the Institute of Soviet and East European Studies at the University of Glasgow, and the Director of the Research Center for Socialist Theory and Movement. In contrast with David Schweickart and James Lawler, he vigorously opposes market socialism. He argues that market socialism is not a brand new theory, emerging as early as 1930s; it had later received constant support from Stalinists and social democrats. Currently, after the superficial victory of capitalism declared due to failure of Soviet socialist model, many former Marxists have started to believe that market should be an universal thing every type of economy should adopt. Thus Market socialism has made a comeback. The Marxists like Ticktin have argued that market socialism is not only practically impossible but also denies socialism at all. Ticktin illustrates his opposition to market socialism from the following four aspects:

20   Capital, Vol. 1, Beijing, People's Publishing House, 1975, p. 112.
21   Edited by Bertell Ollman: Market Socialism: The Debate among Socialists, translated by Duan Zhongqiao, p. 53.
22   *Ibid.*, p. 53.
23   *Ibid.*, p. 55.

The Absurd Elements in Market Socialism

Ticktin has argued that market socialists and Marxists primarily hold different views on market and socialism.

As for market, the non-Marxist classical economists who advocate market define market as an economic environment in which buyers and sellers compete with each other. In other words, as long as there are buyers and sellers, markets should exist. But Marxist economists cannot define market in this way. They should define market as a domain where the law of value works, or a place where value is realizable[24]. The two definitions obviously contradict. For Marxists, unless value is involved, exchange per se is not a market relation. For example, for the people who can only use coupons to exchange special goods, the issuance of coupon has nothing to do with market. The necessary conditions for the existence of market are currency, exchange value and value. By this token, the barter system, for example, where a cooperative factory uses its industrial products to exchange agricultural products with a collective farms cannot be the manifestation of market system.

As for socialism, Ticktin points out that for non-Marxist classic economists, socialism is usually defined as nationalization. For Marxists, socialism should be defined as the planning degree of the society . The planning is conceived as the conscious control of associated producers over the society[25]. In other words, surplus products should be controlled by the majority of people through democratic procedures. However, non-Marxist classic economists argue that planning is only an important form used to coordinate producers' goals and it is a technical relation rather than a social relation. Ticktin emphasizes that the decisive difference between capitalism and socialism lies in the status of labor. In the socialist society Labor will become people's primary need rather than a burden. The wage labor will be abolished and labor will certainly become a creative activity. The division of labor will be overcome in two senses: everybody will engage in more than one occupation and everybody will involve in the management of their organization as well as the society as a whole.

The above view indicates that Marxists and non-Marxists differ significantly in interpreting the connotation of market socialism. Non-Marxists think that market socialism is an economy characterized by large-scale nationalization and inter-enterprise market relations, and the operation of this economy should be based on profit and loss. Marxists hold that socialism abolishes the sale of labor power, and laborers control both economy and enterprises. This means that the market no longer controls labor, and the capital market, value and currency no longer exist. Therefore, the concept of market socialism is quite absurd.

---

24   *Ibid.*, p. 65.
25   *Ibid.*

Some people argue that market had already existed before capitalism and will continue to exist after capitalism, so market can be separated from the capitalist economy which is based on accumulation and profit. For Ticktin, in Marxist sense, markets had existed before capitalism, but only in immature forms, and these forms have grown mature in capitalist system. Market was extremely limited before capitalism, so it is only a secondary and insignificant attribute of the then economic system. Although different kinds of retail and wholesale markets had existed before capitalism, no large-scale commodity production had emerged. Therefore, in the pre-capitalist period, an exchange value already exists, but generally speaking, value does not exist. This situation indicates market is inseparable from its social relations, i.e.: the relations between capital and labor[26].

Market Socialism Completely Opposite to Socialism

Ticktin has argued that the difference between Marxists and market socialists are mainly manifested in the following two basic opposite points of view.

Firstly, socialism certainly eliminates the value-creating abstract labor and the phenomenon that particular workers are degraded into machines or subordinated to production process . Marxists think that workers should be the masters of the production process[27]. In the socialist society, workers work because they feel responsible for the current social system and their enterprises and since their work becomes more individualized and creative. For workers labor becomes a means to realize their individuality. In this social system, people enjoy equality in income and social management, and the character of social relations is humane. By contrast, in the market socialism, workers are subjected to accumulation and profit rate, and they have to compete with their colleagues for jobs, for higher standard of living conditions and for promotion. For market socialists, workers are first considered as consumers who realize higher standard of living through market. Competition and pursuit for profit is considered as the guarantee for economic efficiency, enterprise managers receive higher incomes as a reward for their functions. Since market socialism degrades laborers into competing machines, it is unequal and inhuman.

Secondly, and more fundamentally, Marxists believe that in a socialist society, economy is operated according to the principle of meeting people's increasing needs[28]. The concept of "need" should be understood in a broad sense. It includes all kinds of people's demands from leisure to creation and is not limited to satisfaction as simple consumption. In a society with market economy, exchange value, value and currency are per se purposes, whereas capital accumulation does

---

26 *Ibid.*, p. 67.
27 *Ibid.*
28 *Ibid.*, p. 68.

not have any necessary link with people's welfare. When the economy is backward, it is true that monetary incentives and wealth accumulation may promote industrial and technical development, but it only means that the increase of the power and material interest of the people who control the means of production in the society. But as for the poor, they can guarantee their interests only through struggle. Therefore, profit orientation will extremely distort the human values. Firstly, due to capitalists' or managers' leadership, money- making contradicts people's direct democracy. Secondly, the argument that competition somehow leads to a better consumer satisfaction is doubtful. Under market condition, profit orientation only means maximum increase in surplus product and prices of goods. The only result will be that manufacturers get control of the market and only sell those products profitable to them. They will produce those products with high-quality for the rich, while with poorer quality for the common laborers. Furthermore, under market conditions, social production is unplanned and the goal of making money is realized in an anarchic way. As known to all, Adam Smith had envisaged an invisible hand which will bring about an increase of the wealth in the whole society, but he had failed to see that this invisible hand also brings about colossal militarization, bureaucracy, massive unemployment, and cause millions of people living on the brink of starvation and while at the same time crises of excess demand where also excess food products are destructed. Undoubtedly, it is ridiculous to say that money-making and personal greed will automatically lead to public welfare for the majority.

For Ticktin it is not worth discussing with market socialists, because they lack common ground, particularly on the essence of socialist society and the ultimate objective of socialism. From a Marxist point of view, under contemporary conditions, it is impossible that markets can exist outside capitalism. Market relation is not a technology or means but a special social relation between labor and capital. He emphasizes that only two systems are possible: socialism and capitalism. If market socialism is possible, the form in which it controls workers will only be the society completely opposite to socialism[29]. Ticktin has pinpointed that an unswerving socialist should advocate the distinctive and essential characteristics of socialism, of which planning is the most fundamental. Market is the opposite of planning. It does not allow laborers' conscious regulation and control on economy. It relies on the spontaneous and anarchic behaviors of actors among which the ones who play the greatest role will be those who control capital.

Market and the Transition to Socialism

Market socialists often assume that there will be a transition period between capitalism and socialism, while this period certainly possesses the characteristics of past and future: and this transition period is just the market socialism? Whether

---

29   *Ibid.*, p. 72.

market will temporarily exist or not in the transition period as a temporary measure is not is the main difference between market socialists and Marxists. Ticktin argues that as long as market continues to exist, the transition from capitalism to socialism will not occur.

Firstly, because the existence of the market will certainly increase capital's expansion and additionally capital is international and has a world-wide dominance, it will not allow those states who desire to build socialism[30]. Because these countries are economically dependent on the international capital, the transition to socialism will become impossible. Secondly, the further existence of the market will corrupt the public sector of the economy, thus hampering the transition to socialism, because the further existence of market requires allowing a private sector in the economy and there will be a situation in which the public sector and private sector of the economy co-exist and compete with each other. These two sectors both have their strong points and weak points. In competition, each of them will try do its best to strengthen its own position in production and sales and weaken the other. Once they co-exist together in an economy, the public sector will inevitably be corrupt. As known to all, the scandals related to corruption in public sector have become an epidemic in the 20th century. It is because the profit in public sector is restricted, while it is almost unrestricted in the private sector. Consequently the managers in public sector will inevitably get "kickbacks" from private contractors. In the end, market socialism will certainly cause to bureaucracy. The essential characteristics of socialism include adequate and direct democracy. Only when exchange value of commodities is abolished, can the decision on surplus products be made through conscious regulation and control, thus enables adequate and direct democracy. Therefore, the essence of the transition period should be gradual elimination of exchange value and improvement in the planning of the economy. The existence of market requires the existence of a social group which will manage surplus products, and a bureaucratic group which obtains a controlling status and power in regulating the markets and this group will gradually restrict and eliminate the power of working class. This will certainly hinder transition to socialism. The transition period must be a period in which bureaucracy is defeated. Accurately speaking, this is because bureaucracy represents the old society rather than the new society[31].

All in all, Ticktin believes that as long as market continues to exist, there will be no transition to socialism, and the only result will be further existence of capitalism.

---

30 *Ibid.*, p. 73.
31 Ibid., p. 81.

Market Socialism Cannot Bring Efficiency

After the collapse of socialism in the Soviet Union and Eastern Europe, some scholars have started to argue that socialism is certainly inefficient, but it guarantees sufficient employment, social services, welfare for the majority, free education and guarantees minimum wages for the working classes; on the contrary, they argue that markets bring efficiency, and may improve people's living standards in a certain period. Therefore, the marriage between the market and the so-called socialism may utilize the advantages of the both. Ticktin has pointed out that, in fact, just like many marriages, this marriage is also based on a series of illusions[32].

Firstly, the socialism they base themselves is restricted by "only Soviet socialism". But, it has nothing to do with the socialism envisaged by Marx. More strictly speaking, it should be called Stalinist socialism. In Marx's point of view, socialist society is a society directly managed by producers, but in former Soviet Union, the surplus products in the society were controlled by a minority of elites. In the former Soviet Union, even those things which seemed positive had serious defects. For example, medical services were not distributed equally among various social groups; the majority of the people have only enjoyed a low-level medical service. Similar problems have occurred in education services. Also the non-existence of unemployment was due to the inefficiency in the socio-economic system. Besides, it is noteworthy that the implementation and protection of these majority interests could be guaranteed by the pressure of common people and were not the essential characteristics of the Stalinist social system. These advantages for the people were instruments —the ruling means- to maintain this inhuman social system.

Secondly, market socialism cannot bring efficiency. Some advocates of market socialism mention that there was no real currency in the former Soviet Union and thus economic accounting would be either impossible or extremely difficult, because all economic decisions were based on rough or non-relevant information. Thus they deduce that the socialism without markets will be inefficient and that only markets with currency exchange and where supply-demand law operates can offer reasonable accounting methods and enable effective decisions. However, Ticktin argues that market socialism also cannot ensure efficiency. In addition to its above defects market socialism is also prone to insurmountable problems just in markets. Market will certainly fuel the conflicts between capitalists and workers and between employers and employees. Under the conditions of sufficient employment, monetary stimulation to promote people to get jobs will be weakened, particularly, for those non-skill related jobs and those risky/unhealthy jobs. Pursuit for profit by enterprises will drive them to stop the production of quality products needed by consumers. Even the production of food will face serious

---

32   *Ibid.*, p. 82.

problems caused by the greed for profit. The outbreak of Mad Cow Disease in Britain is a very good example.

Some market socialists argue that market may provide proper signals for producers and consumers, thus guarantees a more effective allocation of resources. Ticktin refutes that, arguing that market can only provide signals related to currency possessed by actors, and poor people without currency cannot give signals related to their real needs or demands. The richer groups holding more currency will increase their demands and this will push the prices upward and market will be distorted. The market will always serve the rich, because it is the best mechanism to make money and profit. One example is the production of Concorde type luxury planes in France which were only affordable by the rich people. In fact in this way, important resources are wasted by the rich. In addition, for the market efficiency, the unemployment mechanism will be maintained to push down the wages which will undoubtedly discourage less talented laid-off people. When unemployed masses and idle machines increase, periodic economic depressions will become inevitable. Competition also causes a huge waste of manpower and resources thus hindering more reasonable regulation of division of labor in the industry. The economic competition for profits between rival states will inevitably cause large-scale militarization and periodic wars.

Ticktin thus concludes that planning and market are incompatible and mixing them will not produce any desirable prospect and the experience in Eastern Europe and the former Soviet Union has fully demonstrated this point.

4. BERTELL OLLMAN

Bertell Ollman is the professor of politics at New York University and a famous Marxist. He thinks that the essence of capitalism rests with market relations, and realizing socialism requires eliminating market relations. Accordingly, he firmly opposes market socialists, and systematically and profoundly criticizes market socialism focusing on the issue, whether market can be preserved during the initial establishment of socialism.

Market Socialism, an Inaccessible Utopia

What is market socialism? Ollman points out that there are different versions of market socialism. "What makes them market societies is that buying and selling, however restricted, continues to go on for commodities and labor power and, in some market socialism versions, even capital markets exist. And money continues to be the mediator among individuals and the reflector of their desires. What makes these societies socialist is that the capitalist class has been removed from its dominant position in society. In the more popular version, workers own and/

or control the enterprises where they work or can elect their managers, and effect decisions which were previously made by capitalist owners or their managers. The capitalists, as a distinct class, are not abolished and in cases where small scale private sector remains, their powers are not severely restricted."[33] Nevertheless, he claims that all versions of market socialism are utopia inaccessible to socialism.

Ollman argues that under market socialism, although enterprises are collectively owned and jointly controlled by workers, these enterprises do not have essential differences from capitalist enterprises. As co-owners of their enterprises, the workers, like any capitalist, will buy raw materials, hire labor, and sell finished goods. Although these activities will not take much of their time, this will provide workers with completely new experiences , especially buy and sell labor power and buy and sell commodities, this on the other hand will make them assimilate some similar experiences those practiced by workers under capitalism. Furthermore, when a jobless worker first applies for a job he will be treated as an outsider by the collective who owns the enterprise, the fear and exclusion he will feel will be all too familiar. The collective, after all, will only hire new people when they believe their work will increase enterprise profit. In a co-operatively owned enterprise, the interests of the individual worker and the interests of the collective do not coincide, because while certain individuals may desire to work shorter, or at a slower pace, etc., but the collective may force him to work longer and faster so that it can lead the competition among the enterprises. The interests of an individual worker will have less weight when compared with the interests of the collective which aims profit maximizing, due to the logic of the market. Under such circumstances, the actual experience of worker's working conditions will have no difference from the current capitalism, although he is the owner in the collective enterprise which buys and employs his labor[34].

Ollman has pointed out that, in all versions of market socialism, market for commodities is not touched and models offer least changes there. The new relations of ownership do not affect the fact that, like in the current capitalist society, it will be individuals those who will decide what to buy, compare and choose commodities on the basis of their price, and compete with individuals to reach the best deal. They will constantly desire more money so that they can buy more, or desire to have stronger power and status to buy more. As now, they will continue to worship money as something that gives them this power. And in order to be stronger in the competition for commodities and money, they will develop also a kind of indifference for the needs of others. Consequently they will continue to view consuming more commodities and more money as the criterion for success, as in capitalism—will never feel satisfied. As a result, the greed and indifference displayed in their deals with each other in the market will continue to determine

---

33   *Ibid.*, p. 113-114.
34   *Ibid.*, p. 114-115.

human nature. All these will make it extraordinarily difficult to raise workers' class consciousness, and especially harm their class solidarity.

Ollman admits that the workers as co-owners of their enterprise will have new experiences. To the extent that their relations with their co-workers within the enterprise are cooperative and democratic, these experiences could be very empowering and positive. But as the co-owners of an enterprise, however, their relations to those outside—to people who are applying for a new job, or to those who represent other enterprises with whom they are in competition, or against final consumers who consume their products—will be similar to that of a collective capitalist. Marx had also evaluated the cooperative factories of his day and commented that cooperative factories turn "associated laborers into their own capitalists"[35]. This view also applies to the collective enterprises owned by workers under market socialism. Under market socialism, "with the aim of maximizing profits, workers, as collective capitalists, are likely to behave rather like capitalists of today"[36], i.e. producing what sells, producing for those who have the money to buy and ignoring the needs of those who cannot afford. Workers participating in these activities directly, or even indirectly, will more or less share those profits that typically go to the capitalist class. By turning workers into collective capitalists, market socialism brings another alienation for them making them think as capitalists and thus adds to their original alienation as workers, although reforms the latter only slightly. Now, they also practice the worries and anxieties caused by competition among capitalists; they also need to manipulate consumers and themselves as workers with the pursuit of highest possible profit; they also practice the greed for money, turning a blind eye to the human needs of others. Marx had aptly characterized competition among capitalists as "avarice and war between the avaricious"[37]. The same description can be applied to the competition between worker groups as collective capitalists in market socialism.

Ollman does not deny that there are some important differences between market socialism and market capitalism, because any market socialist society is likely to distribute many commodities—such as education, health care, and perhaps even partly capital for investment—on the basis of social needs and not based on profit first criterion. Likewise, one would expect "fairer" treatment for some social groups that are currently discriminated against in capitalism and a greater degree of support for those who are the losers in market competition. However, he emphasizes that the new practice people have in selling their labor power and buying commodities, together with the new practice they have as co-owners of

---

35 Capital, Vol. 3, p. 498.
36 Edited by Bertell Ollman: Market Socialism: The Debate among Socialists, translated by Duan Zhongqiao, p. 117.
37 Collected Works of Karl Marx and Frederick Engels, Chinese Version Edition 1, Vol. 42, Beijing, People's Publishing House, 1979, p. 90.

their enterprises, are likely to create the way of thinking and attitudes that are very similar to what exists under capitalism. Also, as in today's capitalist society, these unhealthy tendencies will spread to other areas of life, family life, politics, culture and education. The attempt to educate the people with socialist values will only achieve modest results in the face of exchange practices in the market conditions which teach them other lessons. In this case, "people will neither be able to build socialism nor to live according to its precepts in any consistent manner"[38].

Ollman has asked: The mode of thinking inspired by the existing market—is it compatible with the way of thinking, feeling and values required for socialism? At its simplest, can people develop mutual concern and solidarity needed to coope- rate effectively while maintaining indifference and lusts for personal advantages which make them good competitors? At any given moment, it is probably possi- ble to observe such contrasting qualities inside the same personality, but this mix will be an extremely volatile and delicate one. Market related thoughts will simply spread throughout the entire working day, the problems which these thoughts deal are never wholly resolved and attitudes that accompany them—especially the greed, the fear and the anxiety—cannot be turned on or off with wishful philosophizing . Neither, beliefs or values or emotions are easy to be placed in isolated compartments, and when they are faced with their opposites often a batt- le for dominance will occur. People's ability to respond to those moral values that make socialism possible will diminish with the increase of material incentives and money relations. As long as market and its ways of thinking exercises daily rein- forcement on people's practice in market exchanges, the development of socialist values, and hence socialist practice in any sphere, cannot proceed long. If market socialism cannot lead to socialism, it is an utopia at most.

Inadequate Analysis on Capitalism, Communism, Socialism and Socialist Revolution

Ollman has argued that the main reason why market socialists have come to favor such a solution which is both overly modest and unworkable is their inadequate analysis on capitalism, communism, socialism and socialist revolution.

As for capitalism, Ollman points out, market socialists do not realize how strongly capitalism, its practices and ways of thinking , attitudes and of its problems are related with capitalist market relations, and, consequently, how hugely will preser- ving the market, any market intervene in the building of socialism.

Here, "the fundamental error in their analysis is to equal capital with capitalists which is the current form of capital, and not see that capital, as a relation of

---

38   Edited by Bertell Ollman: Market Socialism: The Debate among Socialists, translated by Duan Zhongqiao, p. 118.

production, can also be embodied in the state ownership (as in state capitalism) or even in workers' cooperatives (as in market socialism)"[39]. Capital is a self-appreciating wealth category by nature so that wealth is not employed to satisfy human wants but to create more wealth. What's ultimately crucial is its inherent, intrinsic purpose, and not who owns it. It is how capital functions in the pursuit of that goal that gives the society most of its capitalist colors and problems. In fact, the market, through which the newly created wealth(capital) which initially appears in commodities form returns to the owners of the means of production in the form of capital, "this is the more important feature of capitalism than its being privately owned"[40]. Thus, ownership may be transferred to the state (as occurred in history with nationalized industries in many countries) or to workers' cooperatives, but if the market remains essentially intact and untouched most of the problems associated with capitalism will continue to exist.

As for communism, Ollman has pointed out that market socialists fail to grasp "how radically different socialism as a transitional form should be from capitalism,"[41] if it is to prepare the foundations for future communism. Since most market socialists do not believe that communism can be possible in any case, this argument will unlikely make them think. Ignoring the necessary ties between communism and socialism, however, remains to be an important reason for the moderate reforms proposed in the name of market socialism.

As for socialism, Ollman points out that "market socialists, like most non-socialists, generally confuse the planning under market socialism with the central planning that existed in the Soviet style economies[42]. Succeeding and sublating capitalism, a major pre-condition for the success of socialism, socialist planning as envisaged by Marx should utilize the advantages of advanced industrial and organizational level, highly skilled and educated working class, relative material abundance, and the deep rooted socialist culture and tradition. Regretfully, market socialists just ignore this point and neglect the negative preconditions possessed and offered by developed capitalist societies in advanced countries for the realization of socialism.

As for socialist revolution, some market socialists think that in future socialist society, workers will not actively participate and effect crucial political decisions, including choosing economic planners and determine the main priorities of the plan, thus they conclude that the planned economy feasible on the basis of democracy is unrealizable. At this point, Ollman has argued that the market socialists "are simply expecting the same human attitude —with which they are familiar

---

39   *Ibid.*, p. 122.
40   *Ibid.*.
41   *Ibid.*, p. 123.
42   *Ibid.*

– in the future society"[43]. They cannot imagine the significance of a successful revolution participated and made by people and its effect in the formation their class consciousness. For Ollman, given the enormous power possessed by the capitalist class, for a victorious socialist revolution, the majority of workers need to attain class-consciousness, which involves, among other things, recognizing their common interests, developing greater mutual solidarity and collective behavior, and acquire certain degree of political awareness, as well as a stronger sense of individual responsibility when changing the old. But these "are just the same qualities that will possibly enable building socialism after the revolution, including democratic central planning."[44] Ollman argues that market socialist analyses on capitalism, communism, socialism, and the revolution, almost without exception, have one thing in common: the treatment of each development period in virtual isolation from the others. If capitalism, socialism, and communism are internally related stages in the historical evolution, the vantage point of an analysis on socialism, or any of its important features, should start by capitalism, paying special attention to the problems it poses for socialism and the material preconditions it establishes for solving them. An approach to socialism that begins with the analysis of market under capitalism, immediately poses other questions such as: organic linkages between market and the accumulation of capital, exploitation, alienation, and class struggle. This false approach manifests very clearly how the market, so construed, is responsible for many of the worst problems in capitalism—economic crisis, unemployment, poles of wealth and poverty, ecological destruction, exaggerated greed, corruption, etc. Considering the essential identity between capitalist relations and market relations, it is impossible to conceive the market as a neutral means for realizing social policies under market socialism.

Starting out to investigate socialism from the aspect of capitalism, therefore, has an additional advantage in that it enables us to give due attention to the enormous achievements realized by capitalism as well as recognizing its impossibility in influencing the shape of the future society . In the sphere of the market, the most important of these capitalist achievements include advanced distribution and communication networks and the technology needed to integrate their functioning , modern patterns of resource allocation, extensive planning mechanisms within private corporations and planning related to public departments, the advanced organizational skills of economic and financial operators, and of course, the huge amount of wealth which is already in the pipeline as well as all the potential material sources available to produce much more. The possibility of economic planning in socialism— let alone evaluated— cannot be fully grasped: its already existing preconditions, the main existing problems such planning should address which will be inherited from the capitalist society by socialism . Market socialists, on the other hand, almost without exception, approach the question of

43 *Ibid.*, p. 124.
44 *Ibid.*

market in socialism from the vantage point of failures observed in Soviet style regimes, and conclude that, if plan seems to cause the failure, the solution can only be replacing plan with the market. But why should reforms, tailored to the conditions in the Soviet Union fit today's advanced capitalist society? To persuade people that market socialist solutions – "which is assumed to cure the problems of a failed socialism"— would apply to today's capitalist society, they abstractly ignore the historical specific characteristics of the Soviet style system, and also simply ignore the advantages for building socialism in an advanced post-capitalist society. Ollman emphasizes that a direct and unrestricted attack on the market and all its drawbacks is an absolutely indispensable means in developing socialist consciousness. "People's turn to socialism will only emerge through the rejection of all market relationships."[45]

Marx and Market Socialism

Ollman also argues against market socialism basing himself on Marx's relevant expositions and has refuted the assertion that Marx himself was a market socialist. He has argued that their confusion is derived from Marx's two passages: one is about his positive evaluation on the workers' cooperatives in capitalism, and secondly his affirmation that a restricted market would continue to operate for a short period after the socialist revolution.

Ollman also affirms that workers' co-operatives enable workers' control over their working conditions and strengthen the solidarity among them in the enterprise, and in this way partly reduce their alienation. In capitalism, those who own the enterprise decide what to produce, what to charge, whom to employ, what to pay them, and so on, and this applies whoever the owner is. As we can see, the market is presupposed here. If one tries to retain these powers for workers in enterprises under socialism, the market will remain, but there would be lesser scope for large scale economic planning. Is this Marx's vision of a socialist society? Marx had indeed written: "to save the working masses, cooperative labor ought to be developed to national level and fostered by national means."[46] But he had also claimed that cooperative enterprises "turn the associated laborers into their own capitalists, i.e. by enabling them to use the means of production for the employment of their own labor."[47] Just earlier, in this same work, Marx had noted that workers' cooperatives "reproduces and must reproduce [...] all the shortcomings of the prevailing system."[48]

---

45   *Ibid.*, p. 129.
46   Marx and Engels Selected Works, Edition 2, Vol. 2, Beijing, People's Publishing House, 1995, p. 606.
47   Capital, Vol. 3, p. 498.
48   *Ibid.*

Marx had recognized that late capitalism might develop an extensive network of workers' cooperatives. Both the rise of the credit system and the greater efficiency achieved in workers' co-operatives, these facts had encouraged Marx to envisage such a scenario. The achievements by cooperatives would also provide an important evidence that the workers are capable of running the enterprises on their own, and that the capitalists, as a class of owners, are not essential for the production process. But, apart from the workers' greater participation in economic decision making, they provide only few indications on what socialism is and how to establish socialism. In addition, those members of workers' co-operatives could seriously dampen their desire to join a socialist revolution. Aware of this, Marx was very critical of German socialist Ferdinand Lasalle's plan to organize state finance workers' co-operatives, he had commented "it is of no value as an economic measure, while at the same time it extends the system of guardianship, corrupts a section of the workers, and castrates the workers' movement". Marx was cautious against placing workers in the same relation to capital as capitalists, since workers' co-operatives confuse them with the same experiences as capitalists, and thus with many similar ideas and attitudes, besides offering them other positive practices and interests as workers. But the resulting mix could cool their revolutionary activities. Experiences over the last hundred years by workers' co-operatives suggest that Marx's fear was not unjustified while their participation in the political activities has been remarkably weaker. Despite all the progressive qualities Marx had observed in workers' co-operatives and his support for this economic arrangement because it gave some important arguments for socialism, Marx did not believe that it provides us either with a model for socialism or a useful strategy develop class struggle against capitalism.

Besides misunderstanding Marx's selective praise for workers' co-operatives in capitalism, the claim that Marx was a market socialist is a misreading of his evaluations on the market under socialism. Here, market socialists, who quote Marx for their views, appear to have conflated three different issues:

1) Is the market to be completely abolished immediately after the workers' government assumes power?

2) If some kind of market continues to exist by the beginning of socialism, how to deal with it and how long will it last?

3) Will the market continue to exist throughout the whole socialist stage as a socialist form of allocating resources and exchanging goods?

In fact the answers Marx had given to the first two questions have been mistakenly treated as answers to the third question which deals with the long-term compatibility of the market with socialism.

As to the first question, it is quite clear that Marx foresaw substantial sections of the market continuing to function right after the socialist revolution. In the Communist Manifesto, for example, his proposition on what the new socialist government should socialize immediately were quite modest—banks, means of transport and communication, and the unused land[49]. This leaves most of the economy, at least in the initial phase in private hands but the property owners' decisions on all matters would be strongly regulated by an economic plan (which is established at the same time), the newly nationalized banks, new laws on those things as wages, working conditions of the workers, pollution, etc. It is clear that in this phase, markets for commodities, labor market, and even capital market, although regulated and modified by new laws, continue to operate.

The crucial question, then, is how will the socialist government deal with the remaining private sector? As indicated above, at the very beginning of socialism, regarding distribution there will still be some people who will be allowed to earn a share from what society produces according to their property assets and not according to their labor contribution. And society will also allow capitalists to participate in production giving them jobs to earn their lives. This major exception – to earn a share according to their property assets—will probably last till their private property on means of production will be transferred to public ownership without causing a disrupt in the production process. To achieve this end, public enterprises led by the socialist government will compete with the remaining private ones, as well as putting some pressure on the latter through bank loans, high taxes, and strict laws[50]. These measures may likely drive most capitalists to bankruptcy or sell their companies to the state in a relatively short time. One of the major reforms Marx believes should be immediately necessary after the revolution is the abolition of inheritance of wealth producing property[51]. When the generation of private owners is eliminated, their companies will all return to public. As a result of these measures and the other strategies mentioned, within forty to fifty years, at most, the entire economy will be socially owned.

From even this brief sketch we can see that a substantial part of the private sector will continue to exist for a short period after the revolution and that it will be allowed to allocate resources and exchange goods through some kind of market. Like all markets, it would create a market mode of thinking, and people's activities in this market would be the main source of alienation. Fortunately, people's practices in other spheres of life at this time will produce many new ideas and attitudes opposing that alienation and other socialist values will flourish with the constantly expanding socialized sector of the economy, and it means these practices and values becomes gradually dominant. In this new era, what guarantees the

---

49   Marx and Engels Selected Works, Edition 2, Vol. 1, p. 293-294.
50   *Ibid.*
51   *Ibid.*

eventual ascendance of a fully socialist mode of thought is the increase of all sorts of communal and cooperative practices.

Only after all the property related to production is gathered under the control of the entire working class can socialist distribution be organized according to the principle, "from each according to his ability, to each according to his work". Only after this distribution principle is established can socialism really begin. If socialism is a transitional stage to communism, the first several decades after the socialist revolution can best be understood as a transition to socialism. As a transition, it contains the elements of both capitalism and socialism, but since it is too short and may involve several sudden changes it can hardly be considered as a separate stage. This period can also be evaluated as a distinctive "moment" at the very beginning of socialism, a moment in which the final prerequisites for socialism are being established or alternatively, it can be viewed as the continuation of the socialist revolution itself, a kind of mopping up operation directed against the last vestiges of capitalist forces and privileges by employing proletarian state power. By extending the class struggle into this first moment of socialism, in each country and around the world, also manifests Marx had in his mind termed by him as the "permanent revolution". It is obvious that Marx clearly did not believe that some forms of market will continue to exist throughout the whole socialist period.

Finally, Ollman has remarked that market socialists in fact regard market as a tool which can be changed at will and which can generate anticipated effects. Even if we regard it as a machine or tool, the crucial issue is: is it more like a can opener or a meat grinder? One is in our hands and we can control it; the other controls us and we are in it, or even worse. Market socialists evaluate market as a can opener, but it is more like a meat grinder[52].

5. MARKET SOCIALISM IN BRIEF

The above is a brief introduction on the debate by contemporary American and British Marxists on market socialism. This argument with great theoretical and practical significance offers valuable ideas for all the Marxists and socialists in the world and also to those who strive to build and develop socialism in socialist countries including China.

Firstly, Chinese Marxists have chosen a special road of building socialism after learning from several bitter lessons in their practice and this road emphasizes a road which suits to several important characteristics of this country and people which is termed as "building socialism with Chinese characteristics ". The above

---

52   Edited by Bertell Ollman: Market Socialism: The Debate among Socialists, translated by Duan Zhongqiao, p. 139

debate will greatly help Chinese Marxists theoretically to have a more clear understanding on the relation between market and socialism and deepen our understanding on Deng Xiaoping's ideas on the relation between market and socialism and their effect on the development of Marxism in China. Currently, China is still in the process of transformation from a traditional socialist planned economy to a socialist market economy. To smoothly complete this transformation and achieve further steps in building socialism, it is certainly necessary to theoretically figure out the relation between market and socialism. In this issue, Chinese Marxists were fettered by the traditional Marxist concept and interpretation for a quite long time which had equaled market economy with capitalism, and planned economy with socialism. It was Deng Xiaoping who had first explicitly negated this old concept in China, but Chinese Marxists are yet to theoretically develop more systematic and scientific explanations on Deng Xiaoping's ideas. In this regard, reviewing the views of Marxists in the world on the relation between market and socialism undoubtedly may broaden our thought and provide a new angle of view.

Secondly, the market socialism models introduced by contemporary British and U.S scholars are undoubtedly based on the current status of highly developed capitalist countries, which has essential different conditions in which China's socialist market economic system is being established. However, this difference does not mean their views have no value of reference for Chinese Marxists. On the contrary, as they explore the consequences of combination between market and socialism and so do we, their exploration certainly has something worthy of learning. Learning from their theoretical research results will certainly promote our practices and achievements in China.

Lastly, this debate enables Marxists to correctly observe the new changes and ideas occurring in the global socialist movement after the abrupt changes in the Soviet Union and Eastern Europe, and proves our confidence in the certain victory of socialism over capitalism. The debate on market socialism in Western developed capitalist countries enlightens us that the collapse of socialism in Soviet Union and Eastern Europe does not prove that the capitalist system is the best, but in contrast, socialism is still an ideal social form pursued by many people including those in developed capitalist countries. We may say that the emergence of market socialism somehow is a sign indicating socialist movement is again entering into a period of revival after the period of low tide and also proves that socialism still has a great vitality.

REFERENCES

• Marx and Engels Selected Works, Edition 2, Vol. 1-4, Beijing, People's Publishing House, 1995.
• Capital. Vol. 1. Beijing, People's Publishing House, 1975.
• Capital. Vol. 3. Beijing, People's Publishing House, 1975.
• Edited by Bertell Ollman and translated by Duan Zhongqiao. Market Socialism: The Debate among Socialists. Beijing, Xinhua Publishing House, 2000.

CHAPTER X

DEBATES ON NEW IMPERIALISM

As known to all, the term "imperialism" is derived from the term "empire" and means the expansive activities of certain powerful states, particularly colonial expansionism. In 1902, J. A. Hobson had published his book Imperialism simultaneously in London and New York. In the book, he had asserted that imperialism supersedes capitalism of free competition, and introduced the concepts of "new" and "old" imperialism, by making comparative studies on them he had concluded that "the new imperialism does not differ in any vital point from its old example" (the expansionism of Roman Empire). Lenin had highly praised Hobson's argumentation. Obviously, the concept of "new imperialism" has been used as early as the 20th century, only the then intention was slightly different from the present one. In that time, the main purpose was to distinguish it from the "old" imperialism. In other words, the "new imperialism" referred to the capitalism in the new stage emerging in late 19th century and early 20th century; while the "old imperialism" referred to the expansionism of ancient Roman Empire. 100 years has passed since the emergence of the concepts of "new imperialism" and "old imperialism" by early 20th century. According to the view of British scholar Chris Harman, from the imperialism in Hobson's days till present, imperialism has experienced two major evolutions: the first is the "imperialism in World War II" and the second is the imperialism occurring between late 1960s to early 1970s. Apparently, after a century, those features which were called "new imperialism" in early 20th century have become "old imperialism", and the features of imperialism with new characteristics are called "new imperialism". The contemporary "new imperialism" mainly refers those theoretical concept or doctrines created and spread by the spokesmen of British and American governments, i.e.: the concepts for strengthening their military capability to force other countries accept their "imperial policy" favorable to American corporations as advocated by "neoconservative" ideologists. It is a kind of imperialism different from the "new imperialism" in early 20th century. Below we will review those abundant researches made by Marxist and leftist scholars.

1. THEORIES AND CHARACTERISTICS OF NEW IMPERIALISM

British and the American Theories

The propositions on the "theories of new imperialism" include the British version and American version. The British version was created by Robert Cooper, senior foreign affairs adviser of British Prime Minister Tony Blair in his booklet *Reorganization of the World Order*. In this article, Cooper proposes that in order to overcome the threat of terrorism, the United States and Britain should establish "new imperialism" which should intervene at any corner of the world through military means. He stresses if terrorists and criminals use non-democratic countries as bases to carry out activities, it is necessary for the West to launch a preemptive armed and military intervention. Cooper also preaches that restoring world order is the mission of liberal democracy, and a new colonial policy is needed to reform the civilization and governance of backward countries. In this regard, he stresses that the European Union must take actions, just like ancient Rome which provided laws and civil rights for the ruled areas in order to expand its ruling. Cooper stresses that, compared to the 19th century, the opportunity and necessity of imperialism has not changed at all[1]. Clearly, Cooper's proposition is exactly the same as the expansionist policy US adopted in recent years. They both beat the drums for the "salvation by new imperialism". He wrote that in the ancient world, empire meant order and civilization and outside the empire were barbarism and chaos. However, the empire which only pursued stability could not help or adapt to the changes and ultimately was replaced by a new international order which emphasized competition and balances of power. But the internal structure of this order system was also not stable. With the collapse of the balance of power between the United States and the Soviet Union in 1989, this order has perished and a new form of empire has emerged— it is stable and allows changes and still represents order and civilization[2].

Moreover, Cooper has ridiculously divided the countries in the world into three types: "pre-modern" countries, mostly former colonial countries, such as: Somalia and Afghanistan; "post-modern" countries, such as: European countries, Canada and the United States; ordinary "modern" countries, such as: China, India and Pakistan. Among those three types of countries, the second type countries, i.e. countries under Post-modernism system have no internal security problems, but are under the threat of modern and pre-modern countries, i.e.: the threat from

1   Fuyong: Crisis of the Empire, Beijing, Zhaohua Publishing House, 2005, p. 12.
2   *Ibid.*, p.14.

the pre-modern and modern worlds. Cooper also believes that in such areas, "chaos is the norm and war is a way of life. In so far there are governments which operate in a way similar to an organized crime syndicate". Therefore, a "defensive imperialism" becomes feasible and necessary. We can view the West's response to Afghanistan in this light. What is more, in the face of a crisis, the Post-modern states get used to apply double standards[3].

Post-modern Imperialism

According to Cooper's theory, today's new imperialism can also be called "Post-modern imperialism" and Post-modern imperialism takes two forms. One is "voluntary imperialism" in economic realm and the other is "imperialism of neighbors". The former is promoted by the IMF and the World Bank; the latter is the UN protectorate jointly established by the Post-modernism states when they feel they face threats. The expansion of the European Union in Eastern Europe is the combination of the two types of Post-modernism imperialism, which can be called "cooperative imperialism".

The American-version "theories of new imperialism" are advocated by some officials and official scholars of the American government. Richard Haass, director of policy planning for the State Department has presented a dedicated research on how to justify acts of intervention in his book Intervention: *The Use of American Military Force in the Post-Cold War World* (1994). After the "9.11" event, he has explicitly proposed "limits of sovereignty", concocting a basis for neo-imperialist acts of aggression. Haass stresses that the sovereignty of each country should be attached and restricted with a series of obligations, such as: not killing the human subjects of its nation and not supporting terrorism. The countries which fail to fulfill these obligations shall be deprived of their sovereignty and their right not to be intervened. The United States and other countries should be given the right of intervention[4]. This is the "theory of intervention" in the current American foreign policy. To make excuses for this "theory of intervention", Haass calls the present era an era of worldwide relaxation of limits. Therefore, the United States may act in order to stabilize the situation here and there and play its role. Haass shamelessly clamored military actions would lead to conflicts with enemy superpowers, but America had gained immunity against this risk and could easily intervene. When asked about the limitation of American strength, Haass answered that the United States could do anything but not everything[5]. In his book *The Reluctant Sheriff* (1997), he has further stressed that the United States is a "sheriff", while "police" is the "coalition of the willing", sheriff and police do not need to worry too much about law, but they must carefully avoid violating

3   *Ibid.*, p. 15.
4   *Ibid.*, p.12.
5   John Bellamy Foster: The New Age of Imperialism. Xinhua Digest, 2004 (20).

the policies and actions of American Security Maintenance Council. Haass also thinks that the United States is on the top position of the world and possesses an obvious hegemony but United States cannot stop the emergence of new global powers. Thus the only wise long-term strategy would be Madeleine Albright's "assertive multilateralism" and Haass' "sheriff plus police" solution. In November 2000, he has published an article titled "Imperial America" in Atlanta. In the article, he has illustrated how America should work out an "imperial diplomatic policy" and use its surplus power to expand its control over the world. Although Haass denies the possibility of a lasting and long-term hegemony, he still believes US should take the advantage of its current special opportunity to reshape the world and consolidate its global strategic assets. This means the necessity of worldwide military intervention. He has even asserted that imperial expansion is not more dangerous than excessive expansion. Just based on this idea, Haass has supported American government's invasion of Iraq in 2002 and argued that the governments which could not control terrorism in their land are failed, and lost the normal status of sovereignty, including the right to stay on their land; other governments, including American government, could employ the right of intervention. When terrorism exists, this might even lead to the defensive right for the preemptive attack[6]. Besides, Washington Post columnist Sebastian Mallaby, American President George W. Bush and United States Secretary of Defense Donald Rumsfeld have all publicly advocated and supported those theories of new imperialism.

To sum up, the main argumentations of new imperialism include:

(1) New imperialism is American imperialism and America is the "only empire" and the "last empire" in today's world; Just like conservative Andrew Bacevich has commented : "Like it or not, America today is Rome."

(2) Restoring world order is the mission of liberal democracy. New imperialism can intervene at any corner of the world through military means.

(3) "Theory of failed states" was introduced. These states should be deprived of sovereignty and the right not to be intervened. The intervention of new imperialism in these states is justified and rationalized.

(4) The new imperialist countries are the "Post-modern" countries. Post-modern countries are under the constant threat of "pre-modern" countries and "ordinary modern" countries. New imperialism should get used to apply double standard and should resort to the old cruel methods – use of force, preemptive attacks, cheating, and so on against the countries except Post-modern countries.

---

6   *Ibid.*

(5) The strategy of new imperialism should concentrate its energy on preventing the emergence of a potential future global competitor.

Cooper and Haass are both official brains who have coined the theory of new imperialism and also the spearheads promoting new imperialism. American and British governments fully follow those theories designed by Cooper and Haass. American left-wing scholars have pointed out that after the "9.11" event in 2001, the disposition to carry out massive military interventions to promote the expansion of American power had become the consensus of the ruling class. The state administration's *National Security Strategy* statement, transmitted to Congress in September 2002, promotes the principle of advanced dissuasion against potential enemies and declares: "The United States must and will maintain the capability to defeat any attempt by an enemy [...] which attempts to impose its will on the United States, our allies, or our friends. [...] Our forces should be strong enough to dissuade potential adversaries from pursuing a military build-up in the hope of surpassing, or equaling, the power of the United States."[7]

Characteristics of New Imperialism by Left-Wing Scholars

American leftist scholar John Bellamy Foster and Indian leftist scholar Arundhati Roy has summed up the characteristics of contemporary new imperialism.

Foster thinks that the imperialism of the late nineteenth and early twentieth century was distinguished mainly by two features: (1) the breakdown in British hegemony, and (2) the growth of monopoly capitalism, or a capitalism dominated by large monopolistic firms, caused by the concentration and centralization of production. Capitalism is of course a system uniquely determined by the drive to accumulate capital, which accepts no bounds to its expansion. Capitalism is on the one hand an expanding world economy characterized by a process that we now call globalization, while on the other hand it is divided politically into numerous competing nation-states. Further, the system is polarized at every level as the center and periphery. From its beginning in the sixteenth and seventeenth centuries, capital within each nation-state at the center of the system was driven by the need to control raw materials and labor forces in the periphery. In the monopoly stage of capitalism, nation-states and their corporations strive to have open doors in the world economy and as wide possible for their own investments, although they try to avoid their competitors benefit from that: "open for myself closed for others". This competition over spheres of influence and control creates a scramble in the various parts of the periphery; the most known example is the scramble for Africa in the late nineteenth century in which all of the Western European powers of the era were involved. Imperialism, however, continued to evolve beyond this classic phase, which lasted till the Second World War and

---

7   *Ibid.*

subsequent decolonization movement. And in the 1950s and 1960s imperialism entered into a new phase with its own historically specific characteristics. The most important of these was that the United States replacing British hegemony in the capitalist world economy. The United States has utilized its hegemonic position to establish the Bretton Woods institutions—the General Agreement on Tariffs and Trade, the International Monetary Fund, and the World Bank—with the intention to consolidate the economic control exercised by the center states, and the United States in particular, over the periphery and hence the entire world market[8].

For this, Indian scholar Arundhati Roy also argues that "for the first time in history, a single empire with an arsenal of weapons that could obliterate the world in an afternoon has established a complete, uni-polar, economic and military hegemony. It uses different weapons to break open different markets. There is not a country on earth that is not caught in the cross-hairs of the American cruise missile and the IMF's checkbook. Poor countries that have geopolitically strategic value for the Empire, or have a 'market' of any size, or infrastructure that can be privatized, or, God forbid, natural resources of value—oil, gold, diamonds, cobalt, coal—must do as they are told or can become military targets. Those with the richest natural reserves face the most risk. Unless they surrender their resources willingly to the corporate machine, civil unrest will be fomented or war will be waged"[9]. Roy pointed out that new imperialism had the following outstanding characteristics:

Roy and New Imperialism

Firstly, executives of the concerned companies influence foreign policy decisions. Roy has commented in her article that at least nine out of the thirty members of the Bush Administration's Defense Policy Board were related to companies that were awarded large military contracts between 2002 and 2003. George Shultz, former Secretary of State, was the chairman of the Committee for the Liberation of Iraq and also on the board of directors of the Bechtel Group, the largest engineering and manufacturing company in the United States. Before the war that American military "liberated" Iraq has ended, Bechtel signed a $680 million contract for reconstruction of Iraq. Likewise, other large American companies like Enron and Halliburton have undertaken infrastructure services business and radically reduced those jobs for native people, and meanwhile Iraq's "democratically elected" leaders have watched the scene.

---

8   *Ibid.*
9   Arundhati Roy: Main Characteristics of New Imperialism. Foreign Theoretical Trends, 2004 (7).

Secondly, new imperialism generates a new racism. Roy writes, unlike before, new imperialist does not need to trudge around the harsh colonies risking malaria or diarrhea or other tropical diseases. The racism of old imperialism is outdated. New imperialism generates a new racism. The tradition of "turkey pardoning"[10] in the US is a wonderful allegory for this new racism. That is to use colonial elites, wealthy immigrants, investment bankers, some famous artists, some writers and the immigrant originated persons like Colin Powell or Condoleezza Rice to maintain its governance. This new racism adopts a new genocide: new genocide can be facilitated by economic sanctions. Without butcher knives, the new genocide can kill more people. A very good example is the economic sanctions against Iraq which have caused food and drug shortage and claimed more than half a million children's lives.

Thirdly, corporate media becomes a part of the project in new imperialism. Roy thinks that except Iraq, millions of people have become the victims of imperialist wars in Latin America, Africa, Central Asia and Southeast Asia. Every war Empire wages becomes a "just war". This, in large part, is due to the role of the corporate media. It's important to understand that the corporate media does not just support the neo-liberal project. Media is part of the neo-liberal project. For example, if India is chosen as the target for a "righteous" war, those facts : about 80,000 people have been killed in Kashmir since 1989 most of them by Indian security forces, and most of them Muslim, and in March 2003 more than 2000 Muslims were murdered on the streets of Gujarat, women were gang-raped and children were burned alive and 150,000 people were driven from their homes while the police and administration has just watched or sometimes actively participated; and no one has been punished for these crimes and the government which has ignored all these was re-elected [...] all of this could make perfect headlines in the international newspapers as a reason for war. Next we know, our cities will be leveled by cruise missiles, our villages fenced in with razor wires, US soldiers will patrol in our streets [...].

Roy's summary on the characteristics of new imperialism is indeed penetrating. Canadian scholar Ellen M. Wood has also written that new imperialism is American imperialism. This imperialism in essence is a global economic order and a management system including many countries. As the rule of global capital is facing serious threats from the volatility in the world economy, imperialist hegemony has to overcome this contradiction and support that multinational economic order. Military power plays a great role but this is the very place where imperial strategy faces with serious problems.

---

10 "Turkey pardoning": Since 1947, on each Thanksgiving Day, American Turkey Federation will send a pair of turkeys to President. The president will eat one and pardon the other as a gesture of generosity. The pardoned turkey will live its whole rest life in the Frying Pan Park in Virginia.

All in all, left wing scholars believe that new imperialism is a modified version of old imperialism. Today's "new imperialism" and the "old imperialism" – the "new imperialism" in early 20th century are the same in essence, only today's imperialism has made some "modifications", but its nature has never changed.

2. THE "9.11" EVENT: THE TURNING POINT

The "9•11" event is both a bad thing and a lucky thing for the American neo-conservatives. It is a bad thing because terrorism has brought a loss of prestige for the United States in the whole world, being such an armed-to-teeth imperialist country. It is a lucky thing because neoconservatives have found an excuse to expand U.S military strength, increase military expenditures and launch wars. American neoconservatives influence American politics, its economy and military institutions through the Project for the New American Century, the Heritage Foundation and other think tanks as well as their famous newspaper Weekly Standard. They have contributed to a series of war policies decided by the American government: initiated a return to the policies in the Reagan era and significantly increase defense expenditures; establish missile defense system; label China, Serbia, Iran, Iraq and North Korea as "authoritarian regimes" or "axis of evil" countries and adopt a "defensive containment" strategy against them. After the "9•11" event, American government has taken advantage of people's insecurity feelings to get its policy approved in the Congress without any resistance. America's "Star Wars" plan has existed for a long time and the country had waged many unjust wars before the "9•11" event, such as: the Kosovo War on Balkan Peninsula, the Afghanistan War in the hinterland of Central Asia and the Gulf War in 1990s, but after the "9•11" event, ignoring the objection by the public in the world, the United States has openly trampled on the Charter of Organization of United Nations and outrageously invaded Iraq in 2003 without any solid evidence. Since then, the nature of the war policy carried by the United States has transformed from quantitative change to qualitative change – into the war of new imperialism.

The "9•11" event has marked the beginning of the war of new imperialism. Famous French Marxist George Labica has pointed out: "After the "9•11" event, the international community has started an unprecedented chorus. A few months later, people gradually came to know this chorus was not an ordinary voice but a voice of cruel duel, similar to 'Crusade' expeditions"[11]. In fact, it indeed was the warning of war climate. George W. Bush has clearly announced: "2002 will be a year of war." All these have not occurred by accident. Shortly after the fall of the Berlin Wall which had symbolized the "realistic existence of socialism", liberalism, i.e.: market dominance has won the victory. In order to make liberalism

---

11   George Labica: Révolution et Démocratie, French Cherry Season Press, 2003, p. 95.

more acceptable and provide it with another facet different from inclement profit pursuit and brutal competition, it was camouflaged and the concept that market, democracy and law have equal values was coined. In this way, market was legitimized under the pretext of democracy and widely practiced under the coat of law. The precondition for borrowing money from and lending money to developed countries is the strict observation of "human rights". Western powers' seemingly "very moderate" armed conflicts are galvanized with "humanistic characteristics" and propagated as restoration and establishment of democracy. The overall intervention is presented as a post-disease treatment rather than invasion. However, after the "9•11" event, everything has changed. The cautious verbiage was discarded and the charming camouflage is removed. Behind the sacrosanct laws, the most fundamental rights were ruined by the war of invasion in Afghanistan, so were the inter-state system and the international law. The anti-terrorism coalition has shown great generosity to its member states. Globalization of security measures was in vogue and every concrete measure was given a new content: from telephone tapping, legalization of body search to a blacklist of terrorist states and organizations. Terrorism, this common enemy, has caused a strong convergence between the left and right wings – security issue as the core issue during elections. Despite the UN laws, the United States has regarded unilateral "legal defense" as its duty. It has imposed "the democratic" system on Afghanistan, but in fact it was an "invisible" war: American soldiers did not allow journalists to take photos and the news on death toll was prohibited. After September 11, breaching democracy and trampling on international laws becomes a common occurrence. Safeguarding the value of Western civilization is to destroy everything with bombs and buy everything with dollars. The moment for controlling global energy and militarizing economy has come. George W. Bush has in fact realized the plan proposed by Zbigniew Brzezinski in his book "The Grand Chessboard", i.e.: conquering Asia is about to control the fate of the world[12].

After the "9•11" event, the United States has started to adopt "military unilateralism". American scholars Max Fraad Wolff and Richard Wolff have written in their article titled "The Rise of Military Unilateralism": since 2000, the crash in the stock market and problems of macro economy have dragged American economy to a recession and the unemployment rate has risen continuously. At home, Bush administration has faced a sluggish economy, a pessimistic and disappointed working class. Abroad, decades' long false policies and diplomacy of neo-liberalism has turned many nations against United States, while the "9•11" event has provided a golden opportunity for Bush administration to solve these problems and change the U.S policies significantly. Max Fraad Wolff and Richard Wolff believe that the surging patriotic sentiment in the United States in fact is to shift the discontent caused by domestic economic depression to new foreign "enemies". These "enemies" are those who have different beliefs, minority people and those

12   *Ibid.*, p. 95-101.

nations who are demonized since they dislike the American-style democracy. Relying on the public's hatred against terrorism, Bush administration has launched the wars in Afghanistan and Iraq, and by extensively utilizing its diplomatic powers in the world opened the road to military unilateralism[13].

William Bloom, a renowned American politician, has keenly summarized the "achievements" of invasions by the United States after the "9•11" event: In 2001-2002, the United States has established military bases in Afghanistan, Pakistan, Kazakhstan, Uzbekistan, Tajikistan, Kyrgyzstan, Georgia, Yemen and Djibouti. In 2003, the United States has launched the war of invasion in Iraq and meanwhile located a large number of forces there and also established military bases in Iraq.

As soon as the Cold War had ended in late 1980s and early 1990s, the United States has established military bases in Saudi Arabia, Kuwait, Bahrain, Qatar and the United Arab Emirates; in 1999, it has established military bases in Kosovo, Albania, Macedonia, Hungary, Bosnia and Croatia. In addition to these military bases in every corner of the planet after the World War II, the United States had become an unmatched hegemony in the world. If it plans, it may attack any target, anywhere. Therefore, Bloom defines the behavior of American government as War profiteer. Although Cold War has ended, the expected "peace dividend" did not appear. In the past decades, American government has claimed that the only reason why it waged wars, spent for huge military buildup and overthrew the governments of other nations by military coups was that it was dealing against the plots of international communism. However, Soviet Union has collapsed, Warsaw Pact has disappeared, the satellite states in Eastern Europe have become independent and the former communists have become capitalists, but American policy is not changed in the least. The Warsaw Pact opposite to NATO no longer exists, but NATO is still there and moreover its military presence and military strength has significantly expanded covering more countries and regions. Therefore, Bloom asserts that the whole thing in fact is a trick. Soviet Union and the communism were not the targets attacked by Washington and so-called communist plots which were never the real cause for attacks. The enemies were and today still are any government, movement and even individual that stands in the way of expansion of American empire, no matter how the United States labels calls them—communism, rogue states, drug traffickers or terrorists[14]. Though the end of the Cold War, American imperialism still prepares for wars and starts wars, big or small.

---

13   Huang Xiaowu: Summary of the 2004 Fourth International Marxist Conference. Foreign Theoretical Trends, 2004 (12).
14   William Bloom: American Empire after the Cold War. Foreign Theoretical Trends, 2004 (10).

British scholar Alex has analyzed that the American strategy was already formed before the "9•11" event in 2001. In other words, America's plans for hegemony on other states was brewed in the 20 years before the "9•11" event. As disclosed by O'Neal, a member of Bush administration, as early as Bush administration was elected, it had determined to destroy Iraqi regime. The occurrence of the "9•11" event was just a great opportunity for the implementation of that plan. Therefore, on the very day when the twin towers were destroyed, US Defense Secretary Donald Rumsfeld has approved the operation to raid Iraq. This proves that the Cold War against Soviet Union and communism waged by the United States was faked and today's hot war against terrorism is faked, too. Clearing obstacles and realizing its dominance over the world is the real intention of the United States.

Motives behind the War in Iraq

French scholar Ignacio Ramonet has made a comprehensive analysis on America's motives for the war in Iraq. He thinks that the Unites States has three motives for its invasion of Iraq:

The first, preventing links between "rogue states" and terrorism had become an urgent concern for the American government. For this purpose, the United States has worked out a "preventive war strategy" in September 2002. This plan states that terrorists always have the advantages to attack regardless of time and location. The only feasible defense is to find them wherever they are and destroy them before they intend to mount an attack. This is the theory advocated by the former CIA director James Woolsey. He has emphasized that the new principle against the asymmetric battle started by terrorism should be "advanced dissuasion" or "preventive war"[15].

The second aim was to control the Gulf and its natural resources. More than two thirds of the world's known oil reserves are in Gulf States. For the developed countries, particularly the US with its greedy appetite for oil, the Gulf is a critical region to assure economic growth and maintain its way of life domestically. The US has declared that any attack on the Gulf States would be direct threat to its vital interests. Former American president Jimmy Carter had outlined the US policy in the Gulf: "Any attempt by any outside force to gain control of the Persian Gulf region will be regarded as an assault on the vital interests of the US, and such an assault will be repelled by any means necessary, including military means."[16]

The third, through this war, US have intended to establish its worldwide supremacy. For years Bush's advisers have hypothesized that the US could become the sole

---

15   Ignacio Ramonet: Three Questions about US-led Iraqi War. Foreign Theoretical Trends, 2003 (4).
16   *Ibid.*

global imperial power. When the Cold War had ended, although most strategists have favored a diminishing role for US armed forces, they have suggested giving priority to restructure and further modernize the military arsenal by relying on new technologies and utilize war threat as a foreign policy tool. They have expressed their hopes for US enjoying freedom against the old multilateral -political arrangements framework. That is why they had urged Bush to abolish multilateral arrangements like the Kyoto Protocol, the Anti-ballistic Missile Treaty, the Treaty Banning Nuclear Power and other treaties. It is not difficult to foresee that next step would be to reject the authority of the Security Council[17].

German Mexican social activist and social politician Heinz Dieterich asserts that the "9•11" event has changed the relation among big world powers, and thus America has initiated a new order targeting the Third World. The order of the Third World has the following features: (1) US has strengthened control over the Middle East region; (2) Central Asia became an expansion area for the US; (3) South Asia may become another victim of "American century"; (4) Russia may try to join NATO, EU and WTO in the future; (5) US promotes FTA of American Continent and Columbia Program in Latin America to force Latin America remaining as its geopolitical life sphere ; (6) American and European imperialists use suppression tools and state terrorism to prevent the world from reaching a consensus on democratic policies; (7) Afghanistan war brings American and European bourgeoisie together to jointly deal with the Third World; (8) European integration is accelerated; (9) Further armament of NATO in fact infringes and bypasses international laws set by the United Nations; (10) The interests of China, Japan and even all mankind are excluded (11) US aims to consolidate its hegemony; (12) The communication and relations in the process of Globalization progress under the framework of global militarization[18].

3. SAMIR AMIN ON ASYMMETRIC GLOBALIZED LIBERAL SYSTEM

Egyptian scholar and famous Marxist world system-dependency- theorist Samir Amin believes that the US is systematically carrying out a hegemonic program. This hegemony is being established on the basis of a double-standard "asymmetric globalised liberal system". Below we will introduce his views.

Amin has first disclosed the hegemonic program of the US. From the 1980s on, and with the collapse of the Soviet system, the ruling class in the United States, Democrat or Republican, has begun drawing up a hegemonic program. Encouraged by its military power, and without any competitor capable to temper

17   *Ibid.*
18   Xu Shicheng: View of Heinz Dieterich on a Number of Contemporary Theories. Foreign Theoretical Trends Journal, 2003 (5).

its fantasies, the US has chosen to reinforce its domination by deploying a military strategy aiming "planetary control". An early series of interventions — in the Gulf, Yugoslavia, Central Asia, Palestine and Iraq – has started this plan which includes endless wars labeled as "made in the USA" and planned and decided unilaterally by Washington.

What closely accompanies this program is a certain political strategy. The political strategy which serves the hegemonic program of the US includes the following aspects: firstly, the US has designed the pretexts for the implementation of this program. These pretexts are "fighting against terrorism", "against drug trafficking" or "against weapons of mass destruction". On the surface, the US raises the banner of "justice", and fights against terrorism and drug trafficking, and the production of illegal mass destructive weapons, but in fact, it itself is produces, possesses and uses these weapons. U.S has used A-bomb at Hiroshima and Nagasaki to take the revenge for the Pearl Harbor attack by Japan, it has used chemical weapons in Vietnam and threatens others by further use of nuclear weapons in the future conflicts.

Secondly, it advocates the doctrine of "advanced dissuasion war". America regards "advanced dissuasion" strategy as its privilege which no one else should attempt. The US not only formulates but applies, rudely trampling on the United Nations Charter, which forbids wars except in cases of legitimate self-defense, and allows military interventions only under strict conditions, and stipulates that any response should be measured controlled and provisional. However, the wars initiated by the US since 1990s completely violate the above U.N provisions. Amin has concluded: "Indeed, the United States, with the support of several countries, is already treating the United Nations as former fascist states have treated the League of Nations."[19] Thirdly, the US advocates a "Master Race" and praises itself as the "Master of the Planet". In the eyes of the Washington establishment, the people of the United States and those of Israel are the "Master Races", while other peoples are all "Red Skins" (the contemptuous name reserved for the Native Americans). These people have the right to exist only when they do not frustrate the expansion of US-based multinational capital. Otherwise, the United States will crush any resistance by using any and every means, even extermination if necessary. If it is a question of making an additional 15 million dollars in profit for the American multinationals at the expense of 300 million victims, then there will be no hesitation. So, Amin has concluded: "the "rogue state" par excellence is none rather than the United States itself."[20]

---

19   Samir Amin: Asymmetric Globalised Liberal System and American Hegemony. Foreign Theoretical Trends, 2003 (11).
20   *Ibid.*

Amin illustrates the hegemonism of the United States under the term of an asymmetric globalised liberal system. He thinks that the economic growth during Clinton administration, which was vaunted as the result of "liberalism", in fact was largely faked, because several reasons had contributed to this result. Firstly, it had depended on capital transfers from its rich partners which also meant stagnation in those partner economies. In other words, The "American miracle" was exclusively a growth in consumption expenditures by the rich and increasing social inequalities. Secondly, it had depended on plunder. Amin has pointed out, the "advantage of the US is that of a predator". The deficit of the US has increased year after year from USD 100 billion in 1989 to USD 450 billion in 2000. The US has covered its deficit by foreign loans obtained by peaceful or forced means. That means Washington has employed various means to make up its deficiencies, including repeatedly and unilaterally violating the liberalism principles, it has largely imposed arms exports to its subaltern allies, and gained extra profits from oil trading by trade tricks. Amin has pointed out that the main part of the American trade deficit is covered by capital flows from Europe, Japan and the Southern countries — plus the additional funds –interest payments–from indebted countries in the periphery of the world system; in fact these countries were forced to a development based on foreign depts. These continuous capital and interest inflow feed the parasitism in American economy and society and allows continuous short term breathing for this superpower. Thirdly, US play "asymmetric" liberal games. The United States, Europe and Japan all preach globalised neo-liberalism, but the US hardly accepts to fairly share fairly those benefits of its leadership with its allies. On the contrary, it seems to treat seems its allies as vassals. Therefore, Amin suggests that the assumption that 'the liberal card game should, or could, be played "honestly" by all and things will thus get better' is a sheer illusion.

A result of American neo-liberal policy is that it can cover its trade deficit by pumping its financial surplus elsewhere in the world, but US applies this policy only very selectively when deciding countries to invest. These are the imperial hegemonic principles of American "asymmetric globalised liberal system".

Finally, Amin has clearly expressed his opposition to American hegemony in his famous article. He believes the militarist program currently adopted by the United States threatens all peoples. Halting the US militarist program becomes, therefore, a major aim and responsibility for all. Success in this struggle will depend on the following two aspects: Firstly, help people everywhere to see the truth behind liberal illusions. The World Bank propagates democracy, good governance and reduction of poverty and favors Washington and tries to boost liberal globalised economy and its illusions, but people should firmly believe that there will never be an "authentically liberal globalised economy. Progressive people should reconstruct a Southern Front so that the people across Asia, Africa and Latin America unite and liberate themselves from the illusions of the asymmetric globalised liberal system that will allow the nations of the Third World overcome the trap of their "backwardness". Secondly, the combat against US imperialism and against the US militarist program is a combat shared by all peoples of the world , its major victims are located in Asia, Africa and Latin America, but includes the peoples of Europe and the Japan who are forced to subordinate positions, and also to the people of North America.

Amin, an enlightened left-wing scholar originating from the Third World, has done unremitting researches on developed countries' unequal trade and capital transactions and their exploitation on developing countries. When American hegemonists have started a new aggressive strategy against other nations, he has timely and profoundly disclosed the hegemonist misdeeds of the United States which inspire people and deserves high respect.

4. JOHN BELLAMY FOSTER AND THE NEW AGE OF REVOLT

Famous American scholar John Bellamy Foster is another influenced researcher on new imperialism who also edits the famous left-wing journal Monthly Review. He has pointed out that the United States resorts to its advanced military strength and economic and financial strengths to maintain its hegemony in the world, but this does not mean its hegemony will be stable and lasting. On the contrary, this imperialism is approaching to its "last moribund stage" and this process mainly manifests itself as: (1) The contradictions among the United States, Europe and Japan is escalating; (2) American government is increasingly alarmed against the potential threat from China; (3) The United States attempts to take challenge by means of enlarging its geopolitical range of hegemony and coaches the national sovereign powers of other countries in a strategy favorable to expand the US hegemony. Therefore, today's world is a world led by American hegemonic imperialism and dominated by global monopoly capital. People were -never before–so grimly faced with a clear choice between destructive barbarism and humane socialism[21]. The United States uses its advanced military power to settle in all parts of the world, which intensifies all kinds of contradictions. These contradictions mainly include:

(1) The contradictions between the US and other developed capitalist countries deepen. After the "9•11" event the US have pumped great enthusiasm for the "anti-terrorism war", invaded Afghanistan and intruded Iraq. This has aroused repulsion by the people in the whole world, including allies like France and Germany; the subsequent trade war has also aggravated the contradiction between the US and its partner nations. The poll organized by BBC in 2004 indicates that 55% of the British citizens think that the US "is a threat to peace"; the same

21 John Bellamy Foster: Monopoly Capital and the new Globalization. Foreign Theoretical Trends, 2003 (6).

survey has also revealed that the 60% of Indonesians, 71% of Jordanians and 25% of Canadians thought the United States was a bigger threat, compared to Al-Qaeda Group.

(2) The contradictions between the US and developing countries deepen. Not only Iran, Libya, Venezuela and Cuba oppose the US, but also the other developing countries, the Arab World in particular also express their discontent towards it. The survey by the famous Pew Research Center in Washington indicates that 53% of the people in the world believe that the "9•11" event was the direct result of American policy; 60~80% of the leaders of political parties and social organizations in Eastern Europe, Russia and Latin America believe that the "9•11" event was due to American's own fault; even in the US, 18% of the people hold the same view. People's discontent to the US, the sole superpower, grows day by day. In fact, before the "9.11" event, the United Stated had sowed much grudge in the world. Famous American writer Gore Vidal said to a Reuter reporter after he published *Perpetual War for Perpetual Peace* (2001) in Italy that in this not long book, he enumerated nearly 400 attacks which the American government launched on other countries. All these were undeclared wars. The reason for the wars was that these states have harbored communists[22]. Vidal also said that in order to maintain its position as a superpower and control the world, US has adopted immoral practices for decades. Now this practice is directed against American people.

(3) The contradiction between American ruling class and the vast majority of American people also deepens. The "9•11" event was a heavy blow at the United States. After the twin towers symbolizing the high status of USA in world finance collapsed in New York, the New York Stock Exchange has stopped trading completely and the stock markets in Europe and some other countries and regions has plummeted. At least billions of dollars of investment funds handled by more than one hundred financial institutions in the World Trade Center has perished, and thousands of topnotch analysts, economists and traders working in the Wall Street have lost their lives. All these have created a serious impact on the American financial market. Firstly, it was a blow at the financial investment sector and secondly it was a blow at the American tourism and aviation industry. A poll organized after the "9•11" event has revealed that 54% of American people were pessimistic on the future of the U.S economy; 78% of were afraid of losing their jobs or find new jobs; 51% of them were dissatisfied with the current trend in the country. People were generally worried about economic slump and the threat of war and terrorism[23].

The acts of the US are criticized by the enlightened people both inside and outside the United States. Famous American scholar Noam Chomsky has analyzed the

---

22   Fu Yong: Crisis of the Empire, p. 50.
23   *Ibid.*, p. 69.

global hegemony of the United States in his book *Hegemony or Survival: America's Quest for Global Dominance* published in November 2003. He has written that America's unilateralism, dismantling of international agreements, state terrorism and militarization of the space are coherent with its motive of global dominance. "The reasons people hate the United States do not conform what President Bush says: they object to progress and liberty; resist selection and culture; dislike music and joyance; discriminate women and are blind followers of a religion; even despise all Jews and the Muslims who refuse the so-called doctrines distorted by them". Chomsky has refuted Bush's words: "Mr. Bush, it is all because of you and your alliances, as well as your conducts". In his book, Chomsky has blasted against the American diplomatic policy and the makers of this policy and accused Bush administration's anti-terrorist war as the extension of traditional external intervention.

Famous American left wing scholar Edward W. Said has questioned: is the United States totally behind Bush's belligerent diplomatic policy and his dangerous, ignorant and pragmatic views? Will America's identity never be changed? The world people is expected to co-exist with the military power of US, but does the US also offer them anything which could allow them to live peacefully together with the U.S without fear? He has observed US from another angle and evaluates it as a state full of disputes and turmoil. He argues that it is more accurate to understand US as a nation which is experiencing a serious identity conflict. This identity conflict is similar to those occurring in other regions of the world. The US perhaps has won the Cold War, but the result is far from clear and the struggle is far from closure[24].

Bellamy Foster points out that this new age of US imperialism generates its own contradictions, amongst them are attempts by other major powers to increase their influences, which resort to similar belligerent means, and all sorts of strategies adopted by weaker states and non-state actors applying "asymmetric" forms of warfare against USA . Rather than achieving a new "Pax Americana" the United States may be paving the way to a new global holocaust. Therefore, the greatest hope in these dire circumstances could be a rising tide of revolt from below, both in the United States and in the globe. Following the events in Seattle in November 1999, the growth of the anti-globalization movement has dominated the world stage; in February 2003, the largest global wave of anti-war protests in human history broke out. Never before has the world's population risen up so quickly and in such massive numbers to fight against and stop the imperialist war. "The new age of imperialism is also a new age of revolt." "the strategy of the American ruling class to expand the American Empire cannot possibly succeed in the long run, and will prove to be its own—we hope not the world's— disintegration."[25]

---

24   Edward W. Said: America and Arab World. Foreign Theoretical Trends, 2003 (6).
25   John Bellamy Foster: The New Age of Imperialism. Xinhua Digest, 2004 (20).

Wallerstein and Anti-system Movements

Famous American world system theorist Immanuel Wallerstein has pointed out that, when the modern world-system is in a structural crisis, four kinds of anti-system movements will occur. These movements have manifested themselves in the protests and demonstrations against Seattle Meeting in November 1999. These forces include the Old Left, trade unions, new social movements and anarchist groups. Following Seattle, the continuous demonstrations around the world against inter-state G 8 meetings with the neo-liberal agenda has in turn led to the establishment of the World Social Forum. This new anti-systemic movement has joined all the previous types and new groups organized in a local, regional, national and transnational pattern (The Old Left, new movements, human-rights organizations, and those others which do not fall into these categories). Their slogan is "Another World is Possible".

Wallerstein believes that such a period of transition has two characteristics that determine the anti-system struggle strategy. The first is that those in power will no longer try to preserve the existing system (thus system is doomed to self-destruction); rather, they will try to ensure that the transition leads to the establishment of a new system that will replicate the worst features of the existing one—its hierarchy, privileges and inequalities. The second fundamental characteristic is that the period of system transition possesses deep uncertainties, and it is impossible to know what the outcome will be. History is on no one's side. Each individual acting on our side can affect the future, but we do not and cannot know how others will act to affect it, too[26]. Therefore, Wallerstein has put forth his strategic considerations in four aspects:

Firstly, we should constantly and openly debate the transition and that outcome we hope for. In this conjuncture, the role of intellectuals will be important. The World Social Forum should encourage this debate.

Secondly, an anti-system movement cannot neglect the short-term defensive action, including electoral activity. The motive and justification for the defensive action should not remedy the failing system but rather aim to prevent its negative effects from getting worse in the short run.

Thirdly, interim, middle-range goals in the right direction have to be established including ultimate goal and political, psychological goals. One of the most important goal is to move towards selective, but ever-widening, decommodification. Industries, especially failing industries, should be decommodified.

---

26   Immanuel Wallerstein: New Revolts against the System. Foreign Theoretical Trends, 2003 (4).

Fourthly, we must develop the comprehensive meaning of our long-term aims and at the same time strive for a world that is relatively democratic and relatively egalitarian. We need to discuss it, outline it and experiment with alternative structures to realize it[27].

Based on his strategic considerations, Wallerstein pins his hope for World Social Forum and believes that WSF is a platform for action and the most important social movement in the world and only World Social Forum has the opportunity to play a substantial role.

In conclusion, in the United States where contemporary new imperialism is popular, there is also a wave of criticism and revolt. The goals of this trend concentrate on the following:

Firstly, disclose the imperial ambitions of United States. American scholar David Ray Griffin presents those facts which demonstrate American empire has existed for a long time in his book *America Dominated Non-benevolent Empire*, and believes that the US has had those imperial ambitions since the United States of America was just founded, and it has also caused the extermination of about 10 million indigenous Indians. Chomsky also believes that the United States has not currently become an empire but since long, at least after World War II.

Secondly, reveal the motives of new American imperialism. At this point, Chomsky's critique is most comprehensive and profound. He thinks that many reasons have contributed to the formation of American imperialism, but the most important one is resource drive, because only when the resources are controlled, others will surrender. More than 150 years ago, the US has occupied today's Texas and about one half land of the Mexican Kingdom, mainly because it aimed to control cotton resources urgently needed by Britain so as to control Britain. Today's Iraqi war is for the control on oil resources. Just like US Deputy Defense Secretary Paul D. Wolfowitz has commented related to Iraq, the United States had no choice, because this state was floating on a sea of oil.

Thirdly, disclose the main features of expansionism by American imperialism under new historical conditions. It is an economic imperialism and ideological imperialism based on military hegemony. Harry Magdoff had explained this feature and offered a lot of economic data. He thinks that the expansion of imperialism in late 20th century was manifested as the globalization of monopoly capital. Achieving the goal of control through economic hegemony not only seems softhearted and voluntary and is more realistic, which can avoid high costs and high risks as in old imperialism; besides, it also helps capital accumulation which cannot be achieved through military means.

---

27   *Ibid.*

Fourthly, try to find a way and solution to overcome imperialism. American left wing scholars think that if the people in the world, including those in the United States, do not fight back, it is extremely likely that the American empire being formed will become a global empire, even a fascist empire. Well, how to prevent the formation of the empire? One proposition is to establish global democratic government like Griffin's model; another proposition is to adopt "democratizati-on of economic order" and grassroots democracy and spurn the mindset of eco-nomics and its supremacy; another proposition is that as imperialism is rooted in capitalism, eliminating capitalism could be the only way to eliminate imperialism[28].

Fifthly, disclose American government's true nature such as its armament strate-gy, war preparations and misleading people. In his book *New American Militarism: How Americans are Seduced by War* (2005), Andrew J. Bacevich, a graduate of West Point, Vietnam War veteran and professor at Boston University, has profoundly disclosed that the new American militarism manifests itself in four different ways: (1) Endless expansion of military power. The present-day Pentagon budget is 12% larger than the average defense budgets in the years of the Cold War era. By 2010 its budget will exceed the Cold War average by 23%. That is to say, in each of the coming few years, American military expenditure will be twice as much as the annual military expenditure during the Cold War. (2) The quest for military dominion: The new American militarism also manifests itself through an increa-sed propensity to use force, in fact leading to the normalization of war. Since the advent of the new Wilsonism, however, self-restraint regarding the use of force has completely disappeared. During the 43-year entire Cold War era from 1945 to 1988, large-scale U.S. military actions abroad have totaled a scant six events, but in the 15 years from 1989 to 2003 nine major military interventions have occurred. Those do not include the open or hidden "non-conventional wars" operated by 2500 special force soldiers in 40-50 countries in the world. (3) U.S has established the "new aesthetic of war". The "old aesthetic of war" was viewed as barbarism, brutality, ugliness and sheer waste, while the "new aesthetic of war" is presented as a "spectacle" and a kind of sport for "spectators". The manipulation of infor-mation overturns the proposition that warfare is risky. In other words, the appli-cation of high war technology in war expels people's fear of war and even offers a feeling of games. These have greatly promoted war. (4) U.S boosts the reputation of military forces and soldiers. This new aesthetic in turn has contributed to a remarkable boost in the status of military institutions and soldiers. For example, George W. Bush is a "warrior-president". The trust of the public on military forces has risen rapidly. A great many photos of the men and women wearing American army uniform are published in famous magazines. Above evaluations by Bacevich has aroused great sensation and increased the awareness of people against US militarism.

---

28   Wu Weifu: Contemporary Anti-imperialist Thoughts in the United States. Social Sciences Abroad, 2005 (4).

Sixthly, a mass wave of public opposition is rising. In November 2005, a large-scale public demonstration against war broke out in the United States which implies the rise of a new anti-war movement in the United States. Most American people love peace. From 1960s-1970s, they ever opposed American government's invasion in Vietnam and boycotted the Vietnam War through large-scale anti-war movement. Today, observing American government is sinking deeper into the mire of war; absolutely, they do not sit and watch.

Outside the United States, a trend opposing capitalist globalization and imperialism has formed. For example, in the "International Meeting of Communist and Workers' Parties" held in Athens, Greece in June 2003, the representatives from 59 communist and workers' parties have unanimously agreed to struggle against war and capitalist globalization which was one of the main themes of the meeting. The meeting has reached a consensus on condemning the United States, Britain and their allies' military intervention in Iraq and occupation of other countries and denounced the invasion of imperialism and their rude trampling on international laws and principles. The meeting has emphasized that the militarism in international relations becomes increasingly dangerous and under the dominance of increased hostilities interventionism, use of force, the threat of new military conflicts is growing. NATO, guided by the "advanced dissuasion" doctrine, continues its expansion and has become a "global cop" under the command of American imperialist hegemony. The whole mankind has become the attack target of modern imperialism and it threatens peace, security and stability of many regions on the planet. The meeting has also emphasized that more active measures should be taken to strengthen the solidarity and cooperation between communist and workers' parties and the coordination between people's movements. At the meeting, some other suggestions were raised, for example: to take concerted actions and jointly oppose the Unites States and European Union plans to control the economy of the Arab World; and launch a campaign to oppose imperialism's attempt of economic, cultural and political colonization of the Third World. The meeting has called for deeper coordination and cooperation between communist parties and workers' parties in the world and wider coordination among democratic movements, the anti-imperialist movement, the anti-monopoly movement and the anti-capitalist movement in order to increase their joint actions.

This indicates that all the peaceful people in the world have sharpened their vigilance, observing the true colors of new imperialists and have formed a sizable trend of resistance. The beginning of the new age of imperialism is also the advent of a new age of revolt. This is the common approach of many people in the World.

REFERENCES

• Samir Amin: Asymmetric Globalised Liberal System and American Hegemony. Foreign Theoretical Trends, 2003 (11).
• William Bloom: American Empire after the Cold War. Foreign Theoretical Trends, 2004 (10).
• John Bellamy Foster: The New Age of Imperialism. Xinhua Digest, 2004 (20).
• John Bellamy Foster: Monopoly Capital and New Globalization. Foreign Theoretical Trends, 2003 (6).
• George Labica: Révolution et Démocratie. French Cherry Season Press, 2003.
• Arundhati Roy: Main Characteristics of New Imperialism, Foreign Theoretical Trends, 2004 (7).
• Edward W. Said: America and Arab World. Foreign Theoretical Trends, 2003 (6).
• Immanuel Wallerstein: New Revolts against the System. Foreign Theoretical Trends, 2003 (4).
• Wu Weifu: Contemporary Anti-imperialism Thoughts in the United States. Social Sciences Abroad, 2005 (4).
• Fu Yong: Crisis of the Empire. Beijing: Zhaohua Publishing House, 2005.

CHAPTER XI

AN ANALYSIS
ON "COLOR REVOLUTIONS"
BY NEW IMPERIALISM

In the eve of the 21st century, "color revolutions" have occurred in Georgia, Ukraine and Kyrgyzstan successively and shows a trend of spreading over to other countries in Central Asia as well as Belarus and has even threatened Russia. This new mode of regime changes manipulated by the United States have aroused the attention of people in the world and especially alarmed the countries of CIS (Commonwealth of Independent States). What is the nature of "color revolution"? What is the role of the United States? What is the consequence? How to prevent it? All these questions need careful research.

1. AN OVERVIEW ON COLOR REVOLUTIONS

"Color revolution" is a term indicating regime changes largely "promoted" by the Western powers. In my opinion, it cannot be called "revolution", because it is a kind of coup to overthrow current regime through peaceful "street politics"–violence is not excluded, but is not the major way-. Similar strategies are also applied in other parts of the world and countries which have several serious conflicts with US and the major western powers, but we will focus on those in Asia and Europe. Notably, such coup has happened in Georgia, Ukraine and Kyrgyzstan in three years in a row.

In November 2003, Georgia held a parliament election and the force supporting Eduard Shevardnadze has won the majority of votes. Under the support of US-led Western countries, Saakashvili, the opposition leader and former justice minister of Georgia, did not accept the election result under the pretext of fraud in the parliament election, triggering to a volatile domestic situation. On the afternoon of November 22, while Shevardnadze was making a speech at the establishment ceremony of the new parliament, the demonstrators led by the opposition have stormed the parliament and required abdication of president Shevardnadze. 28 hours later, the opposition succeeded in the "forced abdication" and Shevardnadze quitted his presidency. In the follow-up elections, Saakashvili has won and became the Georgian president. He adopted a thorough pro-American policy and the relations between Georgia and Russia have worsened quickly. As a demonstrator from the opposition waved a red rose symbolizing peace, this coup resulting in regime change through "street politics" was named the "Rose Revolution".

In October 2004, Ukraine held a presidential election. The United States vigorously supported opposition candidate Yuschchenko. Notably, American non-governmental organizations have assigned hundreds of experts to help Yuschchenko through election. US Congress has passed a bill on October 4, calling on American administrative authority to affect Ukraine by using all available influences and channels. However, the result of the first round elections has indicated that no one got a majority of votes, so it was decided to go for a second round voting on October 21. On October 23, the preliminary count of ballots indicated the incumbent Prime Minister Viktor Yanukovich has received 49.53% of the votes and the opposition leader Yuschchenko 46.66%. On October 24, the Central Election Committee announced Viktor Yanukovich as the elected president. This result aroused great discontent in the United States and other Western countries. European Commission Chairman Jose Manuel Barroso has immediately rebuked the counting results announced on October 23 as not reflecting the real will of Ukrainian constituency and threatened it might affect the relations between Ukraine and EU. US Secretary of State Colin Powell has also declared that U.S does not admit the election result announced on October 24, criticizing that the election did not conform to international standards, and added that it was still not late for the Ukrainian authorities to find a solution which respects to the will of Ukrainian people; "United States earnestly hopes Ukrainian authorities seize this opportunity". Meanwhile, by the support and encouragement of US-led Western countries, despite of the ballots, on October 23, Yuschchenko suddenly appeared on the stage and declared himself as the president in the special parliament meeting held to discuss the election disputes. After that event, he led his supporters to march from the central square of the city towards the president office and besieged the president office. They confronted with police. On October 24—the electoral day, the supporters of Yuschchenko have gathered at Kiev's Independence Square where they had prepared tents. They held a protest rally. As soon as the election result was announced, they raised demands for a re-election. Under such circumstances, Ukraine decided to hold the second presidential election. Yuschchenko won this election. As Yuschchenko supporters used the symbol of orange castanea and orange flags (city flower of Kiev) this regime change was named as an "Orange Revolution".

In February 2005, Kyrgyzstan held parliament elections. Among 75 elected parliament members, about 30 were representatives of pro-government camp, while not more than 8 belonged to the opposition supported by the West. The opposition which obtained support from the United States accused the government by fraud and manipulating the election. However, the Kirghiz government denied this accusation and insisted that the election was just and transparent. In the end, the opposition took the streets and organized mass protests for more than several days. In the southern state named Jalalabad, the demonstrators occupied governor's office of the state and the government building in Osh City on February 10. Later, the police chased away the demonstrators. The two sides collided. As a result, dozens of people were injured, including 3 policemen, and more than 200 people were arrested. On February 20, the opposition again organized a large-scale protest and occupied the police office and government compound. In other areas of Kyrgyzstan, street protests on various scales also took place. In capital Bishkek, about 1500 demonstrators attended a street protest on February 19. By February 24, the situation of Kyrgyzstan had changed abruptly so that about 10,000 opposition supporters went on strike in capital city Bishkek. On February 28, the demonstrators have stormed main government buildings and demonstrating against Askar Akayev. Thus President Askar Akayev was forced to leave for Russia as a refugee and opposition announced the seizure of political power. Kurmanbek Bakiev was appointed acting president and prime minister. As this coup has occurred in the season when primrose (city flower of Bishkek) blooms, it was also called "Yellow Revolution".

As a matter of fact, before the "color revolutions" in these three countries, similar events had also occurred in the Federal Republic of Yugoslavia in 2000. Yugoslavian President Slobodan Milosevic had always opposed the policies of US-led western countries and was viewed as an eyesore by the United States. After the Kosovo War, the United States had supported the opposition in Yugoslavia and coached them to employ "total street politics". Thus opposition frequently took the streets and demanded Milosevic stepping down. However, Milosevic was not a corrupt person and enjoyed a honest image in the public. The opposition could hardly find any excuse to topple him down. In 2000, Yugoslavia held a presidential election. This was seen as the best opportunity to remove Milosevic from his office. Under the circumstance of 78 days' bombardment by NATO and continuous sanctions by Western countries, Yugoslavia had suffered economic deterioration and many people were uneasy and favored change. The United States took advantage of this opportunity and openly declared and promised that if Milosevic stepped down, the Western countries would lift the sanctions and provide aid. Under the substantial support offered by United States and EU, the opposition launched a strong offensive. In the end, the opposition leader Vojislav Kostunica was elected president. Under the temptation of USD 3 billion aid, finally Vojislav Kostunica sent Milosevic, this eyesore of the West to Hague Tribunal in Holland. This was also a "color revolution", only it was not named after a "color".

Encouraged by the "color revolutions" in these countries, the oppositions in other CIS countries and Mongolia were also encouraged and activated. Similar activities organized by opposition in order to seize power were seen in Belarus, Kazakhstan, Uzbekistan, Azerbaijan, Mongolia and Russia. The US-led major capitalist countries also took advantage of this tense domestic situation in those countries to intervene actively in the domestic affairs of these countries and supported oppositions openly without any disguise. For example, the United States considered Lukashenka's regime in Belarus as the "obstacle to the democratic process in Belarus". C. Rice has publicly claimed Lukashenka's government as the "last real dictatorship in Central Europe" and "now it is the time to make a change". On November 24, 2005, Lukashenka disclosed to the media that Western countries attempted to bribe him and offer him personal safety to persuade him to give up the presidential elections in 2006 which was sternly refused by him. By the encouragement of the United States, on the next day after Kyrgyzstan "Yellow Revolution" won, the opposition in Belarus took the streets for protest and has launched a "White Revolution" (also known as "Snow Revolution"). As Lukashenka had taken early measures, the opposition could not succeed. In Russia, the United States decided to earmark more than four million dollars in 2006 to support the development of other political parties and NGOs. In addition, tens of million dollars were allocated into "Economic Support Fund", with specified use for "human right and democracy". After the key opposition figure and former Prime Minister Mikhail Kasyanov returned back from his trip in the United States, his bank account had sharply increased by millions of dollars. Following the success of the "color revolutions" in Georgia, Ukraine and Kyrgyzstan, the oppositions in Russia, Belarus, have rapidly increased their activities. Certainly, this has aroused an alarm in these countries. They have designed several measures to prevent the occurrence of "color revolution"[1]. In today's

---

1   For example, the National Assembly of Belarus had deliberated a bill on January 25, 2006, aiming to prevent "color revolution". The main content of the bill includes the following: Individuals who deliberately fabricate and spread false information about Belarus and organize illegal parades or assemblies will be more severely punished; any person who attends any illegal assembly or provides economic support for it will be subject to a maximum three years' imprisonment; anybody who spreads misleading information through radio, TV or other channels will face a maximum five years' imprisonment. Lukashenka also stated that strengthening president's effective control over army was an important guarantee for domestic peace and stability. For a long time, Russian President Putin has keenly followed America's support to Russian opposition. He has on many occasions stressed that some nations appropriated a huge amount of money to support the political activities of some social organizations in Russia, "all the activities involve sensitive issues and Russian government know very well the real intention of the contributors; and Russian government will strictly forbid foreign states to fund the political activities inside Russia". In December 2005, Russian State Duma officially approved a NGO law. This law stipulates:

international arena, the "color revolution" and the anti-"color revolution" struggles still continue.

Historical Roots and Velvet Revolutions in Eastern Europe

In retrospect of the history, coups in which opposition "peacefully" overthrows a regime through "street politics" by external support and promotion of US-led Western countries has long existed and is not something new at all. A typical example is the political upheaval in Soviet Union and the countries in Eastern Europe in the late 1980s and early 1990s, in which socialist regimes were toppled down. All the oppositions in these countries had seized political power by the support and encouragement of US-led Western capitalist countries, with the connivance and collaboration of the "humanistic-democratic socialist" elements inside communist parties and through mass assembly, demonstration, parade, workers' strike, students' strike and other activities. For example, in the former Soviet Union, in 1989 alone, the Yeltsin-led "democratic bloc" had organized 5300 mass assemblies and demonstrations with 12,600,000 participants. In Czechoslovakia, the opposition had organized a 34,000-people demonstration opposing Czech government on November 17, 1989 – in the anti-fascist day and demanded Czech communist leaders' stepping down. After since, the demonstrations in Prague had never stopped and there were often hundreds of thousand participants. On November 23, Czech opposition "Civil Forum" had organized a mass demonstration with 300,000 attendants in Prague. Under this pressure, the Czech Communist Party was forced to retreat till surrender. The opposition in Bulgaria was also too weak, but by the support of the West, they rapidly grew stronger following the abrupt changes in the situation in other countries in Eastern Europe. In the beginning, they were only able to organize a demonstration with not more than thousand people. By February 25, 1990, the opposition organization "Union of Democratic Forces" had been able to hold an anti-communist march by participation of about 250,000 people and forced the Bulgarian Communist Party to step down. Protest activities had frequently happened in other countries, too and their strength was increasing. Just by this "street politics" methods, the oppositions had

---

all non-governmental organizations and non-profit organizations must be registered in Russia; related national state departments shall have right to randomly check their activities and finances and immediately revoke them in case they are found committing unlawful acts; in case any non-governmental organization does any activity not conforming to its registered constitution will immediately be banned; the government will monitor the cash inflow of above USD 5000 for each NGO. These stipulations imply that the Putin government was timely aware about the moves of non-governmental organizations and thus prevent the penetration and influence by the forces of the US and West. This law became a fuse which triggered Western countries' accusations on Putin government's breach of democracy and destruction of human rights. Azerbaijan and Kazakhstan have also taken strict measures to prevent "color revolution". In recent elections in these two countries, although the oppositions were ready to make trouble, much stir had not occurred.

easily seized political power. The easy victories had even surprised the opposition members themselves. In all of these countries except Yugoslavia where civil war had occurred due to ethnic contradictions and in Romania where minor blood-shed conflicts were seen, all the regime changes were realized in a "peaceful" manner and were termed as "Velvet Revolutions"[2], which means sliding as stead-ily and smoothly as on velvet from socialism to capitalism. In Chinese politics this phenomena is termed as "peaceful evolution" strategy led by imperialism.

Differences between "Color" and "Velvet Revolutions"

In terms of their nature, "Color Revolutions" and "Velvet Revolutions" have principle differences. The "Velvet Revolution" in Soviet Union and the countries in Eastern Europe have caused fundamental changes in the social system. This "revolution" has turned the regimes of socialist states into the regimes of bour-geoisie dictatorship and has transformed the socialist system in these countries into a capitalist system. But the "color revolutions" occurring in several countries in the 21st century were all lived in capitalist countries and not changed the nature of the social system. It was the content among different ruling cliques within the realm of capitalist system. In these struggles a pro-American clique has replaced an anti-American clique or the clique which has not supported America as pleased and has seized the political power. Therefore, in terms of the nature of regime and social system, no fundamental change has occurred. However, these "revolu-tions" do share some common points, including the most prominent two points. Firstly, the methods applied for the regime change is same. In these two types of "revolutions", the oppositions have all resorted to "street politics", i.e.: or-ganizing mass demonstration, assembly or strike, occupying squares or besieging and even storming government departments and buildings , to "peacefully" over-throw current regime and wrest political power. Secondly, more importantly, these two types of "revolutions" were both manipulated by the United States (mostly by the United States, although sometimes including the EU), the oppositions

---

2   The "Velvet Revolutions" as termed by the West can be traced back to the Czech Revolution in 1968, i.e.: the so-called "Prague Spring". At that time, Alexander Dubcek, the First Secretary of the Czechoslovakian Communist Party had proposed "humanistic-democratic socialism" as the guiding ideology and goal of socialist reform. This attitude had implied that the reform might give up original socialist road. Evaluating the possible future prospects, the West believed Czechoslovakia might realize capitalism without abrupt turbulence and move smoothly to capitalism as velvet. Later, the former Soviet Union had sent troops to Czechoslovakia, preventing the "Prague Spring" on which the West had laid great hope. Here I should mention that the issue was not correctly handled by the former Soviet Union but it is another debate, I will not involve due to the scope of this book. In the glossary of the Western politics, "Prague Spring" was indeed a "Velvet Revolution" as often quoted by them and parallel evaluations are made for the later "Color Revolutions". Of course, "Velvet Revolutions" and "Color Revolutions" have important differences in terms of their connotation and related to international political context.

have received support and instigation politically, economically, mentally and even behaviorally, and their activities were suited into the global strategy of the United States, realized American intention and conformed to American interests. Therefore, they were a part of American plots for global hegemony. In this sense, the "Color Revolutions" in the 21st century were nothing but the continuation of the "Velvet Revolutions" in the 20th century. For this reason, some people interchangeable term them as "Color Revolutions" or "Velvet Revolutions". Thus we may combine these two "revolutions" and study them together as an important content of the United States' practice of hegemonism under the new world politics.

Many reasons have contributed to the "color revolutions" in these countries, including internal causes and external causes. According to materialistic dialectics, internal cause is the fundament, while external cause is the condition. The most fundamental reason for "color revolution" is the internal contradictions in these countries. As the saying goes, the fly does not bite the seamless egg. After all, the strongest external cause takes effect only through internal cause. Internal factors were the main reasons for the upheaval occurring in the Soviet Union and those socialist countries in Eastern Europe. In these countries, the lapses and drawbacks faced during socialist practice had aroused people's discontent, providing opportunities for anti-socialist hostile forces. More importantly, the new revisionist political elements who had seized the leading positions in the ruling parties – humanistic-democratic socialist elements had turned a blind eye on the fundamental principles of Marxism, abandoned the socialist road and employed a series of measures which helped and supported hostile forces which aimed to seize the power, and as a result, the situation had suddenly and rapidly turned worse, and the hostile forces had quickly seized power. In contrast, in those countries where "color revolution" have occurred in the 21st century, the economy was badly managed and was highly corrupted, people's life could not be improved, social security was deteriorated, political situation was turbulent and internal domestic contradictions were serious. This has laid the foundations for the "street politics" by opposition. Here, I will not make a more detailed analysis on the internal causes for the "color revolutions" in these countries. I will study the role of the United States in the "color revolutions" mainly from the strategy of the United States' quest for global hegemony, i.e.: how the United States had a hand on promoting the "color revolution" in these countries. I will also give some suggestions on how China should guard against "color revolutions".

2. "COLOR REVOLUTIONS" AND THE UNITED STATES

"Color revolutions" have occurred in different countries. On the surface, it has appeared as the fight by the people of those countries for "democracy" and regime change, but behind them, there is a common manipulator –the United States, the "color revolution" follows American interests and surrender to America's strategic requirements.

Manipulations for "color revolutions" are determined by the essence of American imperialism. The United States is an imperialist country ruled by monopoly bourgeoisie. Its fundamental interest lies on external expansion and hegemonism. Marx had pointed out: "Following the development of capitalism, the bourgeoisie will break the limitation of countries and nations and expand throughout the world, and its inherent pursuit of profit will compel to constantly exploit new world markets and try to subordinate all nations". External expansion is the objective and necessary requirement of the capitalist mode of production. Since the end of the Second World War, the United States has greatly enhanced its economic and military strength and become the strongest developed capitalist country in the world. Consequently, the United States has adopted the strategy of world hegemony. The United States has always claimed that its ideology is the truest in the world and its social system is the most reasonable on the planet. Never will it tolerate the existence of the ideologies and social systems antithetical to its own. It always aims to popularize its ideologies and social system in other countries and fill the "outside" world with its spiritual products. Since after the collapse of Soviet Union, the United States has secured its position as the "sole superpower" and no country alone can challenge it, so it obviously hastened its steps to establish global hegemony and a uni-polar world structure. The serious imbalance in international political power configuration has made American imperialism more offensive, aggressive and adventurous. Former American President Bill Clinton has commented: "After all, we are the only superpower in the world. We must lead the world."[3] After the "9•11" event, George W. Bush has publicly claimed that in this new world, the only road to peace and safety was the road of military actions[4]. These comments fully disclose the outrageous and tyrannical essence of the United States. The "sole superpower" position of the United States will not be fundamentally changed in a short run, and meanwhile this global hegemonism cannot be changed in a short term.

---

3   Liu Jindun: American National Strategy, p. 848, Shenyang, Laoning People's Publishing House, 1997.
4   Fu Yong: Crisis of the Empire, p. 29.

The US realizes hegemonism by two methods. One is the use of force, such as: its military action in Iraq; the other is the peaceful methods by pushing some countries gradually but steadily to the goal set by the United States as if moving on velvet cloth. Practice proves that the former method is too 'costly" and has undesirable effects; while the latter method is featured by lower costs, greater effect and less resistance and can easily be accepted by the "international community". Since the United States has launched the Iraq War, it has spent more than 200 billion dollars, lost more than 2000 American lives and offended many of its allies in the West, but it has still not reached its goal yet and furthermore, it has created many undesired after-effects. By contrast, in Ukraine, the United States has achieved a greater effect by spending only about 200 million dollars and without any casualties. As a bonus, it also won unanimous support from its allies. Obviously, the latter method is more lucrative. After weighing the pros and cons, unless absolutely necessary, the US will certainly prefer realizing its wish of leading and lording over the world through "peacefully" overthrowing the anti-American regimes or those regimes which do not sufficiently support America, and support those absolute pro-American figures to climb to the reins of government[5]. The series of "color revolutions" were directed by the United States according to its needs for world dominance.

In all "color revolutions", the United States has played the card of democracy. All the occurred "color revolutions" share a common feature: at first, the United States would put the labels as "undemocratic", "autarchic", "non-human" or "violator of human rights" on the regime , it does not desire, and then instigate the opposition to stand up for democracy. It is quite illusive. Who does not want and resist democracy?

By the upheavals in the Soviet Union and the countries in Eastern Europe occurring in late 1980s and early 1990s, the United States has used this trick; in early 21st century, it has also played this trick in Yugoslavia, Georgia, Ukraine and Kyrgyzstan. For instance, in the Soviet Union, Yeltsin who wanted desperately to overthrow the regime of the Communist Party of the Soviet Union had claimed himself a "democrat", attacked socialism as a totalitarian and despotic system and

5   The Milosevic regime of Yugoslavia was anti-American and sought for the sovereignty of Yugoslavia, so it is quite understandable that the United States had planned deliberately to overthrow it. However, the Shevardnadze regime of Georgia was not against America. This figure who had helped Yeltsin to overthrow Soviet Union in fact favored the American system in his heart, but why did the United States aim to remove him? This is because he had his feet in two powers and showed "kindness" to both America and Russia, which was intolerable for America. The United States was determined to promote a 100% pro-American person to replace him. The wily Shevardnadze has still complained even after he was removed from the office that he was the firmest supporter of American policy and complained why he was badly treated like that. He did not understand that in order to lord over the world, the United States needed those figures with complete loyalty to it. The case of Askar Akayev in Kyrghizstan somehow is similar to that of Shevardnadze.

regarded the fall of the communist party and the collapse of Soviet Union as the victory of democracy, while the US-led Western countries had provided constant support to Yeltsin in the name of safeguarding democracy.[6]

On 7th of October, 1989, in Berlin, the capital of socialist Germany (German Democratic Republic), the slogans raised by the demonstrators who obtained support from the US outside the venue of national celebration reception was "democracy". On October 9, 70,000 people had attended a demonstration in Leipzig. Their demand was also the realization of "democracy". All socialist regimes in Soviet Union and the countries in Eastern Europe had changed by "street politics" demanding "democracy". In the 21st century, the United States also resorted to demands for "democracy" or "fair elections" to force down the anti-American Yugoslavian Milosevic regime and the original regimes of Georgia, Ukraine and Kirghizstan, which were pro-America, but not thoroughly enough. For example, in the election storm in Ukraine, when opposition supporters were asked why they support Yushchenko, many of them have answered that support-ing Yushchenko was to support democracy. The United States also attempted to use this time-tested trick in China. In May 2005, before Condoleezza Rice visited China, she clamored in Japan that China should have a timetable for its democratization process. These historical experiences warn Marxists that they must carry out an extensive education on Marxist democracy concepts among the communist parties, cadres and masses of working people and intellectuals , theo-retically draw a clear demarcation between proletariat democracy and bourgeoisie democracy, correctly evaluate and criticize bourgeoisie democracy and disclose the true colors of the "democracy" advocated by the United States; meanwhile those countries which are in the stage of building socialism should take practical and effective measures to creatively carry forward and strengthen socialist democ-racy and truly reflect the status of the people as the masters of the country and state . In the face of the aggressive "color revolution" policies promoted by the United States, this work is imperative.

In order to realize "color revolutions", the United States has never stinted money. In each and every country where "color revolution" has occurred, the opposi-tion received financial support from the United States without exception. All the activities against the current regime, including ideological advocacy, "street poli-tics" and election, were too costly, and the opposition normally did not have the

---

6 Ironically, when Yeltsin denounced the U.S White House, dissolved the parliament, abolished constitution and killed 150 people in October 1993, the United States which always paraded "democracy" did not raise any objection and continued to praise Yeltsin government as a model for democracy. Apparently, America's standard for "democracy" is always guided by American interests: nothing is "democratic" if it works against American interest; everything is "democratic" so far as it tallies with American interests. This perhaps can be a note for the democracy approach of the Western states.

finance and had to rely on the United States. On this issue, the United States was generous and did not hesitate to spend a fortune.

As reported by Oriental Morning Post, the United States always oppose other countries providing funds for the political activities in USA, but it concocted various pretexts to provide huge fund support to the so-called "democratization development" in other countries. Each year, the American government spends about one billion dollars for "promotion of democracy". In 1992, American Senate passed the Freedom Support Act. Later on, through many "single programs", the US has provided various kinds of financial support to the former Republics of the Soviet Union. In 1993-1994, the US has spent more than nine billion dollars on the special support used to help the "democratic reforms" in the CIS countries. Above 3/4 of the fund was provided for the incentives aiming private enterprises, NGOs, "independent media" and other private organizations in these countries. On November 4, 2005, American Senate has voted the "Finance Bill for Overseas Actions, Export Fund Management and Relevant Projects in 2006". The bill has approved the Department of State to provide USD 9.5 millions of financial appropriation for the so-called "National Endowment for Democracy" program in 2006. This bill has particularly listed Russia and other countries belonging to the former Soviet Union as the targets of "support".

In Ukraine, when the Yushchenko-led opposition needed to gather the people to capital Kiev in order to organize a mass demonstration, through non-governmental organizations (Soros Foundation for example) the US spent money for renting cars, providing service charges for every demonstrator (it was said that the charge was $10/day, much higher than local actual wages) and putting up tents on the square over night for the demonstrators. During the "Rose Revolution" in Georgia, by the help of NGOs, the US had prepared all the conditions in advance, for example: how much money it should spend, which anti-government organizations it should sponsor and with whom it should cooperate.

In Kyrgyzstan, a few years before the new parliament election, the US had begun to support the opposition with a strong finance. Reportedly, in 2004 alone, the US has provided USD 12 million aid to Kyrgyzstan. During the turbulence in Kyrgyzstan, Stephen Young, American Ambassador in Kyrgyzstan had submitted a report on the situation of Kyrgyzstan to the US Congress. In the report, he said that during the parliament elections in Kyrgyzstan, the US had spent five million dollars in the activities of promoting "democracy" and to support opposition candidates and he appealed to American government to allocate USD 25 million more funds. The Information Center of the U.S. Department of State has declared on March 24, 2005 that Bush administration would give continuous support to the "economic and democratic reforms" in Kyrgyzstan, and would provide USD 31 million aid in 2005. Apart from the direct assistance of the government, the United States also provided huge fund to the Kirghiz opposition through government-funded "non-governmental organizations". There were more than ten American NGOs in Kyrgyzstan. Some of them had set up a dozen branch offices throughout the country. According to statistics, since the founding of independent Kyrgyzstan, the United States had provided various kinds of materials and fund support totaling above USD 700 million. Meanwhile, some European countries (such as: Britain, Holland and Norway) have also provided economic aids to the so-called "democratic movements" and to support building of "civil societies" in Central Asian countries. By now, Kyrgyzstan has become a Central Asian country receiving the highest per capita aid from the West.

In order to overthrow Lukashenko regime in Belarus, American government has allocated USD 89 million in 2005 to support the "independent media", opposition groups, domestic organizations and business groups in Belarus; in 2005, American Senate has announced that USD 50 million of fund would be earmarked to support the opposition in Belarus.

American NGOs have played a tremendous role in "color revolutions". It is worth noting that America's preparation for "color revolution" was usually completed through NGOs, particularly in the stage of ideological preparation works. Under the disguise of cooperation, educational or academic exchanges or sponsorship for scientific research, the foundations brainwash certain figures and seek for appropriate candidates they can manipulate in the future. These activities appear innocent but aims are covert and subtle. Their effect will be seen at crucial historical moments. But, many countries including those socialist ones sometimes undermine these activities and not carefully handle and observe these international foundations and sacrifice fundamental principles for small gains.

There are various kinds of American NGOs which play roles in "color revolutions". Carnegie Foundation, Fund for Peace, National Endowment for Democracy and Eurasia Foundation are some names among them. The most active and typical one is the Soros Foundation. The founder of Soros Foundation is the well-known finance speculator George Soros. He has founded the Open Society Fund in 1979. Gradually this organization was developed into Open Society Institute, with its headquarters in New York. The activity plans of Soros Foundation in each country or region are jointly determined by members of local steering committee, Soros and the advisory board of the Open Society Institute through discussions. By now, Soros Foundation has established branches in Europe, Asia, Latin America and Africa. Its activities cover more than 60 countries and regions. Normally, the Open Society Institute provides long term plans and strategies. And then local Soros foundations will be responsible to implement them. They have huge allocated huge finance for activities (USD 500 million for the Institute and USD 400 million for the Foundation). They both observe one principle: building and maintaining the infrastructure and public utilities for open society. Some people have criticized pointed: "open society is nothing but a signboard, its aid programs and poverty reduction discourse is merely cosmetic. The real intention of Soros is to output American ideology and values to those nations which are "not democratic enough" stir up "a surge of democracy" and pave a road for his financial speculation through change of state power, because in a "closed" society, Soros cannot find opportunities for financial speculation".

After Soviet Union had collapsed, Soros Foundation started its plots in CIS countries. In 1990, it founded International Renaissance Foundation in Ukraine to engage in "democratic penetration". By 2004, the foundation had spent USD 82 millions and set up a head office in capital Kiev and branches in 24 areas; in 1992, Soros Foundation has entered Moldova to promote the values of the West; in 1993, it chose Kyrgyzstan which was dubbed "island of democracy in Central Asia" to mainly foster independent media in the country and quickly expand its influence through health, cultural and educational sectors; in 1994, it marched into Georgia, officially establishing its presence in Transcaucasia. At present, it has four major organizations in Georgia capital Tbilisi, including International Soros Science Education Program and branches in four areas; in 1995, Soros extended its feelers to Kazakhstan, a large nation in Central Asia, attempting to turn it into a bridgehead for its expedition to Central Asia; in 1996, it entered Uzbekistan. Considering the strategic position of Transcaucasia, Soros Foundation has included Azerbaijan and Armenia into its global network in 1997.

In Russia, Soros did not set up its foundation in the beginning. Instead, it carried out charity activities through International Cultural Promotion Foundation and International Foundation for Science. Later in 1995, Russian Soros Foundation was founded. By the end of 2002, this foundation had set up nearly 10 research institutions in Russia, including Pushkin Library Foundation and Cultural Policy Research Institute in Moscow, Likhachyov Foundation in St. Petersburg, and Open Siberia Charity Foundation in Siberia.

Although Soros Foundation carries its activities in CIS countries under different banners, its central aim is to blaze forth the democracy and liberal values of the United States, promote the "democratic construction" in these countries and promote the establishment of pro-American regimes. After resignation, Shevardnadze revealed with anger to media that an ambassador told him that Soros forked out USD 2.5 million~3 million of cash fund for the launch of the "Rose Revolution". At the end of 2004, "Orange Revolution" broke out in Ukraine, Paul, a member of the House of Representatives, revealed in his testimony at the House International Relations Committee that the Ukrainian Open Society Institute attached to Soros Foundation had played an important role in the launch of "Orange Revolution" and Yushchenko was a member of the board of directors of this institute. Paul also disclosed that in the past two years, the US had provided more than USD 65 million of political fund for Ukrainian opposition through Ukrainian Open Society Institute and other NGOs. In March 2005, the shocking "Yellow Revolution" had occurred in Kyrgyzstan. In fact, the Kirghiz Open Society Institute under Soros Foundation had done a lot of work for the promotion of "democracy" in Kyrgyzstan since a long time ago. This institution set up many "electorate political activist" organizations throughout Kyrgyzstan. These organizations were engaged in anti-government and anti-president activities in all parts of the country. They have also established many independent media and publishing agencies to spread rumors about the corruption of Askar Akayev and his family and tarnish the reputation of Askar Akayev among the people[7].

Independent Media

US-sponsored "independent media" plays an important role in "color revolutions". To realize ideological penetration, the US pays great attention to the role of media, particularly establishes independent media by financial support in the targeted countries. The U.S. Department of State announced on August 3, 2005 that it would initiate a special program to "promote the development of independent media in CIS countries". This program was funded by American International Human Rights and Democracy Foundation. The fund was initially about USD 10 million. American embassies would be responsible to carry out this program. In fact, the US had started such attempts long before. In July 2005, the US has established three "democratic information centers" in the American University and other centers in Bishkek, aiming to consolidate and reinforce the democratic process in Kyrgyzstan. The U.S. Department of State has announced that these three information centers help Kirghiz electorates to learn about the international standards for electoral rights and democratic elections. Later on, the United States has provided USD 613,000 to set up five more information centers. In Kazakhstan, the US has spent USD 557,000 and established a "news plant" and used Internet to help the independent media in Kazakhstan. In Uzbekistan, the US had planned to spend USD 80,000 for the establishment of a "social center" which provides free counsels for criminal suspects so as to help "foster the leading role of law in national political life". In Tajikistan, the US had spent USD 887,000 and set up five independent radio stations, providing technical support and organizing broadcast program database.

In the past "color revolutions", the independent media supported by the United States has played an important role. During the "Rose Revolution" in Georgia,

---

7　The above information about Soros Foundation is quoted from the article "Promote 'Color Revolutions': Soros Foundation Penetrates the Globe" written by Tang Yong, Changzhe and Wang Honggang and published in Global Times, 2005-04-20.

the "Rustavi-2" TV Station supported by the West was the mouthpiece of Saakaschwili. Soros Foundation also funded several newspapers and TV stations in Tbilisi and donated more than one million dollars to "Rustavi-2" TV Station for live reporting and broadcast. A Georgian opposition leader who has participated in the "Rose Revolution" told a reporter that without the support and involvement of independent media, the "color revolution" in Georgia would not have been so smooth. During the "Orange Revolution" in Ukraine, the "Channel-5" supported by the West had always been the firm supporter of Yushchenko.

Many independent media companies in Kyrgyzstan are supported by the West. For example, the Osh TV Station in the south Kyrgyzstan, which profusely covered the election campaign of the opposition councilors, had received financial aid from the U.S. Department of State. There is also a radio station in Kirghiz language, which is attached to Radio Free Europe but funded by the American government. The newspaper MSN run by opposition was the key factor during Yellow Revolution supported by the American government. On the eve of parliament elections in Kyrgyzstan, this newspaper published a photo of President Askar Akayev's "luxury mansion" which was under construction. This has aroused people's discontent towards Askar Akayev government. Under the support of the United States, opposition leaders distributed this newspaper all over the country and also free of charge. After the "revolution" has started, this newspaper surprisingly printed 200,000 copies a day; but Kyrgyzstan has only 5 million people. This newspaper has not only published full speeches of opposition candidates before the election but also stirred up the clashes in later turmoil. It has covered the "uprising" in the south with full exaggeration, appealed to the people to attend demonstrations and informed assembly time and locations.

In order to implement "color revolutions", the US also pays much attention to cultivating core political figures who are able to play a leading role. Polish Walesa, Yugoslavian Kostunica, Georgian Saakaschwili and Ukrainian Yushchenko are all the "leaders" chosen by the US. They have also received their "democratic education" directly in the USA. For example, in the summer of 2003, the United States held a seminar in Belgrade and Georgian Saakaschwili was invited to receive training on the Serbia-style "gentle revolution". A few months later, Saakaschwili has successfully launched the "Rose Revolution" in Georgia and smoothly ascended to presidency. Apart from leaders, the United States also energetically fosters backbone leaders. In March 2000, the United States had organized a "non-violent revolt workshop" at the Hilton Hotel in Hungarian capital Budapest. 24 Yugoslavian opposition leaders had secretly attended it. Under the guidance of experts, they were trained how to organize a strike, how to address masses with effective gestures, how to overcome fear, how to shake the reign of an "autocratic government", and so on. Shortly after they had completed the training and returned to Yugoslavia, they have organized those "street activities" against

A REVIEW ON MARXIST AND LEFT DEBATES

Milosevic. In the autumn of 2004, the United States has assigned more than 1000 activists to prepare for the revolution in 14 cities of Ukraine which were timely cultivated and formed the backbone leaders for the "Orange Revolution".

Before the outbreak of "Yellow Revolution" in Kyrgyzstan, the United States has actively sought and cultivated pro-American politicians. Funded by the United States, "American University" was established in Kyrgyzstan. One of the declared missions of this university is to promote the development of a civil society and provide funds for the exchange projects between the two countries. A great many liberal students, NGO leaders and opposition leaders have visited the USA through these projects to receive further "education". The leading figure of opposition Bakiev was one of them. As early as March 2004, the United States also held many direct meetings and talks with the Kirghiz opposition leaders and pro-West media managers and editors on the preparations for the 2005 parliament and presidential elections. It was afterwards revealed that the then U.S. Department of State has secretly invited Bakiev, Masaliyev, former Kirghiz foreign minister Imanaliev and other people to the USA to personally experience the "democratic process" of American election. When meeting them, Pasco, the Deputy Secretary for Eurasia Affairs has commented bluntly that: "by the general elections in 2005, he guessed and hoped Kirghiz regime should be changed".

In Belarus, in 2003, nearly 200 "democratic activists" have visited the USA to receive training and 50 Belarusian youth have attended the "future leaders" program organized by American government.

Enormous facts indicate that the series "color revolutions" which had occurred from late 1980s to early 1990s were all manipulated by the United States and all were parts of America's colossal chess game for the realization of global hegemony. Departing from the intention and acts of the United States, it will be not very difficult to analyze the essence of "color revolutions".

On the basis of summarizing the experience in "color revolutions", on January 18, 2006, United States Secretary of State Condoleezza Rice explicitly proposed the "transformation diplomacy", which would aim to popularize "color revolutions" in the world. She defined the strategic goal of American diplomacy as supporting democracy in the whole world, stopping tyranny and transforming all countries into "free and democratic countries". I think that the theoretical basis of the above "transformational diplomacy" is that democracy and human right are superior to national sovereignty. The previous norms governing international relations (internal affairs of a country, inviolability of territorial integrity, and so on) are being excluded by this theory. Under the circumstances of globalization, the infringement of democracy and tyranny in a country directly constitutes a threat against the security of the United States, so the United States should have the right for intervention; whereas whether a country is democratic or not will completely be decided by the United States. Once this theory is assured, the United States may do whatever it wants. Rice has also stated that the emphasis of American diplomacy should be shifted to countries including China and regarded China as the main target of "peaceful evolution". The "transformation diplomacy" documents specifies basic working methods, i.e.: face the local public, walk out of embassies, directly exchange ideas with local common people, establish consulate bureaus in cities with a population of above one million people and meanwhile increase aid. In fact, this policy document promotes "color revolutions" in those countries which do not please the United States.

3. STEPS AND TACTICS FOR "COVER REVOLUTIONS"

The "color revolutions" in different countries vary in many details, but they share some common features. To summarize, the past "color revolutions" have largely practiced the following steps.

1) Fabricate and establish a public opinion for overthrowing the current regime. Mao Zedong had once commented that it was necessary to weave public opinion and do ideological work as the first step before overthrowing a regime. A revolutionary class acts accordingly, so does a counterrevolutionary class, too. It is an indispensible truth. All the "color revolutions" covertly supported and manipulated by the United States have adopted this strategy. This ideological work may be analyzed in two categories: the first is to demonize current regime – collect and exaggerate the faults and mistakes of the government work and stir up people's discontent; sometimes repeatedly disseminate the same typical event to deepen people's impression on the "misdeeds" of current regime. During the abrupt changes in the Soviet Union, the hostile forces made a big fuss about the Great Purge[8], and have arbitrarily increased the number of the persecuted people in the Great Purge , elaborately described the persecution process, depicted the details, created an atmosphere of hate and shook people's trust in the current regime. In

---

8 This exaggeration sometimes even goes beyond the limits of common sense. They have propagated that 50 million people had died in the Great Purge during 1930s in the Soviet Union, but the total population of the then Soviet Union was only about 160 million. According to the report by the Ministry of Interior of the Soviet Union prepared by the demand from Nikita Khrushchev, in the period from 1921 to 1954, 3.777.330 persons were accused for the crime of counter-revolutionary activity , of whom 642.980 were sentenced to death and 2.369.220 were sentenced to 25 years' of labor reform and imprisonment. Actually, Khrushchev wanted to attack and accuse the Ministry of Interior in the period of Stalin, so he preferred understate these figures. Later on, again for his political campaign against Stalin, Mikhail Gorbachev initiated a new investigation on the events. But the figures obtained were basically same as the above.

the Eastern European countries opposition has focused on issues of corruption. For example in Bulgaria against Todor Zhivkov, the opposition has enumerated his conducts for misuse of power for private interest. In the end, it was proved that all the alleged conducts were non-existent and imaginary. However, during the turbulence, such information was very effective and has played an enormous role in mobilizing the masses. In the countries where "color revolutions" took place in the 21st century, the oppositions have all wantonly colored up economic deterioration, social polarization and undemocratic politics in order to instigate people's emotion of protest.

The second category probably is more important. It is to indoctrinate American values and beautify American-style democracy and freedom through public propaganda and personnel exchanges so that the vast people will gradually sympathize with the American political and economic system, thus lay an ideological foundation for the establishment of a pro-American regime in the future. This "long-term" ideological strategy is particularly important.

The United States lays much emphasis on ideological propaganda and penetration through mass media and personnel exchanges. As early as late 1950s, Eisenhower without disguise had commented that one dollar spent on propaganda was five dollars worth compared with military costs. Nixon had claimed that the one which plays a decisive role in history was ideology and not the "weapons", and if the United States lost the battle in the spheres of ideology, all weapons, treaties, overseas aids and cultural exchanges would become meaningless. During the upheaval in the Soviet Union and Eastern Europe, the United States had utilized used all kinds of mass media to assault and blemish the socialist practice in these countries, wobble people's belief in socialism, make them long for capitalist political and economic system, confuse their ideas and slacken people's organizations. This was an important condition for anti-socialist forces' smooth seizure of political power. In the recent "color revolutions", the United States has not only used its own media but also vigorously depended on the role of "independent media", and actively promoted the development of "independent media" in these countries. A journalist from the West has pointed out that the reason why Western countries have so enthusiastically supported development of independent media in the CIS countries was nothing but utilizing it to influence ordinary people in those countries, brainwash them and persuade them to so-called American democracy and values. It is just this "outstanding" job done by this kind of independent media that enabled small opposition groups to mobilize tens thousands of people to take the streets for demonstration and storm government buildings. So I can say that in all the color revolutions, ideological work was the spearhead as a common feature.

2) Establishing political organizations. On the basis of fabricating public opinions and confusing people's ideas, opposition organizations were established. With the organization, more people can be influenced. In socialist countries, usually they have set up "loose civil organizations"[9] at first and the "opposition parties" later. Allowing the establishment of the so-called "civil organizations" in fact was to allow organized and open anti-communist and anti-socialist activities; paving the way for the establishment of opposition parties[10] which meant to adopt the multi-party system of core capitalist countries; and the adoption of multi-party system inevitably leads to the removal of communist party's leading position. This has created those conditions for the bourgeois political party to seize political power. In today's capitalist countries, the method is to establish pro-American organizations so that they can lead the civil people to conduct political activities and wait for the chance to wrest power. If they succeed, these pro-American organizations will become the pillars of the new government. For example, in Ukraine, the United States has supported Yushchenko-led "Our Ukraine Movement", and then united all opposition groups to form a force which was strong enough to challenge the government and thus "Our Ukraine Movement", has become the core actor of the "street politics". After they have forced the government to accept re-election and won the election, they have rapidly formed a new government around that organization.

3) Seek and promote an influential and charismatic liberal and pro-American figure as the leader of opposition. In this way, it is possible to attract all walks of people who desire to topple down the current regime and when the time is ripe, this leader can lead the people to attack the current regime and organize a new regime under his leadership. He/she should have an obvious pro-American approach and be "loyal" and a more ideal figure would be someone who has received training in the United States and has close connections with American institutions. Soviet Union's Yeltsin, Polish Walesa, Czech Havel, Georgian Saakaschwili and Ukrainian Yushchenko were all selected and vigorously supported and cultivated by the United States.

---

9   In Soviet Union, as Mikhail Gorbachev was promoting the "democratization" policy, NGOs had sprung up like mushrooms. By the end of 1987, the number of NGOs was above 30,000. This figure had exceeded 60,000 by February 1989 and 90,000 by August 1990.

10   In Soviet Union, the Plenary Session of the Central Committee of Soviet Union Communist Party decided to adopt mulitpartism in February 1990. As a result, more than 200 political parties popped up, including more than 20 national parties. All these parties were opposition parties against communism and socialism. In the upheaval of Eastern European countries, many opposition parties were established, too, such as: Polish Solidarity Union, Hungarian Democratic Forum, Czech Civic Forum and Bulgarian Union of Democratic Forces. It was these opposition parties that organized demonstrations, assemblies, strikes and other "street politics" activities, forced communist party to step down and formed a new government.

4) Take advantage of emergencies or use the elections as opportunity to organize demonstrations, parades, strikes, occupy squares, storm government buildings and other type of "street politics" activities under the banners of democracy and freedom, and force the government to surrender."Street politics" will be presented as a reasonable "one-way road": that means whatever the opposition does is democratic, while whatever the government does infringes democracy till it steps down. When the opposition receives a minority of votes, they will say the election is fraudulent and demand re-election, and if not, it will be un-democratic; all illegal activities (including storming presidential office and parliament building) of the opposition are democratic, while if the government stops the crowd, it will be undemocratic. In a word, for the United States "democracy" means to paralyze the government not favored by it and encourage the pro-American opposition to do whatever they want without restraint. It should be noted that in order to maintain their "enlightened modern image", or feared by the sanctions of the "international community", potential threats to personal and family safety after leaving office, the leaders in many countries usually dare not take firm measures to stop the illegal activities of the opposition. Objectively, this encourages opposition. Therefore, during "color revolutions", such scenes were often seen: the opposition was aggressive, and has raised the level of political demands one after another till the incumbent leader hands over the power; while the leaders of the original regime kept compromising and retreating.

In summary, I think , for "color revolutions", ideological work is the foundation, organizing an influential figure to lead opposition is the key, emergency is the opportunity, and establishing a pro-American regime is the goal.

The United States is well aware of the time-tested laws and tactics of "color revolutions". After the successes in Georgia, Ukraine and Kyrgyzstan, it could hardly wait to target Belarus regime. On April 21, 2005 when Condoleezza Rice has met the Belarusian opposition representatives, she said it was the time to start the change in Belarus. She has pointed to four main directions: support independent media and establish a new mass media; accelerate the development of mass movement; organize a coalition among opposition groups; elect a joint president candidate to contend with the incumbent president Lukashenko in the 2006 presidential election[11]. It was not rare case that the United States Secretary of State personally has given a direct counsel to an opposition. This indicates American practice of "color revolution" has been mature and can be applied anywhere.

---

11   In 2006, Belarus held presidential election. Alexander Lukashenko won the election with an overwhelming majority of votes and frustrated America's plot for "color revolution" in Belarus.

4. CHINA AND "COLOR REVOLUTION" RISKS

In this part of the chapter I will discuss on the issues and risks faced by China in the current international configuration especially from the angle of color revolutions, and I will also add my suggestions to prevent such risks. I think China should seriously deal with American tactics and techniques that promote "color revolution". As China is the only large socialist country in the world, the United States desperately desires to remove it. Considering the conflict in their social systems, the differences in geopolitical interest and ideologies and many other aspects, the US-led Western countries have no reason to allow the existence of a strong socialist China and always try their utmost to create difficulties and hurt China. This is determined by the essence of their class and also decided by their longstanding and deep-rooted anti-communist traditions. Perhaps this desire "will not change in the next 100 years", either. If armed intervention cannot achieve the goal, then "peaceful evolution" will be tried. Just like Deng Xiaoping had commented: "the US-led Western countries are staging a third world war without gun smoke." "Without gun smoke means peaceful evolution of socialist countries"[12]. They do not like China's socialist system. The United States are pressing on with its strategy of westernizing and polarizing China and seek opportunities to launch a "color revolution" in China, while the bourgeois liberal elements in China also desire to prepare some trouble. The "non-governmental constitution amendment" farce in 2003 and the "Velvet Action Committee" established in 2005 are good evidences. Therefore, China should carefully analyze the past "color revolutions" and take precautions before it is too late.

Under current international and national situation, the risk of "color revolution" in China objectively exists. In order to prevent "color revolutions", Chinese people should strengthen the coercive apparatus of the people's state against hostile forces. In case of a political turmoil, it is necessary to activate this apparatus to maintain political and social stability for the benefit of the majority. Deng Xiaoping had analyzed this issue: "proletariat as an emerging class wrests the political power and establishes socialism. Certainly, it will be weaker than capitalism in a rather long period to come. Without dictatorship, it will be unable to resist the offensive by capitalism. To adhere to socialism, we must adhere to proletarian dictatorship. We call it people's democratic dictatorship." "Using the power of people's democratic dictatorship to consolidate people's regime is a just thing and has nothing unjust."[13] Only when we exercise people's power over a tiny minority of people, can we fully guarantee the democratic rights of the overwhelming majority of people. It is just and reasonable to utilize coercive apparatus on a small number of liberal elements who engage in "color revolution" activities ,allow

---

12   Selected Works of Deng Xiaoping, First edition, Vol. 3, Beijing, People's Publishing House, 1993, p. 344.
13   *Ibid.*, p. 365; p. 379.

them to correct themselves, forbid them when they make trouble, and punish those violating criminal laws. These measures cannot tarnish China's reputation.

However, coercive apparatus alone is not enough to deal with "color revolutions"– such an attempt which endangers political stability. China should pay attention to prevent and nip it in the bud since to prevent a "color revolution" is a systematic project. It is a matter concerning whether the ruling Marxist communist party can maintain and consolidate its ruling position. I think at least, constant attention is necessary for the following:

Firstly, China should strengthen the economic foundation its socialist system, and consolidate the dominant position of public ownership while socialist economy is based on public ownership. In the preliminary stage of socialism, it is necessary to have the dominance of public ownership. It is a matter of principle and concerns whether the social system can maintain its socialist nature; it means consolidating and developing the public sector of the economy and enhance and expand state-owned economic sector. It is clear that there is a contention between non-public sector and public sector of the economy to win the dominant position on the economy, private ownership desires to substitute public ownership and become the main part of national economy. Once the public ownership perishes or loses its dominant position, China's social system will certainly lose the nature of socialism and certainly be evolved into a capitalist system. By then, the "peaceful evolution" strategy of imperialism could certainly be realized in an economic sense. We should see that American monopoly bourgeois politicians and ideologists attach great importance to this struggle. They try their utmost to push the private sector to seize the main parts of Chinese economy. For example, former American president Nixon had commented that in economy, China had completed a half journey to a free market system. At present, the two sectors of its economy — private and public — are under life-and-death competition. Moreover, the fight is far from closure. As long as the United States continued to intervene in Chinese economy, it would be able to help private sector gradually wear off the important role of the public sector.[14] In 2000, former American president Clinton also mentioned that the United States should use the opportunity of China's entry into WTO to promote American "values" in China, accelerate the decline of large Chinese state-owned enterprises, support private enterprises to substitute them and help the Chinese people who are fighting for human rights and rule of law, so that China can make "choice" needed by the United States. In China, some people also urge the substitution of the dominant position of public sector by private sector of the economy. For example, when a reform is debated for a strategic adjustment in the state-owned sector of the economy, some people openly suggest "state-out and private-in", the public sector should give way to private sector so far it is needed and public sector should retreat to the position guaranteeing the development of private sector so that the private sector can play a dominant role in national economy. In this battle, it is necessary

---

14   Richard Milhous Nixon: Seize the Moment, Beijing, China Yanshi Press, 2000, p. 162, p. 163 and p. 171.

to maintain a cool head. The dominance of public ownership and the dominant role of state-owned sector of the economy should be considered from a height of preventing "color revolution", because failure will lay an economic foundation for a "color revolution".

Secondly, ideologically, the guiding position of Marxism should be strengthened in the superstructure and ideological works should be enriched. Ideological work and struggle is a complex everlasting effort after since reform and opening-up strategy was decided Chinese Marxists have generally given emphasis on opposing the wrong tendency of dogmatic understanding of Marxism and emancipating mind. In this sphere, great achievements were made but in the reform and opening period the tendency of copying the Western bourgeois ideology and theories have appeared, too. Thus guiding position of Marxism has faced challenges and was weakened. In theoretical works and reform practices, neo-liberalism flooded, and the thought of advocating economic privatization, preaching Western bourgeoisie democracy in politics and demanding liberalization in ideology– which openly negates the Four Cardinal Principles have persuaded a considerable part of public opinion field and affected many people. If these thoughts spread excessively, socialist system would lose its own ideological support and "color revolution" may easily lay an ideological foundation for itself. It is not exaggeration. It has become an urgent task for all Marxists to earnestly study Marxist works, grasp the basic principles of Marxism, criticize and eradicate the influence of those theories by Western bourgeoisie ideology and consolidate the guiding position of Marxism.

Thirdly, the leadership functions at all levels must be firmly controlled by Marxists. This is one of the critical issues concerning whether a Marxist communist party can consolidate its ruling position and prevent "color revolutions". As long as all the cadres of party and government at all levels are loyal to communist party and socialist causes, serve the people wholeheartedly and never seek personal gains, no matter how big fuss domestic and foreign hostile forces make, the socialist regime will be as stable as a mountain. The greatest worry is when the trouble is caused from inside by degenerated cadres and "leaders". The stability of China and the realization socialist reforms should be guaranteed by correct organizational line and the successors who truly adhere to Marxism and party spirit. And when choosing and establishing cadres of a leading body, the people who have earnestly studied Marxism-Leninism and Mao Zedong Thought and can stand the test of struggle should be given the highest priority; it means to put revolutionary spirit in the top place; which is the cadre line of Marxist party. Party and government cadres are not ordinary civil servants who handle concrete affairs regardless of political propensity and political stance. After all, China is striving to achieve socialist construction under the siege of capitalism and today capitalism dominates the world. Under these concrete circumstances, if cadres do not care for politics and do not draw a clear demarcation between socialism and capitalism, they may voluntarily decline to capitalism. It is independent of human conscious-ness. If government departments and state enterprises send their cadres to the United States for training (for example, regard Harvard University as their cadre training base and stipulate no cadre will be promoted if he has not received such a foreign training) and allow them be brainwashed by the United States, it will be exactly what the United States desires. In this case, in the event there is a sign of disturbance or trouble, we will not know which side our cadres will stand on.

Fourthly, the most fundamental task is to consolidate and reinforce the class foundation of Marxist communist party. In a socialist country, "color revolution" in fact is a fierce class struggle. The final result lies on the strength of class forces. It is not correct to be afraid of opposition, because in a society with classes, under the drive of class interest, there will always be some people who oppose socialist causes. Being opposed is not so much fearful, but lack of firm support is more important. In other words, it is terrible that the Marxist ruling party does not have reliable class foundation and mass base. It is decisive for its ruling ability. The fun-damental reason why the communist parties in Soviet Union and the countries in Eastern Europe were at wit's end before the offensive of opposition is that they had adopted a revisionist road to cater for the need of bourgeoisie, completely di-vorced themselves from the masses and lost the support of workers and farmers. As a result, they could not stand the offensive of hostile forces and even collapsed without a serious offensive. In the capitalist society, the situation was the same. The opposition in Kyrgyzstan was not very powerful, but most people remained neutral and stood by. Subsequently, the government collapsed at the first encoun-ter. By contrast, the reason why in Venezuela the Chavez regime can withstand the heavy pressure from the United States and continuous resistance from domestic opposition is that the social policies of Chavez regime support the working peo-ple and Chaves and his party obtain the support of above 70% of the working class. To sum up the lessons from the occurred "color revolutions", it is necessary to consolidate the class foundation of the ruling Marxist party, assure the master status of workers and farmers, protect their interest from infringement, and win the masses to the side of the party and enable them become backbone forces in safeguarding the party and socialist undertakings. This is a basic guarantee to strengthen party's ruling capabilities and prevent "color revolutions".

China- U.S Relations

Fifthly, in diplomacy, Sino-US relations should be properly handled. American foreign policy towards China has a dual features, on the one hand, fundamentally speaking, American ruling group's determined policy of westernizing and socially polarizing China will not change and the attempt to hold back China's development, growth and national unification will not be given up. This is decided by their imperialist nature. Leopards cannot change their spots. But their manifestations, forms, methods and means will change with situation, but as long as the United States is still imperialist, its fundamental policy and desires towards China will not change. Of course the most possible policy will remain as to achieve "peaceful evolution". Without perceiving this point, China will lose the basic standpoint when analyzing Sino-American relations and formulating policies towards the United States. On the other hand, realistic consideration and its economic interests, American monopoly bourgeoisie also needs to contact China and develop relations because capitalists are profit-driven and China, such a gigantic market, is undoubtedly attractive for them. Competing with other countries, the United States needs to develop economic and commercial intercourses with China. Following the rise of China's strength and international status, the United States will need cooperation and help from China when it has to deal with many international issues. Therefore, American policy towards China has two faces: on the one hand, it wants to abandon and on the other hand, it wants to engage China, but these do not happen in parallel and are unequal. The former is fundamental and strategic, while the latter is subordinate to the former. The United States advocates "all-round engagement" and "developing relations". Its primary goal is to exert some possible influence on China's politics. Its essence is to promote westernization and social polarization inside China and induce a Soviet Union-like change in China. An American ambassador in China has openly claimed in his testimony at the U.S Congress: protecting the close trade partnership between China and the United States is good for promoting the free circulation of all kinds of ideologies to China, and bringing more American culture and values into China so that China can accept more of Western values. His testimony is outspoken and offers much food of thought which reveal the real intentions of the United States when it develops economic and trade contacts, cooperation and exchange.

In view of above duality, China should also adopt a dual approach in its foreign policy towards the US and adhere to principles and be tough when a case makes this approach necessary. China should stay vigilant all the time to those who desire to abandon socialism and never slacken vigilance. On the issues of principle, such as: opposing hegemonism and power politics, China should fear nothing because the more you show your weakness, the more aggressive they will be and the more they will humiliate you. As proved by facts, China stands tough on issues of principle; the people who want to abandon it will compromise. Of course, it is necessary to avoid acting impetuously and never make offensive remarks or do offensive things. Here I would like to quote the famous political strategist Mr. Hua's comments: "The struggles should be on just grounds, struggle when it is for your advantage and do it with restraint. The struggles should help to protect your own interest and develop your own forces. On the premise of adhering to principles, we may make necessary compromises. The compromise is not surrender, but a break for the next battle. Therefore, handle problems, wholly, calmly, unhurriedly and properly. Just like boxing, it is inadvisable to beat without breaks. Sometimes, you should slow down a bit." The battle with the United States needs a long preparation. It is necessary to do business with it, too. Adopting dual policies to deal with America's duality is a long-term policy but struggle is absolute, which is decided by the sharp conflict between the two social systems; compromise is relative and conditional and should serve to improve struggle. To sum up, sticking to struggle should be integrated with just holding grounds, seizing opportunities for advantage and keeping restraint and principled stands should also be combined with flexibility.

REFERENCES

• Selected Works of Deng Xiaoping. Edition 2. Vol. 1-2. Beijing, People's Publishing House, 1994.
• Selected Works of Deng Xiaoping. Edition 1. Vol. 3. Beijing, People's Publishing House, 1993.
• Tang Yong, Chang Zhe and Wang Honggang: Promote "Color Revolution": Soros Foundation Penetrates the Globe. Global Times, 2005-04-20.

ABOUT THE AUTHOR

Zeng Zhisheng, male, Han nationality, was born in Guangdong in 1944.

In 1968, he has graduated from Sun Yat-sen University. Between 1986 and 1990, he studied abroad in the Philosophy Department of University Paris X and has obtained his Doctor's Degree. Since the end of June 1991 when he returned to China from France, he is engaged in the teaching and research on foreign Marxism and foreign socialism. In the autumn and winter of 2000, he has continued his researches as a senior visiting scholar in Paris Institute of Political Studies.

At present, he works at Renmin University of China as Director of Philosophy Lab in Marxism Department, professor and doctor's tutor, and is a member of the academic committee of Foreign Marxism Review Journal published by the Center for Contemporary Marxism Abroad in Shanghai Fudan University. Main works: Althusser, Foreign Marxism Compendium of the End of the 20th Century, and Post-Marxism. He has written more than 10 co-authored books and has published more than 70 articles.

www.ingramcontent.com/pod-product-compliance
Lightning Source LLC
Chambersburg PA
CBHW031141020426
42333CB00013B/467